Nguyen Chi Ben

A Study on Vietnam's Intangible Cultural Heritage

VISTA PS, Japan, 2024

Translate:

+ Nguyen Ngoc Tho

+ Nguyen Vi Thuy

+ Nguyen Thi Thu Huong

Proofreading:

+ Nguyen Ngoc Tho

Cover Painting: Tham Nguyen Chi An

Cover: Mai Lan

Contents

INTRODUCTION

Vietnam is a country with 54 ethnic groups, each of whom has a treasure trove of heritage both tangible and intangible, abundant in forms and genres, diverse in values, rich in untapped potential. The existing policy on international integration from the 90s of the 20th century, Vietnam has developed various national dossiers on cultural heritage for submission to UNESCO to be registered in the list of World Heritage and Heritage of Humanity, in accordance with the Convention for the Preservation of World Natural and Cultural Heritage, adopted by the UNESCO General Assembly in November 1972, as well as the Convention for the Preservation of Intangible Cultural Heritage adopted by the same Assembly in November 2003.

In the field of intangible cultural heritage, at the time of writing, Vietnam has had 13 intangible cultural heritages honored by UNESCO as intangible cultural heritages representative of humanity and 2 intangible cultural heritages deemed in need of urgent preservation.

As part of my work responsibilities, since 2003, I and colleagues at VICAS have developed built national dossiers to submit to UNESCO for submission to UNESCO to be registered as intangible cultural heritage representative of humanity. Among them are: *The Space of Gong in the Central Highland of Vietnam; Quan ho Bac Ninh Folk Songs; Giong Festival of Phu Dong and Soc Temples; Worship of Hung Kings in Phu Tho; Vi and Giam folk songs of Nghe Tinh; Practices related to the Viet beliefs in the Mother Goddesses of the Three Realms; The Tug of War (as a multinational heritage).*

Furthermore, I was entrusted by the Ministry of Culture and Information, formerly the Ministry of Culture, Tourism and Sports, to lead research on the collection and preservation of the intangible cultural heritage of 54 ethnic groups in Vietnam, in the national target program on culture.

Therefore, over the past years, I have presented a fair number of essays on the intangible cultural heritage of different ethnic groups in

Vietnam at many international scientific conferences, as well as published in various specialized academic journals in Vietnam and overseas.

In review of released scientific works, I publish the book entitled A Study on Vietnamese Intangible Cultural Heritage with 17 selected projects, concentrating on the 3 following issues:

- Intangible cultural heritage of ethnic groups, such as: Gong culture in the Central Highlands, Quan ho Bac Ninh Folk Songs, Giong Festival of Phu Dong and Soc Temples, Chinese cuisine arts in the South, the role of Community in Water worship practices and eco-tourism, etc.

- Marine cultural heritage in Vietnam

- The preservation and promotion of intangible cultural heritage in Vietnam

Throughout the research process, I fortunately received continuous encouragement from Vietnamese social scientists in the Vietnamese National Cultural Heritage Council, whose chairman is Professor, Doctor of Science, Luu Tran Tieu, scientists-colleagues at the Institute of Culture & Arts (Ministry of Culture, Sports and Tourism), Associate Professor Nguyen Ngoc Tho (National University at Ho Chi Minh City), as well as international social scientists such as Professor, Dr. Tokumaru (Japan), Associate Professor Satomi (Japan), Professor, Dr. Park Yeon Kwan (South Korea), Professor Zheng Xiao Yun (China), Professor, Dr. Hy Van Luong (Canada), Associate Professor Lauren Meeker (USA)… In this joyous occasion of publication, I hereby express my deepest gratitude.

Research on the intangible cultural heritage of Vietnamese ethnic groups is a major scientific field, and my own projects are but a drop in this ocean, the personal musings of an individual that certainly welcomes readers' feedback, commentary, and advice.

Hanoi, Vietnam, August 2023.
Ben Chi Nguyen

PREMISES FOR THE DEVELOPMENT

OF VIETNAMESE CULTURE

Vietnam is situated in Southeast Asia. It borders the People's Republic of China to the North, the People's Democratic Republic of Laos and the Kingdom of Cambodia to the West, and the Pacific Ocean to the East with total coastline of 3.260 kilometers. Its mainland stretches from Đồng Văn at the latitude 23°22' North to the Cà Mau at the latitude 8°30' North of 1,650 kilometers long. Its largest width is approximately 600 kilometers, and the shortest width is about 50 kilometers. In addition to the mainland, the territory also includes thousands of outlying islands and small islands. Its total area is about 332,000 square kilometers, three-quarters of which are hills and mountains with different landforms. In the northwest and northeast regions, there are some mountain ranges extending northeast and northwest. The central region has the Trường Sơn mountain range that extends into the southern region. At both ends of the country, there are two plains named after the two big rivers, the Red River Delta and the Mekong Delta.

Vietnam is a tropical country with a humid monsoon. Hai Van Pass is the dividing line between two different climate zones. It is cold in winter from the Hải Vân Pass to the north, and wet and hot throughout the year from the Hải Vân Pass to the south.

Vietnam is the 13th most populous country in the world. According to United Nations statistics, its population reached 79.7 million in 2002, of which 25% lived in urban areas and the remaining population lived in rural areas. The annual population growth rate is 1.31%. The fate of the population is about 240.7 people per square kilometer.

Vietnamese population structure is young with nearly two thirds of its population at working age. The largest cities are Ho Chi Minh

City (population 5.57 million), Hanoi (over 3 million) and Hải Phòng (nearly 2 million).

As for its administrative division, in Vietnam, there are 58 provinces and 5 cities subordinate to the Central government, including Hanoi, Ho Chi Minh, Hai Phong, Đà Nẵng, Cần Thơ. Below the provinces, there are 625 subordinates including 10,541 communes, wards, and district towns. The entire territory of Vietnam is divided into eight geo-economic regions namely Northeast, Northwest, the Red River Delta, North Central, South Central, the Central Highlands, South East, and the Mekong Delta.

Vietnam is a multi-ethnic country. According to statistics released by the National Bureau of Statistics in 1979, there are 54 races (see table 1).

Table 1: List of Vietnamese Ethnicities

Code	Ethnicity	Other denominations	Main residential areas
(1)	(2)	(3)	(4)
01	Kinh (Viet)	Kinh	All over the country
02	Tày	Tho, Ngan, Phen, Thu Lao, Pa Di	Cao Bằng, Lạng Sơn, Hà Tuyên, Bắc Thái, Hoàng Liên Sơn, Quảng Ninh, Hà Bắc, Lâm Đồng
03	Tai/Thái	Tai, Tai Khao (Thái Trắng), Tai Đăm, Tai Thanh (Man Thanh), Hang Tong (Tai Muong), Pu Thay, Tho Da Bac	Sơn La, Nghệ Tĩnh, Thanh Hóa, Lai Châu, Hoàng Liên Sơn, Hà Sơn Bình, Lâm Đồng
04	Hoa (Hán)	Triều Châu, Phúc Kiến, Quảng Đông, Hải Nam, Hẹ (Hakka), Xa Phang	Ho Chi Minh, Hanoi, Hậu Giang, Đồng Nai, Minh Hai, Kien Giang, Hai Phong, Cuu Long...
05	Khmer	Cur, Cul, Cu, Tho, Cambodia, Vietnamese, Khmer, Krom	Hau Giang, Cuu Long, Kien Giang, Minh Hai, Ho Chi Minh, Song Be, Tây Ninh
06	Mường	Mol, Mual, Moi[11], Moi Bi, Ao Ta (Au Ta)	Ha Son Binh, Thanh Hoa, Vinh Phu, Hoang Lien Son, Sơn La, Ha Nam Ninh

---

[1] The Muong is called by the Thai

07	Nùng	Xuong, Giang, Nung An, Phan Sinh, Nung Chao, Nung Loi, Qui Rin, Khen Lai…	Cao Bằng, Lạng Sơn, Bac Thai, Ha Bac, Hoang Lien Son, Quảng Ninh, Ho Chi Minh, Lâm Đồng
08	Hmong (Mèo)	Meo, Meo Hoa, Meo Xanh, Meo Do, Meo Den, Na Mieo, Man Trang	Ha Tuyen, Hoang Lien Son, Lai Châu, Sơn La, Cao Bằng, Lạng Sơn, Nghệ Tĩnh
09	Dao	Man, Dong. Trai, Xa, Diu Mien, Kiem Mien, Quan Trang, Dao Do, Quan Chet, Lo Giang, Giao Tien, Thanh Y, Lan Ten, Dai Ban, Tieu Ban, Coc Ngang, Coc Mun, Son Dau…	Ha Tuyen, Hoang Lien Son, Cao Bằng, Lạng Sơn, Bac Thai, Lai Châu, Sơn La, Ha Son Binh, Vinh Phu, Ha Bac, Thanh Hoa, Quảng Ninh
09	Dao	Man, Dong, Trai, Xa, Diu Mien, Kiem Mien, Quan Trang, Dao Do, Quan Chet, Lo Gang, Giao Tien, Thanh Y, Lan Ten, Dai Ban, Tieu Ban, Coc Ngang, Coc Mun, Son Dau…	Ha Tuyen, Hoang Lien Son, Cao Bằng, Lạng Sơn, Bac Thai, Lai Châu, Sơn La, Ha Son Binh, Vinh Phu, Ha Bac, Thanh Hoa, Quảng Ninh
10	Jo'rai (Jarai, Gia-rai)	Gio-rai, Cho-rai, To-boan, Ho-bau, H'dung, Chor…	Gia Lai, Kon Tum
11	Ngái	Xin, Le, Dan, Khach Gia	Quảng Ninh, Cao Bằng, Lạng Sơn
12	Êđê	Ra-de, De, Kpa, A-dham, Krung, Ktul, Die, Rue, Bloo, E-pan, Mdhur[2], Bih…	Dak Lak, Phu Khanh
13	Bahnar	Go-lar, To-lo, Gio-lang, (Y-lang), Ro-Ngao, Krem, Roh, Con Kde, A-lacong, Kpang Cong, Bo-nam	Gia Lai, Kon Tum, Nghia Binh, Phu Khanh
14	S'đăng (Xơ-đăng)	Xo-teng, Hdang, To-dra, Mo-nam, Ha-lang, Ca-dong, Km-rang, Con-lan, Bri-la, Tang	Gia Lai, Kon Tum, Quảng Nam, Đà Nẵng
15	Sán Chay (Cao Lan – Sán Chỉ)	Cao Lan, Man Cao Lan, Hon Ban, San Chi, (also called Son Tu but never including the San Chi group in Bao Lac and Cho Ro)	Bac Thai, Quảng Ninh, Ha Bac, Cao Bằng, Lạng Sơn, Ha Tuyen

---

[2] The Mdhur is an intermediate group of the E-de and the Jarai. Some villages of the Mdhur living with Jarai in Cheo Reo, Gia Lai Kon Tum province claim to be the Jarai.

16	K'ho (Cờ-ho)	Xre, Noop, (Tu-lop, Co-don, Chi[3], Lat (Latch), Trinh	Lâm Đồng, Thuan Hai
17	Chăm (Chàm)	Chiem Thanh, Hroi	Thuan Hai, An Giang, Ho Chi Minh, Nghia Binh. Phu Khanh
18	Sán Dìu	San Doo, Trai, Trai Dat, Man, Quan Coc	Bac Thai, Vinh Phu, Ha Bac, Quảng Ninh, Ha Tuyen
19	Hrê	Cham Re, Chom Kre, Luy...	Nghia Binh
20	Mnông	Pnong, Nong Pre, Bu-dang, Di-Pri, Biat, Gar, Ro-lam, Chil	Đắk Lắk, Lâm Đồng, Song Be
21	Jp'rai (Jarai, Gia-rai)	Ra-clay, Rai, Noang, La-oang, Xa-dieng	Thuan Hai, Phu Khanh
22	Stiêng	Xa-dieng	Song Be, Tây Ninh
23	Bru-Vân Kiều	Bru, Van Kieu, Mang Cong, Tri, Khua	Binh Tri Thien
24	Thổ[4]	Kuo, Mon, Cuoi, Ho, Dan Lai, Ly Ha, Tay Pongj, Con Kha, Xa La Vang	Nghệ Tĩnh, Thanh Hoa
25	Giáy	Nhang, Dang, Pau Thin Pu, Na, Cui Chu[5]	Hoang Lien Son, Ha Tuyen, Lai Châu
26	Katu (Cơ-Tu)	Ca-Tu, Cao, Ha, Phuong, Ca-Tang[6]	
27	Giẻ-Triêng	Dgieh, Tareh, Giang Ray, Rin, Trieng, Tre, Ta-rieng, Ve (Veh) La-ve, Ca-tang	Quảng Nam, Đà Nẵng, Gia Lai, Kon Tum
28	Mạ	Chau Ma, Ma Ngan, Ma Xop, Ma To, Ma Krung	Lâm Đồng, Đồng Nai
29	Khmu (Kho-mu)	Xa Cau, Mun Xen, Pu Thenh, Tenh, Tay Hay	Nghệ Tĩnh, Sơn La, Lai Châu, Hoang Lien Son
30	Co	Cor, Col, Cua, Trau	Nghia Binh, Quảng Nam, Đà Nẵng
31	Ta-oi	Ta-oi, Pa-co, Pa-hi, (Ba-hi)	Binh Tri Thien

---

[3] Chil is a local group of the Mnông. Most of the Chil migrating to the South to live with the Cờ-ho claim to be the Cờ-ho while those who stay in their homeland with the Mnông claim to be the Mnông.

[4] This is the name they call themselves, it is unlike Thổ which was used to call the Tày living in Northeast Region, The Thai living in Northwest Region and the Khmer living in the Mekong Delta.

[5] The Cui Chu (Qui Châu) that has a group living among the Nùng in Bảo Lạc are considered the Nung

[6] Cà-tang is the common name various ethnic groups living in an area in Quảng Nam – Đà Nẵng that borders Laos. It is necessary to differentiate this common name from specifi names of ethnicities.

32	Ch'ro (Cho-ro)	Do-ho, Chau-ro	Đồng Nai
33	Kháng	Xa Khao, Xa Sua, Xa Don, Xa Dang, Xa Hoc, Xa Ai, Xa Bung, Quang Lam	Lai Châu, Sơn La
34	Xin-Mun	Puoc, Pua	Sơn La, Lai Châu
35	Hani (Hà Nhi)	U Ni, Xa U Ni	Lai Châu, Hoang Lien Son
36	Ch'ru (Chu-ru)	Cho-ru, Chu	Lâm Đồng, Thuan Hai
37	Lào	Lao Boc, Lao Noi	Lai Châu, Sơn La, Thanh Hoa, Hoang Lien Son
38	La Chí	Cu Te, La Qua	Ha Tuyen
39	La Ha	Xa Khao, Khia, Phlao	Lai Châu, Sơn La
40	Phù Lá	Bo Kho Pa, Mu Di Pa, Xa Pho, Pho, Xa Vo Lao, Pu Dang	Hoang Lien Son, Lai Châu
41	La Hủ	Khu Xung, Co Xung, Kha Quy	Lai Châu
42	Lự	Lu, Nhuon (Duon)	Lai Châu
43	Lô Lô	Mun Di	Cao Bằng, Lạng Sơn, Ha Tuyen
44	Chứt	Sach, May, Ruc, Ma-lieng, A-rem, Tu-vang, Pa-leng, Xo-lang, To-hung, Cha-cui, Tac-cui, U-mo, Xa La Vang	Binh Tri Thien
45	Mảng	Mang U, Xa La Vang	Lai Châu
46	Pà Thẻn	Pa Hung, Tong	Ha Tuyen
47	K'lao (Cơ Lao)		Ha Tuyen
48	Cống	Xam Khong, Mong Nhe, Xa Xeng	Lai Châu
49	Bố Y	Chung Cha, Trong Gia, Tu Di, Ti Din	Hoang Lien Son, Ha Tuyen
50	Si La	Cu De Xu, Kha Pe	Lai Châu
51	Pu Péo	Ka Peo, Pen Ti Lo Lo	Ha Tuyen
52	Brâu	Brao	Gia Lai, Kon Tum
53	Ô-đu	Tay Hat	Nghệ Tĩnh
54	Romăm		Gia Lai, Kon Tum

Source: Ethnology Review. Issue No 1 – 1979, pp. 58-63

I. Periods of development and characteristics of Vietnamese culture

Vietnamese culture is a creative achievement gained by Vietnamese ethnicities through their works and struggles to establish and defend the country for thousands of years history. It is also the result of their cultural exchanges and adaptation of the world civilizations. The development of Vietnamese culture can be divided into following periods:

- Prehistoric period: Vietnam was located in the region called by cultural researchers: Southeast Asian cultural stratum. The typical features of this stratum are Non-Chinese and Non-Indian and its cultural vestiges have been found in current Vietnam and ASEAN countries.

- Early historic period: In this period there appeared three culture – civilizations: the Đông Sơn culture in the Northern Delta, the Sa Huỳnh Culture in the Central Coast and the Đồng Nai – Óc Eo Culture in the South. All the three cultures have gained great achievement the Đông Sơn Culture with its high technique of bronze ware making and Co Loa citadel closely relating to the Hung Vuong Era, the Sa Huỳnh Culture with its high technique of iron ware making technique of gold refining, and so on.

- **The first millennium A.D**: The three aforementioned cultures entered to this period with different ends. The Óc Eo Culture suddenly disappeared in the 7th, or 8th century A.D and left behind only its aureole while the Sa Huỳnh Culture continued to develop with its existing Champa Culture. In the Northern Delta, the ancient Viet lived under Chinese Domination. Therefore, anti-Sinicization and becoming Sinicized was the culture features of this period, together with the descendants of Đông Sơn Culture that was preserved and developed.

- **From the beginning of the 10th century to 1858**: The Đại Việt Culture developed and closely associated with development and existence of monarchist dynasties, and integration between Champa and Đại Việt Cultures in the process of extending southwards. This was the golden age of Han and Nom script literature, architecture of temples, pagoda, and communal house, different traditional forms of performing arts such as *chèo* (popular opera), *tuồng* (Classical opera house), puppetry, and son on. After three periods of its restoration, Đại Việt culture has left a legacy or great names such as Nguyễn Trãi (1380 – 1442), Nguyen Du (1765 – 1820),Nguyen Đinh Chieu(1822-1888), Ho Xuan Huong(1772-1822), etc. Up to now(2023), Vietnam has 08 heritage sites recognized by UNESCO under the 1972 Convention: *Ha Long Bay, Hue Ancient Capital, Hoi An Ancient Town, My Son Sanctuary, Thang Long Imperial Citadel, Ho Dynasty Citadel, Phong Nha Ke Bang National Park, Trang An relics* and 15 heritage sites recognized by UNESCO under the 2003 Convention are: *Hue Royal Court Music, The Space of Gong in the Central Highland of Vietnam; Quan ho Bac Ninh Folk Songs; Giong Festival of Phu Dong and Soc Temples; Worship of Hung Kings in Phu Tho; Vi and Giam folk songs of Nghe- Tinh; Practices related to the Viet beliefs in the Mother Goddesses of the Three Realms; The Tug of War (as a multinational heritage), Don Ca Tai Tu in the South, Art of Bai Choi in the Central region, Xoan singing in Phu Tho, Then ritual of the Tay Nung people Xoe art of the Thai people, Ca tru of the Vietnamese, Bau Truc pottery of the Cham people*

. All of these heritages were found and develop during this period. Also, folk traditions developed vigorous both in genres and forms.

- From 1858 to 1945: French Invasion led to the cultural contact and exchange between Vietnamese and western cultures, mainly French, causing Vietnamese culture change and integrate into mainstream of world culture. This changing process was both voluntary and involuntary. The greatest achievements of this period was the development of the national writing system (Quoc ngu) that evolved from the script of a religious community in the Central region to a national one. The appearance of the printing house and the press changed Vietnamese culture from a gift culture to a culture with commodities. The French colonists eliminated examinations in Chinese ideograph in the South in 1867, in the North 1915, and in the Center in 1918, creating conditions for French cultural influences on Vietnam. The French set up new education on the basis of western scientific progresses and built some infrastructure of cultural institutions like the Opera House in Hanoi and Ho Chi Minh city, Far East College that could create the foundation for the new cultural activities later.

-**From 1945 to 1975:** Vietnamese culture developed in the context of the French resistance and Vietnamese – American war. During the war time, writers and artists had to involve in the national independence cause as soldier. Notably, Marxist-Leninist ideology has been penetrated in cultural life of the country. The People's Democratic State formed its new culture on the basis of the inheritance of traditional cultural essence, building new cultural institution like libraries, museums, cultural house, exhibition halls, clubs to facilitate creativity and consumption of new revolutionary cultural values. Having experienced two holly national resistances, Vietnamese culture is deserved to be in the vanguard of cultures of nations in the world that struggles against the invasion of imperialism and oppression.

According to Nguyen Khoa Diem, Vietnamese culture has the following characteristics[7]:

Firstly, Vietnamese culture is a unity in diversity. From the primeval Southeast Asian stratum in the prehistoric period, three cultures came into being in Vietnamese territory, including Dong Sơn culture (in the North), Sa Huỳnh culture (in center) and Đồng Nai culture (in the South). In early historic period and in the first millennium A.D culture in the Northern part suffered nearly one thousand years of Chinese domination while Champa culture existed in the Central Coast and Óc Eo culture in the South, and then they merged into Vietnamese culture, making up the unity in diversity.

One the other hand, Vietnam is a multiethnic nation with 54 ethnicities belonging to different language families. The Austro-Asiatic language family consist of Viet-Muong, Mon Khmer, Tay-Thai, and Mong-Dao groups and mixed language group including the Lachi, Laha, Colao, and Pupeo. The Austronesian language family includes the Giarai, the Ede, the Cham, the Raglai, the Churu. The Sino-Tibetan

---

[7] Nguyen Khoa Diem (Chief editor), *Building an Advances Vietnam Culture Imbued with National Identity,* National Politic Publishing House, Hanoi, 2001, pp. 29-35.

family consist of Chinese and Tibeto-Burmese groups. Each ethnic group of these language families has its own culture. While ethnicities in Truong Son Highland have their common cultural feature as mortuary statues, grave houses, unique gongs and marvelous epics, the Cham in the Central Coast is proud of its architectural towers, carving and inscriptions. The Khmer in the South have its treasury of Buddhist literature, carving, architecture, or pagodas as cultural centers and many traditional festivals. The Tay – Nung in the Northern uplands have their nice stilt houses, a treasury of folklore. Despite their own nuances, Vietnamese ethnic group have cultural elements in common. For the processes of long-lasting coexistence between them there are cultural alternations. Moreover, the ethnic groups belong to the Southeast Asian cultural stratum.

The unity in diversity of Vietnamese culture us also seen in its motion through space. In its long history, the motion of Vietnamese culture has created such cultural areas as Northwest, North-Viet, Northern Central Coast Highlands and Southern. Each of them has their own traits that do not destroy the common features of Vietnamese culture.

Secondly, the development of culture is attached to cultural constants such as peasant, agriculture, water rice and village. Creating, absorbing and bearing subjects of Vietnamese cultural values are peasants in Northern and Central parts, or tenant's farmers in the South who practice wet water rice cultivation. Together with them Confucian scholars in villages are intellectual people. In the process of development, Vietnamese culture comprises of the two streams: folklore and scholarly culture that are interacted, alternated and penetrated into each other creating the values and identities of Vietnamese culture.

The genealogy of Vietnamese culture is regarded as families, villages and the country. Having close association to their communities is the core mentality of Vietnamese people. Each social unit from family to village, has its own sustainable traits that contribute to the development of the country through its history Vietnamese culture both has its clear features and is ruled by those traits.

Thirdly, lying in the middle of the two North-South and East West axes, the intersection of Chinese and Indian civilizations, Vietnamese culture has adapted (maybe involuntarily) many elements of the two cultures. Starting in the 16th century, especially from the middle of the 19th century, the cultural exchange between Vietnamese and Western cultures brought new layers to Vietnamese culture. Due to those contacts (voluntary and involuntary), Vietnamese culture experienced two big transitions: transition from the Southeast Asia cultural stratum to the East Asian culture in the first millennium A.D; from regional culture. That process makes Vietnamese culture both have its own identity and activities integrate in the world culture.

Due to its special geo-political position that very few countries have had (lying on the intersection of the two North-South and East West axes), Vietnam has been a place of international conflicts: the conflicts between the North and South and the East and the West. Vietnam has been also a place that directly accumulates (maybe forced by invaders) ideologies, political institutions, economic modes, social organizations, cultures, beliefs, life styles of important powers in history and in the contemporary world. In the North- South axis there is China and India, and in the East-West axis there is France, Japan and the U.S. If saying that human resources are strength of the country for integrate with the world, the experiences on conflict and exchanges are likely a striking strength of Vietnamese people.

Fourthly, patriotism and desire to keep pace with human civilization are the most important manifestations that have become a constant in Vietnamese history and existed as a whole. They support each other and struggle and conflict with one another. The historical experiences of many countries have shown that the approach to human civilization may become the way to save a country, or may become the way to lose country. In the 19th century, due to mechanical thinking, some reign that refused to approach human civilization to keep defending our country's independence with backward ideas led our country to a slavery circle. Only President Ho Chi Minh and his comrades could establish a dialectic relationship between patriotism and the requirement to catch up with human civilization, and then they discovered Marxist-Leninism revived the nation's strength, threw off the colonialists' yoke, led the country to take new opportunities.

Under the impact of the two driving forces, in many cases in history, the Vietnamese people's behavior are unusual that surprises foreigners. Although they hate Chinese domination, they are willing to learn the teaching Confucianism. Or although they hate Western colonialism and fight against French aggressors, they look for Marxist-Leninism in the French culture. Only dialectic thinking and wisdom drawn from the blood and tears of various generations help the nation combine elements that can make up the nation's strength. It is not likely a defensive trick, or the opportunism of the Vietnamese people but the manifestation of the two driving forces in a flexible and dialectic interrelation.

Fifthly, if the main motivations of national development are a combination of the patriotism and the desire to keep pace with human civilization, Vietnamese national and cultural traits will be tolerance and harmony.

- Tolerance and harmony in heaven-earth-man world view

- Tolerance and harmony in the spiritual and material world with the different ideologies that have stayed long in national life (Buddhism, Confucianism, Christianity, traditional beliefs, modern scientific thinking etc.). President Ho Chi Minh, the brilliant representative of traditional and contemporary worlds, of the East and the West, was given the noble mission to bring Marxist-Leninism to Vietnam. He combined the revolutionary nature in the doctrine of the working class with the quintessence of the nation and the time to create an unbreakable strength.

- Tolerance and harmony in style and method of creation.

- Tolerance and harmony in institution, in man-to-man and generation – to generation relations.

- Tolerance and harmony among people living in the country.

- Today, it is also the tolerance and the harmony between people different in ownership and in political past, but similar in the objectives of building up a rich nation, a powerful country and a civilized, democratic and just society.

It is not without people who want to have scientific-technological and ideological-cultural revolutions that clear off absolutely opposites as the west do. In Vietnam, there is not such a revolution. In Vietnam there is only a revolution based on Ho Chi Minh ideology to advance ahead by integrating noble values of the nation's and human civilizations instead of "cutting off", or "clearing off".

Beside tolerance harmony, respect for sentimental attachment and ethics is also a notable trait to the nation. Benevolence and righteousness, faithfulness, and love for others always appreciated by Vietnamese people: *Eat the fruits, think of the person who planted the tree (Ăn quả nhớ kẻ trồng cây); Drink water, remember its sources (Uống nước nhớ nguồn); Man who live is a heap of gold (Người sống đống vàng); Man produces wealth but wealth does not produce man (Người làm nên của, của không làm nên người),* and so on. Among the tangible cultural heritage of Vietnam there are thousands of historical cultural vestiges, revolutionist, memorial houses, martyrs cemeteries, that worship people who rendered meritorious services to the country, to the people.

II. Reviewing some issues of Vietnamese culture before 1990

Before 1990, culture can be divided into three following periods:

From 1945 to 1954: our people waged the resistance against the French aggressive colonialists.

From 1954 to 1975: our people carried out two strategies tasks: Building socialism in the North and struggling for liberation of the South to unify the fatherland.

From 1975 to 1990: The country has been unified and conducted the three revolutions: scientific-technological revolution, cultural revolution, revolution in production relation. The country step by step integrates into the world economy through an open door policy, implements market economy, gets rid of the subsidized one.

From 1945 to 1954:

When the culture newly built after the victory of the August revolution began to display its power, our nation started the French resistance. For nine years of resistance, our people almost entirely concentrated on accomplishing resistance tasks. "Everything for the front". "Do everything to defeat the French enemy" were slogans of that time. Because of the war, our culture was split up into regional ones like culture of free fire zones, culture of rear areas and culture of temporarily occupied urban areas. During the resistance war, cultural activities were mainly carried out in rural areas and military units. They were in their essence propaganda of resistance tasks. Patriotism, and national salvation were put first. The men-soldiers theme became a major inspiration for culture and art works in those days.

In 1948, at the second National Cultural Conference Truong Chinh delivered the report of *Marxism and Vietnamese Culture*. It could be called a Cultural Guideline developed on the basis of the Vietnam Communist Party's Cultural Guideline 1943.

In 1959, in a letter sent to painters, President Ho Chi Minh put forth an important idea: *Culture and art are also a front, you (i.e. writers and artists) are soldiers in this front yourselves.*

A main feature of resistance culture was vigorous movements of mass artistic performance. The movements created an exciting and cheerful atmosphere among people and were a source of inspiration for such revolutionary movements as patriotic emulation, accomplishing a feat by killing enemy, continuously increase production, etc. ... to serve the front and make a great contribution to common victory of the nation.

From 1954 to 1975

The Dien Bien Phu Victory put an end to the French colonialist's domination over our country. After peace was restored and the North was emancipated, cultural activities from resistance zones spread out to just taken-over urban areas.

In 1955, the Ministry of Culture was established on the basis of Propaganda and Information Office born right after the August Revolution.

Cultural Institution left by the old regime in Hanoi like the Opera House, the National Library, museum, studio, cinemas, newspaper agencies, radio stations, and so on, were taken over and renovated to serve the new regime.

Culture and art university and colleges were established one after another, where culture and art personnel throughout the country have been trained to become active workers of cultural branches.

National Literature and Art Conferences were important landmarks in the development of the literary and art world all over the country (the 2nd Conference was held in February, 1957, the 3rd in November, 1962 and the 4th in January, 1968). Central associations such as the Architects Association (1948), Writers Association (1957), Fine Art Association (1957), Photographer Association (1965), and Cinema Workers Association (1968) were established in this period.

When American imperialists started a sabotage war by the air force over the North of Vietnam, the whole country waged a national salvation anti-U.S. resistance, cultural tasks of the North that were aimed to serve the revolutionary duty as defeating the enemy with such slogans as "Do everything for victory". "Revolutionary attack", "Aim at enemy to fire". Patriotism and collectivism were put at the forefront. Men-soldiers again took the central place in all culture and art creative works. Mass artistic performance also made considerable contributions: the movement of "Song drown bomb explosion" in the North as well as the movement of "Singing for my compatriots" of the youth in Southern occupied areas left a deep impression on our spiritual life those days.

Evaluating contributions of culture and arts to the cause of national liberation revolution, the 6th National Congress Documents said: "The great victory our nation gained in the national salvation anti-US resistance is not only a victory of sound, political, military lines but also of Party's cultural policy".

A network of cultural institution was set up. Culture and art institute, schools, cultural propagandizing institutions, from central level to local one, like cultural house, clubs, museums, libraries, theatres, cinemas, and so on were modeled in those the Soviet Union.

Cultural Achievements in the Period of 1975-1986

The great victory of the national salvation anti-US. Resistance opened up a significant during point in the national history, gloriously finished thirty years of national defensive war, put an end to more than one century of domination by colonialism and neocolonialism over our country, completed democratic revolution all over the country, and took our country to a new era – an era of independence, unification. The whole country advanced up to the phase of building socialism.

In 1976, the 4th National Congress was held. It laid down lines for socialist revolution in our country in general and for cultural domain in particular that was fully called "ideological and cultural revolution line". Expanding this direction, Truong Chinh wrote: "We consider ideological and cultural revolution as an organic part of the whole socialist revolutionary cause of our country. We should not wait till the time that socialist production relationship, modern infrastructure and advance technology have become firm to make an ideological and cultural revolution, but we should proceed it at the same time, even build it in advance a new culture and a new socialist man to a certain extent under dictatorship of the proletariat".

Socio-historical Characteristics of Our Country in the Decade 1975 – 1986

The most evident characteristic determining the main content of the cause of reconstruction with socialist orientation in our country is: *Our country is a society with small-sized production advancing up to socialism by – passing the stage of capitalist development.*

In leading the domain of culture – literature and arts, our Party always pays great attention to theoretical activities, through which they direct practical ones. The Cultural Guideline of 1943 puts forward three principles: nationalization, science, and popularization that were still preserved in "Marxism and Vietnamese culture" (1948), where Truong Chinh applied Marxist theory on presenting some issue of revolutionary culture – literature and art of our country at that time.

Now, the country is entirely unified. We are carrying out socialist construction that requires to have fully worked-out theories including theory of building a new socialist culture with *socialist content and nationality.*

All the concept of cultural building has been presented in the Documents of the 4th National Congress of Vietnam Communist Party. They are as follows:

a. Concept of culture – literature and art as a part of the revolutionary cause under the Party leadership.

b. Concept of nation in building culture, literature and art;

c. Concept of the people (the masses) in building culture, literature and art;

d. Concept of class character and communist party character in culture literature art;

e. Concept of literature and art attached to the life, reality of socialist literature and art;

f. Concept of building new socialist man;

g. Concept of positions roles, functions, culture – literature and arts;

h. Concept of freedom in creation by writers and artists;

i. Concept of building local cultural life.

Heretofore, there are the nice concepts of culture – literature and art if our Party. This system of concepts was summed up from reality and used to a direct culture – literature and art activities in the first decade after the country has been united. These concepts have led us to go to in the right direction and gain certain achievements.

- Building an organization system of the cultural branch was set up right after the establishment of the Ministry of Culture (1955) and in the South after the South was liberated, from the provincial to the communal levels. Remember that in the 4th National Congress of Vietnam Communist Party, our Party advocated to build an organizational system at the district level. The Congress resolution said: "Make districts become powerful economic agricultural and industrial units, take them as areas for reorganizing, distributing labor combine agriculture with industry, a private economy with collective one, workers with peasants. Make district authorities become a management organ that develops all-sided plans, have its budget, manages production, circulation and life in the district". Therefore, the organization of a cultural branch also has to aim at making district powerful.

- Network of cultural institutions

On the basis of the administrative division, the network of cultural institutions in our country includes four levels: central, provincial, district and communal ones. During the resistance war, some of cultural institutions like libraries, stadia, parks, museums, and so on were built in Hanoi and other provinces: The Vietnam – Soviet Union Friendship Palace of Culture in Hanoi city; Hai Phong Museum in Haiphong city; Museum of ethnology in Thai Nguyen province; So

Viet Nghệ Tĩnh Museum in Vinh City, Nghe An province, 3-2 Theatre in Nam Định City, Nam Đinh province.

When the peace has been restored, all the cities in the country need to build their own cultural institutions like general museums, theatres, stadia, parks, young pioneer houses, etc. …

Pilot cultural house at the district level was built first in Dong Hung district (Thái Bình province), then in other districts of Thái Bình. Besides, Hải Hậu district (Nam Định province), Thu Duc district (Ho Chi Minh city), An Nhon district (Bình Định province) also were the first units of the district cultural houses.

According to statistical data of the Ministry of Culture and Information, the provincial cultural institutions up to the end of the 1980s were listed as follows:

Table 2: Cultural Institutions

Cultural Institution	Up to 1985			Up to 1990		
	Central level/ Province	District/ Town	Commune/ Quarter	Central level/ Province	District/ Town	Central level/ Province
Cultural House	22	153	850	45	216	1,020
Public Library	41	462	870	45	428	1,095
Museum	20			37		
House of traditions		82	84		114	163
Local broadcasting station			8,793			≈ 10,000

Apart from the network of administrative cultural institutions under the Ministry of Culture and Information, there are also those subordinate to military, police forces, and trade union, youth's (young pioneers included), women's organization and of some branches like education, postal service, railway, etc. … Compared to the number of existing districts, towns, communes, quarters, the number of cultural institutions is very few. However, they are of great importance because that was the first time in the new society, people built cultural institutions in residential areas to meet their own cultural needs.

During the resistance war, there were only cultural movements but not cultural institution, so cultural activities were not performed regularly. The existence of cultural institutions in residential areas nowadays show that cultural needs of the people have become indispensable on the one hand, and their cultural activities become more and more intensive on the other hand. Therefore, it requires to improve their quality. However, it is necessary to avoid wasting money by building cultural house that are too big with seven halls, or eight thousand seats as many localities do due to "voluntarism", to "show off accomplishments, to gain great achievements" while cultural activities are not performed there regularly.

Now all cultural activities in our country are aimed to fulfill the task of building socialism according to the slogan of "Fast, strongly, steadily, advance to socialism". The matter of building a new culture, new man is put in the framework of "ideological and cultural revolution" and "scientific – technological revolution". In which, the ideology of collective mastery is highly appreciated in the qualities of new man.

CHARACTERISTICS OF THE WORSHIP OF HUNG KINGS IN PHÚ THỌ PROVINCE

1. Like all elements of folklore, the worship of Hung Kings (雄王) in Phú Thọ is influenced by social and historical factors during its development. What we see through this tradition today is the product of contemporary cross-section observation. Throughout history and space, this tradition has had a lot of movement and transformation. It is the movement and transformation that created the worship of Hung Kings with its own characteristics compared to other cults in the Vietnamese folk mind. In other words, it is these specific characteristics that create value for the worship of Hung Kings in Phú Thọ.

2. The worship of Hung Kings is associated with a very specific space, but on the contemporary geographical boundary of Phú Thọ province, a province in the Red River Delta of Vietnam, with the north bordering Tuyên Quang and Yên Bái provinces, the south bordering Hòa Bình province, the west bordering Sơn La province, the east bordering Vĩnh Phúc province, the southeast bordering Hanoi capital.

2. 1. In fact, the name of Phú Thọ province did not appear until 1903 due to the change of the name of Hưng Hóa province. Changing the geographical boundaries of Phú Thọ province in history is not easy at all. In prehistoric times, Phú Thọ belonged to Văn Lang, one of the 15 regions of Văn Lang Kingdom, which according to legend is associated with Hùng Kings. In the early history, Phú Thọ belonged to Mê Linh district. During the Chinese domination (AD 43-938), Phú Thọ was divided into three areas under the three districts of Mê Linh, Tân Xương, Phong Châu. Beginning in the tenth century, the administrative structure of Đại Việt Kingdom had many changes, the district regime of the previous period of Chinese rule was changed by adopting the 'đạo'

system[8]. 'đạo' was then divided into phủ (prefecture), châu (sub-prefecture), or huyện (district). Phú Thọ region belonged to Tam Giang 'đạo'. From the Lê Dynasty (1428-1788) to the Nguyễn Dynasty (1802-1945), except Thanh Xuyên district (now Thanh Sơn, Tân Sơn and Thanh Thủy districts) and Yên Lập district (now Quy Hóa district) remained under Hưng Hóa province, most territorial lands of Phú Thọ have been moved to Sơn Tây province. The French invaded Vietnam, and in 1891, the Governor-General of Indochina established a new province of Hưng Hóa with the districts of Tam Nông, Thanh Thủy of the former Hưng Hóa province and the districts of Sơn Vi, Thanh Ba and Phù Ninh of Lâm Thao prefecture (a part of Sơn Tây province). In 1903, Hứng Hóa province was changed to Phú Thọ province, consisting of two prefectures (phủ) of Lâm Thao and Đoan Hùng controlling 8 districts (Tam Nông, Thanh Thủy, Sơn Vi, Thanh Ba, Phù Ninh, Cẩm Khê, Hạ Hòa, and Hạc Trì) and two sub-prefectures (châu) of Thanh Sơn and Yên Lập. In 1968, the two provinces of Phú Thọ and Vĩnh Phúc merged into one province: Vĩnh Phú. Since 1996, the two provinces of Phú Thọ and Vĩnh Phúc have been re-established. Up to now, Phú Thọ province includes Việt Trì City, Phú Thọ Town and eleven districts (Cẩm Khê, Đoan Hùng, Hạ Hòa, Lâm Thao, Phù Ninh, Tam Nông, Tân Sơn, Thanh Ba, Thanh Sơn, Thanh Thủy, and Yên Lập) instituted by a total of 277 communes, wards, and district towns. Changing that geographical boundary of Phú Thọ in history creates the geo-cultural position of the province itself in Vietnamese history.

2.2. In the opinion of many geographers, Phu Tho is a midland province, a convergence of three rivers: the Red River (Thao River), Lô River, and Đà River. If you imagine the Red River Delta as a triangle with the bottom of the Gulf of Tonkin, the top of that triangle is Việt Trì city. Cultural researcher Trần Quốc Vượng once remarked quite accurately: "The Red River Delta with the current area of about 15-

---

[8] Which was respectively renamed lộ, trấn, xứ or tỉnh, equivalent to "province" of the present day.

16.000km², formed mainly along the triangular road [...] the Red River is 1.150km long, of which 510km is located on the current territory of Vietnam. The Red River is a relatively large and strong river (up to 30,000m³/second), carrying a huge amount of alluvium, calculated to 130 million tons/year. And Việt Trì city is the first delta triangular peak, and the Red River – Đuống River junction (Dâu gate) near Cổ Loa is the second peak and Hưng Yên city is the current third vertex of the Red River Delta, while the bottom edge of the triangle lies along the coast from Yên Lập district (Quảng Ninh province) to Nho Quan district (Ninh Bình province). Therefore, "The Red River" is understood as a "système" (system); and Việt Trì city and surrounding areas - formerly Vĩnh Phú, is the oldest peak region of the Red River Delta" (Trần, Quốc Vượng 1996, p. 72-3). The geographical - cultural, geopolitical position of Việt Trì city and Phú Thọ province related to the process of Vietnamese conquering the Red River and starting to explore the river delta.

2.3. The sixties and seventies of the twentieth century witnessed great achievements of Vietnamese archaeologists in Phú Thọ. In 1968, professors and students of the Faculty of History, Hanoi University (now VNU University of Social Sciences and Humanities) discovered Son Vi Culture, dating from C14:10.000-20.000 years ago today at the end of the Old Stone Age (Trần Quốc Vượng,1996, p. 74). According to Prof. Ha Van Tan: "Sơn Vi culture is a culture before the Neolithic era and after the early Neolithic period" (Hà Văn Tấn 1997, p. 223). After Sơn Vi Culture is the archaeological culture of Phùng Nguyên which has discovered more than 40 relics in Phú Thọ. Along with the Phùng Nguyên archaeological culture, Phú Thọ also has the archaeological cultures of Đồng Đậu and Gò Mun (Hà Văn Tấn 1997, p. 447-593). Most noteworthy is the archaeological site of Cả village. From 1960 to 1980, archaeologists discovered and excavated twice with a total area of 6.589m², uncovering 311 Dongsonian (Đông Sơn) tombs. Archaeologists agreed that before becoming a burial ground, Cả village was a residential area, a midland center of the Dongsonian culture. Commenting on the relationship between these archaeological cultures, Cung Đình Thanh, a Vietnamese researcher in Australia, said that the brass culture from Phùng Nguyên to Dongson was divided into three phases: Phùng Nguyên culture, about XV century BC; Đồng Đậu and Gò Mun cultures belong to the XIV, XIII and XII centuries BC; and Dongsonian culture reached its peak around the seventh and sixth centuries BC (Cung, Đình Thanh 2003, p. 141).

We reiterate the archaeological data to show that Phu Tho was one of the regions associated with the birth of the state in the Red River Delta region. "The geography of the early state formation in Vietnam" (Trần, Quốc Vượng 2005, p. 123), and "the midland of Việt Trì - Bạch Hạc is the geopolitical center of the ancient Vietnam State during the revolution of copper - iron metallurgy" (Trần, Quốc Vượng 1986, p. 82). In folk consciousness, that state was associated with Hùng Kings and attached to the ancient Văn Lang state. There must be a historical premise in order for the Hùng Kings faith to form and develop. It is true that the essence of the worship of Hùng Kings is a memorial of the history of the next generations with the merits of ancestors.

3. The worship of Hùng Kings in Phú Thọ is a faith that has a special position in the folk consciousness of the people in Phú Thọ.

3.1. The worship of Hung Kings in Phú Thọ is the result of the process of change, deposition of different cultural-faith classes, so that on the cross-section, the worship of Hung Vuong is the worship of the first ancestors of the whole nation-state, not only of the Vietnamese in the Red River Delta but also of the Vietnamese in the Central and Southern regions and a number of overseas Vietnamese communities. Formed in the midland region, the worship of Hùng Kings we observe today is actually the worship of the contemporary section. The cultural and religious layer that we easily observed at the deepest cultural layer in this faith is the worship of mountain gods. The results of the 2010-2011 scientific inventory of the research team led by Prof. Bùi Quang Thanh in Phú Thọ province show that there are 46 relics in 29 communes and 11 districts where the character being worshiped is Hùng Kings. Simultaneously, they discovered 108 other monuments in

52 communes and 12 districts where the character being worshiped is named by beautiful names (titles), such as Đột Ngột Cao sơn thánh vương (Lord Đột Ngột High Mountains), Ất Sơn thánh vương (Lord Ất Mountains), Viễn Sơn thánh vương (Lord Far Mountains), etc. Especially, the tablet at Thượng temple on Nghĩa Lĩnh Mountain also names Hùng Kings under these beautiful names (titles). The legend of Hà Lộc commune (Khải Xuân sub-district, Sơn Vi district, Lâm Thao prefecture, Phú Thọ province) clearly states that Hùng Kings' ordained name was Holy King Hùng Quốc Vương: Lord Grandiose High Mountain - the founding emperor among 18 Hùng Kings of the State of Ancient Việt peoples[9]. The ordained name of Hùng Hi Vương (the Chấn branch) is *Holy Hùng King of Far Mountain - the Holy King of Grace*[10], and of Hùng Hi Vương (the Tốn branch) is *Holy Hùng King of Ất Mountain – the Emperor of Victory Support and Justice*[11]. Noticeably, the legend of Vi Cương commune also recorded the similar beautiful titles of these Hùng Kings. I believe that the cultural and religious layer later merged between the worship of Thần Nông (Agricultural Gods/Earth Gods) and the worship of Hùng Kings.

3.2. The worship of Hung Kings is a belief developed between two dimensions of force: the attitudes of the monarchs and the attitudes of the people in history. It can be seen that the worship of Hung Kings, by its very nature, has a profound consensus between monarchs and the attitude of the people. With the status of the founding ancestors of the people, Hung Kings created this consensus. We can see the attitudes of the monarchs through their actions. Henri Maspero, in his research, believed that the temple of Hùng Kings was established in the Trần

---

[9] In Vietnamese: *Thánh tổ Hùng Vương Nam thiên thượng thánh tiền hoàng đế khai quốc hồng đồ, đột ngột cao sơn, cổ Việt Hùng thị nhất thập bát thế vương*; in Chinese: 聖祖雄王南天上聖皇帝開國宏圖突兀高山古越雄氏一十八世王.

[10] In Vietnamese: *Hùng Vương viễn sơn thánh vương, ân trạch phổ huệ thánh vương*; in Chinese: 雄王遠山聖王，恩澤普惠聖王.

[11] In Vietnamese: *Hùng Vương Ất Sơn thánh vương trợ thắng công bình hoàng đế*, in Chinese: 雄王乙山聖王助勝公平皇帝.

Dynasty (1225-1400). If the first Hung Vuong temple was built in the Trần dynasty, it should have appeared after 1313 (the 21st Hưng Long year) when the Trần dynasty conferred titles for the Gods that Lý Tế Xuyên recorded in *Việt điện u linh* (*Collection of Stories on the Shady and Spiritual World of the Viet Realm*). The royal dynasty which had the most impact on Hùng Kings worship was the Lê Dynasty (1428-1789). According to *The Holy Genealogy 18 Hùng Kings*[12] compiled by the late Academy scholar Nguyễn Cố in 1472, King Hồng Đức's 3rd year title was attached to the year of Canh Tý (Gengzi 庚子年, 1600) – the first year of King Lê Kính Tông by Nguyễn Trọng and duplicated by the ritual officer Lê Đình Hoan. As one can see, this holy genealogy is the first complete document to record the full Hùng Kings period. Along with the holy genealogy are the divine relics (legends) of Hùng Kings. So far, at least, we have found the relics of Hạ Giáp commune, Thanh Thúy commune, Yên Khê commune, Hà Lộc commune, Tiên Cương commune, Vy Cương commune, Hy Cương commune, Nghĩa Cương commune, and Quế Trạo hamlet that were well documented by ancient Confucianists on the legend and worship of Hùng Kings. In addition, we discovered Lê-Trịnh dynasties' orders issued in the first Đức Nguyên year (1674), the 28th Cảnh Hưng year (1767), the 46th Cảnh Hưng year (1785), and another order by King Quang Trung of the Tây Sơn Dynasty in 1789 (the second Quang Trung year). The Nguyễn dynasty (1802-1945) repeatedly ordained villages to worship Hùng Kings. In this research, I quote the ordinations of King Gia Long and King Tự Đức. King Gia Long's ordination wrote:

"This is to ordain officers and all villagers of Chân Lao village of Thanh Ba District to worship Hùng Kings. The worship has already existed in this commune. The villagers must follow the old rules in deploying the worship and expressing the veneration to the Kings […].

---

[12] In Vietnamese: *Hùng đồ thập bát diệp thánh vương ngọc phả cổ truyền*; in Chinese: 宏圖十八葉聖王玉譜古傳.

August 21, the eighth year of King Gia Long (1810)" (God's Seal of Chân Lao village, Vĩnh Chân sub-district, Hạ Hòa district, Phú Thọ province, FQ 4o18/XVI, 45)

Chân Loa village was then ordained one more time by King Tự Đức in the third year of his reign (1850).

The common feature of these dynasties is that they all considered Hùng Kings as the first founding ancestor of Vietnam. Similarly, the Nguyễn Dynasty (1802-1945) maintained the assignment to the governor of Phú Thọ province to preside over rituals of Hùng Kings worship at the temples on Nghĩa Lĩnh Mount.

After 1945, the current Vietnamese government attaches great importance to maintaining the worship and the festival of Hùng Kings temples. At the first year of the young Democratic Republic of Vietnam, Vice President Huỳnh Thúc Kháng went to Hùng Kings Temple to pay rituals. In 1956, the Hùng Kings Temple Festival was solemnly held. Reporter of Xinhua News Agency (China) wrote about the festival with respectful words: "Hung Kings are the ancestors and heroes in the Vietnamese people's mind. Hùng Kings made great achievements in pushing back the invading ethnic groups, promoting the development of the Vietnamese nation. Therefore, every year on the 10th day of the third lunar month, Vietnamese people organize activities to commemorate Hùng Kings."[13]. Since then, the Vietnamese Government has always been interested in the worship of Hùng Kings, from the planning of the historical monument of the master temple to the death anniversary of the Kings.

On the other hand, the attitude of people of all generations with the worship of Hùng Kings is a force from the bottom to make this tradition develop in history. The book *Nam Việt thần kỳ hội lục* (The Collected Records of Miraculous Legends of Nam Viet) written in the

---

[13] Essay of Xinhua News Agency No. 2147, 1956; Documentation of the project *Building the profile of the Worship of Hùng Kings in Phú Thọ*, Vietnam Institute of Culture and Art, computer manuscript.

17th century said that the whole country had 73 villages of Hùng Kings worship, of which 11 were imperially ordained. Hundreds of years later, in 1973, Mr. Nguyễn Ngọc Chương provided really valuable data: "If only counting from Việt Trì to Thao River up to Hạ Hòa, up to Đà river to Thanh Thủy, up to Lô river to Đoan Hùng, at least 432 relics can be counted. Among them were 40 temples to worship Hung King, 77 temples to his wife and children; the number of the temple to worship Cao Sơn and Tản Viên gods and generals is 288 places. In addition, there are 87 other monuments related to historical events of the Hung Kings" (Nguyễn, Ngọc Chương 1973, p. 127). Thus, besides being worshiped in the temples on Nghĩa Lĩnh Mountain, Hùng Kings are is also characters worshiped by people in the villages of Phú Thọ province. The respect for Hùng Kings as the founding ancestors of the nation and the morality of "when one drinks water, one must not forget where it comes from" of the Vietnamese people through generations have made the worship of Hùng Kings develop widely and deeply. In the system of folk beliefs in Vietnam, hardly has any religion got such a characteristic. Perhaps, the cohesion of the community, the perception of a common ancestor of the country is the basis to create that characteristic of Hùng Kings worship in Phú Thọ. In addition, it was the impact of the dynasties before 1945 and the current state that made this worship develop. Remembering history really overcomes emotional complex; religious faith simply becomes a sustainable sense of political-historical significance, a rational awareness that makes the common ancestor of the people and the nation. Today people in many regions of Vietnam often remind each other that:

"Anyone who goes back and forth must remember the common ancestors' anniversary on the 10th of the third lunar month each year"[14].

3.3. The main point of certain worship is about people's faith in the worshiped figure(s). Worshiped figures are always pushed into the sacred realms that are both fanciful and mysterious. At the same time,

---

[14] In Vietnamese: "dù ai đi ngược về xuôi; nhớ ngày giỗ tổ mồng mười tháng ba".

the path to the sanctification of the character to be worshiped will be the path that people in the historical period have historically historicized and legendized the character to be worshiped. The worship of Hùng Kings is the result of a harmonious process of historicalization and mythification. "The reverberation of history" – the English translation of "hồi quang của lịch sử" used by Tạ Chí Đại Trường, has made the process of historicizing the worshiped character even more historical. Indeed, on the Vietnamese land, there is hardly any place that has a geographical-historical position like Phú Thọ province to have opportunities for the process of historical development of such characters. Historical researcher Tạ Chí Đại Trường once made a very interesting comment: "The collective memory of the people has kept the image of the leaders of a pre-colonial country (in some form of political gathering) in which similar forms, although they bear shrinkage or change to a certain extent, remain in place during the Chinese domination period and later, making the memory more consolidated and sustainable." (Tạ Chí Đại Trường 2000, p. 138) The process of mythification is the basis for creating a treasure of folklore in general and myth in particular in Phú Thọ region. The author of *Địa chí Vĩnh Phú văn hóa dân gian vùng đất Tổ* (Vĩnh Phú Provincial Chronicle: folklore of the ancestral land) is completely reasonable to divide the former Vĩnh Phú province (now the two provinces of Phú Thọ and Vĩnh Phúc) into three zones of folklore: Hùng Kings zone, Thánh Tản[15] Zone, and Hai Bà Trưng[16] zone. "In Hùng Kings zone, for example, we see dense appearances of legends, fairy tales, legends about 18 Hùng kings [...]. The festivals here are also mainly ceremonies and folk performances around the stories related to the topic of national construction. There are also many forms of singing, dancing, rituals and customs associated with the oldest life such as tùng-dí

---

[15] Tản Viên Mountain God.

[16] Two female leaders (kings) who gathered the Vietnamese in the Red River Delta to fight against Chinese domination during the period AD 39-43.

dancing [17], deploying howling procession, paying sacrifice to nô-nường[18], organizing procession of Mr. and Mrs. Khíu, opening buffalo-meat party or rice-cake and honey cake parties, etc. [...]". Both of these processes interact with each other, making the worshiped character of the faith even more sacred. In the folk consciousness of the Phú Thọ residents, Hùng Kings are both ancestors, gods and the founders of the country, but also caretakers of the lives of the people, both sacred and close as if they are present with the community in every situation of every human life and in the life of the community following the rotation of the nature of the crop. Therefore, the people of Trẹo village (now in Hùng Sơn town of Lâm Thao District) organized the Hùng Kings procession festival from the temples on Nghĩa Lĩnh Mountain to their village to celebrate Tết[19] on the 24th of the lunar December. They regarded Hùng Kings as indispensable members during the Lunar New Year holidays.

3.4. Phú Thọ, due to its geopolitical and geo-cultural position, has become the center of Hùng Kings' worship. From Phú Thọ, the worship spread to all parts of the country. It is true that the diffusion process takes place in two different waves. From this land of origin, this worship spread to some localities in the North. Then from here, among the residents marching to the Central and the South, those who were psychologically oriented towards the origin adopted the worship. Therefore, many Hùng Kings temples were erected in many places of the present-day Central and Southern regions. Therefore, it can be said that the worship of Hùng Kings is the result of the process of convergence and diffusion as well as spreading and converging, becoming a cult of an entire people of a nation with a strong vitality through time.

---

[17] A ritualistic performance of fertility desire in which unmarried men (usually 18 men) holding wooden phallic figures and unmarried women holding wooden vagina figures rhythmically press both figures on each other in the rhythm of drumming.

[18] Nô: symbolic male genital figure; nường: symbolic female genital figure.

[19] Vietnamese name of the lunar New Year festival.

Conclusion

At the end of the book *Văn hóa Đông Sơn ở Việt Nam* (The Dongsonian Culture in Vietnam), Prof. Hà Văn Tấn wrote: "Nowhere on earth except for a place where there are a people who believe that they have a common ancestor and share a common ancestral temple so that people of the whole nation pay pilgrimage to commemorate their ancestor in a unified day of the year" (Hà Văn Tấn 1994, p. 429). I think it is the respectful contemplation of a leading archaeologist in Vietnam of the worship of Hùng Kings on contemporary observation perspective. As a stream from the distant past of history until today, the worship of Hùng Kings in Phú Thọ has mobilized and received different layers of cultural and belief sediments under the influence of magnetic forces under different dimensions, converging and spreading, to become the driving force of the cause of national unity and solidarity in a common voice of the descendants of Hùng Kings.

Before the Anniversary of Hùng Kings in 2011

Reference

1. Đào, Duy Anh. 1994. *Đất nước Việt Nam qua các đời (Vietnam through generations)*. Huế: Thuận Hóa Publisher, Reprint edition.

2. Hà, Văn Tấn ed. 1994. *Văn hóa Đông Sơn ở Việt Nam* (Đông Sơn culture in Vietnam). Hanoi: Social Science Publisher.

3. Hà, Văn Tấn. 1997. *Theo dấu các văn hóa cổ (Tracing the ancient culture)*. Hanoi: Social Science Publisher.

4. Lê, Tượng; Nguyễn, Anh Tuấn; Phạm, Hoàng Oanh. 2009. *Nước Văn Lang thời đại các vua Hùng* (The Kingdom of Van Lang in the era of Hùng Kings). Published by Department of Culture, Sports, Information of Phú Thọ and Phú Thọ History Association, 2009.

5. Lê, Văn Hảo. 1982. *Hành trình về thời đại Hùng Vương dựng nước* (A Journey to the Hùng Kings era). Hanoi: Youth Publisher.

6. Many authors. 2002. *Tổng tập văn nghệ dân gian đất Tổ* (Folk Arts Collection of the Ancestral lands). Published by Department of Culture, Sports, Information of Phú Thọ and Phú Thọ Folk Art Association, Vol. 3.

7. Many authors. 2005. *Lễ hội truyền thống vùng đất Tổ* (Traditional festivals of the Ancestral lands). Published by Department of Culture, Sports, Information of Phú Thọ and Phú Thọ Folk Art Association.

8. Ngô, Quang Nam & Xuân Thiêm ed. 1986. *Địa chí Vĩnh Phú, văn hóa dân gian vùng đất Tổ* (Vĩnh Phú Provincial Chronicle: folklore of the ancestral land). Việt Trì: Vĩnh Phú Department of Culture and Information.

9. Nguyễn, Duy Hinh. 2004. *Văn minh Lạc Việt* (The civilization of Lạc Việt). Hanoi: Culture and Information Publisher.

10. Nguyễn, Ngọc Chương. 1973. "On the distribution of historical monuments under the reign of Hung Kings". printed in *Hùng Kings building the country*, volume 3, Hanoi: Social Science Publisher.

11. Cung, Đình Thanh. 2003. *Tìm về nguồn gốc văn minh Việt Nam dưới ánh sáng mới của khoa học* (Discovering the origin of Vietnamese civilization under the new light of science). Sydney, Australia: Thought Publisher.

12. Phạm, Xuân Độ. 1939. *Phú Thọ tỉnh chí* (Provincial Record of Phú Thọ). Hanoi: Nam Ký Publisher.

13. Tạ, Chí Đại Trường. 1989. *Thần, người và đất Việt* (Gods, people and land of Vietnam). California, USA: Literature Publisher.

14. Tạ, Chí Đại Trường. 1999. *Những bài văn sử* (Historical writings). California, USA: Literature Publisher.

15. Trần, Quốc Vượng. 1996. *Theo dòng lịch sử, những vùng đất, thần và tâm thức người Việt* (Tracing the history, lands, gods and minds of the Vietnamese people). Hanoi: Culture Publisher.

16. Trần, Quốc Vượng. 1996. "Vinh Phu, geopolitical position and indigenous cultural identity". In *Tracing the history, lands, gods and minds of the Vietnamese people,* Hanoi: Culture Publisher. pp.66-pp.83.

17. Trần, Quốc Vượng. 2000. *Văn hóa Việt Nam: tìm tòi và suy ngẫm* (Vietnamese culture: exploration and thinking). Hanoi: Ethnic Culture Publisher and the Journal of Culture and Art.

18. Trần, Quốc Vượng. 2005. *Môi trường, con người và văn hóa* (Environment, people and culture). Hanoi: Văn hóa – Thông tin Publisher and the Institute of Cultural Studies.

19. Taylor, W. Keith. 1989. *The birth of Vietnam.* University of Califonia Press. The Vietnamese version printed by Da Màu.

20. Văn, Tân; Nguyễn, Linh; Lê, Văn Lan; Nguyễn, Đổng Chi; and Hoàng, Hưng. 1976. *Thời đại Hùng Vương* (The Hùng Kings Era). The second edition. Hanoi: Social Science Publisher.

21. Wolters, W. Oliver. 2001. "Narrating the fall of the Ly and the rise of the Tran Dynasties". In *Issues of Vietnamese history*, pp 105-pp 116, Young Publisher & Past and Present Journal.

22. Wolters, W. Oliver. 2001. "Assertions of cultural well-being in fourteenth-century Vietnam". *Issues of Vietnamese history*, pp 117-pp 160, Young Publisher & Past and Present Journal.

THE DEVELOPMENT OF HÙNG KINGS WORSHIP SPACE: THE RELATIONSHIP BETWEEN HERITAGE SITES AND TOURISM

Vietnam's tourism development is intrinsically related to history and cultural heritage. In Vietnam, these cultural heritages include tangible and intangible parts. Tangible elements can easily become tourism property and generally support the development of tourism, especially cultural tourism. A question raised here is, how do the characteristics of folk beliefs become an element in creating a series of places of worship? Has the sacredness of the religious space associated with historical figures become the basis and spiritual support for people to experience and find their roots?

1. Sacred figures of folk beliefs

In the history of Vietnam, Hùng Kings sare figures with special status. It is impossible to guess when details of Hùng Kings were recorded in the history books. Henri Maspero wrote in his book *the Kingdom of Văn Lang* that Hùng Kings' temple was built during the Trần Dynasty (1225-1400), and speculated that this temple must be built after 1313, it was later than the era when the Trần Dynasty ordered all orthodox guardian gods to be granted titles. The earliest historical document mentioning the name of Hùng Kings was *Việt Sử Lược* (越史略, An Outline of History of the Viet, an anonymous history book written in the 15th century, later cited by the Quan Shu (全書) in the Qing Dynasty in China). It said: "During the reign of Chu Trang vương (周庄王, around the ninth century BC), there was an outstanding man in Gia Ninh who was able to subdue the local tribes with magic, claiming to be Hùng King. He stationed his capital in Văn Lang and named his kingdom 'Văn Lang'. The king was good at politics, knew how to record events by tying the knot of a rope. His kingdom was passed down for 18 consecutive generations. People collectively called all kings as the Hung Kings. Furthermore, the book *Đại Việt sử ký toàn thư* (大越史記全書, Complete History of Great Viet) recorded on Hùng Kings dynasty in one of its chapters – *Ngoại Truyện* (外傳, Unofficial Biography), it said: 'Hùng kings ascended the throne, and named the kingdom 'Văn Lang' […], (they) divided the kingdom into 15 prefectures […] All kings of this period were called Hùng Kings" (Ngô Sĩ Liên 1479/ 1972, p. 61). In the tenth century, Vũ Quỳnh and Kiều Phú in their book *Lĩnh Nam chích quái* had a full report on details of Hùng Kings' Kingdom such as stories of Hồng Bàng clan, the god Đổng Thiên Vương, the story of Nhất Dạ Trạch, bánh chưng-bánh dày cakes, etc. (Đinh Gia Khánh & Nguyễn Ngọc San trans., 1960). All these records indicate that Hùng Kings were the kings associated with the ancient kingdom of Văn Lang, the kings who opened the kingdom of the ancient Vietnamese in the Red River Delta.

In the conception of monarchial dynasties from the fourteenth century to the nineteenth century, Hùng Kings were the patron gods or holy kings who had the merit of building the ancient Văn Lang state. The royal dynasty which had the most impact on Hùng Kings worship was the Lê Dynasty (1428-1789). The original tablet "Hùng đồ thập bát diệp thánh vương ngọc phả cổ truyền (雄圖十八葉聖王玉譜古傳, The Geneology of the Eighteen-Hùng Kings)" was written by Nguyễn Cố - a scholar of the Lê's Royal Academy, in the year of Dragon (1472, the 3rd year of King Hồng Đức's reign), edited by Nguyễn Trọng in the year of the Rat (1600, the first year of King Lê Kính Tông's reign), and copied by Lê Đình Hoan - a member of Board of Rites. It can be said that this genealogy is the first complete document about Hùng Kings and their kingdom. Besides the genealogical records, there are also many divine relics about Hùng Kings. So far, we have found such stories recorded by the Confucian scholars in the communes of Hạ Giáp, Thanh Thúy, Yên Khê, Hà Lộc, Tiên Cương, Vy Cương, Hy Cương, Nghĩa Cương, and Quế Trạo (Phú Thọ province). The edicts of the kings of the Lê-Trịnh period in the first year of Đức Nguyên's reign (1674), the 28th year and the 46th year of Cảnh Hưng's reign (1767 & 1785), and the edicts of the Tây Sơn Dynasty (1789-1802) in the second year of King Quang Trung's reign (1789) also clearly show the circulation of these stories. The Nguyễn Dynasty (1802-1945), the last dynasty, also bestowed ordinations to the villages that traditionally worshiped Hùng Kings.

In folklife, Vietnamese people naturally regarded the worship of King Hung as a national ancestor based on the worship of family ancestors. Four words 'Nam Việt triệu tổ' (Viet Nam First Ancestors) at Thượng Temple in Nghĩa Lĩnh Mountain, Việt Trì city, Phú Thọ province is the evidence to show this tradition of Viet people. In the seventeenth century, the *Nam Việt thần kỳ hội lục* (越南神奇匯錄, Records of Vietnam Miracle) showed that of 73 villages of Hùng Kings worship in today Phú Thọ province, 11 villages were obtaining royal ordinations. Hundreds of years later, Mr. Nguyễn Ngọc Chương provided some thoughtful information in 1973, namely, "from the city of Việt Trì city, if we go upstream the Thao river to Hạ Hòa District, upstream the Đà river to Thanh Thủy District, and upstream the Lô river to Đoan Hùng District, we can identify at least 432 sites related to the worship of Hùng Kings and his people, including 40 temples of Hùng kings, 77 temples of their wives and children, 288 temples of the god Cao Sơn, god Tản Viên, and Hùng Kings' generals, and 87 other temples relevant to historical events in Hùng kings era." (Nguyễn Ngọc Chương 1973, p. 127). In 2010-2011, during a scientific inventory trip in Phú Thọ province, Assoc. Prof. Dr. Bùi Quang Thanh and his colleagues found that 46 sites located in 29 communes of 11 districts worship Hùng Kings, and 108 other sites in 52 communes of 12 districts worship figures bearing the honorable titles that dynasties had ordained to Hùng Kings such as Đột Ngột Cao sơn thánh vương, Ất Sơn thánh vương, Viễn Sơn thánh vương.

The god tablet at Thượng Temple on Nghĩa Lĩnh Mountain also validates Hùng Kings under these beautiful titles. The legend of Hà Lộc commune, Khải Xuân subdistrict, Sơn Vi district, Lâm Thao prefecture, Phú Thọ province, clearly stated that Hùng Quốc Vương's ordained title was *"Thánh tổ Hùng Vương Nam thiên thượng thánh tiền hoàng đế khai quốc hồng đồ, đột ngột cao sơn, cổ Việt Hùng thị nhất thập bát thế vương* (Their Majesty Hùng Quốc Vương, King of the South - the founding king among 18 kings of the State of Ancient Việt peoples)"[20], Hùng Hi Vương (the Chấn branch) *Holy Hùng King of Far Mountain - the Holy King of Grace*[21], and Hùng Hi Vương (the Tốn branch) is *Holy Hùng King of Ất Mountain – the Emperor of Victory Support and Justice*[22]

Therefore, Hùng Kings have collectively become symbols of folk beliefs and sacred figures in the concepts of monarchs and folk communities. With the ups and downs of time, the triple temples on Nghĩa Lĩnh Mountain in Việt Trì City, Phú Thọ Province (Thượng, Trung, and Hạ Temples) have long become the center of the national worship of Hùng Kings.

2. From a belief to the worship space of Hùng Kings

From the central region of Phú Thọ province, this religion has spread to all regions of Vietnam. It can be seen that the diffusion process takes place in two different waves. From the land of origin, this belief first spread to some localities in the North. From here, in the spiritual luggage of the Vietnamese people marching to the South, with the mentality toward the origin, the Vietnamese immigrants in the Central region and later the South also built many Hùng Kings temples in the new lands. Therefore, the worship of Hung Kings is the result of two processes of convergence and spread, then spread and re-convergence, becoming a religion of an entire people, a nation with a strong vitality to this day.

More specifically, the Hùng Kings worship space evolved into two different layers. The first is the spreading wave to the Red River Delta, where there are a series of temples dedicated to Hùng Kings in

---

[20]In Chinese: 聖祖雄王南天上聖皇帝開國宏圖突兀高山古越雄氏一十八世王

[21] In Vietnamese: *Hùng Vương viễn sơn thánh vương, ân trạch phổ huệ thánh vương*; in Chinese: 雄王遠山聖王，恩澤普惠聖王.

[22] In Vietnamese: *Hùng Vương Ất Sơn thánh vương trợ thắng công bình hoàng đế*, in Chinese: 雄王乙山聖王助勝公平皇帝.

the provinces today. In this first wave, the geo-cultural and geopolitical position of the delta is the main cause of the spread.

In Nam Định province, there is a Hùng Kings temple located in Vân Cù village, Đồng Sơn commune, Nam Trực district. Formerly, the temple had been built with bamboo and grass roofing material. By the seventeenth to eighteenth centuries, local people contributed to the reconstruction of this temple with the main material of ironwood on an area of about 2000m². In Nghệ An province, Hùng Kings temple was built in 1831 in Hồng Sơn ward, Vinh city.

The second is the wave of Hùng Kings worship temples spread during the Vietnamese marching to the Central and the South from the 17th century onwards. With the mentality of "Living in the South but always look forwards to Thăng Long capital (Trời Nam thương nhớ đất Thăng Long)" (Huỳnh Văn Nghệ), Vietnamese immigrants gradually built Hùng Kings temples on the new lands. In Thừa Thiên-Huế province, Hùng Kings tablet was taken to worship at Lịch Đại Đế Vương Temple (All-Kings Temple) in Huế citadel in 1823 during the reign of King Minh Mạng (1820-1840). In Khánh Hòa province, the people built Hùng Kings Temple in 1970 and completed it three years later. In Lâm Đồng province, there are now many Hùng Kings temples in Dalat City such as those in Ward 2, in 91 Ngô Quyền street, in Ward 6, in Ward 8, and the triple Thượng, Trung, and Hạ temples in Pren Tourist Area, etc. In the South, Bình Phước province has a temple built in Phú Riềng commune, Bù Gia Mập district. In Đồng Nai province, Hùng Kings Temple was started construction in 1968, completed in 1971 in Quarter 3, Bình Đa Ward, Biên Hòa City. In Kiên Giang province, Hùng Kings Temple was built in 1957 in Đông Bình Hamlet, Thạnh Đông B Commune in Tân Hiệp District. In Cà Mau province, Hùng Kings Temple is located on Highway 63 of Giao Khẩu Hamlet, Tân Phú Commune, Thới Bình District, more than 20 km from Cà Mau City.

In Ho Chi Minh City, there are at least 12 establishments with the worship of Hùng Kings, namely Hùng Kings Temple in Tao Đàn

Cultural Park (District 1), Hùng Kings Temple at 2 Nguyễn Bỉnh Khiêm street (District 1), National Kings Temple at 166/33 Đoàn Văn Bơ (District 4), Hùng Kings Temple at 261/3 Cô Giang street (Phú Nhuận District), Memorial area and Hùng Kings Temple in the campus of Historical and Cultural Park (District 9), Hùng Kings Temple at Suối Tiên Theme Park (District 9), Hùng Kings Temple at Đầm Sen Cultural Park (District 11), Trần Hưng Đạo Temple at 189/1 Tôn Đản street (District 4), Cửu Tinh Temple at 96/24 Tôn Đản street (District 4), Từ Quang Phủ Temple at 384/105/31 Lý Thái Tổ street (District 10), and Hòa Thạnh Communal Temple at 378 Lũy Bán Bích street (Tân Phú District).

Among them, the temple of Hùng Kings at City's Botanic Garden is the most typical. This temple, named Commemorative Temple, was built by the French authorities in 1926 at No. 2, Nguyễn Bỉnh Khiêm Street, Bến Nghé Ward, District 1, Ho Chi Minh City. Initially, the temple was used to commemorate the Vietnamese who served in the army for France, sacrificed in World War I, later changed to Hùng Kings - National Ancestral Kings Temple, then Hùng Kings Temple as today. The second typical temple is the Hùng Kings temple in the Cultural and Historical Park which was started construction on April 21, 2002 and inaugurated on March 10 of the lunar calendar in 2009. This is a large-scale temple and memorial area, and it is a special cultural-belief institution of Hùng Kings worship in the South in the present era.

According to statistics of the Department of Culture and Information at the grassroots level (Ministry of Culture, Sports and Tourism), in 2005, there are 1471 places of worship dedicated to Hùng Kings worship and related people of Hùng Kings period throughout the country (see Ministry of Culture, Sports and Tourism 2005). Currently, in some countries and territories in the world, the overseas Vietnamese community has set up temples to worship Hùng Kings, most notably in San Jose, California (USA) (Karen Fjelstad and Nguyễn Thanh Liêm, 2013, pp.971-pp 983)

Starting from the long-lasting Hùng Kings worship in the native land of Phú Thọ, the cultural space of Hùng Kings worship has been expanded throughout Vietnam. In such a space, many tangible heritage establishments associated with the worship of Hùng Kings have been built in almost all regions of the country. Vietnamese people in the whole country are deeply aware that the cultural heritage associated with Hùng Kings worship (both tangible and intangible) is part of their cultural identity; therefore, they are always responsible for spreading and preserving its values.

3. History commemoration and root-seeking pilgrimage

Historical researcher Tạ Chí Đại Trường made a very interesting comment when writing about the worship of Hùng Kings: "The collective memory of the people kept the images of the leaders of a country before being ruled by foreigners (in some form of political gathering) of which similar forms, albeit shrinking or transforming to a certain extent - remains in place during the Chinese rule (111 BC - 938 AD) and later, making the memory more and more consolidated and sustainable." (Tạ Chí Đại Trường 2000, p. 138). Throughout its long history, Hùng Kings are considered a historical symbol, a spiritual fulcrum of Vietnamese people, and a Vietnamese belief. The most concentrated expression of this belief is to perform the ritual of the commemoration of the death anniversary of Hung Kings at the triple temples of Thượng, Trung, and Hạ on Nghĩa Lĩnh Mountain. In other words, historical memorials are always a constant inspiration in every Vietnamese. It is this attitude that creates a consensus between the court and the people for generations. Phú Thọ people said that in 1600, King Lê Kính Tông (1600-1619) organized the National Ceremony on the anniversary of Hùng King's death at Hùng Temple. According to researcher Lê Tư Lành, in the list of poems collected (considered to be composed under the reign of King Lê Hiển Tông (1715 - 1786) there is the poem named *Untitled* as follows:

In Sino-Vietnamese	Modern Vietnamese	English translation
Quốc tịch Văn Lang cổ Vương thư Việt sử tiền Hiển thừa thập bát đại Hình thắng nhất tam xuyên Cựu trưng cao phong bán Sùng từ tuấn lĩnh biên Phương dân ngung trắc giáng Hương hỏa đáo kim truyền	Nước cũ Văn Lang mờ Vua đầu tiên Việt Xưa Mười tám đời tiếp tiếp Ba sông hợp một bờ Mộ tổ trên đỉnh núi Đền thiêng, non tỏ mờ Dân chúng chăm thờ phụng Khói hương mãi tận giờ	The ancient kingdom of Văn Lang The first Viet kings 18 kings in a line Three rivers gather as one Ancestral tombs at top of the mountain Sacred temples at dim mountain People frequently pay sacrifice Incense smoke lasts till now

The poem is important proof to prove that the worship of Hùng Kings was at least conducted in the Lê Dynasty. Later, the Nguyễn Dynasty (1802-1945) paid attention to renovating and constructing the Hùng temples and continued to hold the national ritual at Nghĩa Lĩnh Mountain in even years. According to the epitaph at Thượng Temple, namely *Hùng Vương từ khảo*, in 1917, the Phú Thọ governor Lê Trung Ngọc had an official letter asking the Ministry of Rites (of the Nguyễn Dynasty) set the date of March 10 (lunar calendar) every year as the national worship day, which is one day before the death anniversary of Hung Kings. Ceremonies of the main day (March 11) were organized by the local people. After 1945, especially after 1954, the organization of Hùng King's anniversary was highly respected by the central government as well as Phú Tho provincial agencies. Therefore, in folk there is a saying:

"Anyone who goes back and forth;

You must remember the common ancestors' anniversary on the 10th of the third lunar month each year"[23].

For the people, it is the spirit of commemorating the history mentioned that makes the majority of Vietnamese people wish to come

---

[23] In Vietnamese: "Dù ai đi ngược về xuôi; nhớ ngày giỗ tổ mồng mười tháng ba".

to Hùng Temple to burn incense and commemorate Hùng Kings. After 1975, many Southern people went on a pilgrimage to Hùng Temple, they recorded in the golden book here as follows:"... We came here with all the dreams of the people and soldiers in the Mekong Delta, the southernmost strip of land in the country: Return to the ancestral land of the ancestral Hùng Kings! We are coming back to our national roots, so much emotion and warm feeling. Today, we would like to say to our ancestors and Uncle Hồ (Hồ Chí Minh) that: Following you, we, the Southerners, have faithfully returned to our common roots.' On October 10, 1986, Mr. Vũ Ngọc Sơn, a Vietnamese American, visited Hùng Temples and gave his note that 'Visiting the land of our ancestors, we are like a drop of blood getting back to the heart'. Ms. Nguyễn Thị Đức, Vietnamese American in California noted 'When I am alive, I want to worship the spirit of the country and our ancestors. When I die, I want to cover my grave overseas with love from my ancestral land" (Hùng Kings Museum & Hùng Temples Historical Vestige Site).

Thus, the commemoration of history functions as a psychological basis for people to make root-seeking pilgrimages. Every year, on the occasion of the Spring Festival, people in every part of the country make pilgrimages to their roots. In the depths of their minds, they consider the act of burning incense at Hùng Temple an occasion to pay tribute to the merits of their ancestors and Hùng Kings - the ancestors who found the ancient Kingdom of Văn Lang. This happens not only with Hùng Temple in Phú Thọ Province but also in the temples of Hùng Kings in other localities which are also very crowded on the occasion of the anniversary of Hùng Kings on the 10th of the third lunar month every year. Vietnamese people in all regions, when there is no condition to return to Phú Thọ to make a pilgrimage to their roots, can go to Hùng Kings temples in localities such as Nghệ An, Thừa Thiên-Huế, Khánh Hòa, Bình Phước, Lâm Đồng, Đồng Nai, Kiên Giang, Cà Mau to show their sincerity to the kings. In Ho Chi Minh City, the authors Nguyễn Xuân Hồng and Nguyễn Hồ Phong conducted in-depth interviews and investigations at Hùng Kings Temple in the city's Botanical Garden (Thảo Cầm Viên) and Vietnam Museum of History (Bảo tàng Lịch sử

Việt Nam tại Tp. Hồ Chí Minh). The study gave us some worthy data to consider:

Year	2005	2006	2007	2008	2009	2010	Total
Visitors	23.288	33.438	28.705	32.708	47.678	46.967	212.784

(Source: Tourist Division of the Vietnam History Museum in Ho Chi Minh City)

The statistics show that an average of 35,464 people visit the local Hùng Kings Temple every year. According to our survey, in the 10 hours from February 19 to 20, 2011, 319 people visited the temple, and 94.0% of them performed incense offering ceremony with their sincerity. One resident told us: "I often come to offer incense here, especially on the full moon and the first day of the month. During Tết and Hùng Kings' anniversary, of course, I need to come. They are our ancestors, how could I forget?" (Nguyễn Xuân Hồng & Nguyễn Hồ Phong 2013, p. 931).

In other words, the root-seeking pilgrimage is cultural tourism. For tourists, what they pay most attention to is the must-go destination: Hùng Kings temples in Phú Thọ and other provinces throughout the country. The temples are an important tangible cultural heritage for people to come to express their historical commemoration. In the worship tradition of Hùng Kings, which is a historical commemorative event, the temple is the "materialization" of such an event. For tourists, they go to Hùng Kings Temple to show their mental state of "drinking water and thinking about the source". This is, in fact, a form of historical commemoration.

4. The worship of Hùng Kings in the village and community-based root-seeking tourism

The worship of Hùng Kings at the beginning must be attached to a large cultural and religious space. The worship of Hùng Kings is the result of a harmonious interchanging process of historicalization and mythification. On the land of Phú Thọ, the ancient Vietnamese people in turn experienced many different cultures. The geo-cultural and geopolitical position of Phú Thọ province has created many different archaeological cultures: from Sơn Vi culture (stone age culture) to

Phùng Nguyên, Đồng Đậu, and Gò Mun cultures (metal age cultures). Scientists are completely accurate when asserting that Phú Thọ is the core land of the ancient Văn Lang Kingdom and the center of origin of the ancient Vietnamese.

It is this historical foundation that initiates the history of a Hùng Kings era. And from that same ground, a mythical process began to emerge. Phú Thọ is the leading locality in the country on folklore treasures of the Hùng Kings period. In the folk consciousness of the Phú Thọ community, Hùng Kings are both ancestors and holy kings, both the founders of the country and the ones who take care of the lives of the people. Hùng Kings are both sacred and close, always present in every situation of every human life and in the life of the community in the rotation of nature and crop.

Communal houses, temples, and shrines (tangible cultural heritages) are places where Hùng Kings worship is practiced at the village level. Statistics of the Department of Culture of Phú Thọ Province in 1964 showed that out of 174 monuments worshiping Hùng Kings in the province, 97 relics were damaged, degraded, or had been burnt by the French colonialists during the war. Results of a scientific survey conducted by Assoc. Prof. Dr. Bùi Quang Thanh and colleagues in 2010-2011 in Phú Thọ province said: "Most of the places of worship that are hundreds of years old are destroyed or seriously degraded... Many ponds, lakes, temples, and shrines related to traces of old ruins are no longer available. For example, the places that were said to be the military training ground of the Hùng Kings period such as those in Tiên Kiên Commune (Lâm Thao District), Đặng Temple in Xuân Viên Commune (Yên Lập District), Đanh Temple in Chính Công Commune and Tân Tiến Temple in Vĩnh Chân Commune (Hạ Hòa District) are no longer protected (see Vietnam Institute of Culture and Arts Studies, Inventory Report: The worship of Hung king's in Phú Thọ province).

It is worth noting that while the attitude of commemorating the history among the people is still profound, the tangible cultural heritage associated with it is seriously degraded. Therefore, the state must urgently restore and modify the system of communal houses, temples, pagodas, and shrines in villages related to Hùng Kings worship in Phú Thọ province. The implementation of historical memorial activities in the community is always associated with tangible cultural heritage. Without a specific material institution, it is difficult to conduct complete historical memorial activities. The tangible heritage of the worship of Hùng Kings is essentially the "materialization" of religious beliefs, and it is also a place for people to practice their faith and show their historical memorial attitude towards the Kings.

Vietnamese people across the country when making the pilgrimage to their roots do not need to go to the temples of Thượng, Trung, and Hạ Temples on Nghĩa Lĩnh Mountain in Việt Trì City but can perform right in their hometown. In other words, it is a form of community-based root-seeking tourism. To do that job, there is a lot of work to be done. In the immediate future we must perform the following tasks:

• Promoting to the highest level the community's role in the restoration of tangible heritage relics related to Hùng Kings, collecting and preserving intangible cultural heritages related to the space of cultural-religious worship of Hùng Kings in the villages of Phú Thọ province.

• Publicly introducing this belief to the public by publishing leaflets, books, CDs, VCDs, DVDs on the cultural and religious space of Hùng Kings worship.

• Connecting all the heritage sites the sacrificial monuments of the Hùng Kings worship into a social network (using computer technology for this link), creating opportunities to introduce more about the worship to create better conditions for the community to make the best pilgrimage back to their roots.

5. Conclusion

Hùng Kings, for many generations, are the central figures of an important religious tradition in Vietnam: the worship of Hùng Kings by the Viet. From characters blending history and legend, especially through the process of sanctification, Hùng Kings have become sacred and fanciful characters, considered strong spiritual support of the Vietnamese nation through history. The historical commemoration is the main reason for the development of this belief in time and space. The tangible heritage relics contain many historical and cultural values, so they become significant tourist destinations. People make pilgrimages to find their roots with respect, through which they appreciate their ancestors and those who openly open the country, and also to have more faith in life so that they continue to step into the future.

Reference

1. Henri Maspero: *The Kingdom of Văn Lang (Le Royaume de Văn Lang)*, Hà Nội, 1948
2. Hùng Kings Museum & Hùng Temples Historical Vestige Site, Archive from Hùng Kings Museum. Phú Thọ Province.
3. Karen Fjelstad and Nguyễn, Thanh Liêm, In *Tín ngưỡng thờ cúng tổ tiên trong xã hội đương đại, nghiên cứu trường hợp thờ Hùng Vương* (The ancestor worship in contemporary society – a case study of Hùng kings in Vietnam), Hanoi: Culture & Information Publisher, 2013, pp. 971-pp 983
4. Ministry of Culture, Sports and Tourism. 2005
5. Ministry of Rites of the Lê Dynasty. 1763. *Nam Việt thần kỳ hội lục* (越南神奇匯錄, Records of Vietnam Miracle).
6. Ngô, Sĩ Liên. 1479/1972. *Đại Việt sử ký toàn thư* (大越史記全書, Complete History of Great Viet), trans. Cao Huy Giu, ed. Đào Duy Anh, Vol. 1. The second edition. Hanoi: Social Science Publisher.
7. Nguyễn, Ngọc Chương. 1973. "Về tình hình phân bố các di tích lịch sử thuộc thời các vua Hùng (On the distribution of historical heritage of Hùng King's area)." In *Hùng Vương dựng nước* (Hùng Kings founded the country), Vol. 3, Hanoi: Social Science Publisher.
8. Nguyễn ,Xuân Hồng & Nguyễn, Hồ Phong. 2013. "Đền thờ vua Hùng, Thảo cầm viên thành phố Hồ Chí Minh,điểm đến tâm linh của người dân Nam Bộ (Hùng Temple in Thảo cầm viên, Hồ Chí Minh city – a spiritual destination of the south people)." In *Tín ngưỡng thờ cúng tổ tiên trong xã hội đương đại, nghiên cứu trường hợp thờ Hùng Vương* (The ancestor worship in contemporary society – a case study of Hùng kings in Vietnam), pp 927- pp 934, Hanoi: Culture & Information Publisher.
9. Tạ ,Chí Đại Trường. 2000. *Thần, người và đất Việt* (Gods, people and the Land of Viet), California: USA, Literature Publisher
10. Trần, Thế Pháp. *Lĩnh Nam chích quái* (嶺南摭怪, Selection of Strange Tales in Lĩnh Nam), trans. Đinh, Gia Khánh & Nguyễn, Ngọc San. 1960. Hanoi,

11. Vietnam Institute of Culture and Arts Studies, *Inventory Report: The worship of Hung king's in Phú Thọ province*, paper.
12. *Việt Sử Lược* (越史略, An Outline of History of the Viet), trans Trần, Quốc Vượng, Hanoi, Literature, History and Geography Publisher, 1961.

OVERVIEW OF THE RESEARCH AND COLECTIONS OF GIÓNG FESTIVAL

1. Preface

Saint Gióng and his worship are a cultural and religious phenomenon, especially for the Việt people living in the Red River Delta and Vietnam. Therefore, for a long time, the research on Saint Gióng and its related cultural relics, legends, and festivals has been paid special attention from academia. In other words, this folklore phenomenon has been studied by many generations of researchers for a long time.

2. The monarchical periods

Until now, it is still difficult to clearly determine when researchers began to study Gióng Festival, which is a cultural and religious phenomenon related to Saint Gióng (Thánh Gióng). The earliest related texts are probably the records of the monarchial Confucianists in the early 18th century. Lê Tắc in *An Nam chí lược* (安南志略, *Brief Annals of Annam*) wrote about Xung Thiên Temple (The Temple of ascending to Heaven) in Phù Đổng as follows: "In Phù Đổng village, there had been many conflicts in the past. Suddenly a person appeared in the village. The villagers respected him and followed him. Then the man led the army to fight the enemy. After he won, he flew to Heaven. He was known as Xung Thiên Đại Vương (冲天大王, King flying to Heaven). The villagers built a temple to worship him" (Lê Tắc 2002, p. 67).

In the 14th century, the legend of Saint Gióng was recorded in Chapter "Ngoại Kỷ" (外纪, Outer Part, dated before 967) of the book *Đại Việt sử ký toàn thư* (大越史記全書, Complete Annals of Đại Việt) as follows: "In the village of Phù Đổng in Vũ Ninh District, there was a wealthy family. They had a son. Even when the son was three years old, he would only eat, not speak or smile. At that time, the country was invaded by powerful enemies. The king ordered messengers to travel to different parts of the country to find people who could help the country defeat the enemy. After hearing the messenger's voice, the child suddenly said aloud and asked his mother to invite the messenger in". The child said to the messenger: "Please, give me a sword and a horse, then the king doesn't have to worry!" The king ordered his people to give the child an iron sword and an iron horse. Following the army, the child immediately rushed out and fought against the enemy at the foot of Vũ Ninh Mountain. Then the enemies began to fight each other and many of them were killed. Those who were still alive knelt in front of him and called him the Heavenly General. Saint Gióng then flew to Heaven on a horse. The king ordered his people to build a temple in his garden to worship Saint Gióng. Later, King Lý Thái Tổ awarded him the title "Xung Thiên Thần Vương (God flying to Heaven)". Now, his temple is located next to Kiến Sơ Buddhist Temple in Phù Đổng village." (Ngô Sĩ Liên 1972, p. 61). In the middle of the 14th century, *Thiền uyển tập anh ngữ lục* (禪苑集英語錄, Records on a Collection of Outstanding Figures of the Zen Community) recorded that monk Khuông Việt (Ngô Chân Lưu) dreamed of meeting Vaisravana (Tỳ Sa Môn Thiên vương) who helped King Lê Đại Hành fight the Song invaders. It can be said that these are the earliest records of the god worshipped in Sóc Mountain, who later merged with Saint Gióng (see *Thiền uyển tập anh ngữ lục* 2001, pp. 61-63).

Similarly, in the 14th century, Lý Tế Xuyên wrote *Việt điện u linh* (越甸幽靈, Collection of Stories on the Shady and Spiritual World of the Viet Realm). Along with 26 stories about other gods in the spiritual pantheon of the Việt people, the work contains the legend of the god worshipped in Kiến Sơ Temple named *Xung thiên dũng liệt chiêu ứng uy tín đại vương* (沖天永烈昭應威信大王) (see Lý Tế Xuyên 1972, pp. 90-93). However, it is still unclear why the legend of Heavenly King of Phù Đổng was not recorded in this work.

In the 15th century, when Nguyễn Văn Chất wrote the continuation of *Việt điện u linh*, the legend of Saint Gióng was added with the title *The Legend of the Heavenly King of Sóc* (see Lý Tế Xuyên 1972, pp. 113-115). Similarly, in the 15th century, Nguyễn Trãi (1380-1442) wrote in *Dư địa chí* (輿地志, Local History) as follows:

"Thiên Đức, Vệ Linh [mountains] are located in Kinh Bắc region... Vệ Linh is another name for Vũ Sơn Mountain. The Heavenly King of Phù Đổng flew from there to Heaven" (Nguyễn Trãi 1969, pp. 200).

In the 18th century, Nguyễn Thư Hiên, i.e. Nguyễn Tông Quai (1692-1766) explained: "People in Thanh Hóa Province said that Tản viên Đại vương (Great King Tản Viên) went from the sea to the mountains; the Heavenly King of Phù Đổng rode a horse flying to Heaven; Chử Đồng Tử took a hat and a stick flying to Heaven; Từ Đạo Hạnh left his mark on the stone to be reborn in Ninh Sơn... They are the four Immortal Saints of Vietnam" (Nguyễn Thư Hiên 1969, p. 201).

Also in the 15th century, Vũ Quỳnh and Kiều Phú recorded the story of the Heavenly King of Đổng village in *Lĩnh Nam chích quái* (嶺南摭怪, Selection of Strange Tales in Lĩnh Nam) with a relatively complete story structure. However, the story did not include the following detail: after heavy rain and windy nights, Saint Gióng's mother went to the garden. She saw and stepped into a strange huge footprint and became pregnant. Vũ Quỳnh and Kiều Phú simply noted that: "There is a rich man over 60 years old who gave birth to a son on the seventh day of the first month of the Lunar New Year". Limited details similar to those are also provided in later versions (see *Lĩnh Nam chích quái,* 1960, pp. 31-34). However, in Act Six of *Tân đính Lĩnh Nam chích quái* (新訂嶺南摭怪, The New Version of Selection of Strange Tales in Lĩnh Nam) wrote that: "The elderly came to the court to report; The Heavenly King Đổng defeated Ân enemies". The author Vũ Quỳnh provided some additional details, namely that: Saint Gióng's maternal grandfather was called Huy, his family name was Đổng; Saint Gióng's mother was called Nàng Thánh. Once, when she went to the edge of the village to pick mulberry leaves, she saw an unusually huge footprint. She tried to fit her feet on it. Back home, she felt anxious and became pregnant. Hùng King bestowed on the child the title *Bắc Bình phá lỗ tướng quân, tổng đốc binh mã đô nguyên súy* (The General who defeated the Northern enemies) (see *Tân đính Lĩnh Nam chích quái* 1993, pp. 80-88).

During the 16th century, the legend of the Heavenly King of Phù Đổng was written in full[24]. Many details only appeared in this version, including the vegetables were grown where Saint Gióng's mother lived; and, the footsteps she tried to adapt to were not on the roadside, but "she saw a strange big footprint on the vegetable in her garden; she was sorry for the young green vegetables and took them home to cook, so she was pregnant". The legend fully recorded the facts that Saint Gióng appeared in the dream of monk Khuông Việt, assisted Lê Hoàn to defeat the Song invaders, assisted Lý Thái Tổ to replace the previous Former-Lê Dynasty, and supported Lê Lợi to defeat the Ming rulers. The legend *Veritable Record of the Heavenly King of Sóc Mountain* tells similar details. Among the god legends compiled by Nguyễn Bính in the first year of the Hồng Phúc first year (1572), only the legend of Thanh Nhàn Temple (Thanh Xuân Commune, Sóc Sơn District) and the legend of Ân Phú commune (Yên Phong District, Bắc Ninh Province) are a bit different in the details of Saint Gióng's birth and growth. In the first legend, Saint Gióng's mother saw a star falling from the sky into her stomach, then she became pregnant and gave birth to Gióng. In the second legend, Gióng's mother dreamed that the halo was fallen (from the sky), she swallowed it. Later, she dreamed of a golden dragon and then gave birth to him.

In 1606, the villagers recorded this legend in the stele *Hiển Linh từ thạch* of Phù Đổng Temple, which was not much different from the legends of previous periods. This stele also helps us understand the worship of Saint Gióng, the hero of Phù Đổng village, in different dynasties (Đinh (968-980), Tiền Lê (980-1009), Lý (1009-1225), Hậu Lê (1428-1527), and Lê-Trịnh (1533-1789) dynasties).

---

[24] This version is kept at the Institute of Hán Nôm Studies, encoded AE. a7/27.

The author of *Thiên Nam ngữ lục* told the legend of Saint Gióng in six and eight syllable verse (thơ lục bát), providing familiar details. However, he provided two specific details that were different from those in other versions. First, he wrote that the first sentence the boy in Phù Đổng village said to his mother was "My real name is the Heavenly King of Phù Đổng", whereas it is most commonly known that the Lý Dynasty bestowed this title upon him. Although at the end of the book, the author wrote that Hùng Kings "offered him title Xung Thiên thần vương (God-King flying to Heaven). This detail means that Đổng Thiên vương (the Heavenly King of Đổng) has assimilated with Xung Thiên thần vương (God-King flying to Heaven). The unique second detail of this book is that Saint Gióng's parents died when he was three months old:

In Vietnamese	English translation
Kể lần ba tháng lỡ làng, Nghiêm	*Since he was three months old;*
đường làm khách suối vàng xa chơi	*His parents passed away*

The author also did not provide details of Saint Gióng's trip to Cáo village on West Lake, nor did he provide details of Gióng's mother's stepping in the giant's footprint. Lê Ngô Cát and Phạm Đình Toái in *Đại Nam quốc sử diễn ca* (大南國史演歌, *Historical Songs of the Great Southern Kingdom*) explained in *Nôm* script the legend of Saint Gióng, providing details similar to those in other versions.

In *Đại Nam nhất thống chí* (大南一統志, *Đại Nam Comprehensive Encyclopaedia*), officials of the National History Bureau of the Nguyễn Dynasty wrote about the god of Vệ Linh Mountain as follows: "Vệ Linh Mountain is where King Đổng flew to Heaven on a horse" (the National History Bureau of the Nguyễn Dynasty 1971, p. 74). They also wrote a familiar detail about the Temple of Heavenly King of Đổng village, confirming that Saint Gióng's mother was "not married; she became pregnant because she stepped on the giant's footsteps" (the National History Bureau of the Nguyễn Dynasty 1971, p. 100). At about the same time, the officials also wrote that "Hùng Kings ordered the construction of a temple in the area to worship him. During the period of King Lê Đại Hành, the Heavenly King of Đổng village supported him to defeat the Song (Chinese) enemy, and King Lê Đại Hành offered him the title "Superior God (First-Rank God)". King Lê Thái Tổ awarded him the title of the Heavenly King. Even today, one can see his temple on Vệ Linh Mountain" (the National History Bureau of the Nguyễn Dynasty 1971, p. 100).

In the early 19th century, Phan Huy Chú compiled *Lịch triều hiến chương loại chí* (歷朝憲章類誌, Charters of the Vietnamese dynasties). He wrote: "Phù Đổng Temple is situated in Tiên Du district" (Phan Huy Chú 1960, Vol. 1, p. 89). He described the legend of Saint Gióng in detail in a way that is not much different from other narratives, with one exception: "(his father) is a famous village, a rich man". He also wrote: "King Hùng awarded him (Saint Gióng) the title of the Heavenly King of Đổng village and ordered people to build a temple in the village to worship him. Many people came to pay sacrifice since the temple is believed to be very sacred" (Phan Huy Chú 1960, Vol. 1, p. 89). Phan wrote about Vệ Linh Mountain as follows: "Ancient legends say that Vệ Linh Mountain is where the Heavenly King of Đổng flew to Heaven. According to legend, the Heavenly King defeated the enemies and then came to the mountain, riding a horse to fly to heaven, leaving a coat hanging on the pine tree. Now, four adjacent communes worship him. It is said that the temple at the foot of the mountain is sacred" (Phan Huy Chú 1960, Vol. 1, p. 91).

Also, during the Nguyễn Dynasty, several geography books were produced in Bắc Ninh Province, such as *Bắc Ninh phong thổ tạp ký* (北寧風土雜記, *Miscellaneous Notes of Bắc Ninh*) and *Bắc Ninh toàn tỉnh địa chí* (北寧全省地志, *Local History of Bắc Ninh Province*), etc. In *Bắc Ninh phong thổ tạp ký*, the details of the legend provided are not much different from other accounts. However, it is worth noting that of the author of this article discovered at Phù Đổng Festival that "every year, two girls are chosen to be enemy generals and 26 girls to be assistants[25]. All of them wear black hats, yellow scarves and red coats... According to the

---

[25] Only choose females, maybe because according to Yin and Yang philosophy, females are Yin, symbolizing enemies.

legend, King Lý Thái Tổ met the Heavenly King of Đồng village while living at this temple. Later when Lý became a king, he recalled the merits of the Heavenly King and ordered to establish this festival to make people visualize the power of the Heavenly King when he was fighting against the enemy (Trần Thị Kim Anh 2009, pp. 54-5).

In *Bắc Ninh toàn tỉnh địa chí*, the author(s) wrote about Sóc Sơn Temple as follows "This temple is located at the highest point of Vệ Linh Mountain, called Sóc Sơn Temple... This is where the Heavenly King flew to Heaven on his horse". The author also distinguished between two temples on the mountain: "the temple at the highest point on the mountain is a place to worship *Đồng Thiên vương - Sóc thiên đại thánh (The Heavenly King of Đồng - the Heavenly King of Sóc);* whereas, the temple at the foot of the mountain worships *Vệ Linh sóc thần phù thánh đại vương" (The God of Vệ Linh Mountain).* In *Bắc Ninh toàn tỉnh địa dư chí* (北寧全省輿地志, *Local History of Bắc Ninh Province)*[26], the author wrote about Sóc Sơn Mountain as follows: "As the legend says, the Heavenly King of Đồng village flew from here to heaven. There are two temples on the mountain called Thượng Temple (Upper Temple) and Hạ Temple (Lower Temple)" (see *Bắc Ninh toàn tỉnh địa dư chí* 2009, p. 92). According to the book, when referring to temples and shrines, the author said that Phù Đồng Temple was dedicated to the Heavenly King of Đồng. When describing this legend, he provided details similar to other versions. However, when describing Sóc Sơn Temple, the author carefully wrote: "According to written records, this mountain is the place where the Heavenly King of Đồng flew to Heaven on a horse. In addition, according to *Trích quái ngoại truyện* (遮怪外傳, *Strange Stories)*, General Tỳ Sa emerged and defeated the Song (Chinese) invaders. King Lê Đại Hành bestowed him the title *Sóc Thiên thần vương* (the Heavenly King of Sóc Mountain) and ordered people to build a temple locally to worship him. There is a temple at the top and another one at the foot of the mountain. The name of gods is not very clear. The title of the Upper Temple is *Đồng Thiên Thiên vương -*

---

[26] Encoded A2889, Institute of Sino-Nôm Institute.

Sóc Thiên đại thánh (the Heavenly King of Đổng – Great Heavenly God of Sóc Mountain). The title of the Lower Temple is Mê Linh tôn thần - Phù Thánh đại vương (God of Mê Linh – Supportive God). Heavenly King of Sóc village, who supported King Lê Đại Hành, was not the acquired Heavenly King of Phù Đổng village. It is also possible that the Heavenly King of Sóc village who assisted King Lê Đại Hành was also due to the epiphany of the Heavenly King of Đổng. In that mysterious world, it is difficult for us to know" (*Bắc Ninh toàn tỉnh địa dư chí* 2009, p. 232). In addition, in the section about temples and shrines, the authors wrote about a temple in the small village of lower Mê Linh hamlet (i.e., Thụ Mã hamlet) dedicated to the Heavenly King of Đổng (see *Bắc Ninh toàn tỉnh địa dư chí* 2009, p. 233). In the section on regional customs, it is mentioned that Phù Đổng Festival is celebrated in Tiên Du District, while a festival is held at the Temple of the Heavenly King of Đổng on Vệ Linh Mountain and another one held at Phù Lỗ (both in Kim Anh District). All these festivals are held in memory of Saint Gióng (see *Bắc Ninh toàn tỉnh địa dư chí* 2009, p. 266-7).

3. The colonial period

In *Bắc Ninh tỉnh địa dư* (北寧省地輿, *Historical facts of Bắc Ninh Province)* written in the 14th year of the Minh Mạng reign, the author(s) wrote about Sóc Mountain, in the section of *Danh sơn* (Well-known moutains), Soc mountain is written in this section, clearly stating that the mountain was the place where the Heavenly King of Đổng had flown to Heaven. In the section *Đền thiêng* (Sacred Temples), the author(s) wrote: "There are two temples dedicated to the Heavenly King of Đổng, one of which is located in Phù Đổng Commune in Tiên Du District, the other one in Vệ Linh Commune of Kim Hoa District (see *Bắc Ninh tỉnh địa dư* 2009, p. 301-2, 307).

In 1877, Trần Gia Du in *Nam Sử chí dị* (南史誌異, *Historical Records of Southern Kingdom*) told the legend of Saint Gióng in the story *Nói về sự tích Thánh Đổng* (*Talk about the legend of Saint Đổng*). The detailed information he provided is almost the same as the other versions, except for the following: "There is an elderly woman, over 60 years old, but no children. One morning, when she visited the fields, she saw a huge footprint in *the middle of the road*. She tried to fit her foot in and became pregnant".

Đỗ Trọng Vĩ (1829-1899) wrote *Bắc Ninh địa dư chí* (北寧輿地志, *Local Historical Facts of Bắc Ninh*) sometime between 1882 and 1885. In the book, he discussed Phù Đổng Festival in Tiên Du district, the festival at Phù Đổng Temple on Vệ Linh Mountain, as well as the festival in Phù Lỗ Sub-district. Special attention should be paid to the following details: "Residents from 7 sub-districts of Kim Anh, Tiên Dược, Phù Lỗ, Hương Đình, Đà Thượng, Cổ Bái, Đông Đồ in Đông Anh District and Đông Bảng Sub-district in Đa Phúc District came to the temple on the same day for the ceremony. They all brought some sticks to defend themselves when necessary. Each different sub-district took a turn to perform its ritual separately. Late sub-district teams often fought each other. In case someone was injured or killed in battle, it was not reported as a crime… For entertainment purposes, colorful flowering trees were made of bamboo. After the ceremony, the participants tried to steal the trees so that they (the trees) could be placed next to the gate of the temple as a charm. During the feast, they chopped the meat and mixed it with eggs, then made horses from the mixture, and then displayed them at the door of the temple to compete for the most beautiful horses" (Đỗ Trọng Vĩ 1997, p. 186).

In 1887, G. Dumoutier (1850 - 1904) published a book of *Légendes historiques de l'Annam et du Tonkin* (Historical legends of Annam and Tonkin) in Hanoi (Dumoutier 1887). In this book, he announced that the legend of Saint Gióng was the translation of a Chinese version, but it did not specify which book or who was the author.

In 1893, E. Sombthay might have based on folk narration when writing "Truyện đền Phù Đổng (The Story of Phù Đổng Temple)" in the work *Ba mươi truyền thuyết và cổ tích Bắc Kỳ* (Thirty Legends and Tales in Tonkin) (see Sombthay 1893).

In 1893, the Frenchman G. Dumoutier became the first Western scholar to study the legend and festival of Saint Gióng. The author described legends, ruins, and festivals in detail, which were all lifelike. Some of his remarks were particularly interesting, such as "It's amazing to see the faces of farmers in northern Vietnam. They usually don't care when they bend over in the fields, and they suddenly change a lot under the influence of religion... Their shy gestures and behavior suddenly change. Often, they appear humble and avoidant. Now, they all appear noble and solemn, and at the same time show this completely secular ceremony, patriotic behavior, and awe of religion (Dumoutier 2009, pp. 148).

In 1893, G. Dumoutier published the work *Etude historique et archéologique sur Cổ-Loa, capitale de l'ancien royaume de Âu - Lạc (réunion de Thục et de Văn-Lang) 255-207 av. J.C.* (Historical and archaeological study on Cổ-Loa, capital of the ancient kingdom of Âu - Lạc (integration of Thục and Văn-Lang) 255-207 BC.) He announced the legend of Saint Gióng with title of a miraculous baby, liberator of kingdom (see Dumoutier 1893. pp. 46-50).

Bắc Ninh tỉnh khảo dị (北寧省考異, Strange Stories of Bắc Ninh Province), which includes the preface written by Phạm Xuân Lộc in 1920, has a very detailed and true description of Gióng festival at Phù Đổng Temple in the chapter "Dân tục thần tích xã Phù Đổng huyện Tiên Du, phủ Từ Sơn, tỉnh Bắc Ninh (The Legends of Phù Đổng commune, Tiên Du district, Từ Sơn Prefecture, Bắc Ninh province)". The chapter includes the following parts: summary of the legends; flag rehearsal; the selection of the 28 female generals (enemies); the selection of the chief general and vice chief general; and opening the festival: fighting & killing the generals. There is also a part dedicated to singing and dancing by Mục Lao (Ải Lao) Troupe. The author's description is quite detailed and real.

In 1921, Phạm Văn Thụ rewrote the tale of Saint Gióng in the work *Sóc Sơn từ phả* (Records of Sóc Sơn). In 1932, in *Monographie de la province de Phúc Yên: Notices du mandarin provincial de Phúc*

Yên (Monograph of Phúc Yên Province: Notices on mandarin of Phúc Yên province) briefly described the legend of the hero of Phù Đổng village (1932). In 1934, Lê Ta (i.e. poet Thế Lữ) wrote an article introducing Gióng Festival at Phù Đổng Temple in the *Phong hóa* newspaper. However, this is a rough article, not a research article. Nevertheless, it can help us understand the atmosphere of Gióng Festival at that time.

In 1938, Nguyễn Văn Huyên published his work called *Le Fêtes de Phu-Dong: Une bataille céleste dans la tradition annamite* (Phù Đổng Festival, a Legendary Battle in the Legends of Vietnam) in French. In 1941, he also published *Les chants et les dances d'Ai-Lao aux fêtes de Phù Đổng* (Ải Lao Singing and Dancing in Phù Đổng Festival). In 1996, both works were translated and published in Vietnamese language. He detailed the legend, the organization of the festival, and the performance during the festival in his previous works. In addition, he provided seven photos and three graphic images to support his description. When reading Nguyễn Văn Huyên's works, it is easy to see that his method is the same as that commonly used in French ethnography in the 1930s. His description is true, true, and detailed. An example of such a detail can be seen in the following description: "In the worship hall, three drums were played. The parade began. There were two command teams in front. This group of 12 children wearing colored shirts carried rattan sticks. The battle is simple. There is a lotus lake between the two dikes. The enemy occupy the lake. On the one hand, there are many mounds on this land. There are three trimmed white sedge mats. In the middle of each sedge mat, there is a bowl turned over, sitting on a blank sheet of paper. The sedge mat symbolizes the plain, the bowl symbolizes the hill, and the paper symbolizes the cloud" (Nguyễn Văn Huyên 1996, pp. 20-1). In his later work, he particularly emphasized *new additions*. He added three songs which were composed by Confucian scholars due to the request of the governor Tiên Du District. Ải Lao Troupe first performed these songs in 1941 (Nguyễn Văn Huyên 1996, p. 66). Two works by Nguyễn Văn Huyên are good examples to provide a realistic, scientific, and detailed description of Gióng Festival in Phù Đổng village.

In 1938, Nguyễn Khánh Trường reserved a part to introduce the legend of the hero of Phù Đổng village in *Legend of principal Gods worshiped in Phúc Yên province (Tonkin)* (Légendes des principaux génies honorés dans la province de Phuc-Yên (Tonkin)) (Nguyễn Khánh Trường 1938. pp. 7-11).

4. Contemporary period

In 1954, in *Đại cương về văn học sử Việt Nam* (Introduction to Vietnamese historical literature), Nguyễn Khánh Toàn also covered some aspects of the legend of Saint Gióng.

In the book *Quan điểm duy vật máy móc và duy vật biện chứng trong cách nhận định một truyện cổ tích* (The Perspective of Mechanical Materialism and Dialectic Materialism in Viewing a Tale), Trần Thanh Mại (1955, p. 12) made many criticisms of the legend of Saint Gióng. He said: "This legend symbolizes the powerful impetus of an emerging young country, a country full of pride that has the ability to defeat its strong enemies with just a whip". Unfortunately, Trần Thanh Mại inaccurately believed that the society in the story of Saint Gióng was a society of feudal autonomy!

In 1956, Nguyễn Đổng Chi highlighted the legend of Saint Gióng in his book namely *Lược khảo thần thoại Việt Nam* (Introduction to Vietnamese Myths). In 1975, he also included this legend in another book entitled *Kho tàng truyện cổ tích Việt Nam* (*The Collection of Vietnamese Fairy Tales*).

In 1957, folklorist Vũ Ngọc Phan included the story of Saint Gióng the book *Truyên cổ Việt Nam* (Vietnamese Fairy Tales). At the same year, Văn Tân and other authors addressed the content and artistic aspects of the legend of Saint Gióng in an edited book entitled *Sơ thảo lịch sử văn học Việt Nam* (Overview of the History of Vietnamese Literature) (Volume I).

In 1963, Nguyễn Hồng Phong published his work *Tìm hiểu tính cách dân tộc* (Understand national character), in which he referred to the legend of Saint Gióng with strong arguments, believed that the legend had an epic essence and expressed our love for peace.

In 1967, researcher Tầm Vu studied the main ideas of the ancient Việt people through several myths and legends. He argued: "Saint Gióng's story clearly proves the patriotism of our ancestors, which has been developed since ancient times" (Tầm Vu 1967).

In 1968, Vũ Tuấn Sán discussed the legend of Saint Gióng through myths. In 1968, Vũ Ngọc Phan identified God of Phù Đổng (i.e. Saint Gióng) as a beautiful and powerful literary image of the country since ancient times.

Toan Ánh was born in the North but moved to the South after 1954. In 1969, he published the book *Nếp cũ: hội hè đình đám* (Old Customs: Festivals), in which he described the festival of Phù Đổng village from his memories and other written materials. Toan Ánh described the festival in the same way as ethnologists. His writing structure ranges from legendary legends and festival performances to detailed descriptions of the preparation and execution of festival tasks. However, compared to the description provided by Nguyễn Văn Huyên decades before that, Toan Ánh's description is somewhat incomplete, e.g., details of the music team leading the parade during the festival (Toan Ánh 1969, p. 112). On the other hand, Toan Ánh's work is more systematic and follows a fixed structure when describing the festival. It provides valuable resources for other authors to study Gióng Festival.

In the same year (1969), Cao Huy Đinh published the monograph *Người anh hùng làng Dóng* [27] (The Hero of Dóng Village), consisting of six chapters as follows:

---

[27] In order to respect the author's point of view, we retained the original version, although our point is to replace "Dóng" with "Gióng". Until now, there are two ways in Vietnamese language to use "Gi" and "D" to write the name of the hero.

Chapter 1: The Country of Trung Châu (Central Plain) tells the story of Saint Dóng;

Chapter 2: From the story of a tribal hero to the legend of a national hero;

Chapter 3: Dóng Festival and hero singing art;

Chapter 4: The legend of Saint Dóng in Vietnamese literature during monarchical and colonial times;

Chapter 5: Contemporary writers' discussion about the legend of Saint Dóng;

Chapter 6: Saint Dóng – a very old but new image in the Vietnamese epic. Professor Nguyễn Xuân Kính provided such accurate comments when commenting on Cao Huy Đinh's approach as follows: "In the 1960s, when many folklorists still looked at folklore from the perspective of literature, Cao Huy Đinh perseveringly proposed a method of on-site investigation in the context of the origin of folklore" (Nguyễn Xuân Kính 1995, p. 130). Nguyễn Xuân Kính reconfirmed that Cao Huy Đinh's research method is a synthetic method (Nguyễn Xuân Kính 1995, p. 131). Special attention should be paid to the fact that, by then, it was the only official large-scale monograph on the legend and Gióng Festival.

In 1970, in Volume 1 (namely, "Folklore") of the textbook *Lịch sử văn học Việt Nam* (History of Vietnamese Literature), the author Đỗ Bình Trị addressed the legend of Saint Gióng generally together with other legends.

In 1973, Đinh Gia Khánh and Chu Xuân Diên published a textbook called *Văn học dân gian Việt Nam* (Vietnamese Folklore), which includes an accurate scientific assessment of the legend of Saint Gióng.

In 1975, Trần Quốc Vượng and Vũ Tuấn Sán published the book *Hà Nội nghìn xưa* (Ancient Hanoi) part of which introduced the hero of Gióng village. Though this section is short, it contains both valuable material and useful research methods (Trần Quốc Vượng & Vũ Tuấn Sán 1975, pp. 57-62).

In 1977, Nguyễn Huy Hồng studied the performances during Gióng Festival to reiterate that the legend of Saint Gióng is an epic story. The author described the details of Gióng Festival in great detail, which is similar to that described by Nguyễn Văn Huyên before the August Revolution (1945) (Nguyễn Huy Hồng 2007, pp. 106-44).

In 1978, Bùi Văn Nguyên studied the legend of Saint Gióng in order to learn more about the significance of fighting against foreign invaders in the legend.

In 1979, when studying the folk performances, Chu Hà confirmed that together with *hát cửa đình*[28], the battle in the Gióng Temple Festival was a large-scale folk performance with a long history. In 1979, Hoàng Tiến Tựu explored the development of the legends of ancient Vietnam fighting and foreign invaders through the legends of Saint Gióng and An Dương Vương.

In 1979, Trần Việt Ngữ published an article "Hội trận đền Gióng (The battle-enacting festival at Gióng Temple)", in which he described a part of Gióng Festival of Phù Đổng Temple. After skipping some of the more familiar details, special attention should be paid to the tiger hunting during the festival (Trần Việt Ngữ 1979, p. 134). In this year, Nguyễn Huy Hồng, another writer, wrote the article "Diễn xướng anh hùng ca Gióng (The Performance of the Epic of Gióng)" on the *Journal of Folklore*.

In 1981, at the Ethnography Conference, Nguyễn Khắc Đạm published an article entitled "Một số vấn đề về Hội Gióng (Some Issues of Gióng Festival)", in which he covered the following issues: the organizers of Gióng Festival and the background of the battle that took

---

[28] Performance to serve the tutelary gods in the communal temple festival in Northern Vietnam.

place during the festival; the number of people involved in the battle; the time and procedure of the battle; the ceremony, the art and discipline of the battle; and the village's expenditure in the battle. Especially, the author said: "...During the entire period of the feudal system, and during the period of French colonial rule, Gióng Festival was regularly organized every year. During the war with the French, due to the unfavorable conditions, the organization of Gióng Festival was not able to be held..." (Nguyễn Khắc Đạm 1981/2009, p. 478).

In 1983, American writer Keith Weller Taylor mentioned the legend of Saint Gióng in *The Birth of Vietnam* and asserted: "Vietnamese people always remember this legend because it expresses their earliest identity as a nation"[29].

Tạ Chí Đại Trường wrote the 28-page monograph namely *Lịch sử một thần tích: Phù Đổng Thiên Vương* (History of a legend: the Heavenly King of Phù Đổng) in 1984. According to the author, the work was completed on September 14, 1984, but not published. It was then included in a French journal, *the New Road*, in 1986, and later reprinted in *Những bài dã sử Việt* (Vietnamese unofficial chronicles) in 1996. The monograph includes the following sections: the scale of the festival and conditions for tracing its origin; the origin of the legend: a fragment of a popular belief system of the mass Buddhist tradition; the Heavenly King of Sóc: a compound story of the God and the shadow of a human God of Phù Đổng village; and the festival from the court: a battle show. In addition to providing a wealth of information resources, the author successfully applied the comparison method to the changes of legends and festivals. The author based much on ancient texts, such as *An Nam chí lược, Đại Việt sử kí toàn thư, Việt điện u linh, Lĩnh Nam chích quái, and Thiền uyển tập anh*, to document the development of the legend of the God of Phù Đổng village. At the same time, the author also "organized the incarnation of the Heavenly King of Phù Đổng village according to the records of different periods" (Tạ Chí Đại Trường 1996,

---

[29] Published in *Lễ hội Saint Gióng* (*The Saint Gióng festival*), Culture and Information Publishes, Hanoi, 2009.

p. 97). The author confirmed that the worship of Saint Gióng originated from the worship of stone trees. This cult of stone trees was later absorbed the Quan Bích sect of Zen Buddhism and was intervened by Lý, Trần, and Lê dynasties, and finally changed the overall structure of the God. "The combination of mystery and reality, and the combination of sacredness and secularity, make the Vietnamese psychologically suitable for transforming the role of natural-human Gods into human-natural Gods." (Tạ Chí Đại Trường 1996, p. 99) Tạ Chí Đại Trường's point of view is that of historians. In addition, he had no opportunity to work on-site at Kinh Bắc region. Therefore, he could not see the different cultural levels and faiths contained in this cult.

In 1984, two writers Nguyễn Văn Khỏa and Lê Trọng Khánh studied the change and expansion of Saint Gióng's legend. Cao Huy Đỉnh had a debate with the two authors, stating that Gióng was not a tribal hero. On the contrary, he (Saint Gióng) "primarily originated as a hero of a country" (Nguyễn Văn Khỏa and Lê Trọng Khánh 1984, p. 170).

In 1985, two authors Đặng Văn Lung and Thu Linh published their work entitled *Traditional and Modern Festival*, and while Gióng Festival at Phù Đổng and Sóc Temples were not the main subjects of their study, they still provided viewpoints and comments on it.

In 1986, Trần Bá Chí published his work "*Hội Gióng đền Sóc (Gióng Festival at Sóc Temple)* with the preface written by the famous historian, Phan Huy Lê. It can be said that this is the first work discussed in details about Gióng Festival at Sóc Temple. In the book, basic facts such as The way to Dóng Festival at Sóc Temple, the history of Sóc Sơn; the legend of Saint Dóng fighting the invaders; Dóng Festival of Dóng Temple and Sóc Temple; contemporary generations' memory and nostalgia for Saint Dóng, etc.

In 1987, Trần Quốc Vượng published his article namely "Căn bản triết lý người anh hùng Phù Đổng và hội Gióng (Basic Philosophy of the Hero of Phù Đổng Village and Gióng Festival)". It is interesting to learn that the author separated the legend and the cultural layers of Gióng Festival in order to indicate its structure and decode the symbols of this cultural and religious phenomenon. He said: "It is an artificial stone column, about 4 meters high, with a small top end, a narrow middle, and a large bottom end, with a tenon-shaped shaft, which is inserted into the bottom of the round stone. There is no doubt that this is the stone structure of the Lý Dynasty, with the symbols of lingam (phallus) and yoni (clitoris), symbolizing fertility and secular power" (Trần Quốc Vượng 2000, p. 247). The author concluded that: "Gióng Festival begins with an ancient belief and agricultural etiquette. It prays for rain and expresses the worship of the sun God. With the passage of time and changes in history, it has become the worship of a hero who fought against the enemy and a performance ceremony for epic spectacles" (Trần Quốc Vượng 2000, p. 250). His conclusion is based on the research results of interdisciplinary research methods and is a proper method in this case study.

In 1989, Tạ Chí Đại Trường published a book entitled *Thần, người và đất Việt* (Gods, People and the Land of Viet). Although the worship of Saint Gióng is not the main focus of this book, the author commented on the legend and its cultural aspects when addressing the changes in Vietnamese folk beliefs (Tạ Chí Đại Trường 1989).

In 1990, Ngô Đức Thịnh and Vũ Ngọc Khánh published the book *Tứ bất tử* (The Four Immortal Gods), In which, the two authors viewed the legend of Saint Gióng and Gióng Festival through the lens of the four Immortal Gods of the Vietnamese people in the Red River Delta, respectively, Tản Viên Sơn Thánh (The God of Tản Viên Mountain), Saint Gióng, Chử Đồng Tử (God of Coastal Region), and Thánh Mẫu Liễu Hạnh (Liễu Hạnh Mother Goddess).

In 1990, Văn hóa dân tộc (Ethnic Culture Publisher), in conjunction with the Central Office of New Lifestyle, published a book entitled *Hội hè Việt Nam* (*Festivals in Vietnam*), chiefly edited by Trương Thìn. This book covers Gióng Festival of Phù Đổng Temple, as well as 17 other traditional festivals celebrated in other parts of the country.

In the book *Địa chí văn hóa dân gian Thăng Long - Đông Đô - Hà Nội* (Folklore of Thăng Long-Đông Đô - Hanoi) published in 1991 edited Đinh Gia Khánh and Trần Tiến, authors legendary story of Saint Gióng in Chapter III (namely "Folk tales"), Ải Lao Singing and Dancing Team in chapter IV ("Folk song and dance"); performance of Saint Gióng fighting Ân invaders in Chapter V ("Games - folk performances"); Gióng Festival in Chapter VI ("Rituals and customs") (Đinh Gia Khánh & Trần Tiến 1991, pp. 103, 154, 182-3, 196, 244).

During his visiting scholarship at Cornell University (the USA) in 1991, Trần Quốc Vượng completed the draft of a book entitled *Truyền thuyết về ông Gióng-trong sách vở và ở ngoài đời* (*The Legend of Saint Gióng - in books and in life*), presenting all his perceptions and reflections of Saint Gióng (see *Gióng Festival*, 2009).

In 1992, a monograph on traditional festivals completed by researchers of the Institute of Folklore (now known as the Cultural Institute of the Vietnamese Academy of Social Sciences), namely *Lễ hội cổ truyền* (Traditional Festivals). The work includes a number of citations related to Gióng Festival at Phù Đổng Temple as significant clues to illustrate the authors' arguments on traditional festivals. The author Lê Trung Vũ devoted section C in Chapter VIII (namely, "Historical events being enacted in the village festival") to describe four separate festivals devoted to Saint Gióng, including Phù Gióng festival in Sen Hồ hamlet, Lệ Chi commune, Gia Lâm district; Gióng Festival at Phù Đổng commune, Gia Lâm district; and Đông Bộ Đầu Gióng Festival in Thống Nhất commune, Thường Tín district. All these festivals are held today within the Hanoi capital. In 1993, at a meeting with the Ministry of Culture and Information, in order to formulate festival regulations, Lê Trung Vũ raised the issue of decoding the contents of Gióng festival.

In 1993, Bùi Thiết published a book entitled *Từ điển hội lễ Việt Nam* (*Dictionary of Vietnamese Festivals'*). Based on texts previously written by other researchers, the author briefly summarizes Gióng Festival of Phù Đổng Temple and similar festival at Sóc Temple.

In the 1995 book *60 lễ hội truyền thống Việt Nam* (60 Traditional Festivals of Vietnam) written by Thạch Phương and Lê Trung Vũ was introduced to readers. In the book, the two authors described five festivals, which are considered "serially held" to commemorate the Heavenly King of Phù Đổng. The five Gióng festivals include the ones in Phù Đổng village, Chi Nam village, Xuân Đỉnh village, Sóc Sơn village, and Đông Bộ Đầu village (Thạch Phương and Lê Trung Vũ 1995, pp. 211-19).

In 1996, Như Hạnh used the method of text comparison to raise a question, that is, how to determine a continuous line to connect Vaisravana (through the Heavenly King of Sóc village) to the Heavenly King of Phù Đổng village. The author compared records of the Heavenly King of Phù Đổng in *Thiền uyển tập anh, Việt điện u linh, Lĩnh Nam chích quái, and Đại Nam nhất thống chí* in order to identify the relationships between Buddhism and folk beliefs through the image of Phù Đổng village's god under the compilation and suplementation of contemporary Confucian scholars. From there, he determined the relationship between Vaisravana, the Heavenly King of Sóc village, and the Heavenly King of Phù Đổng village, in order to learn about the ancient people through the legend of Saint Gióng. In the same year (1996), Phạm Kế published a book entitled *Tứ bất tử* (Four Immortal Gods), reaffirming the values of the worship and legend of Saint Gióng.

In 1997, Lê Văn Kỳ published the monograph on *Mối quan hệ giữa truyền thuyết của người Việt và hội lễ về các anh hùng* (Relationship between the legend of the Vietnamese people and the festival of heroes), in which the author described Gióng Festivals of Phù Đổng, Đông Bộ Đầu, and Phù Linh villages in the third chapter.

In 1998, when compiling the book *Lễ hội Thăng Long* (The Festival in Thăng Long), Lê Trung Vũ included an article on the Saint Gióng festival, which was previously published in *60 lễ hội truyền thống Việt Nam* (60 Traditional Festivals of Vietnam).

In Issue 17 of *Nhân dân cuối tuần Newspaper* published in 1998, Cung Khắc Lược and Lương Văn Kế introduced the entire translation version of the Chinese-script legend at Đông Bộ Đầu Temple, Thống Nhất commune, Thường Tín district[30]. This legend was originally compiled by Nguyễn Bính in 1572. According to the two authors, "the content of the legend of the Heavenly King of Đồng Sóc is quite different from the familiar legend of Saint Gióng" (see Cung Khắc Lược & Lương Văn Kế 1998/2009, pp. 174-82). In the same year (1998), Nguyễn Thế Long published a book namely *Đình và đền Hà Nội* (Communal Houses and Temples in Hanoi), in which the author described Thượng Temple (Upper Temple) and Mẫu Phù Đổng Temple (the Heavenly King of Phù Đổng's Mother Temple) in Phù Đổng Commune, Gia Lâm district, Sóc Temple in Xuân Đỉnh commune, Từ Liêm district, and Sóc Sơn Temple in Phù Linh commune, Sóc Sơn district (see Nguyễn Thế Long 1998, pp. 253-6, 294-4). These are the sites where the worship of Saint Gióng is currently rated as a National Historic Site under the protection of the (former) Ministry of Culture.

In 2000, Doãn Đoan Trinh published a book entitled *Hà Nội: di tích lịch sử văn hóa và danh thắng* (*Hanoi: Historical and Cultural Sites and Sites of Attractions*), in which the author described the site of Phù Đổng village. In addition to the description of the site, the author briefly described the legend and provided detailed information similar to the familiar version (Doãn Đoan Trinh 2000, pp. 309-15). In this book, the author also mentioned Sóc Temple of Xuân Đỉnh commune, Từ Liêm district and Thanh Nhàn Temple of Thanh Xuân, Sóc Sơn district (Doãn

---

[30] This legend, encoded AE. a2/92, is currently stored in the library of the Institute of Sino-Nôm Studies.

Đoan Trinh 2000, pp. 571-2, 607-8). All these attractions are places of worship for Saint Gióng.

In 2000, the Hanoi Management Board of Historical Sites and Sites of Attraction published a book entitled *Di tích lịch sử văn hóa Hà Nội* (Historical and Cultural Sites in Hanoi), in which the authors described the site of Phù Đổng in Phù Đổng commune, Gia Lâm district and the site of Sóc Sơn in Phù Linh commune, Sóc Sơn district (Hanoi, Management Board of Historical Sites and Sites of Attraction 2000, pp. 531-7, 550-7). The descriptions of these sites in the book are invaluable for understanding and investigating the worship of Saint Gióng in these two localities.

In 2001, Nguyễn Thị Hương Liên published her article "Khảo sát thực trạng văn hóa lễ hội đền thờ Saint Gióng - lễ hội đền Phù Đổng (Investigation of the cultural situation of the festival at Saint Gióng Temple - the Festival at Phù Đổng temple)". The new main contribution of this work is that the author has paid attention to the description of the sites, such as Gióng temple, Kiến Sơ temple, Ban Temple, Mother Goddess Temple, and those at Giá Ngự, Đồng Đàm, and Soi Bia, which recorded the royal ordinations and titles granted by different dynasties to Saint Gióng. At the same time, the author based on the bibliography and the description of early researchers to discuss the history of the festival, and to describe the festival from a contemporary perspective on her own observation. Therefore, the author's main method is ethnographic description, without any necessary decoding instructions.

In 2005, Lê Trung Vũ and Lê Hồng Lý published the book *Lễ hội Việt Nam* (Festivals in Vietnam). In describing the festivals in Hanoi, the author described Gióng Festival of Sóc Temple in Xuân Đinh village, Gióng Festival in Sóc Sơn, the festivals of Saint Gióng in Phù Đổng village and Chi Nam village (Lê Trung Vũ & Lê Hồng Lý 2005, p.183-96). Compared with previously published works, their description of the festival is no different. However, it is worth noting that the author introduced the legend of Saint Gióng through the version edited by Nguyễn Bính in the Hồng Phúc reign (1572).

In 2006, Lê Trung Vũ published the work *Hội làng Hà Nội* (Village festivals in Hanoi). In addition to reprinting Lê Trung Vũ's previous works on Saint Gióng's Festival, the book also introduced other festivals held at the Saint Gióng workshop, such as the festival at Xuân Lai temple (Xuân Thu commune, Sóc Sơn district) by Tố Uyên, the festival at Thanh Nhàn temple (Thanh Xuân commune, Sóc Sơn district) by Nguyễn Thị Phương, the festival in Cán Khê village (Nguyên Khê commune, Đông Anh district) by Nguyễn Thị Hồng Hạnh, the festival at Sọ temple (Phù Lỗ commune, Sóc Sơn district) by Nguyễn Thị Phương, the festival in Đồng Xuyên village (Đặng Xá commune, Gia Lâm district) by Vũ Kiêm Ninh, and the festival in Vo village (i.e. Hội Xá village) by Văn Hậu, etc. The description of these Saint Gióng festivals is very important for studying Saint Gióng.

After the previous parts were printed and published separately, the Hanoi People's Committee published the entire series of *Bách khoa thư Hà Nội* (Encyclopedia of Hanoi) in 2008. This series of books was edited by a group of scientists from 1993 to 2000 and included 18 volumes. Volume 14 introduces museums and historical sites. In the third part of this volume, "Some Cultural and Historical Relics in Hanoi," the author described the remains of Phù Đổng (pp. 305-9) and Sóc Sơn Temple (pp. 331-2). In this volume, the author also provided detailed information on the legend of Saint Gióng. For example, an iron horse is 18 feet tall, the iron stick is 7 feet long, and so on. Vol. 17 refers to the customs and festivals of Hanoian people. In Chapter II of this volume, namely "Traditional Festivals", the authors thoroughly described the festival of Sóc (pp. 149-52) and the festival of Gióng (pp. 191-7) in full detail.

In 2009, Nguyễn Thụy Loan published the article "Một tuyên ngôn giữ nước bằng lễ hội ở đầu thời Lý (A declaration to defend the country was announced through the festival during the early Lý Dynasty)." In the same year, Văn Quảng compiled the book *Văn hóa tâm linh Thăng Long - Hà Nội* (The Spiritual Culture of Thăng Long - Hanoi). In Chapter II of the book, "Worshipped gods in Hanoi", the author addressed the character of Saint Gióng - the worshipped god of Sóc Sơn, Gia Lâm, and Từ Liêm communes.

In 2009, a massive four-volume book series entitled *Tổng tập nghìn năm văn hiến Thăng Long* (The Collection of A Thousand Year of Culture of Thăng Long) was launched in Hanoi. In Volume 1, the authors included the essay "Saint Gióng: huyền thoại và sự thật lịch sử (Saint Gióng: the legend of historical truth)" (pp. 1959-60). In Volume 2, the authors included the legend of the Heavenly King of Đồng village (pp. 2399-2400), as well as the Heavenly King of Sóc village (pp. 2410). Also in this volume, the authors included an essay entitled "Hội Saint Gióng (The festival of Saint Gióng)" written by Lê Trung Vũ (pp. 2624-8), as well as the essay "Tứ bất tử (the Four Immortal Gods)" by Phạm Văn Tình (pp....). In Volume 4, the authors introduced the site of Sóc Sơn (pp. 122-3), as well as a monograph entitled "Người anh hùng làng Phù Đổng (The hero of Phù Đổng village)" written by Trần Quốc Vượng (pp. 1415-7), etc.

In 2010, Kiều Thu Hoạch and Nguyễn Chí Bền published an article namely "Gióng hay Dóng (Gióng or Dóng)", in which, based on the phonetic rules and arguments related to the dictionary and the attitude of the community, the two authors confirmed that the Phù Đổng hero's name is Gióng, not Dóng as preferred by some writers.

In April 2010, the Hanoi People's Committee and the Ministry of Culture, Sports and Tourism organized an international conference entitled "Bảo tồn và phát huy lễ hội cổ truyền trong đời sống xã hội đương đại: trường hợp hội Gióng) (Preservation and development of traditional festivals in contemporary society: the case of Gióng Festival)". Nearly 100 domestic and international scholars participated in the Conference. If in 1993 the international conference called "*Lễ hội truyền thống trong xã hội đương đại* (Contemporary Festival of Contemporary Society)" organized by the Vietnamese Academy of Social Sciences, there was no direct mention of Gióng Festival held at Phù Đổng Temple and Sóc Temple, but this international conference attracted many famous scholars, for example, Hoàng Lương, Trần Lê

Bảo, Nguyễn Tri Nguyên, Nguyễn Bích Hà, Bùi Quang Thanh, Lê Thị Hoài Phương, Nguyễn Văn Phong, Đỗ Lan Phương, Đoàn Minh Châu, Vũ Anh Tú, Lê Thị Minh Lý, Từ Thị Loan, etc. These authors addressed different aspects of Gióng Festival at Phù Đổng Temple and Sóc Temple. While Trần Lê Bảo reviewed the values of Gióng Festival from the perspective of cultural heritage, Nguyễn Bích Hà raised the issue that it was the time to retell the legend of Saint Gióng. Similarly, while Hoàng Lương investigated the wishes of the mass, Bùi Quang Thanh studied the national character in Gióng Festival. Besides, Vũ Anh Tú reviewed various cultural layers in Gióng Festival to understand the fertility worship in the festival; Nguyễn Thị Thu Hường simply reviewed the worship of stones during the festival, etc. It can be said that the study of Gióng Festival at this international conference has reached a new level.

In 2010, Prof. Dr. Lê Hồng Lý published his work entitled *Tìm hiểu lễ hội Hà Nội (Understanding the Festivals in Hanoi)*, in which he used a part of Chapter III (namely, "Folk Festivals in the Contemporary Society") to describe Gióng Festival among the nine other traditional festivals of Hanoi. Special attention should be paid to the author's efforts to interpret Gióng Festival in Chapter 5, namely, "Some issues of festivals in Hanoi".

In 2010, Prof. Dr. Nguyen Chi Ben and his colleagues published the monograph *Hoi Gióng at Phu Dong and Sóc temples* (The Gioi publishing house, both Vietnamese and English versions). In addition, concluding, Appendix, the monograph has 6 chapters: Chapter 1 (Overview of the research on the Gióng festival); Chapter 2 (The Gióng festival space); Chapter 3 (Gióng festival of Phudong temple); Chapter 4 (Gióng festival of Sóc temple); Chapter 5 (The Gióng festival in other communes and villages); Chapter 6(Safeguarding and promoting values of the Gióng festival).

5. Conclusion

Therefore, regarding Gióng Festival, it is the birthplace of legends and festivals in the Gia Lâm, Sóc Sơn, Từ Liêm, and Thường Tín regions, and has been studied by Vietnamese and foreign scientists. Hundreds of articles and monographs have been published so far. There are many invaluable works, such as those by Dumotier, Nguyễn Văn Huyên, Trần Quốc Vượng, Nguyễn Tự Cường (i.e. Như Hạnh), Cao Huy Đinh, and Tạ Chí Đại Trường, etc. However, in general, from the perspective of intangible cultural heritage, Gióng Festival is a unique cultural phenomenon of the Viet people in the Red River Delta and therefore has not yet been the subject of any scientific monograph.

References

1. *"Bắc Ninh tỉnh địa dư* (北寧省地輿, Historical facts of Bắc Ninh Province)." In *Địa phương chí tỉnh Bắc Ninh qua tư liệu Hán Nôm* (Local history of Bắc Ninh province through the document in Hán-Nôm), trans. Đào Phương Chi, ed. by Trần Thị Kim Anh, Hanoi: Social Science Publisher.

2. Phạm,Văn Thụ, *Bắc Ninh tỉnh khảo dị* (北寧省考異, Strange Stories of Bắc Ninh Province). 1920

3. *Bắc Ninh toàn tỉnh địa dư chí* (北寧全省輿地志, Local History of Bắc Ninh Province)." In *Địa phương chí tỉnh Bắc Ninh qua tư liệu Hán Nôm* (Local history of Bắc Ninh province through the document in Hán-Nôm), trans. Nguyễn Tô Lan, ed. Trần, Thị Kim Anh, Hanoi: Social Science Publisher.

4. Bùi,Thiết. 1993. *Từ điển hội lễ Việt Nam* (Dictionary of Vietnamese Festivals). Hanoi: Culture Publisher.

5. Bùi, Văn Nguyên. 1978. "Tìm hiểu thêm ý nghĩa cảnh giác chống ngoại xâm trong truyện Thánh Gióng" *Journal of Literature* No 5/1978 in *Lễ hội Thánh Gióng* (Festivals of Saint Gióng), pp. 191- pp. 200, Hanoi: Culture and Information Publisher.

6. Cao, Huy Đinh. 1969. *Người anh hùng làng Dóng* (The Hero of Dóng Village)˙ Hanoi: Social Science Publisher.

7. Chu, Hà. 1979. Conference proceedings: *Diễn xướng dân gian và nghệ thuật sân khấu (Folk Performance and the Art of Theatre).* Hanoi: The Institute of Arts.

8. Cung, Khắc Lược & Lương Văn Kế. 1998. "Phát hiện mới về truyền thuyết Thánh Gióng, Phù Đổng thiên vương cứu mẹ" *Nhân dân cuối tuần Newspaper*, No. 17 (1998), Reprinted in *Lễ hội Thánh Gióng* (Festivals of Saint Gióng), ed. pp 174-182. Hanoi: Culture and Information Publisher.

9. Doãn, Đoan Trinh. 2000. *Hà Nội: di tích lịch sử văn hóa và danh thắng* (Hanoi: historical and cultural sites and sites of attractions). Hanoi: UNESCO Center for the Preservation and Development of National Culture of Vietnam.

10. Dumoutier, G. 1893. *Etude historique et archéologique sur Cổ-Loa, capitale de l'ancien royaume de Âu - Lạc (réunion de Thuc et de Văn-Lang) 255-207 av. J.C.* (Historical and archaeological study on Cổ-Loa, capital of the ancient kingdom of Âu - Lạc (integration of Thục and Văn-Lang) 255-207 BC.). Paris: Ernest Leroux.

11. Dumoutier, G. 1887. *Légendes historiques de l'Annam et du Tonkin* (Historical legends of Annam and Tonkin). Hanoi: mp. F. H. Schneider.

12. Dumoutier, G. 1893/2009. *Une fête religieuse Annammite à Phù Đổng - Revue des histoires des religions N. 1, t. XXVIII (Juil-Aoỳt 1893),* trans. Phan Phương Anh. Hanoi: Culture and Sports.

13. Đinh, Gia Khánh & Trần, Tiến eds. 1991. *Địa chí văn hóa dân gian Thăng Long - Đông Đô - Hà Nội* (Monography of Folklore of Thăng Long-Đông Đô - Hanoi). Hanoi: Hanoi Department of Culture and Information.

14. Đỗ, Bình Trị. 1970. *Lịch sử văn học Việt Nam* (History of Vietnamese Literature). Hanoi: Education Publisher.

15. Đỗ, Trọng Vĩ. 1997. *Bắc Ninh địa dư chí* (北寧興地志, Local Historical Facts of Bắc Ninh), trans. Đỗ Tuấn Anh, ed. Nguyễn Thị Thảo. Hanoi: Culture Information Publisher.

16. Lê,Trung Vũ ed. 1992. *Lễ hội cổ truyền* (Traditional Festivals). Hanoi: Social Science Publisher.

17. Kiều, Thu Hoạch & Nguyễn, Chí Bền. 2010. "Gióng hay Dóng (Gióng or Dóng)." *Journal of Folklore* 1: Hanoi.

18. Lê, Hồng Lý. 2010. *Tìm hiểu lễ hội Hà Nội* (Understanding the Festivals in Hanoi). Hanoi: Hanoi Publisher.

19. Lê, Ngô Cát & Phạm, Đình Toái ,*Đại Nam quốc sử diễn ca* (大南國史演歌, Historical Songs of the Great Southern Kingdom)

20. Lê,Tắc. 2002: *An Nam chí lược* (安南志略, Brief Annals of Annam), Vietnamese trans. Trần Kinh Hòa. Second edition. Huế: Thuận Hóa Publisher and East and West Cultural and Linguistic Center.

21. Lê ,Trung Vũ and Thạch, Phương, 1995. *60 lễ hội truyền thống Việt Nam* (60 Traditional Festivals of Vietnam). Hanoi: Social Science Publisher.

22. Lê, Trung Vũ ed, 1998. *Lễ hội Thăng Long* (The Festival in Thăng Long). Hanoi: Hanoi Publisher.

23. Lê, Trung Vũ & Lê, Hồng Lý. 2005. *Lễ hội Việt Nam* (Festivals in Vietnam). Hanoi: Culture and Information Publisher.

24. Lê, Trung Vũ ed 2006. *Hội làng Hà Nội* (Village festivals in Hanoi). Hanoi: Culture and Information Publisher and Institute of Culture Studies.

25. Lê, Văn Kỳ. 1997. *Mối quan hệ giữa truyền thuyết của người Việt và hội lễ về các anh hùng* (Relationship between the legend of the Vietnamese people and the festival of heroes). Hanoi: Social Science Publisher.

26. Lý, Tế Xuyên 1972: *Việt điện u linh* (越甸幽靈, Collection of Stories on the Shady and Spiritual World of the Viet Realm), Vietnamese trans. Trịnh Đình Rư, ed. Đinh Gia Khánh. Hanoi: Literature Publisher.

27. Many authors. 2009. *Tổng tập nghìn năm văn hiến Thăng Long* (The Collection of A Thousand Year of Culture of Thăng Long). Hanoi: Vietnam Economics Newspaper & Culture and Information Publisher.

28. Ngô, Sĩ Liên. 1972. *Đại Việt sử ký toàn thư* (大越史記全書 Complete Annals of Đại Việt) trans. Cao Huy Giu, ed. Đào Duy Anh. Volume 1, second edition. Hanoi: Social Science Publisher.

29. Nguyễn, Doãn Tuân, ed. 2000. *Di tích lịch sử văn hóa Hà Nội* (Historical and Cultural Sites in Hanoi). Hanoi: National Politic Publisher.

30. Nguyễn, Đổng Chi. 1956. *Lược khảo thần thoại Việt Nam* (Introduction to Vietnamese Myths). Hanoi: Literature, History and Geography Publisher.

31. Nguyễn, Đổng Chi. 1975. *Kho tàng truyện cổ tích Việt Nam* (The Collection of Vietnamese Fairy Tales), Volume IV. Hanoi: Social Science Publisher.

32. Nguyễn, Huy Hồng. 1977/2007. *Diễn xướng dân gian và nghệ thuật sân khấu truyền thống Việt Nam* (Folk Performance and the Art of Vietnam Traditional Theatre), pp. 106-144. Hanoi: The World.

33. Nguyễn, Huy Hồng. 1979. "Diễn xướng anh hùng ca Gióng (The Performance of the Epic of Gióng)". Journal of Folklore, Republished in *Diễn xướng dân gian và nghệ thuật sân khấu truyền thống Việt Nam* (Folk Performance and the Art of Vietnamese Traditional Theatre). Hanoi: The World.

34. Nguyễn, Khắc Đạm. 1981/2009. "Một số vấn đề về Hội Gióng (Some Issues of Gióng Festival)" In *Lễ hội Thánh Gióng* (Saint Gióng festival). pp.478-pp.484, Hanoi: Culture and Information Publisher.

35. Nguyễn, Thế Long. 1998. *Đình và đền Hà Nội* (Communal Houses and Temples in Hanoi). Hanoi: Culture Publisher.

36. Nguyễn, Thị Hương Liên. 2001. "Khảo sát thực trạng văn hoá lễ hội đền thờ Saint Gióng - lễ hội đền Phù Đổng (Investigation of the cultural situation of the festival at Saint Gióng temple - the Festival at Phù Đổng temple)." In *Khảo sát thực trạng văn hoá lễ hội truyền thống của người Việt ở đồng bằng Bắc Bộ* (Investigation of the Cultural Situations of Traditional Festivals of Viet People in the Red River Delta), ed. Nguyễn Quang Lê, Hanoi: Social Science Publisher.

37. Nguyễn, Thụy Loan. 2009. "Một tuyên ngôn giữ nước bằng lễ hội ở đầu thời Lý[31] (A declaration to defend the country was announced through the festival during the early Lý Dynasty)." *Journal of Folklore* 2:

38. Nguyễn, Văn Khỏa & Lê, Trọng Khánh. 1984. "Dóng,anh hùng bộ lạc hay anh hùng dân tộc"; republished in *Lễ hội Saint Gióng* (Saint Gióng festival). pp. 156 - pp. 173, Hanoi, Culture and Information Publisher.

39. Nguyễn, Văn Huyên. 1938. *Le Fêtes de Phu-Dong: Une bataille céleste dans la tradition annamite* (Phù Đổng Festival, a Legendary Battle in the Legends of Vietnam), In *Hội thánh Dóng (Les Pêtes de Thanh Dong)*, Culture and Information Publisher, 2009, pp. 152-226.

40. Như, Hạnh. 1996. Tỳ sa môn thiên vương (vaisravana), Sóc Thiên vương và Phù Đổng thiên vương trong tôn giáo Việt Nam thời trung cổ, No. 1 (San Jose, USA),1986 Republished in *Journal of Buddhism Studies* (Vietnam) 3/1998: 18-23 & 2/1999: 21-24. in *Lễ hội Saint Gióng* (Saint Gióng festival). pp. 137 - pp. 155, Hanoi, Culture and Information Publisher.

41. *Nguyễn Trãi toàn tập* (The Complete Works by Nguyễn Trãi), trans. Phan Duy Tiếp, ed. Hà Văn Tấn. Hanoi: Social Science Publisher.

42. Nguyễn, Trãi. 1969. "Dư địa chí (輿地志, Geography)." In *Nguyễn Trãi toàn tập* (The Complete Works by Nguyễn Trãi), trans. Phan Duy Tiếp, ed. Hà Văn Tấn, Hanoi: Social Science Publisher.

43. Nguyễn, Xuân Kính. 1995. *Các tác giả nghiên cứu văn hóa dân gian* (Vietnamese Folklorists). Hanoi: Social Science Publisher.

---

[31] *Journal of Folklore*, issue 2/2009.

44. Nguyễn, Văn Huyên. 1941/1996, *Les chants et les dances d'Ai-Lao aux fêtes de Phù Đổng* (Ải Lao Singing and Dancing in Phù Đổng Festival)/ Góp phần nghiên cứu văn hoá Việt Nam (Contributions to the Studies of Vietnamese Culture). Hanoi: Social Science Publisher.

45. Nguyễn, Hồng Phong. 1957. *Tìm hiểu tính cách dân tộc* (Understand national character). Hanoi. Literature, History and Geography Publisher.

46. Nguyễn, Khánh Toàn. 1954. *Đại cương về văn học sử Việt Nam* (Introduction to Vietnamese historical literature). Hanoi.

47. Nguyễn, Khánh Trường. 1938. *Légendes des principaux génies honorés dans la province de Phuc-Yên (Tonkin)* (Legend of principal gods worshiped in Phúc Yên province (Tonkin). Hanoi: Impr. du Nord.

48. Phạm, Kế. 1996. *Tứ bất tử* (Four Immortal Gods), Hanoi: Labor Publisher.

49. Phan, Huy Chú. 1960. *Lịch triều hiến chương loại chí* (歷朝憲章類誌, Charters of the Vietnamese dynasties), trans. Vietnam Institute of History. Hanoi: History Publisher.

50. Sombthay, E. 1893. *Ba mươi truyền thuyết và cổ tích Bắc Kỳ* (Thirty Legends and Tales in Tonkin). Hanoi: F. H. S Chneider.

51. Tạ, Chí Đại Trường. 1989. *Thần, người và đất Việt* (Gods, People and the Land of Viet). California, USA: Literature(Văn học)

52. Tạ, Chí Đại Trường. 1996. *Những bài dã sử Việt* (Vietnamese unofficial chronicles). California, USA: Thanh Văn.

53. Tầm, Vu. 1967. "Tư tưởng chủ yếu của người Việt thời cổ qua những truyện đứng đầu trong thần thoại và truyền thuyết (The Main Ideas of Ancient Viet People through the Top Legends and Myths)." *Journal of Literature* 3: 60-71.

54. Vũ Quỳnh. *Tân đính Lĩnh Nam chích quái* (新訂嶺南摭怪, The New Version of Selection of Strange Tales in Lĩnh Nam), trans. Bùi Văn Nguyên. 1993. Hanoi: Social Science Publisher.

55. The Hanoi Management Board of Historical Sites and Sites of Attraction. 2000. *Di tích lịch sử văn hóa Hà Nội* (Historical and Cultural Sites in Hanoi). Hanoi: National Politic Publisher.

56. The Hanoi People's Committee. 2008. *Bách khoa thư Hà Nội* (Encyclopedia of Hanoi). Hanoi: Culture and Information Publishing House and Institute of Research and Dissemination of Knowledge.

57. The National History Bureau of the Nguyễn Dynasty. 1971. *Đại Nam nhất thống chí* (大南一統志, Đại Nam Comprehensive Encyclopaedia), trans. Phạm Trọng Điềm, ed. Đào Duy Anh. Hanoi: Social Science Publisher.

58. *Thiên Nam ngữ lục* (the 17th century), trans. Nguyễn, Lương Ngọc & Đinh ,Gia Khánh. Hanoi: Culture Publisher & Department of Publications (Ministry of Culture), 1958.

59. *Thiền uyển tập anh ngữ lục* (禪苑集英語錄, Records on a Collection of Outstanding Figures of the Zen Community), trans. Ngô, Đắc Thọ & Nguyễn, Thúy Nga,1990. Printed in *Văn xuôi tự sự Việt Nam thời trung đại* (Vietnamese medieval narrative proses), introduction, selection Nguyễn Đăng Na, pp. 59- pp. 96, Second edition. Hanoi: Education Publisher.

60. Toan, Ánh. 1969. *Nếp cũ: hội hè đình đám* (Old Customs: Festivals). Volume 1. Saigon: Nam Chi tùng thư Publishing.

61. Trần, Bá Chí. 1986. *Hội Gióng đền Sóc* (Gióng Festival at Sóc Temple). Soc Son District People's Committee Publishing

62. Trần, Gia Du. 1877. *Nam Sử chí dị* (南史誌異, Historical Records of Southern Kingdom). Hanoi.

63. Trần, Quốc Vượng. 1991. *Truyền thuyết về ông Gióng-trong sách vở và ở ngoài đời* (The Legend of Saint Gióng - in books and in life), in *Lễ hội Saint Gióng* (Saint Gióng festival). pp. 283 - pp. 325, Hanoi, 2009, Culture and Information Publisher.

64. Trần, Quốc Vượng. 2000. *Văn hóa Việt Nam: tìm tòi và suy ngẫm* (Vietnamese Culture: Examination and Thoughts). Hanoi: Culture Ethnic Publisher & Journal of Culture and Arts.

65. Trần, Quốc Vượng & Vũ Tuấn Sán. 1975. *Hà Nội nghìn xưa* (Ancient Hanoi). Hanoi: Hanoi Department of Culture and Information Publisher.

66. Trần, Thanh Mại. 1955. *Quan điểm duy vật máy móc và duy vật biện chứng trong cách nhận định một truyện cổ tích* (The Perspective of Mechanical Materialism and Dialectic Materialism in Viewing a Tale). Hanoi: Lô River Publisher.

67. Trần, Thế Pháp. 1960. *Lĩnh Nam chích quái* (嶺南摭怪, Selection of Strange Tales in Lĩnh Nam), Vietnamese trans. Đinh Gia Khánh & Nguyễn Ngọc San. Hanoi: Culture Publisher & Vietnam Institute of Literature.

68. Trần, Việt Ngữ 1979. "Hội trận đền Gióng (The battle-enacting festival at Gióng Temple)." In *Vùng ven sông Nhị* (The Area along the Nhị River). Hanoi: Hanoi Publisher.

69. Trương, Thìn. 1990. *Hội hè Việt Nam* (Festivals in Vietnam). Hanoi: Ethnic Culture Publisher & the Central Office of New Lifestyle.

70. Văn, Quảng. 2009. *Văn hóa tâm linh Thăng Long - Hà Nội* (The Spiritual Culture of Thăng Long - Hà Nội). Hanoi: Labor Publisher.

71. Văn, Tân, Nguyễn, Hồng Phong, Nguyễn, Đổng Chi, Vũ, Ngọc Phan & other authors (1957). *Sơ thảo lịch sử văn học Việt Nam* (Overview of the History of Vietnamese Literature). Hanoi: Literature History Geography Publisher.

72. *Địa phương chí tỉnh Bắc Ninh qua tư liệu Hán Nôm* (Local history of Bắc Ninh province through the document in Hán-Nôm), trans. Trần Thị Kim Anh, ed. Đinh Khắc Thuân. Hanoi: Social Science Publisher.

THE GIÓNG FESTIVAL OF PHÙ ĐỔNG TEMPLE AND SÓC TEMPLE: REPRESENTATIVE INTANGIBLE CULTURAL HERITAGE OF HUMANITY

The space of Gióng Festival originated in the Kinh Bắc region. Although the geographical division has changed in history, at present, the central area of Gióng Festival is still mainly located on the north bank of the Red River, including the districts of Gia Lâm, Đông Anh, and Sóc Sơn (formerly Bắc Ninh Province, now Hanoi). In Gia Lâm District, Gióng Festival exists in Phù Đổng village (Phù Đổng commune) which, according to legend, was the birthplace of Saint Gióng, as well as in Đặng Xá commune and Lệ Chi commune. In Long Biên District, Gióng Festival is held annually in Hội Xá village (now Phúc Đồng ward). In Sóc Sơn District, Gióng Festival takes place in three different zones, including (1) Sóc Temple-centered area (Vệ Linh village, Phù Linh commune) and the villages of Dược Thượng (Tiên Dược commune), Xuân Dục, Đan Tảo (Tân Minh commune), Đức Hậu village (Đức Hòa commune), Yên Sào village (Xuân Giang commune), and Yên Tàng village (Bắc Phú commune); (2) Sọ Temple-centered area (Phù Lỗ Đoài village, Phù Lỗ commune); and (3) group of villages: Thanh Nhàn village (Thanh Xuân commune), Xuân Lai village (Xuân Thu commune). In Đông Anh District, Gióng Festival is organized in Sơn Du, Cán Khê villages (Nguyên Khê commune), and Đống Đồ village (Nam Hồng commune). In, Gióng Festival is available in Xuân Tảo village (Xuân Đỉnh commune) of Từ Liêm District and in Đông Bộ Đầu temple (Thống Nhất commune) of Thường Tín District. Although Gióng Festival is held in various places as mentioned above, the main figure of the festival is Saint Gióng, the hero of Phù Đổng Village.

All organizers and participants of Gióng Festival of Phù Đổng Temple and Sóc Temple as well as in other villages are Vietnamese wet-rice farmers. They are responsible for creating, organizing and maintaining the Gióng festivals. So far, Vietnam's cultural background in the Red River Delta seems to have not changed, including farmers, wet rice farming, and rural villages. In Sóc Sơn District, agriculture and forestry economy dominate, with a total area of 20,400 hectares, of which agricultural land is 13,835 hectares, forestry land is 6,133,5 hectares, and aquaculture land is 430,6 hectares. In 2001, the total number of households was 53,121, of which 44,320 were engaged in agriculture. In 2003, agriculture occupied an important position in the economies of Gia Lâm and Long Biên. In 2009, Gia Lâm District had 127 villages with 55,000 households, of which 48,000 lived on agriculture. In the districts of Đông Anh, Từ Liêm and Thường Tín, the situation was similar. This explains why the Phù Đổng Village's Gióng Festival has a long life in history.

In fact, Saint Gion is a legendary figure, deified as a symbol of faith. The legend of Saint Gióng has changed over time, not being stable from the beginning. The motif of a hero fighting against foreign invaders, protecting the community, defending the country, being born in an abnormal situation, and growing up suddenly to become a hero in the battle is a very popular pattern in legends of all nations in the world. Synchronously, the legend of Saint Gióng can be divided into three stages, with the following themes:

(a). The Birth:

• The mother found a bigfoot on the farm and was pregnant;

• She was pregnant for more than three years and had a son who was unable to speak or smile at the age of three;

• The boy grew up magically, and relatives and villagers fed him rice and pickled garden eggs.

• In response to the king's appeal, the royal court and village equipped him with iron weapons and tools (iron armor, iron horse, whipping rod) to fight against invaders in battle.

(b). Fighting the invaders:

- He fought in the battle with other soldiers and generals;
- He broke the whipping rod and used bamboo as a weapon to continue fighting;
- He fought against the sea monster.

(c). Reincarnation:

- Ascending to Heaven without any interest in fame or benefits in this mundane world;
- Supporting next dynasties to fight against invaders.

Therefore, it is clear that the legend of Saint Gióng belongs to the motif (theme) of a hero who fought for the community against foreign invaders and was born to be responsible for fighting the Red River Delta community against foreign invaders. The theme takes place in the following order: a hero was born under unusual circumstances → he heard the call to fight foreign invaders → he was armed by the community → he prepared to fight the enemy → he won a battle → he returned home. This is a familiar theme of heroes who fight foreign invaders and bring peace to communities and countries, and this Vietnamese story is not unique. However, the unique theme of the legend of Saint Gióng is that he rose to heaven after winning the battle. This is the most beautiful and romantic theme of the hero fighting invaders, it is rarely seen in many other ethnic groups in Vietnam or in other countries in the world.

The value of Gióng Festival lies in the existence of cultural and religious levels in the myths and festivals of the region. This is actually the worship of natural phenomena. Researcher Cao Huy Đinh spent a lot of time conducting field investigations in the area and recording the stories told by residents: 'This is Saint Đổng's footprint. He is very tall. His head reached the sky, his feet stepped on the ground but his shoulders touched the clouds. He raked the soil into a field, turned the rock into a hill, split the sand into a river, and then walked from one mountain to another. His footprints caused the ground to sink and the rocks fell, his voice sounds like thunder sounded like thunder, his eyes were blazing with fire, and the clouds of his breath spewed out clouds, stormy wind, and thunderstorms. He used to appears on summer days during thunderstorms, when the garden eggs and rice plant in the fields are about to bloom, according to legend. He walked all directions. He went from the west to the east, and there was a western storm. He went from east to west, and there was an eastern storm. He destroyed all rice, eggplants, bamboos, and banyan trees in the garden (Cao Huy Đinh 2003a, p. 198). The natural god kept in folklore as a mythical character reminds us of the story of miracle character(s) in the early history of mankind. Unfortunately, for many reasons, the Vietnamese mythology collapsed during contact with the Chinese culture, it was not systematically preserved like the Bahnar, Jo'rai, Ede ethnic groups in Vietnam, or like those of India and other countries. What remains now includes legendary pieces and verses of this outstanding hero handed down in the Nghệ Region:

In Vietnamese	English translation
Ông tát bể	He emptied the sea
Ông kể sao	He touched the sky
Ông đào cây	He digged the tree
Ông xây rú	He created the forest.

Therefore, the ancient cultural and religious aspects of the ancient Vietnamese in the legend of Saint Gióng are the remains of Saint Đổng's. A natural phenomenon has been legendized to be a legendary figure in commoners' faith. This is why there was an ancient temple dedicated to Saint Đổng in the former Phù Đổng area, and the residents sacrificed him with a bowl of rice, a plate of pickled garden eggs, and a vegetarian meal that was offered every year during the rainstorms (annually on 9th day of the fourth month of the lunar calendar). In the garden egg harvest season, farmers left a *sào* (equivalent to 360 square meters) of garden eggs for him to pick, while in other fields, people put long bamboo sticks with one end cut into cotton-like fibers next to the garden egg plants in order to avoid damaging the entire field when picked the garden eggs. These details remind people of the ritual of worshiping Rice Mother of before the harvest season practiced by the ethnic groups living in Northern Vietnam. In other words, this is a manifestation of the natural god worship of ancient Vietnamese peoples. Saint Đổng is the god of thunder and thunderstorms, so he used to appear on rainy and windy nights. This legend gave birth to Gióng Festival in Phù Đổng village to be organized on the 9th day of the fourth lunar month. Prof. Trần Quốc Vượng made a wise judgment when 'he considered Gióng Festival as a sacrifice to thunderstorms' (Trần Quốc Vượng 1994; 2009, p. 440) because this moment is the last period of the traditional Spring the festival, and the rainy season normally starts at the beginning of the fourth lunar month in the Red River Delta, as local residents describe:

In Vietnamese	English translation
Tháng tư cày vỡ ruộng ra	Land should be plowed out in the fourth
Tháng năm gieo mạ chan hòa	lunar month
nơi nơi	So seed can be cultivated widely in the
	fifth lunar month

Gióng Festival opens a new cycle of rice and crops. People begin to expect rain for new crops, which led to the fact that the ritual of praying for rain is common in their mental life. The famous Soviet researcher X. A. Tokarev once concluded that the ritual of praying for rain is essential in every religion. In addition to the worship of thunderstorms and thunderstorms, Gióng Festival is also related to the worship of trees and stones. All things related to foreign invaders destroyed by Saint Gióng are attached to the stone, including stone horses, and the stone pillars tied to the horses the Ân (the enemy) in Châu Cầu area. The legend recorded by Trần Bá Chí in the Sóc Sơn region shows that all the tools of the Ân enemy were made of stone, and the commander of the Ân was named Thạch Linh (Stony Spirit). A stone cradle, a stone sickle, and a stone pot were connected to Saint Gióng's mother in Đổng Xuyên village. The footprints of Saint Gióng still remain on the rocks of Thanh Nhàn village (Thanh Xuân commune, Sóc Sơn District). This reminds people of the ancient beliefs of the

Vietnamese people. The elders in the area told us that in the past, on the top of Sóc Mountain, there was a very old and sacred temple with a large stone on which the footprints of Mr. Đùng was printed (Trần Bá Chí 1986, p. 40). In 1984, Associate Professor Đặng Văn Lung and Associate Professor Thu Linh pointed out: "The Holy King of Heaven (Xung Thiên thần vương), also known as Saint Đổng, is actually General Stone (Thạch tướng quân) being worshipped in the Phù Đổng village). The name Phù Đổng is explained as Phnom - Núi in the Khmer language, and Pù Đổng - Núi in Tai languages" (Đặng Văn Lung & Thu Linh 1984, p. 98). This point may give us an idea of finding a deeper cultural-belief layer of the ancients, but that does not have to be traces of folk etymology.

Another tradition involving worship of natural phenomena during Gióng Festival is worship of the sun. In the temples of Phù Đổng and Sóc, a white wooden horse is located in the harem of the temple. The white wooden horse symbolizes the worship of the sun. Legendary thinking of the ancients allowed to use the image of horse/chariot to symbolize the sun. It should be emphasized that, for the people who grow wet rice, the worship of the sun is very important. According to Lại Văn Tới, there are 3 bronze drums found among the artifacts discovered in Cổ Loa area namely Xóm Nhồi drum, Cổ Loa I drum and Cổ Loa II drum. It is worth noting that in the middle of the Cổ Loa I drum, there is a 14-pointed star decorated with peacock feather patterns, and 16 long-beak birds flying counterclockwise (see Lại Văn Tới 2000). The image of a 14-pointed star and the birds flying counterclockwise provides evidence for our understanding of the sun worship of the ancient Vietnamese people in Cổ Loa. Therefore, the legends of Saint Gióng and the mascots in the temple remind us of the worship of the sun in Đông Sơn culture, as Professor Trần Quốc Vượng said: "Through the worship of the sun, Đông Sơn cultural traces in Gióng Festival are revealed". The sun in Đông Sơn culture has changed from star symbols and birds flying counterclockwise to the white horse in Gióng Temple and the iron horse in Gióng's legend (Trần Quốc Vượng 2009, p. 440). According to the records of *Bắc Ninh tỉnh khảo dị* (Investigation on anomalous objects of Bắc Ninh province), it is necessary to pay attention to the costume of the " Ấn enemy general","Female generals always wear red clothes and a martial hat"[32]. The one who plays the role of The Holy King of Heaven (Xung Thiên thần vương) also wears the same costume. This is clearly a manifestation of the worship of the sun. The most obvious symbol of the worship of the sun can be seen through a flag game guided by the flag master who symbolizes Siant Gióng. In Đống Đàm and Soi Bia, people organize totally six games, including three games in which the flag master waves the flag by the right hand (*ba ván cờ thuận*) and another three games by the left hand (*ba ván cờ nghịch*). The color of the flag symbolizes the sun, and the movement of the flag symbolizes the movement of the sun in a day: from east to west during the day and from west to east at night. During Gióng Festival, the ceremony Saint Gióng in the battle takes place at noon. According to legend, Saint Gióng started his journey on the battlefield from the east (Châu Sơn) to the west (Sóc Sơn) and finally ascended to Heaven. This is also a hint of the sun moving from east to west as usual.

Traces of the worship of the sun can also be found in the traditional Gióng festival in the village of Đìa (also called Đống Đồ village) in Nam Hồng commune, Đông Anh District. During the festival, the villagers hold a show of *robbing the phết ball (hất phết)*. The phết ball is painted in red, which is taken from the harem by the elders. In the robbing battle, about 20 young men scramble for the ball (giật phết); when the game starts, the ball is thrown into the air, falling up and down as many times as possible. The more the ball is thrown up and down, the happier the villagers are. The elders in the village said that this performance simulated the way that Saint Gióng used to train his soldiers. This performance is also an expression of the worship of the sun of the villagers of làng Đìa.

---

[32] Vietnamese translation (from Han scripture) by Nguyễn Tô Lan, edited by Nguyễn Thị Hường & Đinh Khắc Thuân (Vietnam Institute of Culture and Arts Studies, 2008).

Meanwhile, residents of Lệ Chi village (Lệ Chi commune, Gia Lâm District) organize a wrestling game between the local army (wearing only red loincloths and yellow belts, while the Ân invaders blue loincloths and white belts) on the morning of the 8th day of the first lunar month. In this wrestling show, we pay special attention to the red color of the loincloth which is a reflection of the worship of the sun by the ancient Vietnamese people. In addition to this game, fighting with sticks and fighting for a coconut on top of a bamboo tree during Gióng Festival also refers to the worship of the sun. Unlike the worship of the sun as a national religion, such as the cult of the sun goddess Amaterasu in Japan, the worship of the sun of agricultural residents like the ancient Vietnamese was associated with rituals to pray for crops.

Another religious practice that exists in Gióng Festival is the fertility (fecundity) belief of ancient agricultural residents dating back to the Neolithic Age. According to X. A. Tokarev, a scholar of the Soviet religious studies, "it is one of the oldest, and independent, roots of religious beliefs and rituals associated with sex" (Tokarev 1994, p.141) and has been popular in Southeast Asian traditions. Many objects of this belief have been found by archaeologists in Vietnam. Statues of no-hand but enlarged genitals were found the site of Phùng Nguyên (4,000 years BC). The unearthed stone statue of Văn Điển (Millennium I, BC) turns to be a man with a big penis. On the lid of the Đào Thịnh bronze jar discovered in Yên Bái province (5th century BC), four pairs of men and women were in sexual intercourse. After the process of contact and cultural exchange between Han culture and the culture of ancient Southeast Asian people, traditional fertility beliefs changed in different ways. In the south of the Gianh river, these beliefs were not influenced by Han culture, so hey developed as a separate flow, becoming an important component of the system of local beliefs to this day. We can see evidence of this flow through the linga, yoni worshiped in the traditional towers (kalan) of the Cham people in the Central region, or can be found through the popular graves (tombs) of many ethnic minorities in the Central Highlands. In the Red River Delta, contact and cultural exchange with Han culture took place strongly, even the Trần Dynasty (1225-1400) once ordered the destruction of heterodox cults, forbidding people from worshiping heterodox deities. This caused this belief to be deconstructed, but it did not thus disappear completely. The opinion of the talented ethnologist Nguyễn Từ Chi is completely correct, he said: "male and female mating, the symbol of fertility is not the result of a long and slow cognitive process but is the product of an unpredictable force, suddenly rising from the depths of man, that is the unconsciousness of human beings. In other words, it is the purely inherent instinct of man (Nguyễn Từ Chi 1996, p. 367). Fragments of this belief exist in many aspects of folklore from folk literary to folk arts (including village temple sculpture, folk painting) and folk festivals. Kinh Bắc region, the early home of ancient Vietnamese people, therefore becomes a land where fertility concepts have been vigorously developed. Until 1920, there were records of festivals in which there were widespread manifestations of fertility belief, such as the festivals of Long Khám commune of Tiên Du District (Đông Sơn sub-district), Trường Lâm commune, Cự Linh commune and Phú Thị commune of Gia Lâm District[33], etc. Therefore, it is not surprising that Phù Đổng Temple festival has many vivid expressions of fertility beliefs.

The most obvious expression of fertility belief is that 28 beautiful girls of Phù Đổng village were chosen to play the role of "enemy general". These girls from 10 to 13 years old were selected according to strict criteria: beautiful, obedient, not during the mourning period. Only the most beautiful of them can play the role of the general and deputy general. Prof. Lê Hồng Lý confessed: "A Bulgarian folklore researcher, Professor Radost Ivanova, suggested another idea after watching 28 girls disguised as Ân generals at Gióng Festival and the fight of the flag masters (Saint Gióng's lower generals). He wondered if this was a remnant of the past custom of wife robbery, which still exists in certain ethnic groups in Vietnam and the world? (Lê Hồng Lý

---

[33] The author does not have conditions to check these sites according to the current administrative boundary.

2010, p. 243). In the 1960s, researcher Cao Huy Đinh's field survey of Phù Đổng village showed that boys and girls were set up to chase each other along the riverbank at night after the vegetarian ritual at Thượng temple ended at the village festival on April 7 of the lunar calendar. Boys used to wear loincloths and have their heads bare to avoid being pulled by girls. However, this tradition today is very old, falling into oblivion, only left in the way of teasing between girls and boys" (Cao Huy Đinh 2009, p. 527). This approach is reminiscent of a type of folk singing art (hát Quan họ) in the ancient village of Bắc Ninh, full of fertility ideas. Some songs played at the Phù Đổng Temple Festival by the Ái Lao band also expressed the young man's desire to find his fiance. Holding a fishing rod, a young man from the band sang a song as follows:

In Vietnamese	*English translation*
Người ta câu bể câu sông	Whether one goes fishing in a river
Thì tôi câu lấy con ông cháu bà	or at the sea
Có chồng con, em nhả mồi ra	I just want to fish you, girl
Không chồng con, em cắn, em	If you are already married, release
dứt, em tha lấy mồi	the bait
Khấn giời phù hộ cho tôi	And please bait it if you are single
Để tôi câu lấy một người thanh	May God bless me
tân	For fishing a virgin girl.

Explaining the two last sentences of the song, the author of *Bắc Ninh tỉnh khảo dị* (Investigation on anomalous objects of Bắc Ninh province) added: "The young man was surrounded by soldiers in front of the embankment. While holding a fishing rod, he saw the beautiful girl, stroked her with the fishing rod, and sang the last two sentences of the song for fun."[34] Regarding the fertility beliefs in Gióng Festival, we cannot help but think of the horse tie pole of Ân invaders in Châu Cầu area (now Quế Võ District, Bắc Ninh province). This man-made stone pillar is 4m high, the head is small, with a horizontal line, and the base

---

[34] Vietnamese translation (from Han scripture) by Nguyễn Tô Lan, edited by Nguyễn Thị Hường & Đinh Khắc Thuân (Vietnam Institute of Culture and Arts Studies, 2008).

is large, inserted into a thick cake-shaped stone. The whole structure makes the symbol of linga and yoni.

At the end of the Sóc Temple Festival (Sóc Sơn District), the game of slashing enemy generals is performed. Three girls aged 13 to 16 in of Yên Tàng, Mậu Tàng, Xuân Tàng villages are disguised as enemy generals. The slashing performance started on the evening of the seventh day of the first lunar month. Starting from the top of the mountain, some flags are arranged to display the order signs. According to the instruction of the flags, the person who plays the role of the slashing character is quick to perform slashing moves that have been rehearsed before. At this time, the gongs are noisy, viewers crowded inside and outside the yard. The flags on the mountain flutter stronger, as fast as a cut, a sword is lift up, the female general quickly ran into the bush. At this time, a family member takes her home. The game of splashing enemy generals reminds us a lot of scenes where boys and girls traveled in the mountains in the spring. In other words, it is a manifestation of fertility beliefs and is only visible in fragments of cultural and religious layers of the present time.

In addition to the worship of natural gods, the worship of the sun, and the belief in fertility, the worship of craft ancestors is also essential. In order to understand the worship of craft ancestors around the Cổ Loa region, it is necessary to study it in correlation with beliefs related to Sơn Tinh (the God of Tản Viên Mountain) in Việt Trì region, Saint Chử Đồng Tử in Hưng Yên province, and Holy Mother Goddess Liễu Hạnh in Nam Định province. The cults of Gióng, Sơn Tinh, Chử Đồng Tử, and Liễu Hạnh formed the Four Great Immortals structure in Vietnamese culture. Considering the correlation with this immortal group, the worship of craft ancestors in Cổ Loa region showed a difference. On the two sides of the Red River, if Cổ Loa is the focal point, we will identify the cultural and religious area of Saint Gióng worship (Phù Đổng Thiên Vương). We can only interpret this multi-faceted, multi-meaning, and multi-valued image of Saint Gióng when we put the creativity of the people in the context of the ancient

Vietnamese people who had descended from the mountains to the deltas and built independent state. It is only possible to understand why the hero of Phù Đổng village (Saint Gióng) told the royal messenger to request the King (Hùng King) to arm him a set of iron armor, an iron horse, an iron sword, and whipping rods to defeat the Yin invaders if we consider the metal crafts (including these weapons) made by the Vietnamese in the Cổ Loa region at that time. Many objects made of iron and copper found in Cổ Loa by archaeologists are the most obvious evidence to support this hypothesis. Brass refining technique by ancient Viet people in Đình Tràng, Đường Mây, Bãi Mèn, Xóm Hương, Xóm Nhồi, Mả Tre, and Cầu Vực early reached its peak and turned to forge and iron fabrication (Hoàng Văn Khoán et al. 2002, p. 416; see also Lại Văn Tới 2002). Bronze objects found in Cổ Loa are not big but diverse in types, such as production tools, household appliances, weapons, jewelry, etc. Obviously, from large and heavy Cổ Loa I drums decorated with various exquisite patterns to small objects, this shows the fact that casting and forging techniques were perfected in all stages of product manufacturing. Many red copper products found at Cổ Loa, including hundreds of plowshares and blades, indicate that red copper existed on the basis of the highly developed brass metallurgy technology.

The iron objects discovered at Đường Mây show that the cast iron technology was further developed on the groundwork of copper casting technology. Especially, the iron objects found at the foot of Cổ Loa citadel also imply the birth time of iron metallurgy technology before Cổ Loa citadel was built" (Hoàng Văn Khoán et al. 2002, p. 417-418).

Therefore, craft ancestors can be seen in the portrait of the hero Gióng. The iron horse of the hero of Phù Đổng village roared and burned the bamboo forest in the village, but now all that remains is the ivory bamboo in a corner of the village. Is it a technique to make the craft ancestors spiritual and sacred in people's minds? Therefore, the original portrait of the hero may be a cultural hero, an ancestor of craftsmanship. In other words, the legend of the hero of Phù Đổng village is a mirror image of the achievements of the ancient Vietnamese iron making. They reached the pinnacle of metal processing early, and at the same time created a legend to reflect this achievement. After emigrating to the plains, Vietnam's exploitation of the Red River Delta faced invasion from enemies from the north (China). Is that what has made this cult worship add new layers of cultural alluvium? The late Professor Trần Quốc Vượng is correct in his statement that "The story of the hero of Gióng village whose final appearance is filled with patriotism and the spirit of fighting against invaders and defending the country originated from a legend in a metallurgical region" (Trần Quốc Vượng 1996, p. 18).

Therefore, from the myth fragments of the worship of Saint Gióng, one can imagine that ancient culture and religion flowed layer by layer, and until today it flows to the mainstream of the worship of a hero who defeated invaders. The late Professor Trần Quốc Vượng said: "At present, cultural and mythological heroes are swallowed by human unconsciousness, but the heroes who defeated the invaders are always visible in human consciousness. Similarly, the agricultural ceremony was engulfed by the unconscious, but the hero's performance was vividly reflected in Gióng Festival" (Trần Quốc Vượng 1994, p. 225). The movement and interaction of cultural-religious layers perfected the hero's portrait with the motif expressed in the system of relics and epitaphs until the end of the sixteenth century. The victory over the heroic invaders of Phù Đổng village's hero can be historically divided into two stages:

(1) The stage of fighting against the Ân invaders: In the first stage, due to the demands of history, the boy of Phù Đổng village (Gióng) magically grew up to become a hero. The hero Saint Gióng defeated the invaders from Trâu Sơn Mountain to Quế Võ, from Phả Lại to Gia Lương, and from the Lục Đầu River (Tiên Du, Dông Ngàn, Yên Phong) to the areas around Sóc Mountain. Compared to the process of developing the Red River Delta of the ancient Vietnamese, the battleground Saint Gióng fighting the Han invaders is located in the

north of the current Red River, the fourth branch of the river as noted by *Thủy Kinh chú* in the early Christian era, which refers to the areas of Long Biên, Luy Lâu, Tây Vu, Bắc Đái, Kê Từ, etc. (i.e., Kinh Bắc region). Ancient Vietnamese residents from the midland regions encountered forests, swamps, and forces from the ocean, so they needed a hero of their own. All these details were legendized, so that the later Confucianists transformed him into a national hero. In this regard, researcher Keith W. Taylor made a sharp opinion in *The Birth of Vietnam* as follows:

"Legends of Lac Long Quan, Ong Giong, the spirit of Mount Tan-vien, and Nhat Da Trach were incorporated into Ngo Si Lien's court history in the fifteenth century. All of these legends were by that time encrusted with elaborations stemming from the cultural currents of later centuries (Tran Quoc Vuong, p. 404). These legends were remembered by the Vietnamese because they expressed their earliest identity as a people" (Taylor 1983, p. 6; see also Trần Quốc Vượng 1994, p. 326).

The existence or non-existence of an ethnic community at the dawn of history has caused the cultural and religious layers of agricultural residents to subside, and the cultural-religious layers of anti-foreign hero appears more clearly. This sense of the people was raised by the Confucian scholars after the tenth century, transformed into written and divine works in villages that worshiped Saint Gióng.

Since that time, Saint Gióng has become a very beautiful and majestic anti-foreign hero of the Vietnamese people, as Tam Tam author once said: "Saint Gióng is a beautiful figure of folk art, [...] full of patriotism with hatred of foreign invaders and the will to win. Moreover, Saint Giong was also a hero who fought for the community without caring about his own fame. He incarnated into the sacred realm (the immortal realm) when he had finished fighting the foreign invaders. It is worth noting that the heroic action of Phù Đổng village's hero has become a gathering place for all patriots, which makes the legend of

Saint Gióng become an epic about fighting foreign invaders (Cao Huy Đinh 2003b, pp. 197-213).

(2) Saint Gióng's epiphany to help the later dynasties against foreign aggression to protect the country. Unlike some other historical heroes, Saint Gióng later appeared to help the later dynasties fight foreign invaders, such as helping the Former Lê dynasty (980-1009) to fight the Song invaders, and Lê Lợi against the Minh domination (1408-1427). Stele *Hiển linh từ thạch* engraved in 1606 still in Phù Đổng Temple is a testament to that statement.

In this transformation, the role of monarchy dynasties in Saint Gióng cult was very important. These dynasties ordained this immortal Saint through various ordinations. Particularly at Phù Đổng Temple, in addition to the records of the Confucianists in *Việt Điện U Linh Tập* (越甸幽靈集, Collection of Stories on the Shady and Spiritual World of the Viet Realm, by Lý Tế Xuyên in 1329) and *Lĩnh Nam Chích Quái* (嶺南摭怪, Selection of Strange Tales in Lĩnh Nam, by Trần Thế Pháp in the fourteenth century) describing the dedication of the Lý dynasty (1009-1225) and the Trần dynasty (1225-1400) to Saint Gióng. There are about 20 imperial conferments on Saint Gióng by the Lê dynasty (1427-1789) and the Tây Sơn dynasty (1789-1802) preserved in Phù Đổng temple.

Under the Nguyễn dynasty (1802-1945), *Phù Đổng thiên vương* (Phù Đổng Heavenly King) was continuously conferred by Minh Mệnh, Thiệu Trị, Tự Đức, Bảo Đại emperors. It is worth noting that there are various sacred legends and genealogy about Saint Gióng in the region. Sacred legends of Phù Đổng, Sóc Sơn, Thanh Nhàn and other temples all have were compiled by Nguyễn Bính in 1572 and completed by Nguyễn Hiền in 1740[35]. The dedication of the state and various sacred legends made Saint Gióng more sacred and mysterious throughout the generations and made the process of Saint Gióng's mythicization more

---

[35] Historically, 1740 belonged to the reign of King Lê Hiển Tông. It is not clear why there is such a legend in the legend.

elaborate in the folk mentality. Among the dynasties, the Lý dynasty (1009-1225) played an important role in transforming the mythical hero into a real hero of Phù Đổng village, and he was depicted as an anti-invader hero. Not only was a temple built next to Kiến Sơ Pagoda, but a temple dedicated to Saint Gióng was established by the Lý dynasty in the West Lake area near the capital of Thăng Long.

Throughout the dynasty, Buddhist monks also played a role in sanctifying the heroes of Phù Đổng village. Therefore, the legend of Saint Gióng is also part of the Buddhist culture. According to various legends of the villages, Saint Đổng's large feet printed on the vegetable garden or road may be a cultural trace of Jainism, but others told that Saint Gióng's footprints are on the top of Sóc Mountain, or printed on the stone in Thanh Nhàn village (Thanh Xuân town). According to the legend of Bộ Đầu village, Saint Gióng's mother accidentally stepped on a stone footprint and became pregnant, many people referred this story with the one in Thanh Nhàn village. It is undoubtedly a cultural trace of Jainism, and more importantly, a relic of Buddhist culture. Many people proved that the legend of the god appearing in monk Khuông Việt (Ngô Chân Lưu)'s dream had been integrated with the legend of Saint Gióng. *Thiền uyển tập anh* (A Collection of Outstanding Figures of the Zen Community) recorded this dream while the two Vietnamese books of history *Việt sử lược (*Brief Annals of Vietnam*)* or *Việt điện u linh* (Collection of Stories on the Shady and Spiritual World of the Viet Realm) did not mention it. It is possible that the legend did not exist until the fourteenth century; however, it was found in the text documents compiled by Nguyễn Bính in 1572. The legend of a god appearing in the monk's dream in Khuông Việt in Phù Đổng village recorded the god wearing armor and holding a golden ax, while this god in Xuân Tảo commune's legend was told to hold a golden spear in his left hand and a precious stupa in his right hand. From *Tỳ Sa Môn thiên vương* (Vaisravana) to *Sóc Thiên vương* (Sóc Heavenly King), and then to Phù Đổng Thiên vương (Phù Đổng Heavenly King), this is the process of transforming the image of Saint Gióng under the influence of Buddhist culture (Như Hạnh/Nguyễn Tự Cường 1998, 1998; 2000, pp. 137-155; see also Tạ Chí Đại Trường 1996, pp. 75-102).

The geo-cultural and geopolitical status of the Kinh Bắc region makes this land the birthplace of Buddhism and its earliest development in Vietnam. Therefore, it is indispensable to incorporate Buddhist culture into faith in local hero worship. Regarding Buddhism in the Kinh Bắc region, Vietnamese Buddhist history researchers have confirmed the development of Dâu and Kiến Sơ Schools (sơn môn) in Phù Đổng area from the early AD to the eleventh and twelfth centuries. Dâu Pagoda Schools is divided into 2 branches, ancient and new. The former branch was famous for its monks named Mâu Tử, Khương Tăng Hội, Chi Cương Lương, Tì Ni Đa Lưu Chí, Pháp Hiền, Thanh Biện, etc., and the later Định Không, La Quý An, Pháp Thuận, etc. Kiến Sơ School took place around the beginning of the 9th century. A monk who had previously lived at Tiên Du Mountain named Lập Đức has renovated a Nguyễn family house (Phù Đổng village) into a pagoda. However, it was not until Monk Vô Ngôn Thông (? -826) came to practice that the Kiến Sơ School took shape. Kiến Sơ School is also divided into two sections: the first includes monks named Vô Ngôn Thông, Cảm Thành, and Thiện Hội and the second Vân Phong and Khuông Việt (Ngô Chân Lưu). It is noticeable that monk Khuông Việt (933-1011) joined in the royal mission to consolidate the Đinh dynasty (968-980). While "Dâu Pagoda School applied Dharani to form rather powerful magic practices under the Lý Nhân Tông and Lý Thần Tông periods from the end of the eleventh century to the beginning of the twelfth century" (Nguyễn Duy Hinh 1999, p. 457), Kiến Sơ School was intended to be more of a profane life with deep Zen Buddhism thought rather than a purely religious sect (Nguyễn Duy Hinh 1999, pp. 139-646).

Buddhist monk Khuông Việt is believed to have cultivated Buddhist factors into the legend of Saint Gióng. Because monk Khuông Việt's Zen thoughts focused more on secular life than pure religious philosophy, Saint Gióng became the protector of the country in his dream. The hero of Phù Đổng village is considered to be a "convergence point" between the folk's desire to have a national hero and the attitude of the monk Khuông Việt towards the royal court. In addition, if the Vietnamese migrated from the midland's region down to the Red River Delta (from Việt Trì down to Cổ Loa), Phù Đổng (where Kiến Sơ School was established) and Sóc Mountain are very close to each other, both of which are located on the north side of the current Red River. This explains why the legend of Saint Gióng took shaped in Phù Đổng village rather than in other regions. Kiến Sơ Pagoda was the place where the founding king of the Lý dynasty practiced in his childhood, and where many famous monks of Kiến Sơ School lived. It is now close to Saint Gióng Temple. The pagoda is the birthplace of the hero of Phù Đổng village. The Great Master Khuông Việt and later King Lý Công Uẩn (974-1028) were the factors that had a conscious influence on Kiến Sơ School, which made the school play an important role in the legendary process of the hero Gióng and upgraded him into a national patron god. However, Kiến Sơ School was formed after Dâu Pagoda School, which means that the cultural layer associated with Dâu Pagoda School had spread throughout the region (from Dâu Pagoda to Phật Tích Pagoda), and transformed Phu Dong village, which had followed Brahmanism and then Jainism in the early Christian era, to the Buddhist village. Buddhism with the Great Master Khuông Việt was an important factor in creating the integration of the Saint Gióng legend with the Buddhist culture. He created a special characteristic of both the cult and legend of Phù Đổng village, as Tạ Chí Đại Trường once remarked interestingly: "The God of Sóc Mountain (Vệ Linh) was assimilated to the God of Phù Đổng village" (Tạ Chí Đại Trường, p. 90).

It is from this mythical process that the hero Saint Gióng, who resists foreign aggression, has a new look: a hero who fights against the flood and brings rain to the agricultural inhabitants. The legend and the transformation of the statue of Saint Gióng in the transformation Đông Bộ Đầu Temple (Thống Nhất commune, Thường Tín District) evokes the idea of the god fighting the flood, in which the image of Saint Gióng stepping on two *jiao* dragons (jiao long) is clearly the image of the god fighting the flood. *Bắc Ninh địa dư chí* (*Geography of Bắc Ninh province)*, Đỗ Trọng Vĩ described the ritual of prayer for rain in Đức Hậu commune[36] as follows: Children in the village went to pick fruits, built flocks in the fields, beat drums, tore paper to make flags, and arrange bamboo sticks to make a sedan chair. They went to Mã Temple (also called Vệ Linh Temple) to bring the incense burner back to their altar and prayed for good luck. They did it effectively many times. People said that one day, the children saw a thirsty white-haired old man who asked them for water. The children ran to carry water for him, and the old man named this place Thanh Thủy village (meaning 'pure water') of Đức Hậu ('great virtue') commune. The old man also said, "From now on if there is a drought, you guys come to the temple and tell me, I will take water to reward you." After saying that, the old man disappeared. It is him, the Holy God of Heaven (*Thiên vương)*"[37].

In *Bắc Ninh địa dư chí (Geography of Bắc Ninh province)* (serial number A. 2889 of the Sino-Nom Research Library), a similar record has been found. It clearly affirmed "(The old man) is the incarnation of Đổng Thiên Vương (the Holy King of Heaven of Phù Đổng)" (Đinh Khắc Thuân (ed.) 2009, pp. 276-7). An inscription at Phù Đổng Temple also stated that: "the Holy King of Heaven is written in Chronicles as the noble Saint of generations, so sacrifices mus be performed similarly to the sacrifice of the eight official state-sponsored deities. From the Đinh dynasty (968-980) onwards, the court ordered the mandarins to pray for rain in the hope that the spring would always be full and clean. Especially in drought years, the king sent officials to pray for rain. At that time, it often rained, making all people well-off"[38]. This record completely coincides with the stele *Hiển linh từ thạch* engraved and erected in the sixth year of Hoằng Định reign (1606) at Phù Đổng

---

[36] According to Nguyễn Văn Huyên in *Kinh Bắc's Administrative Geography*, Đức Hậu commune belonged to Phổ Lộng & Đa Phúc District (now Sóc Sơn District, Hanoi city).

[37] Translation (from Han script) by Đỗ Tuấn Anh, edited by Nguyễn Thị Thảo (Hanoi: Culture and Information Publisher, pp. 184-5).

[38] Stela records on Phù Đổng King of Heaven, archived in Institute of Social Science Information, code FQ4o 18, IV, translated by Nguyễn Kim Măng.

Temple: "Previous generations recorded the legend of the Holy King of Heaven on the stele. The sacrifice must be performed in accordance with national regulations, and this God is ranked eighth among the deities in the temple. Every year, the village must appoint young men to prepare for the sacrifice. This activity must continue forever with the country to pray for peace and happiness. Whenever a drought occurs, the rain prayer ritual is carried out effectively, which helps people and everything to multiply and become prosperous".[39]

Thus, over thousands of years of history, Saint Gióng has become a multi-faceted symbol, demonstrating the qualities and actions of a hero against foreign aggression, a patron of crops, a god against floods, a model for loyal and filial virtues, the deity being trusted and worshiped by monarchs and folk of generations, etc. Many layers of cultural-religious sediments have been stacked on top of each other, and then at the present perspective, it is a portrait of an anti-invader hero who is very strong, poetic, and beautiful. The charisma and the attraction of Saint Gióng and Gióng Festival are in that respect.

Gióng Festival is a place where Vietnamese people recreated the heroic victory of the hero of Phù Đổng village. In fact, in the treasure of Vietnamese traditional festivals, there are many festivals commemorating history and heroes fighting foreign invaders. However, those festivals often only hold certain memorial performances or events, but not a whole festival, to commemorate historical figures. The festivals associated with the hero take place in many villages as mentioned above, each one has its own characteristics; however, they all gather into a large picture of the portrait of Phù Đổng village's hero.

In festivals in the villages where Saint Gióng is worshiped, Gióng festival in Phù Đổng Temple has the largest scale. No researcher has confirmed the exact time of the birth of Gióng Festival at Phù Đổng Temple. Đặng Văn Lung and Thu Linh (1984, p. 29) once said that "the operation in Gióng Festival with such well-organized facilities and

---

[39] Stele *Hiển linh từ thạch,* translated by Nguyễn Kim Măng.

good arrangement of soldier-performers' structure might not exceed the Lê dynasty". However, it is hard to believe that it would take until the Lê dynasty to complete this festival. Researcher Tạ Chí Đại Trường asserted: "Such a huge scenario cannot come from Phù Đổng village but must be received from the royal theater that appeared from the Trần to the Lê dynasties, and the later development under the Nguyễn dynasty." (Tạ Chí Đại Trường 1996, p. 95) For one thing, in Vietnamese folklore, the boundary between court culture and village culture is just a blurred line, while festivals are always attached to the village community.

Contemporarily, Gióng Festival of Phù Đổng temple is not only a show but a match with many activities performed in festive language. In other words, Gióng Festival in Phù Đổng temple is like a battle. The creativity of the Vietnamese people in the Kinh Bắc region, in particular, the Red River Delta in general can be said to be a cultural creation of humanity.

The performances of Gióng Festival of Phù Đổng temple are arranged in the form of a battle. The hero led the army to the battlefield, fighting and defeating the enemy's generals, forcing the enemies to surrender, and treating his army to a feast. Troops to the battle in Gióng Festival include *hiệu Trống* (drum master), *hiệu Cờ* (flag master), *hiệu Tiểu cổ (percussion master)*, *hiệu Chiêng* (gong master), *phù giá* (assistants), *đoàn quân áo đỏ* (the army in red), Ải Lao singing troupe; the 28-female-general enemy troop, etc. The festival is held on a huge battlefield enough for the hero to fight the invaders. The battlefield is about 3 km away from Thượng Temple in Đống Đàm and Soi Bia. Each place has three mats on the ground, with a bowl in the middle of the mat facing up on a piece of paper. The mat symbolizes the plain, the bowl symbolizes the hills and mountains, and the piece of paper symbolizes the cloud. The flag master holding the flag danced on the three mats and threw the bowl and paper out of the mats in front of the villagers' jubilant witnesses.

It is worth noting that everything from fighting to participants in the festival is highly symbolic. Gióng Festival at Phù Đổng Temple is a re-enactment of the victory of Saint Gióng, which is expressed by some of the following symbols: dragging the white horse to the battlefield; making loud sounds of gongs and drums, (the flag master) dancing and waving the flags, releasing paper butterflies (from the flags) to symbolize the threats to the invaders; 'splashing' 28 enemy generals, and so on.

Gióng Festival at Phù Đổng Temple, one of the most interesting epics of the Vietnamese, have been sanctified and materialized through unique symbolic and creative performances in Vietnamese history. This makes Gióng Festival of Phù Đổng Temple very valuable. The iron Horse shouting out fire (in the legend) was transformed into a wooden horse painted red (or white) and is now worshipped in Phù Đổng Temple and Sóc Temple. It is brought to the battlefield during the festival. Characters such as *hiệu Trống* (drum master), *hiệu Cờ* (flag master), *hiệu Tiểu cổ* (percussion master*)*, *hiệu Chiêng* (gong master), *phù giá* (assistants), *đoàn quân áo đỏ* (the army in red), members of Ải Lao singing troupe, and 28 female enemy generals are all acted by villagers, this makes Gióng Festival a unique cultural treasure of traditional Vietnam. In the folk literature of many ethnic groups in Vietnam, legends of heroes that defeat invaders, help the people and save the country are popular, but a hero being respectfully worshiped as a leading Saint among other deities and becoming a central figure of a national festival is extremely rare.

Gióng Festival of Phù Đổng Temple, held from the 11th century to the present, is the moral thought of the Vietnamese people and expresses the harmonious combination between nation and family. It also contains the long-standing culture and beliefs of the Vietnamese people, such as fertility beliefs and worship of the rain god.

In Gióng Festival of Sóc Temple, in addition to the ceremony of bathing the statue, a bamboo flower parade is performed. The bamboo flower is made of a piece of bamboo, one end of which is cut into fibers and dyed yellow. The ceremony of slashing generals is symbolically performed by the flag dance.

However, as a battle-like game, Gióng Festival showcases the core peace ideas that the Vietnamese people hope to inherit forever. Because after the battle, weapons are placed in the temple, the army of Saint Gióng and the generals of the enemy happily enjoyed the blessings of Saint Gióng Phù Đổng Temple.

Therefore, it is said that Gióng Festival of Phù Đổng Temple and Sóc Temple is a cultural museum that retains different levels of culture and beliefs. Professor Nguyăn Văn Huyên pointed out at some time before the August 1945 revolution that, "Gióng Festival contains both moral and philosophical thoughts and shows the harmonious union between the family and the country. The festival also aims to achieve peace for the people. This is a festival of peace and prosperity indeed" (Nguyễn Văn Huyên 2009, p. 178). The desire for a peaceful country, the desire for beneficial nature and the abundant crops are the messages that Vietnamese integrate into Gióng Festival. This festival and the noble message are fully capable of bringing this legacy to the whole human community.

3. Especially in the Gióng festivals of Phù Đổng Temple and Sóc Temple, as well as the Gióng festivals of the entire region, we clearly see the subjectivity of the festival. So far, these festivals still retain people's traditional creativeness. Gióng Festival held at Phù Đổng Temple has indeed made an important contribution to the treasures of the Vietnam Village Festival. From the perspective of rural festivals, Gióng Festival has become a regional and a national festival. People created a system containing real and virtual (sacred and ordinary) symbols to reproduce the victory of fighting against foreign invaders to protect a country of legendary heroes, which makes Gióng Festival extremely powerful and attractive. From generation to generation, Gióng Festival at Phù Đổng Temple and other villages is the glue that connects the residents of the village of Saint Gióng with those of other villages in the Red River Delta. People in the area are still shouting:

In Vietnamese	English translation
Mồng bảy hội Khám	The seventh day is the day of
Mồng tám hội Dâu	Khám Festival
Mồng chín đâu đâu trở về hội	The eighth day is for Dâu Testival
Gióng	Wherever you are, please return to
Ai ơi mồng chín tháng tư	join Gióng Festival on the nineth
Không đi hội Gióng cũng hư mất	day
đời.	Do not miss Gióng Festival
	On the 9th of Lunar April.

So far, the subjective role of the community in the festival organization is still very important. Therefore, regardless of whether the historical dynasty consciously intervened in Gióng Festival, the traditional creativity of Phù Đổng Temple's Gióng Festival has been preserved. The fighting process of Gióng Festival is preserved and practiced by Phù Đổng villagers. In the past, there was a notebook in the Phù Đổng Temple which recorded the responsibilities and process of Gióng Festival. Every year, before the festival, the organizers gather to hold a ceremony for Saint Gióng and prepare for the festival based on the notebook. Then the notebook was lost. In the 1990s, the organizers of the festival gathered with the elders, the Fatherland Front, the Party Committee, the People's Committee of the commune to rewrite the content of the festival according to their memory. Compared to the records in Han-script books such as *Bắc Ninh tỉnh khảo dị* (Investigation on anomalous objects of Bắc Ninh province), *Bắc Ninh toàn tỉnh dư địa chí* (*Geography of Bắc Ninh province*), etc., G. Dumoutier's works in 1893, Nguyễn Văn Huyên's works in 1938 and 1941, and legend of Phù Đổng village written at the request of *Viễn Đông bác cổ Pháp* (E'cole Francaise d'Extreme - Orient – EFEO) in 1938, there is not much different. In other words, the community have played a very important part in practicing and protecting Gióng Festival so far.

When organizing Gióng Festival, villagers in the Red River Delta region were fully aware that their intangible cultural heritage was related to lineage and was passed down from generation to generation by practitioners. Every year in the first and the fourth lunar months, residents living in the area where Saint Gióng was born and residents in the area where Saint Gióng was ascended to Heaven should respectfully organize Gióng Festival. In 1893, G. Dumoutier praised Gióng Festival of Phù Đổng Temple. He said: "This is one of the most impressive and touching scenes we have witnessed in Tonkin that remains in everyone's minds. For our aging Europe, will people still be proud of celebrating the historic events before 2000?" (Dumoutier 2009, p. 151).

Conclusion

In short, Gióng Festivals of Phù Đổng Temple, Sóc Temple and other villages in the region fully meet the standards of a representative human intangible cultural heritage as inscribed by the Intergovernmental Committee under the 2003 UNESCO Convention (at the 5th session from November 15 to November 19, 2010 in Nairobi, the capital of the Republic of Kenya). The inscriptions of the elements particularly provide the villagers of Saint Gióng cult in particular and the people of Vietnam in general with the responsibility to protect and promote the values of human representative intangible cultural heritage, because since November 16, 2010, Gióng festival has belonged not only to Vietnamese people but to the whole world.

Reference

1.   Cao, Huy Đỉnh. 2003a. "Người anh hùng làng Dóng (The hero of Dóng village). "In *Cao Huy Đỉnh, tác phẩm được giải thưởng Hồ Chí Minh* (Cao Huy Đỉnh and his works of Hồ Chí Minh Award), Hanoi: Social Science Publisher.

2.   Cao, Huy Đỉnh. 2003b. "Chương 1: Đất nước vùng trung châu kể chuyện ông Dóng (Chapter 1: The story of Saint Dóng in the Red River Delta.", In *Người anh hùng làng Dóng* (The hero of Dóng village), pp. 197-213. Hanoi: Social Science Publisher.

3.   Cao, Huy Đỉnh. 2009. "Người anh hùng làng Dóng (The hero of Dóng village)." In *Lễ hội Thánh Gióng* (Saint Gióng Festival), pp. 485- pp. 632, Hanoi: Culture and Information Publisher.

4.   Dumoutier. G. 1893/2009. "Một lễ hội tôn giáo nước Nam(tại làng Phù Đổng,Bắc Kỳ)",Revue de l'History des religionns, In *Lễ hội Thánh Gióng* (Saint Gióng Festival) trans. Phan Phương Anh, pp. 365 - pp. 374. Hanoi: Culture and Information Publisher.

5.   Đặng, Văn Lung & Thu Linh. 1984. *Lễ hội truyền thống và hiện đại (Traditional and contemporary festivals)*. Hanoi: Cultural Publisher.

6.   Đinh, Khắc Thuân (ed.). 2009. *Địa phương chí tỉnh Bắc Ninh qua tư liệu Hán Nôm* (Local geography of Bắc Ninh province in Sino-Nom documents). Hanoi: Social Science Publisher.

7.   Hoàng, Văn Khoán, Lại, Văn Tới & Nguyễn ,Lâm Anh Tuấn. 2002. *Cổ Loa, trung tâm hội tụ văn minh sông Hồng* (Cổ Loa, center of the Red River civilization). Hanoi: Culture and Information Publisher & Institute of Culture.

8.   Lại, Văn Tới. 2000. *Các di tích đồng thau và sắt sớm khu vực Cổ Loa thời đại kim khí đồng bằng Bắc Bộ* (Early sites of brass and iron of Cổ Loa area in the metal age of the Northern Delta). Doctoral thesis in History. Hanoi: Institute of Archaeology.

9.   Lê ,Hồng Lý. 2010. *Tìm hiểu lễ hội Hà Nội* (Studying Hanoi festivals). Hanoi: Hanoi Publisher.

10. Nguyễn ,Chí Bền. 2011: "Gióng Festival of Phù Đổng Temple and Sóc Temple: representative intangible cultural heritage of humanity", *Journal of Cultural Heritage* 1:

11. Nguyễn, Duy Hinh. 1999. *Tư tưởng Phật giáo Việt Nam* (Ideology of Vietnamese Buddhism). Hanoi: Social Science Publisher.

12. Nguyễn ,Từ Chi. 1996. "Từ một vài "trò diễn" trong lễ-hội làng (From some "acting performances" in village festivals)." In *Góp phần nghiên cứu văn hóa và tộc người* (Contributions to the studies of culture and ethnic groups), pp. 359 - pp. 374, Hanoi: Culture and Information Publisher & Journal of Culture and Arts.

13. Nguyễn, Văn Huyên. 2009. "Hội Phù Đổng, một trận đánh thần kỳ trong truyền thuyết Việt Nam – 1938 (Phù Đổng festival, a magical battle in Vietnamese legends - 1938)." In *Hội Thánh Gióng* (Gióng Festival). Trans. Trần Đinh & Đỗ Trọng Quang, pp. 152 - pp. 226 Hanoi: Culture and Information Publisher.

14. Nguyễn, Văn Huyên. *Địa lý hành chính Kinh Bắc* (Kinh Bắc's Administrative Geography).trans Nguyễn Khắc Đạm, culture and Information Department Bắc Giang, 1997:

15. Như Hạnh (Nguyễn, Tự Cường). 1998/1999. "Tỳ Sa Môn thiên vương (Vaisravana), Sóc Thiên vương và Phù Đổng thiên vương trong tôn giáo Việt Nam thời trung cổ (Sa Môn thiên vương (Vaisravana), Sóc King of Heaven and Phù Đổng King of Heaven in medieval Vietnamese religion)." *Journal of Buddhism Studies* 2&3; reprinted 2008 in *Lễ hội thánh Gióng* (Gióng Festival), pp. 137 - pp. 155, Hanoi: Culture and Information Publisher.

16. Tạ, Chí Đại Trường. 1996. "Lịch sử một thần tích: Phù Đổng thiên vương (History of a legend: Phù Đổng King of Heaven)." In *Những bài dã sử Việt* (Articles of folk Vietnamese history), pp. 75-102. California: USA, Thanh Van (Thanh văn).

17. Tạ, Chí Đại Trường,1989,*Thần, người và đất Việt*, (Gods, man and the land of Vietnam). California: USA.Literature(Văn học)

18. Taylor, W. Keith. 1983. *The Birth of Vietnam*. Los Angeles/ London: University of California Press.

19. Tokarev, X. A. 1994. *Các hình thức tôn giáo sơ khai và sự phát triển của chúng* (Early forms of religion and their development). Vietnamese translation by Lê Thế Thép. Hanoi: National Politics Publisher.

20. Trần ,Bá Chí. 1986. *Hội Gióng đền Sóc* (Gióng Festival of Sóc Temple). Published by People's Committee of Sóc Sơn District.

21. Trần, Quốc Vượng. 1994. "*Căn bản triết lý người anh hùng Phù Đổng và hội Gióng (Basic Phylosophical basis of the Hero of Phù Đổng village and Gióng Festival).*" In *Tìm hiểu di sản văn hóa dân gian Hà Nội* (*Studying Hanoi folklore heritage*), pp. 203-225. Hanoi Publishing House. Reprinted 2009 in *Lễ hội Thánh Gióng (Saint Gióng Festival),* pp. 435-448, Hanoi: Culture and Information Publisher.

22. Trần, Quốc Vượng. 1996. "Vài suy nghĩ tản mạn về trống đồng (Some refections on drums)." In *Theo dòng lịch sử* (On the historical flow), pp. 17 - pp. 38. Hanoi: Cultural Publisher.

23. Trần, Quốc Vượng,2000 "Từ tư duy thần thoại đến tư duy lịch sử (From mythical thinking to historical thinking)." In *Văn hóa Việt Nam: tìm tòi và suy ngẫm* (Vietnamese Culture: Examination and Thoughts). Hanoi: Culture Ethnic Publisher & Journal of Culture and Arts, pp. 263- pp 269.

24. *Bắc Ninh tỉnh khảo dị* (Investigation on anomalous objects of Bắc Ninh province), Trans : Nguyễn, Thị Hường,Nguyễn, Tô Lan dịch, ed: Đinh Khắc Thuân,trong *Địa phương chí tỉnh Bắc Ninh qua tư liệu Hán Nôm* (in *Monographie Bac Ninh province through Han Nom documents),*2009, Hanoi, Social Science Publisher.

25. Đỗ, Trọng Vĩ, *Bắc Ninh địa dư chí* (Geography of Bắc Ninh province). Trans. Đỗ Tuấn Anh,ed Nguyễn Thị Thảo. 1997, Hanoi: Culture and Information Publisher.

FOLK BELIEFS IN THE GIONG FESTIVAL IN VIET NAM

The legend of the hero will serve as the core of the festivals relating to him. Layers of culture and religion remain from the development of these festivals. The Gióng festivals, held in the villages of Phù Đổng, Hội Xá, Đặng Xá (Gia Lâm district), Vệ Linh (Phù Linh commune), Dược Thượng (Tiên Dược commune), Xuân Dục, Đan Tảo (Tân Minh commune), Đức Hậu (Đức Hòa commune), Yên Sào (Xuân Giang commune), Yên Tàng (Bắc Phú commune), Phù Lỗ Đoài (Phù Lỗ commune), Thanh Nhàn (Thanh Xuân commune), and Xuân Lai (Xuân Thu commune) in Sóc Sơn district; Sơn Du, Cán Khê (Nguyên Khê commune) and Đổng Dồ (Nam Hồng commune) in Đông Anh district; Xuân Tảo (Xuân Đinh commune) in Từ Liêm district; and Đông Bộ Đầu (Thống Nhất commune) in Thường Tín district, all have Phù Đổng village's hero - Thánh Gióng - as its main character.

The shrine dedicated to Thánh Gióng at all the aforesaid relics, excluding that in Sóc Temple, which is something different, is always located in the central chamber (See *Appendix of Temple Diagrams at Relics*).

According to Nguyễn Minh Ngọc and Hoàng Thu Hương, the seven statues in the central chamber of Sóc temple are named *Thần tướng* (Divine General), *Ngọc nữ* (Fairy), *Tỳ Sa Môn thiên vương* (Vaisravana), *Thánh Gióng, Vu Điền quốc vương* (King Vu Điền), *Tiên đồng* (Angel), and *Thần tướng*[40] (Divine General). Meanwhile, Nguyễn Thị Thanh Hòa labeled them as *Phù Đổng thiên vương* (Heavenly King Phù Đổng), *Vu Điền quốc vương* (King Vu Điền), *Tỳ Sa Môn thiên vương, Nữ Oa Bộ Thiên, Na Tra thiên tử* (Heaven's Sơn Na Tra), *Tả*

---

[40] *New Findings on Archaeology in 2004*, Social Sciences Publisher, Hanoi, 2005.

Xiên xiên lực sĩ,, and *Hữu vạn vạn tinh binh[41].* We have doubts about the disorder of the shrine at Thượng temple because the temple in Sóc Sơn has been embellished several times. According to the geography books such as *Bắc Ninh toàn tỉnh địa dư chí, Bắc Ninh phong thổ tạp ký* and *Bắc Ninh tỉnh địa dư* on Bắc Ninh province, at the end of the 19th century, the locality was home to two temples and to the integration process, transforming *Tỳ Sa Môn thiên vương* into *Sóc thiên vương* and then into *Phù Đổng thiên vương,* as implied by Như Hạnh quite profound analysis[42]. The shrine to Thánh Gióng at the temple of Sọ (Thanh Nhàn village) embodies the image of Thánh Gióng holding a bamboo stick, whereas the shrine at Đông Bộ Đầu temple, Thống Nhất commune, Thường Tín district, is differently designed. The statue of Thánh Gióng here is colossal, holding a sword in his right hand, carrying a valuable tower in his left hand, and treading on the head of two monsters, which reminds the viewer of the status of an anti-flood deity merged into Thánh Gióng. Is it true that Vũ Phương Đề was sound to write in *Công dư tiệp ký* in the 18th century: "Ever since *Thiên vương* rode his iron horse up to heaven, he has made his reputation brilliant. Is it possible that his mother was caught by the monsters? Maybe, there appeared another deity who was hallowed like *Phù Đổng thiên vương,* and thus used this title as his pen name. Please let me express my shallow opinion here for the distinguished readers to study"[43].

Legends and shrines at the vestiges of Thánh Gióng will dominate the sacred objects surrounding them and the development of the Gióng Festival in the villages where Thánh Gióng is worshipped.

---

[41] *Initial Studies on Seven Statues in Thượng Temple of Sóc Temple's Relics Complex, Sóc Sơn, Hanoi,* Major Thesis, Department of History, University of Social Sciences and Humanity, Electronic Manuscript, 2007, pp.12.

[42] See also *Tỳ sa môn thiên vương* (vaisravana), *Sóc thiên vương* and *Phù Đổng thiên vương* in "Religions of Vietnam in Middle Ages" in *Festival of Thánh Gióng,* Culture and Information Publisher, Hanoi, 2009, pp. 137–155.

[43] Translated by Đoàn Thăng, in *General Collection of Hán Script Novels of Vietnam,* Thế Giới Publisher, Hanoi, 1997, Vol. 1, pp. 543.

The cult addressed to natural phenomena is first mentioned. After all-out efforts to travel and study the delta, scholar Cao Huy Đinh recorded narrations from the regional inhabitants: "This is God Đồng's footprint. He was an extraordinary big man, whose head was able to contact the sky, while his feet touched the ground and shoulders reached the clouds. He raked the ground into fields, piled up stones into hills and dredged sand into rivers. His step connected the peaks of mountains. His footprint resulted in subsidence on stones and holes in the ground. His voice sounded like thunder. His eyes were bright like a flash. He breathed out black clouds and violent wind and rain. He used to appear on rainy and windy days when eggplants fruited. He went in various directions, sometimes straight and sometimes revolving. Western and eastern cyclones occurred, respectively, when he traveled from West to East and vice versa. He beat rice, dropped eggplants and broke unaccountable bamboo and banyan trees"[44]. The figure of a natural god is engraved in the people's mind as a legendary model. This is the motif of a miraculous character closely linked with the primitive age of the history of mankind. Regretfully, the Viet people's legends, for some reasons, have dissolved into separate pieces of legendary figures in their contact with Northern culture, instead of consolidating into a system like the legends of the ethnic groups of Bana, Gia Rai and Êđê, etc., in Vietnam, of India or some other countries. Children's verses in the Nghệ region (Central Vietnam) used to refer to such preeminent persons:

Ông tát bể

Ông kể sao

Ông đào cây

Ông xây rú

(The man who bailed out water from the sea

---

[44] *Hero of Dóng Village*, in Cao Huy Đinh's collection of works winning the Hồ Chí Minh Award, Social Sciences Publisher, Hanoi, 2003, pp.198.

The man who counted stars

The man who dug trees

The man who developed forests)

It is possible to say that the traditional cultural and religious layers of the ancient Việt people in the legend of Thánh Gióng trace back to God Đồng. People have hallowed a natural phenomenon into a belief and a character for worship. It is not by chance that Phù Đổng village formerly had an old shrine to God Đồng, who was offered a bowl of rice, a plate of eggplants and other vegetarian dishes on the ninth of fourth lunar month (stormy time). At eggplant harvest time, God Đồng was reserved a *sào* (equivalent to 360 square meters) of eggplants for him to pick when he came back. Meanwhile, adjoining fields were protected from the destruction of God Đồng by long bamboo sticks, whose one end was smartly whittled into fibers like cotton fixed next to eggplants. Such detail reminds one of the ceremonies of the northern ethnic minority groups, who gave rites to the Rice Mother prior to harvesting their rice. In other words, the ancient Việt people followed the belief in natural gods. As a god of thunder and lightning, God Đồng subsequently turned up on stormy nights. Such a reason has given birth to the event of the Gióng festival in Phù Đổng on the ninth of the fourth lunar month. How utterly sensible Prof. Trần Quốc Vượng is when proclaiming the Gióng festival "as a time of storm"[45]. It is because, in the North, the spring festival closes to an end the dry season, while the early fourth lunar month signals the arrival of the rainy season:

Tháng tư cày vỡ ruộng ra

Tháng năm gieo mạ chan hòa nơi nơi.

"The fouth lunar month is the time to plough the field

---

[45] "Basic arguments of Phù Đổng village's hero and Dóng Festival", in *Festival of Thánh Gióng*, Culture and Information Publishing House, Hanoi, 2009, p. 440. Its copy is excerpted from *Study on Folklore Legacy of Hanoi*, Ha Noi Publisher, 1994, pp. 203–225. The author used materials to write about the Gióng festival.

May is the time to sow rice everywhere".

The Gióng festival marks the start of a new cycle of rice plants, as well as new crops. People need it to rain for their crops. Such expectations have realized into a rain praying ceremony in people's cultural and religious life. And as X.A. Tocarev, a (former) leading USSR scholar of religions, said: such ceremony exists in all religions.

The Gióng festival also takes reverent care of stone plants, in addition to natural gods. Everything in relation to the foreign aggressors Thánh Gióng killed was associated with stone. It was a stone horse. It was also in a stone pillar where the horses of the Yin enemy were kept in Châu Cầu. According to Trần Bá Chí's notes on Sóc Sơn, Yin invaders were led by Thạch Linh and their instruments were all made of stone. A stone bed and stone sickle were close to the mother of Thánh Gióng in Đồng Xuyên. The hero's footprint was left on a large rock in Thanh Nhàn (Sóc Sơn). All of this indicates an age-old religion of the Việt people. Local notables told that the top of Sóc Mountain used to be home to an exceedingly sacred ancient shrine with a large rock. Tradition has it that a deep footprint of Mr. Đùng was printed on the rock[46]. We are not clear about the source of materials on which professor Đặng Văn Lung and Thu Linh based the statement: "It is *Xung thiên thần vương*, or God Đổng, who is Thạch General (worshipped in Phù Đổng village). Many people believed Phù Đổng was Phnom-Núi (Mountain), based on the Khmer language system, while some others explained he was Pù Đổng-Núi based on the Tai-Dai language"[47]. Such ideas urge us to look back on a deeper layer of culture and religion, but without even a few hallmarks of folk explanation.

Sacrifice to the sun, along with natural phenomena, is shown in the Gióng festival. Both Phù Đổng and Sóc temples have a white wooden horse at their shrine, which symbolizes faith in the sun.

---

[46] Trần Bá Chí: *Gióng of Sóc Temple*, Sóc Sơn District People's Committee, 1986, pp. 40.

[47] *Traditional and Modern Festivals*, Culture Publishing House, Hanoi, 1984, pp. 98.

Legendary thought relies on the image of the horse/horse vehicle to represent the sun. Such belief is considered very important for those living mainly on rice cultivation. According to Lại Văn Tới, there were three kettledrums amongst the objects found in Cổ Loa, including one from Xóm Nhồi and two others from Cổ Loa I and Cổ Loa II. Cổ Loa I kettledrum stands out from the others. At the center of its surface is a relief of a 14-pointed star. Each point is designed with peacock feathers, while its hoop has 16 long-beaked birds flying anticlockwise[48]. The designs of the 14-pointed star on the kettledrum's surface, and the birds flying anticlockwise, show us the belief in the sun once pursued by the ancient Việt people in Cổ Loa. The legend of Thánh Gióng and sacred objects reminiscences one about the respect for the sun in the culture of Đông Sơn. As Prof. Trần Quốc Vượng explained: "The cult of the sun is a outline of Đông Sơn at the Gióng festival. Đông Sơn 'sun' has shifted from a symbol of "a star on the surface of a kettledrum, with birds flying anticlockwise, to the image of a white horse at Gióng temple and an iron horse in the legend of Gióng"[49]. It is necessary to study the costumes of the "enemy generals" through *Bắc Ninh tỉnh khảo dị* (*Monography of Bắc Ninh*): "Those who acted as female Generals should wear red clothes and a military hat"[50]. And those who played the part of *Thiên vương* also wear clothes of the same color, which altogether originates from the belief in the sun. In which, the performance of the commanding flag by the Flag Master (who represents Thánh Gióng) is the most visible symbol of such belief. At Đồng Đàm, he shows three dances of the flag in a clockwise direction and three others in a anticlockwise direction. The flag's color signifies the sun. The "beating" of the commanding flag implies the daily temporal movement of the sun, which goes from East to West in

---

[48] See *Cổ Loa-based Vestiges of Bronze and Iron at the Metal Age of the Red River Delta*, Ph.D. thesis on History, Institute of Archaeology, Hanoi, 2000.

[49] "Basic arguments of Phù Đổng village's hero and Dóng Festival", in *Festival of Thánh Gióng*, Culture and Information Publisher, Hanoi, 2009, pp. 440.

[50] Translated by Nguyễn Tô Lan, edited by Nguyễn Thị Hường and Đinh Khắc Thuân, manuscript, Vietnam Institute of Culture and Arts Studies, 2008.

the daytime and from West to East at night. The performance of Thánh Gióng entering the battlefield takes place when the sun is at its highest (that is, midday). The hero's journey from East (Châu Sơn Mountain) to West (Sóc Mountain), before flying to heaven, also indicates the movement of the sun from East to West.

Expression of faith is also found in the *hất phết* game [fighting over a ball] at the festival in Đìa (Đống Đồ) village, Nam Hồng commune, Đông Anh district. This game is regularly held at the festival in honor of Thánh Gióng. The *Phết* has an olive shape and colored red. The village's elders conduct a ceremony to carry the *phết* from its harem to the playground. Some 20 young men compete to catch the *phết* and toss it up into the sky. The more times the *phết* moves up and down, the more joyful the villagers feel. The elders said that Thánh Gióng formerly trained his army using this game, which also presently displays Đìa villagers' devotion to the sun.

In the meantime, Lệ Chi villagers (Lệ Chi commune, Gia Lâm district) compete in wrestling on the eighth of the first lunar month. Players coming from the hosting army are half-naked, wearing a red loincloth and yellow belt, while the opposite side, acting the role of Yin aggressors, is bare to the waist, wearing a green loincloth and white belt. Red reflects the ancient Việt people's belief in the sun. The ceremony of fighting with sticks to attain a coconut on the peak of a bamboo tree also stems from similar reasons. Unlike the cult of the sun as a national religion, such as that to the sun goddess of Japan, Amateraxu, the fact that agricultural citizens, like the ancient Việt people, held the sun in veneration is closely connected to their aspirations for good crops.

Popular at the Gióng festival in all villages, is the fertility cult, which is ranked amongst the oldest religions of agriculturalists. Born during the Neolithic era, it is, as said by X. A. Tocarev, "one of the most ancient, but independent, roots of beliefs and religious ceremonies close to sexual relations". At the ancient layer of Southeast Asian culture, it is fairly progressive. In Vietnam, archaeologists have uncovered quite a large number of objects belonging to this religion[51]. The stone statue excavated from the archaeological site of Phùng Nguyên (4,000 years BC) has two hands, not a big sex organ, removed. The other, dug up in Văn Điển (the 1st millennium BC), shapes a man with very large genitals. On the surface of the Đào Thịnh copper jar, dug up in Yên Bái province (in the 5th century BC), is the image of four couples having sexual intercourse. The fertility cult varies in different ways when cultural exchanges between Han and ancient Southeast Asian residents occur. In the South of the Gianh River, under no influence of Han culture, it has so far developed naturally as a flow or a component of the system of local beliefs. We can take the cases of *linga* and yoni, worshipped by Chăm people in the towers (kalan) in Central Vietnam, and sepulcher statues popular in the Central Highlands, as good examples. Meanwhile, the Red River delta witnessed cultural exchanges. The Trần dynasty (1266-1400), amongst some others, even ordered the elimination of obscene words, and strictly prohibited people from worshipping vulgar deities, which deformed, but failed to eliminate, the religion. Famous ethnographer Nguyễn Từ Chi was completely right in saying that: "Man and woman's sexual relations, a symbol of the fertility cult and reproduction, are not a result of a long-term and moderate process of awareness, but rather an offspring of an unanticipated power, which unexpectedly rises up from the bottom of the human heart and the layer of human unconsciousness. It is instinct and nothing but instinct"[52]. The religion's small pieces have persisted in various forms of folk culture ranging from literature to art (sculpture of communal houses and folk pictures) and festivals. The Kinh Bắc region, where the ancient Việt people set foot early, is the place where such religion prospered. Until 1920, *Bắc Ninh tỉnh khảo dị* still recorded religion-based festivals like those held in Long Khám commune, Đông

---

[51] *Primary Religious Forms and their Development*, Vietnamese version by Lê Thế Thép, National Political Publisher, Hanoi, 1994, pp.141.

[52] "From some "performances" in village festival, in *Contributions to the Study of Culture and Ethnicity*, Culture and Information Publishes, Culture and Arts Magazine, Hanoi, 1996, pp. 367.

Sơn chief town, Tiên Du district; Trường Lâm commune, Gia Lâm district; Phú Thị commune, Gia Lâm district, and so on[53]. For such reasons, it should not be deemed unusual to see signs of the fertility cult at the festival at Phù Đổng temple. The selection of 28 beautiful girls from Phù Đổng village to play the role of the "enemy's female Generals" is a most perceptible symbol of this religion. The strictly nominated girls must be between 10 and 13 years of age, nice and pretty, and come from a "pure" family. The Commander in Chief and Second in Command must be the most beautiful girls of all. Professor Lê Hồng Lý said that: "After watching the performance of the 28 Yin enemy's female Generals at the Gióng festival and the battle of the Masters (Gióng's Generals), Professor Radost Invanova, a Bulgarian folklore scholar, offered a suggestion. He wondered if it was past practice to rob a wife, as found in several ethnic groups in Vietnam and worldwide"[54]. According to documents of field studies, undertaken by scholar Cao Huy Đinh at the Phù Đổng festival on the seven of the fourth lunar month during the 1960s, the sacrifice at Thượng temple with vegetarian dishes "is followed by the practice of men and women catching one another at the river ground at night. The men's side always wore loincloths and kept bareheaded to prevent them from being pulled by the opposite side. This age-old custom grew so faded that it is now no more than teasing between men and women[55]. The practice partly reminds us of the practice of *hát trùm đầu* (female and male singers of Quan họ folk songs), with kerchiefs or blouses covering their head, singing challenge-and-response phrases), filled with fertility characteristics, in the ancient *Quan họ* villages of Bắc Ninh province. Some of the songs sung by the Ải Lao troupe at the Phù Đổng Festival

---

[53] I have not yet managed to update these localities according to the present administrative structure.

[54] *Studying Festivals of Hanoi*, Hà Nội Publisher, 2010, pp. 243.

[55] "Hero of Dóng village", in *The Festival of Thánh Gióng*, Culture and Information Publisher, Hanoi, 2009, pp. 527.

display the aspirations of young men and women to find a good partner. A person in the troupe holds a fishing rod while singing:

Người ta câu bể câu sông

Thì tôi câu lấy con ông cháu bà

Có chồng con,em nhả mồi ra

Không chồng con,em cắn,em dứt,em tha lấy mồi

Khấn giời phù hộ cho tôi

Để tôi câu lấy một người thanh tân

"Others arrive at sea and river to catch fish

While I just want to marry your child

Married woman ignores call

Unmarried woman reply call at once

May God bless me!

Enable me to get married to a maiden".

The author of *Bắc Ninh tỉnh khảo dị* clarified the final two aforementioned sentences: "This person, who was surrounded by troops in front of the dyke, was carrying a fishing rod. When seeing a beautiful girl, he directed the rod towards the girl, singing the two verses, as a way of making fun"[56]. In terms of the fertility cult at the Gióng festival, it would be a mistake to overlook the pillar to which the Yin enemy's horses were tied in Châu Cầu (presently in Quế Võ district, Bắc Ninh province). This artificial stone pillar, some four meters tall, is stuck on a round flagstone, symbolizing *linga* and *yoni*.

Meanwhile, the festival at Sóc temple (Sóc Sơn district) finishes with the performance of beheading generals. Three girls aged 13 to 16, from the three villages of Yên Tàng, Mậu Tàng and Xuân Tàng, are

---

[56] Translated by Nguyễn Tô Lan, edited by Nguyễn Thị Hường and Đinh Khắc Thuân, manuscript, Vietnam Institute of Culture and Arts Studies.

appointed to the role of enemy generals. The ceremony begins in the evening of the seventh of the first lunar month. The commanding flags send out signals from the top of the mountain. Accordingly, the person who is assigned to cut off the generals' heads quickly repeats the fluently trained steps. At the same time, sound of drums and gongs are echoing, while a sea of viewers congregate. The commanding flag is repeatedly waved and a stroke of sword is brandished as quickly as lightning. Immediately, the female general runs swiftly into a hidden area, before having her family members take her home[57]. The practice of beheading generals has some resemblance to the scene of local young men and women walking to enjoy the spring atmosphere on the mountains. In other words, it is a manifestation of the fertility cult, which remains nowhere, but in small pieces of cultural and religious layers.

The cult of the trading forefather goes along with that of the natural gods, the sun and the fertility cult. In order to learn about it in Cổ Loa and surrounding areas, it is essential to study it in relation to others regarding Sơn Tinh in Việt Trì, Chử Đồng Tử and his two wives in Hưng Yên, and Thánh mẫu Liễu Hạnh in Nam Định. In regards to the four immortals, the worship of the trading forefather in Cổ Loa is something different. The two banks of the Red river, placing Cổ Loa as its heart, are the cultural and religious areas dedicated to Thánh Gióng (or *Phù Đổng thiên vương*). It will be impossible to decode the character of Thánh Gióng, with different appearances, meanings and values, unless people's creativity is linked with the fact that the Việt people flocked to the delta to set up their own state. It will also be impossible to know the reason why Phù Đổng village's hero asked the messenger to tell Hùng King that he needed an iron horse, an iron whip and iron armor to defeat the aggressors, unless such weapons are intermingled in the fact that Việt people in Cổ Loa already had succeeded in the

---

[57] "Gióng Festival of Sóc Temple", in *Lễ hội Thánh Gióng*, Culture and Information Publisher, Hanoi, 2009, pp. 470-471.

manufacture of metal instruments. Let's take the depot of copper arrows excavated by archaeologists in Cổ Loa as an example. "In Cổ Loa, during the time when the Hùng Kings were building up Văn Lang state, the ancient Việt in Đình Tràng, Đường Mây, Bãi Mèn, Xóm Hương, Xóm Nhồi, Mả Tre, and Cầu Vực, developed the brass refining technique to its highest level and adopted these methods to manufacture iron products"[58]. Moreover, brass items found in Cổ Loa are not large in number, but are diversified in category, including production tools, utensils, weapons, and jewelries. Obviously, from the large heavy kettledrum of Cổ Loa I, with sophisticated designs on its surface, to smaller objects, one can see that local casters had completely mastered casting techniques or, in other words, felt completely confident in professional skills. Bronze products, including hundreds of ploughshares, as well as shovels, discovered in Cổ Loa, prove their appearance on the basis of its highly developed brass refining techniques.

In view of this, the stamp of a trading forefather can be vaguely seen from the portrait of Thánh Gióng. The iron horse of Phù Đổng village's hero shouted out fire, burning clusters of local bamboo trees and leaving clumps of glossy yellow bamboo trees growing there today. Is it a legendary story that makes the trading forefather distinct and sacred in the eyes of his followers? For this reason, his initial appearance may be that of a hero of culture or as a trading forefather. In other words, the legend of Phù Đổng village's preeminent child is

---

[58] Hoàng Văn Khoán, Lại Văn Tới and Nguyễn Lâm Anh Tuấn: *Cổ Loa, the Rendezvous of Red River Civilization*, Culture and Information Publishing House and Institute of Culture, Hanoi, 2002, pp. 416. See also *Cổ Loa-based Vestiges of Bronze and Iron at the Metal Age of the Red River Delta*, Ph.D. thesis on history, electronic manuscript, Institute of Archaeology, Hanoi, 2000.

[59] Ibid, pp. 417-418, also Lại Văn Tới: Ibid.

reflected in the metal manufacturing achievements of the ancient Việt people, who reached the pinnacle of the technique and, at the same time, wrote down the legend of such an achievement. When heading to flat land to explore the Red river delta, they confronted the Northern aggressors. Is this the reason why new layers of culture were added to the faith in this forefather? Late Prof. Trần Quốc Vượng said: "The story of Gióng village's hero, whose last image is imbrued with patriotism and strong determination to join all the people in defending the home village, stems from the legend of a metallurgy area of blacksmiths"[60]. His remarks are correct in this case.

From the small pieces of legends in the cultural and religious areas devoted to Thánh Gióng, ancient streams of culture and religions can be imagined flowing smolderingly like artesian waters activated so far, but under a main stream of the cult of the enemy-fighting hero. According to the late professor Trần Quốc Vượng, "the cultural and legendary hero has entered the unconscious now, while the enemy-fighting hero perpetually appears in people's awareness. Similarly, the agricultural ceremony has drifted into the past, while the performance of the hero is an indispensable part of the Gióng festival"[61]. The movement of cultural and religious layers has portrayed an enemy-fighting hero with motifs popular in stories of the gods and epitaphs during the late 16th century. The victories of Phù Đổng village's hero are temporally divided into two phases as follows:

- *Fighting against the Yin aggressors on earth*:

The historical context in this phase required the boy of Phù Đổng village to grow up rapidly into a hero, who beat the invaders from Trâu Sơn Mountain, Quế Võ and Phả Lại to Gia Lương, Lục Đầu river, Tiên Du, Đông Ngàn, Yên Phong, and surrounding Sóc Mountain.

---

[60] "Some thoughts on the kettledrum", in *Following the Flow of History*, Culture Publisher, Hanoi, 1996, pp. 18.

[61] "Basic arguments of Phù Đổng Village's Hero and Dóng Festival", in *Study on Folklore Heritage of Hanoi*, Hà Nội Publisher, 1994, pp. 225.

Comparing this with the exploitation of the Red river delta by the ancient Việt people, one can see that the battlefield where Thánh Gióng combated against the Northern invaders lies in the North of today's Red river – that is, the fourth branch of the Red river during the early Christian era, as noted in *Thủy Kinh chú*. They are exactly the places of Long Biên, Luy Lâu, Tây Vu, Bắc Đái, and Kê Từ, etc. (that is, the later Kinh Bắc region). The Việt people from the midlands, who flocked into the delta with its dense forests and swamps, and lurking forces from the sea, desired to have their own hero. The Confucian scholars of future generations built up the figure of a national hero based on all of these legendized elements. "The legends of Lạc Long Quân, Mr. Gióng, Mountain God Tản Viên, and Nhất Dạ Trạch, were all introduced in an historical textbook written by Ngô Sĩ Liên in the 15th century. They were all condensed, relying on the cultural flows of the following centuries. Such legends are engraved in Vietnamese people's minds due to the fact that they manifest the very first identity of the Vietnamese *as a nation* - emphasized by the editor"[62]. In *The Birth of Vietnam*, Keith Weller Taylor passed accurate remarks upon such case. The existence or inexistence of a national community at the dawn of history sunk the cultural and religious layers of agricultural citizens, while floating the figure of an enemy-fighting hero, at the same time. This common sense was heightened and transmitted by post-10th century Confucian scholars into the written documents and stories of the gods in the villages of Thánh Gióng. And it is Thánh Gióng who has become an exceptionally mighty hero of the Vietnamese. Author Tầm Vu stated that Thánh Gióng undoubtedly appears as a deeply impressive figure in folk art. He was brimful of patriotism, hatred for enemy and strong determination for victory. He also fought for the peace of the community, but took no care for fame and fortune, joining himself into eternity upon the completion of his mission. Notably, the army led by Phù Đổng village's

---

[62] *The Festival of Thánh Gióng*, Culture and Information Publishing House, 2009, pp. 326.

hero proved a gathering of all patriotic persons, which deepens the legend of Thánh Gióng into an epic in the aggressor fighting tradition[63].

- Appearing to help royal dynasties to defeat the enemy:

Unlike other heroes, Thánh Gióng turned up to help the First Lê dynasty drive away the Song enemy, Lê Lợi (1385-1433) to squash Ming invaders, and so on. *Hiển linh từ thạch bia* inscribed in 1606, which remains at Phù Đổng Temple today, provides a good example of his support.

Royal dynasties played a pivotal role for Thánh Gióng as a result of two phases. They all consecrated their immortal saint with conferment letters. In addition to the notes of Confucian scholars in *Việt điện u linh* and *Lĩnh Nam chích quái* on conferment by the Lý and Trần dynasties, Phù Đổng Temple alone has been conferred by the following dynasties:

King Lê Thần Tông, on August 26 during the fifth year of Dương Hòa (1639): one decree.

King Lê Chân Tông, on February 28 during the secong year of Phúc Thái (1646): one decree; and, on July 17 during the third year of Phúc Thái (1647): one decree.

King Lê Thần Tông, on May 13 during the fourth year of Thịnh Đức (1656): one decree.

King Lê Huyền Tông, on April 18 during the eighth year of Cảnh Trị (1670): one decree.

King Lê Gia Tông, on July 29 during the third year of Dương Đức (1674): one decree.

King Lê Hy Tông, on June 24 (intercalary month) during the fourth year of Chính Hòa (1683): one decree.

---

[63] See also Cao Huy Đinh: *Hero of Dóng Village*, Chapter 1: Stories of Mr. Dóng in the Delta, Social Sciences Publisher, Hanoi, 2003, pp. 197-213.

King Lê Dụ Tông, on August 10 during the sixth year of Vĩnh Thịnh (1712): one decree.

King Lê Thuần Tông (Lê Duy Phương), on December 10 during the fourth year of Vĩnh Khánh (1732): one decree; and, on May 27 during the fifth year of Long Đức (1736): one decree.

King Lê Hiển Tông, on July 24 (1740) during the first year of Cảnh Hưng: one decree; on July 25 during the third year of Cảnh Hưng (1742): one decree; on August 8 during the 28th year of Cảnh Hưng (1767): one decree; on December 16 during the 38th year of Cảnh Hưng (1777): one decree; and, on May 16 during the 44th year of Cảnh Hưng (1783): one decree.

King Lê Mẫn Đế, on March 22 during the first year of Chiêu Thống (1787): one decree.

King Nguyễn Huệ, on March 27 during the third year of Quang Trung (1790): one decree; and, on March 29 the fifth year of Quang Trung (1792): one decree.

King Nguyễn Quang Toản, on May 21 during the fourth year of Cảnh Thịnh (1796): one decree.

The Nguyễn dynasty (1802–1945), from the time of Minh Mệnh, Thiệu Trị, and Tự Đức Kings to Bảo Đại King, decided to confer a title to *Phù Đổng thiên vương*. It is necessary to focus on the compilation of stories of the god and epitaphs relevant to Thánh Gióng. All the temples of Phù Đổng, Sóc Sơn and Thanh Nhàn, etc., have stories of the god supposedly compiled by Academician Doctor Nguyễn Bính during the first year of Hồng Phúc (1572), and later copied from the originals by Nguyễn Hiền during the sixth year of Vĩnh Hựu (1740). (In reality, 1470, the first year of Cảnh Hưng, was during the reign of King Lê Hiển Tông. Stories of the god refer to this year for reasons unknown - Author's notes). Royal conferment letters and stories of the god relating to Thánh Gióng have further consecrated him in the eyes of generations, aiming to deepen and perfect the legendary image of Thánh Gióng amongst the masses.

The idolization of the aggressor fighting hero has, therefore, brought him the new missions of an anti-flood hero and mild weather creator for farmers. The transformation of the stories of Thánh Gióng and his statue at the shrine of Đông Bộ Đầu temple (Thống Nhất commune, Thường Tín district) followed the motif of an anti-flood god. The statue of the hero treading on the heads of two monsters also indicates the posture of this god. In *Bắc Ninh địa dư chí* (Geography Book of Bắc Ninh], Đỗ Trọng Vĩ wrote about a rain praying ceremony in Đức Hậu (Nguyễn Văn Huyên in *Địa lý hành chính Kinh Bắc* (Administrative Geography of Kinh Bắc), noting that Đức Hậu commune belonged to Phổ Lộng chief town, Đa Phúc district, which is present day Sóc Sơn). "Local children picked fruits and built religious stages on the fields. They beat drums, folded flags from paper and designed tormentors from bamboo, before reaching Mã (Vệ Linh) temple where they carried incense burners onto the stage and found some miracles. Legend has it that a white-haired man came to beg for water from local children who were playing together. The children competed with one another to help the old man quench his thirst. The man called the village Thanh Thủy and the commune Đức Hậu, and told the kids: "From now on, if drought happens, please come to see me at the Buddhist temple. I will award water to you all". After saying this, he disappeared. He turned out to be *Thiên vương*. The epitaph at Phù Đổng Temple was inscribed with the following words: "*Thiên vương* in *Sử ký* (Records of the Historians) is a famous god for all generations, so he will be worshipped as the eight gods were. From the Đinh dynasty onwards, mandarins were assigned to conduct a rain praying ceremony in the correct way, which helped fortify the course of the stream. Similarly, in years of drought, the king ordered his mandarins, along with some young men, to pray for rain. It usually rained then. All the people enjoyed a life of peace and prosperity"[64]. Such words coincide

---

[64] Copied from epitaphs on *Phù Đổng thiên vương*, preserved at the Institute of Social Sciences Information, Code FQ4o 18, IV, 42, translated by Nguyễn Kim Măng.

completely with those inscribed on the epitaph, *Hiển linh từ thạch bia*, built in Phù Đổng temple in the sixth year of Hoằng Định (1606): "The legend of *Thiên vương* was recorded by all dynasties. As a national ceremony, the cult of him was ranked at the eighth position in the temple. Every year, young men were entrusted to prepare customary offerings to pray for a peaceful country and wealthy people. A rain praying ceremony was regularly conducted in the event of drought. And rain poured down to help all living things reproduce"[65].

Thousands of years have passed. Thánh Gióng has become a symbol of different roles. He acts as a hero against foreign aggressors, a crop guardian, a mild weather supplier for rural areas, an anti-flood god, a kind carrier of loyalty, and so on. Different layers of culture and religion have gone under the surface, offering their seat to the portrait of nice, mighty and poetic hero against aggressors.

---

[65] *Hiển linh từ thạch bia*, translated by Nguyễn Kim Măng.

OVERVIEW ON COLLECTION AND RESEARCH OF
QUAN HỌ BẮC NINH FOLKSONGS

Quan họ Bắc Ninh folk songs (hereafter "*Quan họ*") is one of the intangible cultural heritages of Vietnamese people. It is a highly rated heritage and very attractive to many people. Therefore, many generations of collectors, social science researchers, especially folklorists, are interested in studying *Quan họ*.

1. Literature Review

Quan họ's research process can be divided into four stages, including the period before 1954, the period from 1954 to 2005, the period from 2005 to 2009, and the period from 2009 to the present.

1.1. The period before 1945

At present, there is no consensus between folk literature researchers and collectors on "When was *Quan họ* born?" The earliest literature on *Quan họ* was from the middle and late 19th century, most of which came from the history books of Confucian scholars in the Nguyễn Dynasty. In *Đại Nam nhất thống chí* (大南一統志, *Đại Nam Comprehensive Encyclopaedia)*, officials of the National History Bureau of the Nguyễn Dynasty recorded some melodies some folk songs that are considered to be *Quan họ Bắc Ninh folk songs* in the section "Bắc Ninh Customs". Another book written by Nguyễn Thăng in the late Lê and Nguyễn dynasties, *Kinh Bắc phong thổ ký* (京北風土記, *Records on Customs of the Kinh Bắc region*), is one of the Chinese-script books that study the communal customs of people in the Quan họ region. This work subsequently included in the book *Thiên tải nhàn đàm* (千載閒談, Talk on a-thousand-year history) in the sixth year of the Gia Long reign (1807). The author briefly mentioned the custom of "Xuân Ổ village women luckily welcome men home"[66]. This detail was then explained in the Nôm-script book entitled

---

[66] In Vietnamese: *Gái hát làng Xuân Ổ đón được trai về nhà lấy làm may.*

Kinh Bắc phong thổ ký diễn quốc sự (京北風土記記演國事, *The interpretation of national facts in "Records on Customs of the Kinh Bắc region"*) as follows:

In Vietnamese	English translation
Gái Xuân Ổ thói hàng có mấy	*Only some Xuân Ổ girls are lucky*
Rước được trai mừng ấy có duyên[67]	*They happily welcome men home because they have established friendship*

Similarly, Đỗ Trọng Vỹ in *Bắc Ninh toàn tỉnh địa dư chí* (北寧全省興地志, Local History of Bắc Ninh Province) wrote about Tiên Du district as follows: "Xuân Hội, Lũng Sơn, Hoài Bão, Trung Mầu, and Chi Ne communes all have village singing teams. In springs, people in Lũng Sơn and Lũng Giang communes carry out processions and organize folk games; boys and girls gather to sing at the communal houses…" People in the area have a saying: "High trees get wind at the middle of the trunks. I am so happy to meet you this time[68]". The author also recorded villages with singing habits in Yên Phong District, which we can guess that they are Quan họ songs:

In Vietnamese	English translation
Nhất ngon là mía Lan Điền	*The best is the sugar cane planted in Lan Điền*
Giai khôn đứng đấy, gái hiền ngồi đây[69]	*Smart boys should stay there while good girls should sit around here*

It is worth noting that *Bắc Ninh tỉnh khảo dị* (北寧省考異, Strange Stories of Bắc Ninh Province) written by Phạm Xuân Lộc in the same period recorded the *Quan họ* custom of Viêm Xá village (ie, Diềm village) as follows: "Every year on January 4th, villagers organize the ceremony of *Lễ khai xuân* to celebrate two tutelary gods. On August 10, they continue to hold another ceremony called *Lễ nhập tịch* to worship these two gods.

The men and women of Viêm Xá commune have made friends with the Hoài Bão commune in Tiên Du District. Men and women from each

---

[67] Translated by Trần, Văn Giáp (1971, pp. 41, 57).

[68] In Vietnamese: Cây cao gió đánh lưng chừng, gặp anh từ đấy vui mừng từ đây.

[69] See Đỗ Trọng Vỹ (1997, pp. 171-4)

village gathered to form a singing team; each team consisted of 10 young men and 10 young women. Each team is a singing group ready to join the village festivals". "When the Viêm Xá commune held *Lễ khai xuân* or *Lễ nhập tịch* ceremonies to celebrate the village gods, the villagers chose a young man to bring betel nuts to Hoài Bão commune and invited their singing team to sing the *Quan họ* festival at Viêm Xá commune. However, only 10 young men from Hoài Bão commune joined Viêm Xá commune's ceremonies, the other 10 women of Hoài Bão group did not participate. Therefore, in the *Quan họ* singing festivals of Viêm Xá commune, only Hoài Bão men sang together with Viêm Xá women. On the contrary, during the festivals of Hoài Bão Commune, the commune also chose a man with betel nuts to invite men and women of Viêm Xá commune. The women of Viêm Xá commune did not go. Instead, only selective village men came to sing *Quan họ* folk songs with Hoài Bão women. If there were many singing women in the village, 4 to 5 of them could sing together in one song (Đinh Khắc Thuân 2009, p. 363).

Chu Ngọc Chi (1928)'s *Hát Quan họ* (Performance of *Quan họ*) is the first work to introduce *Quan họ* in chữ Quốc ngữ (the Vietnamese national language). The author introduced 5 *Quan họ* songs and 7 *hát Đúm* songs. In fact, each song contains multiple versions. In this book, the author wrote the lyrics without musical notation. Dương Quảng Hàm in his book entitled *Việt Nam văn học sử yếu* (An outline of Vietnamese literature history, 1951) also used a part to mention the *Quan họ* singing custom in Bắc Ninh and Bắc Giang (Dương Quảng Hàm 1951, p. 24). In 1953, musician Nguyễn Đình Phúc collected Quan họ songs directly from *Quan họ* artisan Nguyễn Thị Nguyên (see Lê Ngọc Chân 2002).

1.2. The period from 1954 to 2005

In 1954, the Central Culture and Art Troupe invited some national singers to sing folk songs and make CDs. In 1955, Mr. Nguyễn Đình Phúc said that he already collected more than 60 folk songs in the Bắc Ninh region. In early 1956, the Army Arts Department sent musicians Nguyễn Đình Tấn, Nguyễn Viêm, and Lưu Khâm to 11 *Quan họ* villages in Bắc Ninh to investigate and study local folk songs. In June 1956, musicians Lê

Yên and Lưu Hữu Phước led a group of people to visit 18 villages in *Quan họ* region and collected 314 songs, of which 290 songs were published by the Bureau of Arts.

In 1960, the Ministry of Culture's Music and Arts Publishing House published three volumes about Quan Ho. Quan ho artisans performed a total of 60 songs with a complete musical note system provided by Nguyen Viem, all of which were then accepted by the Department of Music Research of the Ministry of Culture.

In 1962, a group of writers including Lưu Hữu Phước, Nguyễn Văn Phú, Nguyễn Viêm and Tú Ngọc included many *Quan họ* songs in the book *Dân ca Quan họ* (*Quan họ* folk songs). They introduced totally 36 songs of the introductory phase (of a full Quan họ singing performance), 75 songs of the middle phase, 127 songs of informal voice, 11 song of ending phase, and 76 songs of unknown type. They only have lyrics and no musical notes.

In 1965, Hoàng Tiêu published 48 new *Quan họ* folk songs in the appendix of his BA. thesis in history.

In 1971, folk literature researcher Vũ Ngọc Phan introduced two types of full folk songs: (1) songs with repeated, prolonged sounds or auxiliary words (4 songs) and (2) songs without any insertion (26 songs) (Vũ Ngọc Phan 1971).

In 1987, 25 traditional *Quan họ* folk songs and many other new *Quan họ* songs were introduced in the book *Những làn điệu Dân ca Quan họ quen thuộc* (Popular tunes in *Quan họ*) renamed by musicians Công Miêng, Thế Công, and Hùng Việt.

In 1997, two authors Trần Linh Quý and Hồng Thao published 17 *Quan ho* folk songs in the textbook *Tìm hiểu Dân ca Quan họ* (A study on *Quan họ* folk songs), in which the two authors produced musical notes based on the performance of rural artisans in the *Quan họ* region.

In 2000, the work *300 bài Quan họ* (Three hundred folk songs) with a musical notation system created by Hồng Thao was published by the

National Conservatory of Music in Hanoi. The carefully prepared book is the product of the author's lifelong research and collection of *Quan họ*.

In 2000, Trần Chính published 161 *Quan họ* songs in the work *Nghệ nhân Quan họ làng Viêm Xá* (*Quan họ* artisans of Viêm Xá village), which were performed by artists of the 20th-century Viêm Xá (Diềm) villagers. Instead of using musical notation, he accurately wrote down the lyrics spoken by the artisans and even reiterated worn-out words. In short, this is an important systematization of the author in recording *Quan họ* folk songs.

Also in 2000, in the book *Một số vấn đề về Văn hóa Quan họ* (Some issues of *Quan họ* culture), two writers Lê Danh Khiêm and Hoắc Công Huynh published their *Quan họ* song collections, which were classified according to their sound types, including 19 "standard" songs, 176 "informal" songs, 9 "farewell" songs. They also introduced 19 *Quan họ* folk songs with the 'standardized' voice with a full musical notation provided by Trần Ngọc Sơn, Hoắc Công Huynh, Nguyễn Mạnh Thắng, Nguyễn Trọng Tỉnh, and Nguyễn Văn Thanh. In the same year, Nguyễn Trọng Ánh introduced 17 *Quan họ* songs in the work *Âm nhạc Quan họ* (*Quan họ* music). After listening to the real performance of the *Quan họ* artisans, he made a musical notation system himself.

In 2001, in the book *Dân ca Quan họ, lời ca và bình giải* (*Quan họ* folk songs: lyrics and interpretation), Lê Danh Khiêm introduced 213 *Quan họ* tunes with a total of 308 songs.

1.3. The period from 2005 to present

In 2005, Nguyễn Trọng Ánh introduced 45 *Quan họ* songs with the full musical notation in the appendix of his Ph.D thesis on arts entitled *Những giá trị âm nhạc trong hát Quan họ* (The musical values in *Quan họ* folk songs performance).

In 2005, Đinh Thị Thanh Huyền re-introduced songs of 36 *Quan họ* sound types from a narrative and introduced 41 *Quan họ* sound types composed by Diềm villagers, which were obtained during her field visit in the Bắc Ninh area.

In 2006, in the work *Không gian Văn hóa Quan họ*(Cultural space of *Quan họ*), Hoắc Công Huynh introduced 10 *Quan họ* folk songs of "farewell" types, which he wrote and recorded on musical notation system.

In 2008, Department of the Local Culture (Ministry of Culture, Sports and Tourism) published *Thống kê lễ hội Việt Nam* (Vietnam Festival Statistics). In this book, Bắc Ninh province contributed 332 festivals, 86 of which are dedicated to *Quan họ* folk songs performance (Department of Local Culture 2008, pp. 105-145). Specifically, there were 27 *Quan họ* festivals out of 64 festivals in Yên Phong district, 14 out of 91 in Quế Võ district, 18 out of 22 in Bắc Ninh city had, 27 out of 51 in Tiên Du district, 3 out of 67 in Gia Bình district, 7 out of 65 in Lang Tài[70]. There were 513 festivals in Bắc Giang Province, including 20 *Quan họ* festivals. Specifically, there are 11 out of 100 festivals in Hiệp Hòa district were Quan họ festivals, 5 out of 115 in Lạng Giang district, 2 out of 34 in Lục Nam district, while in Tân Yên district, Việt Yên district, and Bắc Giang city, each district had only one *Quan họ* festival. It is worth noting that the five *Quan họ* villages on the north bank of the Cầu River in Việt Yên district did not have *Quan họ* folk song festival (Local Cultural Office 2008, p. 47-104).

1.4. The period from 2009 to 2018

Since *Quan họ Bắc Ninh Folk Songs* being recognized by UNESCO in September 2009, the collection of *Quan họ* is still the focus.

2. A review of research

Among the popular cultural activities of the Vietnamese people, *Quan họ* is the most studied topic. According to the statistical data about *Quan họ* in *Vùng Văn hóa Quan họ* (The cultural region of *Quan họ*)[71] (see Institute of Culture and Information & Bắc Ninh Department of Culture and Information 2006, pp. 1100-60), there are more than 700

---

[70] Particularly for the villages in Gia Bình and Lang Tài districts, Quan họ has only developed in recent years.

[71] The author of this article got a lot of information from the book's bibliography. The author really wants it love to thank its authors.

documents related to *Quan họ* so far. When previous researchers studied *Quan họ*, they believed that *Quan họ* was a universal phenomenon, even part of regular cultural activities. They neither classified it as a folk song nor named it another special art. Such research can be divided into three periods: before 1954, 1954-2005, and 2005-2008.

2.1. The period before 1954

In Vietnam script, namely *chữ Quốc ngữ*, the first person to mention *Quan họ* as Lim Festival in Vietnamese script is Vũ Bằng. His seemingly simple article entitled "Hội Lim (Lim Festival)" published on *the An Nam Review* in 1931, describing the negative aspects of the festival and the performance of *Quan họ*. Due to the lack of a full understanding of Lim Festival at the period of over-emphasis of Lim Festival's shortcomings, the text actually caused prejudice against Lim Festival (ie. *Quan họ*). Two years later, Việt Sinh published his book *Nghe hát Quan họ một đêm ở Lũng Giang* (A night enjoying *Quan họ* performance in Lũng Giang) in 1933.

In 1934, Nguyễn Văn Huyên mentioned Lim Festival at the beginning of his doctoral thesis, with the theme *Hát đối đáp nam nữ thanh niên* (Interactive singing among young people). The author's ethnographic record did help us visualize Lim Festival at the time. He wrote: "The natural forest farm becomes a big stage and the singing festival normally starts in the early evening. Such *Hátđối* music festivals (interactive singing) in Vietnam are not popular in spring but are more often held in autumn" (Nguyễn Văn Huyên 1934, p. 370).

In 1937, Minh Trúc published his monograph called *Hát Quan họ* (*Quan họ* singing performance) in 8 issues of the *Trung Bắc Tân Văn*, particularly Issue5692 (March 4, 1937), Issue 5963 (March 5, 1937), Issue 5964 (March 6, 1937), Issue 5967 (March 10, 1937), Issue 5969 (March 12, 1937), Issue 5971 (March 14, 1937), Issue 5974 (March 18, 1937) and Issue 5976 (March 20, 1937). During a visit to *Quan họ*'s performance, he took notes of himself as a real participant. "In the beginning, I participated in the *Quan họ* event, and was invited to sing *Quan họ*. The *Quan họ* singing night began with various voices, deep voice high-pitched voice, prolonged voice, bouncing voice, etc." Such a book is the first to give a comprehensive introduction to *Quan họ* songs and *Quan họ* festival.

In 1940, Nguyễn Duy Kiện wrote an article about the forest festival and published it on *Việt Báo*. In the same year, Mạnh Quỳnh published his article writing on Lim Festival on *Trung Bắc Tân Văn Sunday.*

In 1943, Toan Ánh wrote an article about *Quan họ* songs, namely "Hát *Quan họ*, một lối chơi xuân thú vị ở vùng Bắc Ninh (*Quan họ's* performance: Bắc Ninh's New Year's entertainment)", published in *Phong lưu đồng ruộng (Joys on the fields)*, accompanied by 20 folk games and other popular performances (see Toan Ánh 1992, p. 7-14). This is not a basic science research project. The author mainly wrote it in the style of an on-site note, which gives readers a glimpse into the *Quan họ* art.

In 1953, Thanh Lãng introduced *Quan họ* performance as one of the most popular categories of folk songs in Vietnam in the book *Văn học khởi thảo - văn chương bình dân* (Introduction to popular literature).

2.2. The period from 1954 to 2005

Nguyễn Đình Phúc was the first musician to conduct a field trip and subsequently publish a paper on *Quan họ*. Probably before 1954, when he exchanged ideas about *Quan họ* with artisan Nguyễn Thị Nguyên, he was impressed with this art, which prompted him to conduct field visits right after the anti-French war (1954). Based on such fieldwork notes, Nguyễn Đình Phúc was the first person to publish research essays on *Quan họ*, such as "Tính chất đúng đắn, tập thể của hát *Quan họ* (The accuracy and collectiveness of Quan họ songs performance)", "Các giọng Quan họ(Voice types of *Quan họ*)", "Thêm một vài ý kiến về các giọng *Quan họ* (Some additional ideas on *Quan họ* voice types)", and "Để góp phần vào vấn đề nghiên cứu *Quan họ* (A contribution to the study of *Quan họ*)". It is undeniable that these publications represented the first enlightenment and meticulous thoughts about *Quan họ* cultural heritage, and Nguyễn Đình Phúc was the first person to point out the attributes of *Quan họ* music after 1954.

In early 1956, the Bureau of Military Music sent musicians Nguyễn Đình Tấn, Nguyễn Viêm, and Lưu Khâm to carry out the task of collecting *Quan họ* folk songs. As a result, the book *Tìm hiểu Quan họ* (A Study on *Quan họ*) written by the three authors was published, which included "a set of literature on folk songs and general concepts". This book was introduced and discussed by Tử Phác in the article "Góp ý kiến về *Quan họ* (Comments on Quan họ)" in *Music Journal* (see Tử Phác 1956).

In 1956, the Ministry of Culture organized a study of *Quan họ*. Many musicians such as Lưu Hữu Phước, Nguyễn Viêm, Tú Ngọc, and Nguyễn Văn Phú went to *Quan họ* villages to collect and study folk songs. A series of notes on *Quan họ* were published in *the Music Journal* during the period, such as "Mấy ý kiến trao đổi về nâng cao và phát triển *Quan họ* (Some ideas on strengthening and developing *Quan họ*)" by musician Nguyễn Đình Tấn (1956).

In 1956, Lưu Khâm wrote about origin and performance of *Quan họ* in the book named *Tìm hiểu nguồn gốc và sinh hoạt của Quan họ* (A study on origin and performance of *Quan họ*) (1959). In the same year, Tú Ngọc wrote the book *Các giọng trong Quan họ* (Voice types in *Quan họ*) (Tú Ngọc 1956).

In 1957, the Lê Quý Đôn group introduced *Quan họ* Bắc Ninh in their book *Lược thảo lịch sử văn học Việt Nam* (Introduction to the History of Vietnamese Literature) as follows: "Some beautiful folk songs played in *Quan họ Bắc Ninh* region are often called *Quan họ Bắc Ninh*" (Lê Quý Đôn 1957, p. 40). In the same year, a group of authors including Văn Tân, Nguyễn Hồng Phong, Nguyễn Đổng Chi and Vũ Ngọc Phan published the work *Sơ thảo lịch sử văn học Việt Nam* (A brief introduction on Vietnamese Literature). When introducing various types of folk songs of the North, the authors referred to aspects of *Quan họ Bắc Ninh* such as hypothesis on origin of *Quan họ*, content and forms of *Quan họ folk songs*, etc. Despite the short writing, the author has outlined the issues that need to be raised about *Quan họ*.

Trần Văn Khê wrote his own article "*Quan họ* Folk Song Performance" in Paris in 1958 based on the available texts in Vietnam, introducing the main characteristics of *Quan họ* (Trần Văn Khê 1958).

At the same time, in 1959, Nguyễn Tiến Chiêu published his paper "Tìm hiểu nguồn gốc *Quan họ* (Research on the origin of *Quan họ*)" in Saigon. Based on the previously published references, he proposed 06 theories originating from the entire *Quan họ Bắc Ninh*, and put forward ideas on these theories. He concluded that "*Quan họ*'s art probably appeared during national production and was formed in the villages of Bắc Ninh province at the end of the eleventh century. Quan họ's founder might have been a popular artist" (Nguyễn Tiến Chiêu 1959).

In following year, 1960, in Sài Gòn city, Nguyễn Tiến Chiêu continued his publishing of the writing *Lời ca Quan họ* (*Quan họ* lyrics). In the same year, in Hanoi city, Phạm Phúc Minh published the book *Tìm hiểu ca nhạc dân gian Việt Nam* (A Study on Vietnamese folk songs), in which he introduced folk songs of Kinh ethnic group nationwide, including a general idea on *Quan họ* performance as follows:" Quan họ is now gaining popularity not only in Vietnam but also abroad" (Phạm Phúc Minh 1960, p. 15).

In 1962, in Huế, Lê Văn Hảo published his essay entitled "Nguồn gốc và tiến hóa của hát *Quan họ* (The origin and evolution of *Quan họ*) (Lê Văn Hảo 1962). It can be said that this is a carefully prepared and rich paper on Quan họ. Most importantly, due to historical conditions at the time, the authors were unable to visit Bắc Ninh province. In the following year, Lê Văn Hảo released his essay "Vài nét về truyền thống của hát *Quan họ* trong truyền thống văn hóa dân gian (A brief introduction to folk song performance in traditional folklore)" (Lê Văn Hảo 1963).

Six years after fieldwork by musicians from the Music Research Bureau, in 1962, the Art Department of the Ministry of Culture published the *Dân ca Quan họ*(*Quan họ* folk songs) written by Lưu Hữu Phước, Nguyễn Viêm, Tú Ngọc and Nguyễn Văn Phú. It can be said that this was Quan họ's first comprehensive study at the time. With Quan họ songs listed last, the book was divided into many chapters, such as Study on the original homeland, organization, and rules of *Quan họ*; Study on the sound, content, and methods of *Quan họ*'s voice performance; Study on the birth and development processes of *Quan họ*; Study on the content and artistic value of *Quan họ*, etc.

In the North in 1965, Hoàng Tiêu in his BA. Graduation thesis discussed some aspects of *Quan họ Bắc Ninh*, such as the basic conditions of the development of *Quan họ*, ways of organizing and performing *Quan họ* songs; the cultural aspects of the Bắc Ninh people are expressed through *Quan họ*; the development process of *Quan họ* after the August Revolution (1945); and an appendix of 48 *Quan họ* folk songs (both old and new songs), as well as a description of the living environment of *Quan họ* performances, and the mythology of Y Na village. Although it was written within the framework of a university graduation thesis, it was a very good research work for *Quan họ*.

In 1969, Toan Ánh described the relationship between *Quan họ* Bắc Ninh and *Hát văn* his book entitled *Cầm ca Việt Nam* (Vietnamese Music and Songs) published in Saigon. He intentionally described the performance of *Quan họ Bắc Ninh* in relation with Hát ví in general, Hát ví in Nghệ Tĩnh in particular, Hát trống quân, Hát cò lả, etc. (Toan Ánh 1969, pp. 111-36). The author discusses many aspects of the *Quan họ* art, such as the voice of the *Quan họ* singers, the season of the *Quan họ* festival, and the way people invite people to perform and/or participate in the *Quan họ* festivals, etc.

In 1972, in Volume 1 (namely "Folk literature") of the textbook *Lịch sử văn học Việt Nam* (A history of Vietnamese Literature), the authors discussed folk songs of the ethnic Kinh (Viet) people, affirming that each region had its own local folk song. They said: *"Quan họ Bắc Ninh* stands out amid others" (see Toan Ánh1976, p. 40). The author reviewed the three theories about the origin of *Quan họ*, and briefly introduced the singing technique, singing style, and symbolic gestures of *Quan họ* (to meet the requirements of textbooks).

They reconfirmed two theories on the origin of *Quan họ* and briefed on the fashion of performing, picturing because this is a textbook of Vietnamese folk literature (see Toan Ánh 1976).

Also in 1972, Đinh Gia Khánh and Chu Xuân Diên published their literary textbooks entitled *Văn học dân gian* (Folk Literature). In Vol 1, when discussing the development of folk literature in history, the authors concluded that "The interactive responding singing between young men and women was popular in the Trần dynasty. This kind of singing provided singers with wonderful word creation skills. Among the popular folk song genres, *Quan họ* is the one to be mentioned" (Đinh Gia Khánh& Chu Xuân Diên 1972, p. 229). The authors confirmed that Quan họ had originated during the Lý dynasty. In Volume 2, when discussing the creativity of folk literature, the authors discussed the creativity of the *Quan họ* artisans of Bồ Sơn and Y Na villages (Đinh Gia Khánh& Chu Xuân Diên 1972, pp.229-30, 390).

After four conferences on *Quan họ* held in 1965, 1967, 1969 and 1971, Hà Bắc Department of Culture (now divided into Bắc Ninh and Bắc Giang provinces) published the book *Một số vấn đề về Dân ca Quan họ* (Some Issues on *Quan họ* folk songs) in 1972, consisting of 28 essays written by 25 authors. This is probably the first book published by Hà Bắc Department of Culture on *Quan họ*, which includes several valuable papers, such as Văn Cao's "*Con sáo sang sông* theo phong cách *Quan họ* (The song *Con sáo sang sông* in the style of *Quan họ*)", Cao Huy Đỉnh's "Bàn thêm về đặc trưng của Dân ca *Quan họ* (Further discussion on characteristics of *Quan họ folk songs*)", Lê Thị Nhâm Tuyết's "Mấy ý kiến về tìm hiểu nguồn gốc Dân ca *Quan họ* (Some ideas on the origin of *Quan họ folk songs*)", Tô Vũ's "Sưu tầm và nghiên cứu âm nhạc *Quan họ* (Collection and Study on *Quan họ* Music)", Vũ Ngọc Phan's "Mấy ý kiến sơ bộ về Dân ca *Quan họ* (Primary ideas on *Quan họ*)", etc.

In 1972, in Saigon, Phạm Duy published the book *Đặc khảo về dân nhạc ở Việt Nam* (Special survey on folk music in Vietnam), in which he discussed the origin, characteristics, voice types, tunes, and melodies of *Quan họ* (Phạm Duy 1972, pp. 99- 105).

In 1973, Lê Sĩ Giáo selected Lim Festival as his subject in his Bachelor of Arts degree's thesis entitled *Sơ bộ khảo sát hội Lim trước Cách mạng tháng Tám* 1945 (A brief survey on Lim Festival before the August Revolution 1945). He divided the thesis into three main parts, namely "A brief on historical geography, economic geography, and social relation of the Lim area before the August Revolution (1945)", "the performance of Lim Festival before the August Revolution", and "Conclusion". In addition to the main discussion, the author also added four maps as an appendix. It is worth noting that the author carefully described the performance of *Quan họ* on Lim Festival.

In 1974, Cao Huy Đỉnh published his work *Tìm hiểu tiến trình văn học dân gian Việt Nam* (A Study on the Evolution of Vietnamese Folk Literature), in which he discussed *Quan họ* in Chapter 4. He emphasized the evidence of folk art presented on the ancient bronze drums (fifth century BC to the second century AD), as well as the evidence of folk art presented in *Quốc Âm Thi Tập* (國音詩集, National Language Poetry Collection) by Nguyễn Trãi (1380-1442), suggesting that "The custom of exchanging love between young people that has created opportunities for young men and women to perform folk poetry and new songs must be very old and popular" (Cao Huy Đỉnh 1974, p. 87). According to him, *Quan họ* belongs to such type of singing art.

In 1974, Toan Ánh published the book *Nếp cũ: hội hè đình đám* (Old customs: festivals) in Saigon. The author described Lim Festival in terms of general introduction, *Quan họ* performance, the origin of *Quan họ*, the seasons of *Quan họ* singing, the reasons for *Quan họ* performance, *Quan họ* artisans, singing competition, the ways to invite ones to perform and/or participate in *Quan họ* folk songs in a festival or invite friend home to sing overnight, making friends among the "brothers" and "sisters", returning to Lim Festival, etc. Among other festivals, the author listed festivals in 17 villages in Võ Giàng, Yên Phong, Việt Yên, and Tiên Du districts of Bắc Ninh and Bắc Giang provinces (Toan Ánh 1974, pp. 186-8). In 1974, he continued releasing the article "Hội Lim với tục hát *Quan họ* (Lim Festival and *Quan họ* performances)" in *Oriental Monthly Review* (vol 31& 32/1974).

In 1974, musician Lê Yên participated in a debate with several authors, revolving around the analysis of *Quan họ* songs in the article entitled "*Qua việc phân tích mấy bài Quan họ* (From the analysis of some *Quan họ* folk songs)". Also under this trend, musician Nguyễn Viêm replied with the article "*Bàn về giá trị một bài hát* (On the value of songs)". *Arts Study Review*, vol 4/1974). Two years later, musician Hồng Thao responded to both Lê Yên and Nguyễn Viêm in the article "Nhân việc phân tích mấy bài *Quan họ* (On the occasion of analyzing some *Quan họ* folk songs)" on *the Journal of Art Studies* 4 (1976).

In 1976, after the first visit to the motherland (from France), Trần Văn Khê went to Bắc Ninh and wrote the article "*Sau khi thăm quê hương Quan họ - Vài nhận xét về quá trình nghiên cứu Dân ca Quan họ* (After visiting *Quan họ* homeland: some comments about the research process of *Quan họ* folk songs)".

In the two years of 1977 and 1978, Hồng Thao published several essays on Quan họ, such as "Dân ca *Quan họ* với sự giao lưu nghệ thuật (*Quan họ* and arts exchange)", "Về tổ chức và đặc điểm của lời ca trong dân ca *Quan họ* (About organization and features of *Quan họ* lyrics", and "Về sự ra đời và phát triển của dân ca *Quan họ* (About the origin and evolution of *Quan họ*)" on music- and art-related journals.

In 1978, Đặng Văn Lung, Hồng Thao and Trần Linh Quý released the book *Quan họ, nguồn gốc và quá trình phát triển* (*Quan họ*:the origin and evolution). The work is divided into six chapters, including (1) A glimpse at the styles of Quan họ; (2) Further investigation on the "standard" (*Quan họ* songs); (3) In-depth study on the customs and conceptions (of *Quan họ*); (4) History (of *Quan họ*); (5) On the melodies of *Quan họ*; and (6) Quan họ artisans.

In 1978, Quang Lộc reconsidered the theme of the origin of *Quan họ* in Hà Bắc's Creative Journal through the article "Thử tìm hiểu nguồn gốc Dân ca *Quan họ* (Let's study the origin of *Quan họ*)".

In 1980, Đặng Văn Lung successfully defended his Ph.D thesis entitled "*Quan họ - nguồn gốc và quá trình phát triển* (*Quan họ*: the origin and evolution process). Besides the introductory and primary Commentary, the thesis was divided into 7 chapters, namely *Quan họ* in the life of Hà Bắc people; Highly-developed forms of *Quan họ*; Complete and diversified *Quan họ* melodies; Passionate love songs; Myths on origin of *Quan họ*; Overview of the custom of making friends in *Quan họ*; and Study on the term "*Quan họ*".

In 1981, Tô Nguyễn and Trịnh Nguyễn presented an overview of *Quan họ* in terms of the name, origin, performance techniques, and *Quan họ* singing festivals in the book *Kinh Bắc - Hà Bắc* (see Tô Nguyễn & Trịnh Nguyễn 1981, pp: 92-120).

In 1982, the works of many authors *Địa chí Hà Bắc* (Local history of Hà Bắc) was published, in which Đặng Văn Lung wrote the section "*Quan họ*". Within the scope of this section, he could only briefly introduce the basic theme of *Quan họ* (Đặng Văn Lung 1982, pp. 610-2). In the same work, Lê Hồng Dương wrote about the custom of making friends among *Quan họ* villages and Trần Linh Quý wrote about village festivals. Because of their deep understanding of Hà Bắc and *Quan họ* art, both of them provided accurate descriptions of these two topics.

In 1983, Ngô Duy Cương completed his graduation thesis on the subject *Tìm hiểu nghệ thuật phổ thơ sáu tám trong Dân ca Quan họ* (An investigation on the six-eight style [72] verse in *Quan họ*) at the Hanoi Conservatory of Music. Although this is just a graduation thesis, the work is actually a new insight into *Quan họ*.

During the years of 1985-1989, Nguyễn Đình Bưu released a number of articles working on *Quan họ*, including "Bàn thêm về ca *Quan họ* (Further discussion on *Quan họ*)" (1985) "Ý nghĩa của từ "*Quan họ*" (Meanings of the term "*Quan họ*")" (1986), "Ca nhạc và *Quan họ* (Music and *Quan họ*) (1989), etc.

---

[72] Verse written in pairs, one of which contains six words, the other eight. The last word of the first sentence must match the sixth word of the second sentence.

In 1986, Tô Ngọc Thanh and Hồng Thao co-authored the book *Tìm hiểu âm nhạc dân tộc cổ truyền* (A study on traditional music). In this work, Hồng Thao's writing includes "Canh hát hội Lim (A *Quan họ* performance in Lim Festival), (Talk about *Quan họ* singing" comprising "Đêm Y Na không ngủ (A sleepless night in Y Na)", Gặp gỡ diễn viên đoàn Dân ca Quan họ (Meeting the artists of the Folk Songs Troupe)". (see Tô Ngọc Thanh, Hồng Thao 1986). This is a note report written by knowledgeable collectors and researchers so that the beauty and remaining issues of *Quan họ* singing were successfully communicated.

In 1986, the Hà Bắc Department of Culture and Information held a scientific seminar on festivals. Among 18 papers presented which were then published in the book *Hội xứ Bắc* (the Kinh Bắc region's festival) (1988)[73], Lê Văn Kỳ discussed *Quan họ* festivals held in the Kinh Bắc region in "Thử tìm hiểu một vài đặc điểm về hội lễ ở Hà Bắc (Let's try to explore some characteristics of the Hà Bắc festival)". The author is quite reasonable when claiming that "*Quan họ* is actually a typical performance in Vietnam, representing optimism, a healthy lifestyle and the pure feelings of countrymen" (Lê Văn Kỳ 1988, p. 36).

In 1989, the Hà Bắc Department of Culture and Information continued to publish *Hội xứ Bắc* (Kinh Bắc region's Festivals)[74]. Among the three festivals mentioned, Khổng Đức Thiêm proposed Lim Festival in "Hội Lim, hồn nước gọi ta về (Lim Festival, the national soul is calling us)". Compared with the notes of Vũ Bằng and Nguyễn Duy Kiện on Lim Festival before August 1945, Khổng Đức Thiêm's paper is excellent. He detailed the activities of Lim Festival in this paper.

In 1990, Lê Chí Quế, Võ Quang Nhơn and Nguyễn Hùng Vĩ co-authored the text book *Văn học dân gian Việt Nam* (Vietnamese folk literature) at Hanoi University. In the section of romantic folk songs, the authors concisely wrote about *Quan họ*, including the custom of making friends, phases of a *Quan họ* performance show, and places of performance.

---

[73] Also called "Volume 1".

[74] Also called "Volume 2".

They asserted that "*Quan họ* is the peak of Vietnamese folk songs" (Lê Chí Quế et al. 1990, p. 246-7).

In 1994, Tú Ngọc wrote *Dân ca người Việt* (Vietnamese folk songs), in which *Quan họ* art was discussed in several pages, among other types of folk songs of the Vietnamese.

In 1994, Hồng Thao mentioned again the issues of the name and origin of *Quan họ* in the article entitled Hồng Thao "*Quan họ*: tên gọi và nguồn gốc (*Quan họ*: the name and origin)". In the essay "Sắc thái Quan họ và phong cách dân ca Việt (Particular features of *Quan họ* and the style of Vietnamese folk music", He incorporated *Quan họ* into the broad framework of Vietnamese folk music to extract its unique characteristics.

In the same year, Phạm Phúc Minh mentioned *Quan họ* in the work *Tìm hiểu dân ca Việt Nam* (Understanding on Vietnamese folk songs). In this book, he gave a brief description of *Quan họ*'s concept, lyrics, and music content (see Phạm Phúc Minh 1994, pp. 211-2).

In 1994, Nguyễn Phương Châm published an article "Về hiện tượng Dân ca *Quan họ* Hà Bắc (About the "phenomenon" of Hà Bắc's *Quan họ* folk songs)" in *Folklore Journal*. At the same year, under the resolution of the Hà Bắc People's Committee, the Quan họ Cultural Center was established. At this time, the Hà Bắc Department of Culture and Information published a small guide book entitled *Trung tâm văn hóa Quan họ* (the Quan họ Cultural Center). In this book, 27 articles on *Quan họ* and *Quan họ* culture were presented; however, all of these were actually speeches, not quite scientific papers.

In 1995, Thạch Phương and Lê Trung Vũ complied and edited the book *60 lễ hội truyền thống Việt Nam* (Vietnam's 60 traditional festivals). In the 60 most representative festivals considered, the authors described Lim Festival from indoor and outdoor (on the mountain, on boats) performances and vegetarian cooking competitions (see Thạch Phương & Lê Trung Vũ 1995, pp. 95-101).

In 1997, Trần Linh Quý and Hồng Thao released the textbook *Tìm hiểu dân ca Quan họ* (A study on *Quan họ*) for students of culture and arts.

In addition to the 16 selected *Quan họ* songs provided in the appendix, the work includes three main parts, namely, "Hometown, principles, and customs of *Quanhọ*", "The lyrics of *Quanhọ*" and "Music in *Quanhọ*".

In the same year, Hồng Thao presented another piece of work named *Dân ca Quan họ* (*Quan họ* folk songs). In addition to the Introduction written by Tô Ngọc Thanh, this work consists of 10 chapters, namely, Chapter 1: "Basic features of practices and customs of *Quan họ*"; Chapter 2: "The existence and evolution of *Quan họ*"; Chapter 3: "The essence and characteristics of *Quan họ* lyrics"; Chapter 4: "The essence and characteristics of *Quan họ* music"; Chapter 5: "The relationship between lyrics and music in Quan họ"; Chapter 6: "From traditional to modern *Quan họ* songs"; Chapter 7: "Art exchange"; Chapter 8: "A phenomenon of diversified folk culture"; Chapter 9: "Discussion on the meanings of the term '*Quan họ*'"; and Chapter 10: "The reservation, introduction, research, and development of *Quan họ* after the August Revolution 1945" (see Hồng Thao 1997).

In 1998, Lê Toàn successfully defended his Doctoral Dissertation on *Quan họ: truyền thống và đương đại* (*Quan họ*: tradition and contemporary)[75] in Russia. Previously, he completed his graduate thesis named *Tìm hiểu một số thủ pháp Quan họ hóa trong những bài Quan họ hóa có nguồn gốc du nhập* (A study on *Quan họ*-ized techniques in imported *Quan họ* songs) at the Hanoi Conservatory of Music in 1989.

In 1998, in response to the 30th anniversary (1969-1999), the Bắc Ninh *Quan họ* Troupe released a program called *Sum họp trúc mai* (The reunion of bamboo and apricot[76]) There are two articles to mention, namely, "Đoàn Dân ca *Quan họ*: ba mươi năm hoạt động và trưởng thành (The

---

[75] According to the regulations of the Ministry of Education and Training, all graduate students who are about to graduate must submit a copy of the thesis. Unfortunately, we cannot find this work at National Library (No. 31, Tràng Thi Street, Hoàn Kiếm District, Hanoi). Therefore, we know nothing about it. The title and year of defense are provided by Lê Toàn. We are very grateful to him.

[76] In Vietnamese culture, the pair of bamboo and apricot symbolizes the long-lasting friendship between men and women.

Bắc Ninh Quan họ Troupe: 30 years of working and growing) by well-known artisan Thuý Cải, and "Niên biểu ba mươi năm Đoàn Dân ca *Quan họ* (Thirty-year chronology of the Bắc Ninh Quan họ Troupe) by musician Hoắc Công Huynh. Through these two articles, we can gain a deep insight into how a folk culture and folk singing group in the national workforce has long promoted the *Quan họ* love duet.

In 2000, Nguyễn Trọng Ánh released his research work entitled *Âm nhạc Quan họ* (Music of *Quan họ*). In addition to the introduction written by Phạm Minh Khang, the book consists of 5 chapters, namely, Chapter 1: "A generic system of folk song melodies", Chapter 2: "Structural form", Chapter 3: "The modality of *Quan họ*", Chapter 4: "Quan họ melodies" and Chapter 5: "The relationship between music and verse". It is undeniable that this is a large-scale study that fully examined the music of *Quan họ*. The author was, of course, faithful and diligent in the field of *Quan họ* music. Prior to this, he defended the graduate thesis on the topic *Những bước đầu tìm hiểu về một số vấn đề thuộc giai điệu của âm nhạc Quan họ* (Preliminary steps in studying *Quan họ*'s musical melody) in 1984, and the MA thesis in Musicology on the topic *Điệu thức trong âm nhạc Quan họ* (Musical modality in *Quan họ*) in 1996. Therefore, it is said that Nguyễn Trọng Ánh's research is a new scientific contribution to the study of Quan họ's music.

Trần Chính published his master's thesis in folk culture literature in 2000, namely *Nghệ nhân Quan họ làng Viêm Xá* (Quan Ho artisans of Viêm Xá village). The first part of the book was to analyze the theme "Nghệ nhân *Quan họ* làng Viêm Xá" (*Quan họ* artisans of of Viêm Xá village), including three chapters, namely, "Viêm Xá: a representative village of *Quan họ*", "*Quan họ* artisans in the community of Viêm Xá village", and "Characteristics of the way Viêm Xá's artists perform *Quan họ*". In fact, this research is highly valued for its approach. Talking about Bắc Ninh means talking about *Quan họ* artisans. However, before Trần Chính, only Trần Linh Quý, a research expert, had studied this issue. In Trần Linh Quý's research, *Quan họ* artisans were the core but generic subject of academic research while Trần Chính personally conducted an on-site survey and research on the artists in a specific village using fieldwork methods. As a result, his only 100 pages of research work contributed greatly to the study of *Quan họ*.

In the same year, *Quan họ* Cultural Center in Bắc Ninh issued another collection, namely *Một số vấn đề về văn hóa Quan họ* (Some issues of Quan họ culture). The book contains 11 articles written by Lê Danh Khiêm, Trần Đình Luyện, Lê Thị Chung, Hoắc Công Huynh, Lê Viết Nga, and Đức Miêng, etc., presenting the overall view of *Quan họ* in terms of a cultural heritage and particular aspects such as music, lyric, performance, clothing, music, etc.

In 2001, Lê Danh Khiêm made the book *Dân ca Quan họ, lời ca và bình giải* (*Quan họ*:lyric and interpretation), including two main parts: Voice of *Quan họ*, and Lyric and interpretation. The author explained and analyzed 106 popular words and phrases in Quan họ songs. Obviously, this research is the result of the hard work of the author who has devoted himself to the research of *Quan họ* almost all his life.

From 1995 to 2000, overseas Vietnamese scholar Lê Ngọc Chân surveyed Quan họ in Bắc Ninh. Then, in 2002, he successfully defended his doctoral dissertation in music research at the University of California, Berkeley, namely "*Quan ho singing in North Vietnam: A yearning for resolution*. The doctoral thesis comprises of 8 chapters, including (1) Introduction, (2) *Quan họ* singing in ritual-Festivals in Bắc Ninh region, (3) National Identity an The dissrtation comprises orald folk music institutionalization, (4) Institutionalization of Quan ho tradition and music, (5) *Quan họ* Songs and Performances, (6) The *la rằng* songs, (7) Characteristics of today's *Quan họ* songs and their cultural historical implications, and (8) Understanding *Quan họ* songs and practice as sociocultural dialectic.

In 2002, the musician Đức Miêng proposed the collection *Yêu một Bắc Ninh* (Love a Bắc Ninh) based on his articles previously released the Bắc Ninh Newspaper. In the book, he provided singing skills and typical *Quan họ* villages to spread knowledge to the public.

Also in 2002, the Bắc Giang Department Culture and Information published the work *Lễ hội Bắc Giang* (Bắc Giang's festivals). In describing the festivals in the Việt Yên district, the author focused on the festivals in the village of Thổ Hà. In addition to folk cultural activities, *Quan họ* were also performed at the festivals (see Ngô Văn Trụ ed. 2002, pp. 496-512). Nonetheless, the book did not mention five *Quan họ* villages s on the north side of the Cầu River.

In 2003, the Bắc Ninh Department Culture and Information and the editor-in-chief Trần Đình Luyện jointly published the book *Lễ hội Bắc Ninh* (Bắc Ninh's festivals). The book described 49 festivals of Bắc Ninh, including some villages that perform *Quan họ*, for example Nhồi festival, Ó festival, Yên Mẫn festival, Lim festival, and Diềm festival, etc. Even if this work could not cover all festivals in 44 Quan họ villages, it is obviously valuable for those who study *Quan họ*.

In the same year, Đỗ Thị Thuỷ's Master of Arts thesis *Văn hóa làng Diềm* (Culture of Diềm village) was published at Hanoi Culture University. In addition to Introduction, Conclusion, References and Appendix, her thesis consists of 3 chapters, namely, (1) Conditions affecting the formation of traditional culture in Viêm Xá village, (2) Elements that shape the traditional culture of Viêm Xá village, and (3) The preservation and development of traditional values in the current innovation process. It had the same research theme as Trần Chính's Master of Arts thesis, but due to the different research methods used, this thesis has established its own position. The traditional culture of Diềm village was deliberately described among the 49 *Quan họ* villages in the region.

In 2003, in a local magazine the Kinh Bắc people, Nguyễn Thượng Luyến wrote a short article, namely "Đi tìm nguồn gốc Dân ca *Quan họ* (Discovering the origin of *Quan họ* folk songs)". The author asserted that "The origin of *Quan họ* folk songs formed in the Lim area was created by the Governor Đỗ Nguyễn Thụy" (Nguyễn Thượng Luyến 2003, p. 70). In fact, the author was a little early to conclude the origin of a complex cultural phenomenon like *Quan họ*.

On November 2, 2004, in cooperation with the Bắc Ninh Department of Culture and Information and the Tiên Du District People's Committee, a scientific conference on "*Hội Lim, truyền thống và hiện đại* (Traditional and Modern Festivals)" was held. The conference proceedings were published, including 21 research papers (out of the 29 papers totally). It can be said that this is the first time many aspects of Lim Festival has been studied. However, this is not a systematic study of the entire *Quan họ* cultural space.

2.3. The period from 2005 to 2009

In 2005, the Ministry of Culture and Information (today's Ministry of Culture, Sports and Tourism), the Bắc Ninh Provincial Party Committee and People's Committee developed a policy document that has established a national file to be submitted to UNESCO to recognize Bắc Ninh's *Quan họ* culture as an intangible heritage of humanity. A series of tasks have been carried out, such as compiling a collection of research works on Quan họ and publishing a photo book called *Bắc Ninh vùng Văn hóa Quan họ* (Bắc Ninh: *Quan họ* Cultural Area), etc.

It was also in 2005 when the researcher Trần Linh Quý announced his own essay on Dân ca *Quan họ* (*Quan họ* folk singing) in *Bắc Giang Folklore Journal*. On an 86-page book, the author summarized his lifelong understanding of *Quan họ* from the following aspects: *Quan họ* area, a set of 'standard' principles in *Quan họ*, customs, practices, selected song lyrics, etc. It can be said that this is a detailed scientific paper on Quan họ, which was written by one of the two Vietnamese researchers who has devoted his life to the study of *Quan họ*.

In the same year, Đinh Thị Thanh Huyền successfully defended her master's thesis in history on the topic *Trang phục trong sinh hoạt văn hóa Quan họ (làng Diềm, xã Hòa Long, huyện Yên Phong, tỉnh Bắc Ninh* (Costume in *Quan họ* cultural activities: a case study of Diềm village, Yên Phong district, Bắc Ninh province). In this thesis, the authors presented an overview on natural conditions and habitants of Diềm village in Chapter 1, festivals and *Quan họ* cultural activities as the survival and development environment of *Quan họ* costumes in Chapter 2, classification and expression of *Quan họ* costumes in Chapter 3, cultural values and preservation of *Quan họ* costume in the last chapter (Chapter 4). If there is more investment in the content in Chapter 3, the paper will be more successful, because this is the first and most comprehensive research in the study of *Quan họ* clothing. It is worth noting that this appendix is composed of many clothing drawings used in *Quan họ* including clothes, camisole, shirts, and belts.

In 2005, the Bắc Ninh Provincial Culture and Art Association published a book entitled *Về văn học nghệ thuật dân gian Bắc Ninh* (On folk culture and arts in Bắc Ninh) (vol.1). The book included Lê Danh Khiêm's article, namely "Văn hóa *Quan họ*: tổng hòa của các loại hình văn hóa truyền thống làng xã Bắc Ninh (*Quan họ* culture: synthesis of folk culture forms in the villages of Bắc Ninh province). As a passionate researcher in *Quan họ*, he introduced a valuable article about *Quan họ*. This article evaluated *Quan họ* from a cultural point of view. The ideas includes *Quan họ* culture and behavior culture, *Quan họ* culture and trust culture, *Quan họ* culture and festival culture, *Quan họ* culture and community's behavioral culture, and *Quan họ* culture in relation to other traditional folk songs and music.

Within this book, Nguyễn Khắc Bảo wrote the article "Nguyễn Du viết về *Quan họ* (Nguyễn Du's writing on *Quan họ*). From the term "*Quan họ*" that Nguyễn Du mentioned in the verse "Văn tế Trường Lưu Nhị nữ" (Funeral oration on two ladies in Trường Lưu), Nguyễn Khắc Bảo asserted that "*Quan họ* is a set of folk melodies (songs) of the closed group of performers (họ) being passed from generation to generation. It was created, nurtured and developed (quan) by talented people in the villages of the Kinh Bắc region" (Nguyễn Khắc Bảo 2005, p. 288-9).

In 2005, Lê Trung Vũ and Lê Hồng Lý published the book *Lễ hội Việt Nam* (Festivals of Vietnam), which introduced 17 traditional festivals in Bắc Ninh. Among the 17 traditional festivals, the author introduced four total festivals, including Xuân Ổ Village Festival, Lim Festival, Diềm Village Festival, and Nội Duệ Village Festival.

Also in 2005, at the Annual Folklore Bulletin Conference of the Institute of Cultural Studies (Vietnamese Academy of Social Sciences), Lê Cẩm Ly presented the paper "*Quan họ* trong sinh hoạt văn hóa tín ngưỡng ở làng Diềm (*Quan họ* in religious and cultural activities in Diềm Village". In this article, the author described four festivals in Diềm Village (Viêm Xá Village), including Hưng Sơn Pagoda Festival; Ngọc Temple & Cùng Temple Festival; Vua Bà Temple Festival; and Diềm Village Communal Temple Festival (see Lê Cẩm Ly 2005, p. 528-38). Also at this event, Phạm Thị Thủy Chung presented the paper "Sông Tiêu Tương với văn hóa Kinh Bắc (The Tiêu Tương River and the Kinh Bắc culture)". By referring to written texts and field investigations, the author traced the ancient cultural activities along the Tiêu Tương River (a river that played an important role in Quan họ culture) (see Phạm Thị Thủy Chung 2005, p. 19-33).

In early 2006, it was the first time that an international conference on the preservation of the *Quan họ* Bắc Ninh folk song cultural space was held in Hanoi. A total of 11 foreign scholars and 49 domestic scholars participated. At the end of the year, all participating papers were published in the book *Không gian Văn hóa Quan họ bảo tồn và phát huy* (The *Quan họ*Cultural Space: preservation and improvement). It can be said that the conference marks an important step in the research of Quan họ.

In 2006, after receiving the resolution establishing the UNESCO national file issued by the Ministry of Culture and Information (today's Ministry of Culture, Information, and Tourism), some working projects were implemented under the cooperation of the two provinces of Bắc Ninh and Bắc Giang and the National Institute of Culture and Art. The concept of "*Quan họ* cultural space" was also clarified. Concerning this term, Trần Linh Quý wrote an article entitled "Không gian văn hóa *Quan họ* và các làng *Quan họ* phía Bắc sông Cầu (*Quan họ* cultural space and *Quan họ* villages in the north of the Cầu River). Although it was not very convincing, the author tried to explain the term "cultural space" in the case of *Quan họ*. In addition, he also discussed some characteristics of the *Quan họ* villages in the north of the Cầu River. In this article, he proposed to include these 5 villages in the list of "old" *Quan họ* villages. He honestly admitted that "no matter how different it is from the number of 5 villages that I suggested in 1971, I actually realized my mistake" (Trần Linh Quý 2006, p. 250).

In 2006, the research work *Không gian văn hóa Quan họ* (Cultural space of *Quan họ* singing) was published (see Lê Danh Khiêm ed. 2006). In addition to Introduction, Forewords and a number of *Quan họ*'s "giã bạn" songs written and transcribed by Hoắc Công Huynh, the book consists of 4 core essays, namely, "Origin of *Quan họ* cultural activities" by Lê Danh Khiêm, "Festival activities in Quan họ villages" by Lê Thị Chung, and "The formation, development process and some basic characteristics of the intangible culture of Diềm village" by Lê Danh Khiêm. In fact, this is a study of *Quan họ*'s general cultural activities, which is based on the basic concepts defined by the Ministry of Culture, Sports and Tourism; however, it is a collection of random papers on the same subject, not a systematic research work. Therefore, it lacks the methodological issues of cultural space and the basic foundation of the *Quan họ* cultural space.

In 2006, Nguyễn Thụy Loan published her monograph named *Dân ca Quan họ: một di sản độc đáo*(Quan họ Bắc Ninh folk singing: a unique heritage). As an expert in the history of Vietnamese music, her monograph is considered to be the comprehensive research work of *Quan họ* in terms of culture and art. She asserted: "*Quan họ* Bắc Ninh is a unique intangible heritage that represents the idyllic beauty of Vietnamese culture. *Quan họ* is a unique intangible heritage, not only because it includes high-value art works of human, but also contains useful meanings and values and its diversity. UNESCO's endorsement also means a reasonable assessment and appreciation of the cultural space created and preserved by the Vietnamese people during the history" (Nguyễn Thụy Loan 2006, p. 852-3).

In 2005, in the Hanoi Conservatory of Music, Nguyễn Trọng Ánh successfully defended his Doctoral dissertation entitled *Những giá trị âm nhạc trong hát Quan họ* (Music values in *Quan họ* singing). It can be said that Nguyễn Trọng Ánh is a prominent scholar and has always been devoted to the research of *Quan họ* music. Therefore, the dissertation highly synthesized his wide and in-depth knowledge of *Quan họ* Music. The 194-page dissertation is divided into 4 chapter : Native land, forms of *Quan họ* activities, and system of *Quan họ* tunes (chapter 1), The relationship between music and literature (chapter 2), Organization (chapter 3), and Melodies (chapter 4). Compared with his Master of Arts thesis and the book *Âm nhạc Quan họ* (*Quan họ* Music) previously published by the Hanoi Conservatory of Music, this thesis perfectly embodies the foundation of *Quan họ* art.

On October 17, 2006, Bắc Ninh's Department of Culture and Information held a scientific workshop on "*Quan họ, thực trạng và giải pháp bảo tồn* (*Quan họ*: Current situation and preservation solutions)". This is a seminar aimed at investigating public opinion about the national movement to protect the *Quan họ* culture. Bắc Ninh's Department of Culture and Information received more than 30 papers and published abstract book to serve the workshop. Especially in the process of discussing the protection and improvement of the *Quan họ* cultural heritage, at the workshop, the speeches of artists of *Quan họ* villages and Bắc Ninh's *Quan họ* Troup, such as Nguyễn Quý Tráng, Nguyễn Khánh Hạ, Nguyễn Văn Quỳnh, Nguyễn Công Dứa, and Tạ Thị Hình, were highly valued.

In 2006, Unfortunately, the author seemed not having enough necessary materials to study, so that she couldn't find out the beauty of such a cultural activity in Bắc Ninh province. Unfortunately, the author seems not to have enough necessary materials to learn, so that she cannot find the beauty of this cultural activity in Bắc Ninh Province.

Also in 2006, in Volume 3 of the Journal of Cultural Heritages issued by Office of Cultural Heritages (formerly as Ministry of Culture and Information), Lê Danh Khiêm wrote the article "Bảo tồn và phát triển *Quan họ*: những chặng đường đã qua (Preservation and Development of *Quan họ* - past journeys)". The author divides the preservation and development of *Quan họ* into five stages, respectively, 1945-1965, 1965-1969, 1969-1982, 1982-1992; and 1992-2006. In terms of administration, his writing was full of high-quality materials. However, in terms of science, the author did not discuss and analyze enough on the preservation and improvement of *Quan họ* Bắc Ninh.

After spending a long time in Vietnam, in 2007, Lauren Meeker defended her doctoral dissertation entitled "*Musical transmissions folk music, mediation and modernity in Northern Vietnam* "at the University of Columbia. Through a large number of picture descriptions and examples, the dissertation emphasized the "Emerging musical voices" in chapter 1, "Circulation and technique" in chapter 2, and "Technics and returns" in chapter 3. From an anthropological point of view, the author puts forward some valuable new views on the transmission of *Quan họ*. Based on the dissertation, Lauren Merker published the book *Sounding out heritage: cultural politics and the social practice of quan họ folk song in northern Vietnam* in 2013.

In 2007, Phạm Trọng Toàn successfully defended his doctoral dissertation (Cultural studies) on the theme *Tương đồng và khác biệt giữa hát xoan, hát ghẹo Phú Thọ và Quan họ Bắc Ninh* (Similarities and differences among *hát xoan* and *hát ghẹo* in Phú Thọ and *Quan họ* in Bắc Ninh)". The dissertation comprises of three chapters, respectively, the cultural space and native lands of *hát xoan, hát ghẹo* and *Quan họ*, the cultures of *hát xoan, hát ghẹo* in Phú Thọ and *Quan họ* in Bắc Ninh, and the hypothesis of historical evolution and the relationship between *hát xoan, hát ghẹo* and *Quan họ*. It can be said that Phạm Trọng Toàn is the first researcher to conduct a comparison between *hát xoan, hát ghẹo* and *Quan họ*, finding out the similarities and differences between them, and providing explanations for these problems. However, the author's explanation is not very clear in terms of archaeology and ethnicity.

In 2007, Ngô Đức Thịnh published his article entitled "*Quan họ*: một hiện tượng xã hội tổng thể (*Quan họ*: a general social phenomenon) in the *Journal of Cultural Heritage Studies*. This is a short article, but due to its proper scientific perspective, it is able to bring a new approach to the study of *Quan họ* of Bắc Ninh. He asserted "*Quan họ* was originally a ritual singing [...]. *Quan họ* is a ritual folk singing type, closely related to the agricultural society." (Ngô Đức Thịnh 2007)

In 2007, Đinh Khắc Thuân introduced the book *Bắc Ninh tỉnh khảo dị* written by Phạm Xuân Lộc to the public. This is a Chinese-script book that plays an important role in studying *Quan họ*.

2.4. The period from 2009 to 2018

Since 2009, the study on *Quan họ* has continued to grow strongly. In 2009, the National Center for Cultural Research, Conservation, and Promotion announced the work of *Tìm về cội nguồn Quan họ* (Discovering the origin of *Quan họ*), chaired by Hoàng Chương and his colleagues. This is a ministerial-level research project funded by the Federation of Vietnam Science and Technology Associations.

In 2010, Lê Danh Khiêm - a researcher who has been engaged in *Quan họ* research since graduating from university, published the work Lê Danh Khiêm. 2010. *Dân ca Quan họ, lời ca và bình giải (Quan họ:* lyrics and commentary).

In 2011, Lâm Minh Đức released the work *Từ ngữ -điển tích Dân ca Quan họ* (Words and stories about *Quan họ*). This is a very significant book in presenting and annotating the words and stories of *Quan họ* folk songs.

In 2012, under the sponsorship of the Vietnam Folklore Association, Trần Linh Quý organized his papers on Quan họ published in the past few years into a book entitled *Trên đường tìm về Quan họ* (On the way back to *Quan họ*). It can be said that this work includes all the outstanding works of the author Trần Linh Quý, who is a lifelong researcher of *Quan họ* folk songs in Bắc Ninh and Bắc Giang today. The book is divided in six parts, namely, Part 1: "*Quan họ* cultural space", Part 2: "Customs and principles in *Quan họ* singing", Part 3: "*Quan họ* artisans at the end of the twentieth century and the early twenty-first centuries, Part 4: "*Quan họ* on the way to recover" Part 5: "System of *Quan họ* performance", and Part 6: "Preservation and promotion the *Quan họ* cultural heritage in contemporary life". This work really made a huge contribution to the process of studying folk songs.

In 2015, Đinh Thị Thanh Huyền successfully defended her doctoral dissertation *Tục chơi Quan họ (xứ Kinh Bắc) xưa và nay* (The practice of *Quan họ* in the past and present) at the University of Social Sciences and Humanities - Vietnam National University in Hanoi. The dissertation includes four chapters, namely, Chapter 1: "Literature review, theory and research method", Chapter 2: "The practice of *Quan họ* now and then in Diềm Village (Viêm Xá)", Chpater 3: The practice of *Quan họ* now and then in Bịu Village (Hoài Thị), and Chapter 4: "The culture of *Quan họ*: tradition, transformation, and preservation". This dissertation continued to contribute to the study of *Quan họ*. In 2017, the Vietnam Folklore Association published this work.

In 2016, Trần Minh Chính defended his doctoral dissertation on the theme *Sinh hoạt Văn hóa Quan họ làng (qua trường hợp làng Quan họ Viêm Xá)* (Cultural activities in *Quan họ* villages (Taking Viêm Xá Village as an example) at the Hồ Chí Minh Institute of National Politics. The dissertation was divided into four chapters, including Chapter 1: "Literature review, theoretical basis and research methodology", Chapter 2: "The *Quan họ* cultural activities in traditional Viêm Xá Village", Chapter 3: "The *Quan họ* cultural activities in the present Viêm Xá Village", and Chapter 4: "Preservation and enhancement the *Quan họ* cultural activities at the present day". It has indeed contributed to the research of *Quan họ* cultural activities in *Quan họ*'s research process. In 2017, the author published the dissertation in the book and renamed the first chapter.

In the same year, Chu Thị Huyền Yến successfully defended her doctoral dissertation in Sociology on the theme *Một số yếu tố xã hội tác động đến việc bảo tồn các giá trị truyền thống của Quan họ* (Some social factors affecting the preservation of *Quan họ*'s traditional values) at the University of Social Sciences and Humanities - Vietnam National University in Hanoi. The dissertation includes four chapters, namely, Chapter 1: "Literature review", Chapter 2: "Theoretical basis and research methodology", Chapter 3: "Preserving traditional values of *Quan họ*", and Chapter 4: "Basic factors affecting traditional conservation activities *Quan họ* and some solutions to improve protection performance". The dissertation approaches and presents the traditional values preservation activities of *Quan họ* in the Kinh Bắc region.

In 2016, Bùi Quang Thanh conducted a research project called *Nghiên cứu nghệ nhân Quan họ trong quá trình bảo tồn và phát huy di sản Dân ca Quan họ ở hai tỉnh Bắc Ninh và Bắc Giang* (Studying Quan họ artisans in the process of preserving and promoting the Quan họ Folk Heritage in Bắc Ninh and Bắc Giang provinces), a project sponsored by the Vietnam National Science and Technology Funds. The draft of the project has not published; however, some research outcomes were included in the book *Dân ca Quan họ: di sản văn hóa phi vật thể đại diện của nhân loại* (*Quan họ*: representative intangible cultural heritage of humanity) (edited by Nguyễn Chí Bền) in 2018.

In 2017, Bắc Ninh Cultural Center published the book *Bảo tồn nghệ nhân Quan họ* (Nurturing *Quan họ* artisans). It can be said that this is an encouraging effort of specific researchers of Bắc Ninh Cultural Center such as Lê Thị Chung, Nguyễn Thị Hương, Nguyễn Hữu Huynh, Nguyễn Sỹ Tuấn, etc.

In 2017, Lương Công Lý, Nguyễn Thị Vân, and Dương Thị Hóa compiled the book *Triết lý nhân sinh trong Văn hóa Quan họ* (Life philosophy in *Quan họ* culture). The work consists of two chapters, namely, Chapter 1: "Life philosophy in *Quan họ* culture: theoretical and practical issues", and Chapter 2: "The content of human philosophy in *Quan họ* culture and solutions to preserve and promote the values". Compared to a monograph, the book is a bit thin with only 176 pages (size 14.5 x 20.5cm) but it is quite valuable because the authors have set a new research direction in *Quan họ*.

In 2018, Nguyễn Đắc Toàn successfully defended his Doctoral dissertation on the topic *Nghệ nhân Quan họ trong đời sống văn hóa đương đại* (*Quan họ* artisans in the contemporary cultural life) at the National Institute of Culture and Art. The dissertation consists of four chapters, including Chapter 1: "Literature review and theoretical basis",

Chapter 2: "Artisans in traditional *Quan họ* cultural activities", Chapter 3: "The current situation of *Quan họ* artisans in the contemporary cultural life", and Chapter 4: "On the role of *Quan họ* artisans in *Quan họ* culture and its changing trend". The dissertation is a research work that mainly studied the transformation of *Quan họ* artisans from traditional to modern.

At the same year (2018), Hà Chí Cường defended his Doctoral dissertation on the theme *Biến đổi của Văn hóa Quan họ trong thời kỳ hiện nay* (Change of *Quan họ* culture in the current period) at the Hanoi University of Culture. There are four chapters in the dissertation, including Chapter 1: "Literature review, theoretical basis and overview of the study area, Chapter 2: "Bắc Ninh cultural sub-region and *Quan họ* traditional culture", Chapter 3: "The reality of today's *Quan họ* cultural change", and Chapter 4: "Factors affecting *Quan họ* culture change and raised problems". This dissertation is a typical study on the change of *Quan họ* culture in the current context.

In 2018, Nguyen Chi Ben (ed) published the book *Bac Ninh Quan Ho Folk Songs, a representative intangible cultural heritage of humanity.* The book was edited by him, 440 pages long, including introduction, conclusion and 7 chapters:

Chapter 1: Looking back at the situation of collecting and researching Quan Ho folk songs in Bac Ninh

Chapter 2: Historical and cultural space of Bac Ninh Quan Ho folk songs

Chapter 3: Origin and development process of Bac Ninh Quan Ho folk songs

Chapter 4: Quan ho village and cultural elements

Chapter 5: Quan Ho artisans

Chapter 6: The human values of Quan Ho Bac Ninh folk songs

Chapter 7: Protecting and promoting the representative intangible cultural heritage of humanity

3. Conclusions

It can be said that the process of collecting and researching *Quan họ Bắc Ninh* culture has been going on for more than 100 years. Generations of collectors have made great efforts to collect and research so that we can capture the relatively sufficient number of *Quan họ* songs. From the notes of Confucian scholars at the end of the 19th century to the notes recorded by Lê Danh Khiêm's group, in fact, this is a long road in the career of collecting *Quan họ* songs. As for the collections and research on village festivals in *Quan họ* region, another long journey has been gone from the notes of Vũ Bằng in 1931 to Lê Thị Chung in 2006. We have established a foundation for festivals in *Quan họ* villages in order to capture the true essence of *Quan họ* cultural activities. In the field of research, *Quan họ* is an attractive discipline for generations of researchers. There were 6 PhDs working on *Quan họ* in total. Two of them were foreigners. Three of them defended abroad and the other three defended in Vietnam. Compared with other folk cultures, the research of Quan họ has achieved many achievements. Researchers have clearly defined the subject of *Quan họ*'s content, form, performance, and value. The active preservation and improvement of *Quan họ* have attracted a lot of attention. However, it is very important to conduct a comprehensive discussion to study *Quan họ* as a complete phenomenon. As for the collection task, it is time to summarize the complete collection of *Quan họ* songs. This means that collectors and researchers in *Quan họ* must continue working hard to support this significant intangible cultural heritage. This is a difficult but very practical task.

Reference

1. Bắc Ninh Cultural Center. 2017. *Bảo tồn nghệ nhân Quan họ* (Nurturing *Quan họ* artisans). Bắc Ninh.

2. Bắc Ninh Culture and Information Department. 2006. *Quan họ, thực trạng và giải pháp bảo tồn* (Quan họ: Current situation and preservation solutions). Bắc Ninh: Conference Proceedings.

3. Bắc Ninh Provincial Culture and Art Association. 2005. *Về văn học nghệ thuật dân gian Bắc Ninh* (On folk culture and arts in Bắc Ninh) (vol. 1)

4. Bắc Ninh's Quan họ Cultural Center. 2000. *Một số vấn đề về văn hóa Quan họ* (Some issues of Quan họ culture). Bắc Ninh.

5. Bắc Ninh Quan họ Troupe. 1998. *Sum họp trúc mai* (The reunion of bamboo and apricot). Bắc Ninh.

6. Nguyễn, Chí Bền ed, 2018, *Dân ca quan họ Bắc Ninh, di sản văn hóa phi vật thể đại diện của nhân loại (Bac Ninh Quan Ho Folk Songs, a representative intangible cultural heritage of humanity)*, Hanoi: Social Science Publisher.

7. Cao, Huy Đỉnh. 1974. *Tìm hiểu tiến trình văn học dân gian Việt Nam* (A Study on the Evolution of Vietnamese Folk Literature). Hanoi, Social Science Publisher.

8. Chu, Thị Huyền Yến. 2016. *Một số yếu tố xã hội tác động đến việc bảo tồn các giá trị truyền thống của Quan họ* (Some social factors affecting the preservation of Quan họ's traditional values). Ph.D. Dissertation. Hanoi: the University of Social Sciences and Humanities - Vietnam National University.

9. Đặng, Văn Lung; Hồng Thao & Trần, Linh Quý. 1978. *Quan họ - nguồn gốc và quá trình phát triển*(Quan họ - origin and evolution). Hanoi: Social Science Publisher.

10. Đặng, Văn Lung. 1980. *Quan họ - nguồn gốc và quá trình phát triển* (Quan họ: the origin and evolution process). Ph.D Thesis. Hanoi.

11. Đặng, Văn Lung. 1982. "Quan họ." In *Địa chí Hà Bắc* (Local history of Hà Bắc). Bắc Ninh: Hà Bắc Provincial Library.

12. Đinh, Thị Thanh Huyền. 2005. *Trang phục trong sinh hoạt văn hóa Quan họ (làng Diềm, xã Hòa Long, huyện Yên Phong, tỉnh Bắc Ninh* (Costume in Quan họ cultural activities: a case study of Diềm village, Yên Phong district, Bắc Ninh province). Master's Thesis in History. Hanoi.

13. Đỗ, Thị Thuỷ. 2003. *Văn hóa làng Diềm* (Culture of Diềm village). Master of Arts thesis. Hanoi: Hanoi Culture University.

14. Đỗ, Trọng Vỹ, *Bắc Ninh toàn tỉnh địa dư chí* (北寧全省輿地志, Local History of Bắc Ninh Province), ed. Nguyễn Thị Thảo, trans. Đỗ Tuấn Anh. Hanoi: Culture and Information Publisher.

15. Đức, Miêng. 2002. *Yêu một Bắc Ninh* (Falling in love with Bắc Ninh). Hanoi: Music Publisher.

16. Chu, Ngọc Chi. 1928. *Hát Quan họ* (Performance of Quan họ). Hanoi: Phúc Văn Hiệu publishing.

17. Department of Local Culture (Ministry of Culture, Sports and Tourism). 2008. *Lễ hội Việt Nam* (Festivals of Vietnam). Hanoi:

18. Dương, Quảng Hàm. 1951. *Việt Nam văn học sử yếu* (An outline of Vietnamese literature history). Second edition. Hanoi: Ministry of Education Publishing.

19. Đinh, Gia Khánh; Chu, Xuân Diên. 1972. *Văn học dân gian* (Folk Literature). Vol. 1. Hanoi: Professional College and High School Publisher, Hanoi.

20. Đinh, Khắc Thuân ed. 2009. *Địa phương chí tỉnh Bắc Ninh qua tư liệu Hán Nôm* (Local history of Bắc Ninh through Sino-Nôm texts). Hanoi: Social Science Publisher.

21. Đinh, Thị Thanh Huyền. 2017. *Tục chơi Quan họ (xứ Kinh Bắc) xưa và nay* (The practice of Quan họ (region Kinh Bac) in the past and present). Hanoi: Fine Arts Publisher.

22. Hà Bắc Department of Culture and Information. 1995. *Trung tâm văn hóa Quan họ* (the Quan họ Cultural Center). Bắc Ninh.

23. Hà, Chí Cường. 2018. *Biến đổi của Văn hóa Quan họ trong thời kỳ hiện nay* (Change of Quan họ culture in the current period). Ph.D. Dissertation. Hanoi: the Hanoi University of Culture.

24. Hoàng, Chương. 2009. *Tìm về cội nguồn Quan họ* (Discovering the origin of Quan họ). Hanoi: Theater Publisher.

25. Hồng, Thao. 1976. "Nhân việc phân tích mấy bài Quan họ (On the occasion of analyzing some Quan họ folk songs)." *Journal of Art Studies* 1(January-March).

26. Hồng, Thao. 1977. "Dân ca Quan họ với sự giao lưu nghệ thuật (Quan họ and arts exchange)." *Journal of Arts Studies* 2.

27. Hồng, Thao. 1977. "Về tổ chức và đặc điểm của lời ca trong dân ca Quan họ (About organization and features of Quan họ's lyrics)." *Journal of Arts Studies* 15.

28. Hồng, Thao. 1978. "Về sự ra đời và phát triển của dân ca Quan họ (About origin and evolution of Quan họ singing)." *Journal of Ethnic Studies* 2.

29. Hồng, Thao. 1994. "Dân ca Quan họ và phong cách dân ca Việt (Particular features of Quan họ songs and Vietnamese folk music style)." *Journal of Music Studies* 2.

30. Hồng, Thao. 1994. "Quan họ: tên gọi và nguồn gốc (Quan họ: the name and origin)." *Vietnam art forum* 4.

31. Hồng, Thao. 1997. *Dân ca Quan họ* (Quan họ folk songs). Hanoi: Music Publisher.

32. Many authors 2006. "Thư mục nghiên cứu Không gian văn hóa Bắc Ninh (Research directory of Bắc Ninh Cultural Space)." In *Vùng Văn hóa Quan họ Bắc Ninh* (Quan họ Bacninh Cultural Space). Hanoi Institute of Culture and Information & Bắc Ninh Department of Culture and Information Publishing.

33. Khổng, Đức Thiêm. 1989. *Hội xứ Bắc* (Kinh Bắc region's Festivals). Vol.1. Bắc Ninh: the Hà Bắc Department of Culture and Information.

34. Lâm, Minh Đức. 2011. *Từ ngữ - điển tích Dân ca Quan họ* (Words and stories about Quan họ folk songs). *Hanoi:* Culture and Information Publisher.

35. Lê, Cẩm Ly. 2005. "Quan họ trong sinh hoạt văn hóa tín ngưỡng ở làng Diềm (Quan họ in religious and cultural activities in Diem Village". *The Folklore Bulletin*, ed pp.528-538. Hanoi: Social Sciences publishing house.

36. Lê, Chí Quế; Võ, Quang Nhơn & Nguyễn, Hùng Vĩ. 1990. *Văn học dân gian Việt Nam (Vietnamese folk literature)*. Hanoi, Hanoi General University bookshelf.

37. Lê, Danh Khiêm. 2005. "Văn hóa Quan họ: tổng hòa của các loại hình văn hóa truyền thống làng xã Bắc Ninh(Quan họ culture: synthesis of folk culture forms in the villages of Bắc Ninh province)." In *Về văn học nghệ thuật dân gian Bắc Ninh* (On folk culture and arts in Bắc Ninh) (vol.1). ed. the Bắc Ninh Provincial Culture and Art Association, pp. 240-pp.281. Hanoi.

38. Lê, Danh Khiêm ed. 2006. *Không gian văn hóa Quan họ* (Cultural space of Quan họ singing). Bắc Ninh: Center of Culture and Information.

39. Lê, Danh Khiêm. 2006. "Bảo tồn và phát triển Quan họ: những chặng đường đã qua (Preservation and Development of Quan họ - past journeys)", *Cultural Heritage Studies 3*.

40. Lê, Danh Khiêm ed. 2001. *Dân ca Quan họ, lời ca và bình giải* (Quan họ folk songs: lyrics and commentary). Bac Ninh Quan Ho Cultural Center Publishing), Bắc Ninh.

41. Lê, Hồng Dương ed, 1982 . *Địa chí Hà Bắc* (Local history of Hà Bắc). Bắc Ninh: Hà Bắc Provincial Library.

42. Lê, Ngọc Chân. 2002. *Quan ho singing in North Vietnam: A yearning for resolution*. Ph.D. Dissertations. Berkeley, CA.: University of California at Berkeley.USA.

43. Lê, Quý Đôn group. 1957. *Lược thảo lịch sử văn học Việt Nam* (Introduction to the History of Vietnamese Literature) (vol. 1). Hanoi: Construction Publisher.

44. Lê, Sĩ Giáo. 1973. *Sơ bộ khảo sát hội Lim trước Cách mạng tháng Tám 1945*. BA thesis. Hanoi.

45. Lê, Trung Vũ, Lê, Hồng Lý. 2005. *Lễ hội Việt Nam* (Festivals of Vietnam). Hanoi: Culture and Information Publisher.

46. Lê, Văn Hảo. 1962. "Nguồn gốc và tiến hóa của hát Quan họ (Origin and the evolution of Quan họ)." *University Gazetteer of Huế University* 28.

47. Lê, Văn Hảo. 1963. "Vài nét về truyền thống của hát Quan họ trong truyền thống văn hóa dân gian (A brief introduction to folk song performance in traditional folklore)". *University Gazetteer of Huế University* 29.

48. Lê, Văn Kỳ. 1988. "Thử tìm hiểu một vài đặc điểm về hội lễ ở Hà Bắc (Let's try to explore some characteristics of the Hà Bắc festival)." In *Hội xứ Bắc* (the Kinh Bắc region's festival). Vol.1, Bắc Ninh: the Hà Bắc Department of Culture and Information.

49. Lê, Yên. 1974. *Qua việc phân tích mấy bài Quan họ* (From the analysis of some Quan họ folk songs)." *Arts Study Review* 2.

50. Lương, Công Lý; Nguyễn, Thị Vân & Dương, Thị Hóa. 2017. *Triết lý nhân sinh trong Văn hóa Quan họ* (Life philosophy in Quan họ culture). Hanoi: Ethnic Culture Publisher.

51. Lưu, Hữu Phước; Nguyễn, Viêm; Tú, Ngọc & Nguyễn, Văn Phú. 1962. *Dân ca Quan họ* (Folk song of Quan họ Bắc Ninh). Hanoi: the Art Department of the Ministry of Culture Publishing.

52. Lưu, Khâm; Nguyễn, Viêm & Nguyễn, Đình Tấn. 1956. *Tìm hiểu Quan họ* (A Study on Quan họ Bắc Ninh). Hanoi: People's Army Publisher.

53. Lưu, Khâm. 1959. *Tìm hiểu nguồn gốc và sinh hoạt của Quan họ.* (A study on origin and performance of Quan họ Bắc Ninh).

54. Mạnh Quỳnh. 1940. "Hội Lim (Lim festival)". *Trung Bắc tân văn chủ nhật* (Sunday New Literature of the North and the Central Vietnam) No. 1.

55. Many authors. 1972. *Lịch sử văn học Việt Nam* (A history of Vietnamese Literature). Hanoi: Education. Reprinted in 1976.

56. Many authors. 1994. *Dân ca người Việt* (Folk songs of the Vietnamese). Hanoi: Music Publisher.

57. Many authors. 1988. *Hội xứ Bắc* (the Kinh Bắc region's festival), vol. 1. Conference proceedings. Bắc Ninh: Hà Bắc: Department of Culture and Information.

58. Meeker, Lauren. 2007. *Musical transmissions folk music, mediation and modernity in Northern Vietnam*. Ph.D. Dissertation. NY.: University of Columbia Press, USA.

59. Ngô, Đức Thịnh. 2007. "Quan họ: một hiện tượng xã hội tổng thể (Quan họ: a general social phenomenon)." *Journal of Cultural Heritage Studies* 3.

60. Ngô, Văn Trụ (ed.). 2002. *Lễ hội Bắc Giang* (Bắc Giang's festivals). Bắc Giang city: Bắc Giang Department of Culture and Information.

61. Nguyễn, Duy Kiện. 1940. "Hội Lim (Lim festival)" *Việt Báo* No 1059.

62. Nguyễn, Đắc Toàn. 2018. *Nghệ nhân Quan họ trong đời sống văn hóa đương đại* (Quan họ artisans in the contemporary cultural life). Ph.D. Dissertation. Hanoi: National Institute of Culture and Art.

63. Nguyễn, Đình Bưu. 1985/1986. "Bàn thêm về ca Quan họ (Further discussion on Quan họ)." *Journal of National Culture* 3 (1985) & 4 (1986).

64. Nguyễn, Đình Bưu. 1986. "Ý nghĩa của từ "Quan họ" (Meanings of the term 'Quan họ')". *Kinh Bắc Journal* 6.

65. Nguyễn, Đình Bưu. 1989. "Ca nhạc và Quan họ (Music and Quan họ)." *Theater* 10.

66. Nguyễn, Đình Phúc. 1956. "Tính chất đúng đắn, tập thể của hát Quan họ (The accuracy and collectiveness of Quan họ songs performance)." *Văn nghệ* (Culture and arts) 114.

67. Nguyễn, Đình Phúc. 1956. "Các giọng Quan họ (Voice types of Quan họ)." *Văn nghệ* (Culture and arts) 116.

68. Nguyễn, Đình Phúc. 1956. "Thêm một vài ý kiến về các giọng Quan họ (Some additional ideas on Quan họ voice types)." Music Journal 10 & 11.

69. Nguyễn, Đình Phúc. 1961. "Để góp phần vào vấn đề nghiên cứu Quan họ (A contribution to the study of Quan họ)." *Văn hóa* (Culture) 11.

70. Nguyễn, Đình Tấn. 1956. "Mấy ý kiến trao đổi về nâng cao và phát triển Quan họ (Some ideas on strengthening and developing Quan họ)." *Music Journal* 10.

71. Nguyễn, Khắc Bảo. 2005."Nguyễn Du viết về Quan họ (Nguyễn Du's writing on Quan họ). In *Về văn học nghệ thuật dân gian Bắc Ninh* (On folk culture and arts in Bắc Ninh) (vol.1). ed. the Bắc Ninh Provincial Culture and Art Association, Hanoi.

72. Nguyễn, Phương Châm. 1994. "Về hiện tượng Dân ca Quan họ Hà Bắc (About the "phenomenon" of Hà Bắc's Quan họ folk songs)." *Folklore Journal* 4.pp 16-18.

73. Nguyễn, Thụy Loan. 2006. *Dân ca Quan họ: một di sản độc đáo* (Quan họ Bắc Ninh folk singing: a unique heritage). Hanoi: Institute of Culture and Information & Bắc Ninh Department of Culture and Information.

74. Nguyễn, Thượng Luyến. 2003 "Đi tìm nguồn gốc Dân ca Quan họ (Discovering the origin of Quan họ folk songs)", *The Kinh Bắc People* 2.pp 68-70.

75. Nguyễn, Tiến Chiêu. 1959. "Tìm hiểu nguồn gốc quan họ Bắc Ninh (A Study on the origin of Quan họ Bắc Ninh.)" *Encyclopaedic* No. 65, Sài Gòn.

76. Nguyễn, Trọng Ánh. 1984. *Những bước đầu tìm hiểu về một số vấn đề thuộc giai điệu của âm nhạc Quan họ* (Preliminary steps in studying Quan họ's musical melody). BA. Thesis. Hanoi.

77. Nguyễn, Trọng Ánh. 1996. *Điệu thức trong âm nhạc Quan họ* (Musical modality in Quan họ), MA thesis in Musicology. Hanoi.

78. Nguyễn, Trọng Ánh. 2000. *Âm nhạc Quan họ* (Music of Quan họ). Hanoi: the Hanoi Conservatory of Music.

79. Nguyễn, Trọng Ánh. 2006. *Những giá trị âm nhạc trong hát Quan họ* (Music values in Quan họ singing). Hanoi: the Hanoi Conservatory of Music.

80. Nguyễn, Văn Huyên.1934. *Hát đối đáp nam nữ thanh niên* (Interactive singing among young people). Ph.D. Dissertation, France.

81. Nguyễn, Viêm. 1974. "*Bàn về giá trị một bài hát* (On the value of songs)". *Art Study Review* 4.

82. Phạm, Duy 1972. *Đặc khảo về dân nhạc ở Việt Nam* (Special survey on folk music in Vietnam), Modern Publisher, Saigon.

83. Phạm. Phúc Minh. 1960. *Tìm hiểu ca nhạc dân gian Việt Nam* (A Study on Vietnamese folk songs). Hanoi. Music Publisher.

84. Phạm, Phúc Minh. 1994. *Tìm hiểu dân ca Việt Nam* (Understanding on Vietnamese folk songs). Hanoi.Music Publisher.

85. Phạm, Thị Thủy Chung. 2005. "Sông Tiêu Tương với văn hóa Kinh Bắc (The Tiêu Tương River and the Kinh Bắc culture)". *The Folklore Bulletin*, pp.19-33. Hanoi: Social Sciences.

86. Phạm, Trọng Toàn. 2007. *Tương đồng và khác biệt giữa hát xoan, hát ghẹo Phú Thọ và Quan họ Bắc Ninh* (Similarities and differences among *hát xoan* and *hát ghẹo* in Phú Thọ and *Quan họ* in Bắc Ninh). Hanoi, Ph.D. Dissertation Vietnam Institute of Culture and Arts.

87. Phạm, Xuân Lộc. 1920. *Bắc Ninh tỉnh khảo dị* (北寧省考異, Strange Stories of Bắc Ninh Province). trans. Trần Văn Giáp. Bắc Ninh: Department of Culture.

88. Quang, Lộc. 1978. "Thử tìm hiểu nguồn gốc Dân ca Quan họ (Let's study the origin of Quan họ)". *Hà Bắc Journal* 9.

89. Thạch, Phương & Lê, Trung Vũ (ed.). 1995. *60 lễ hội truyền thống Việt Nam* (Vietnam's 60 traditional festivals). Hanoi: Science Society Publisher.

90. Thanh, Lãng. 1954. *Văn học khởi thảo - văn chương bình dân* (Introduction to popular literature). Hanoi (Phong trào văn hóa xuất bản) publishing culture movement.

91. The Ministry of Culture, Sport, and Tourism. 2005. *Bắc Ninh vùng Văn hóa Quan họ.* (Bắc Ninh Quan họ Cultural Area).

92. The National History Bureau of the Nguyễn Dynasty. 1971. *Đại Nam nhất thống chí* (大南一統志, Đại Nam Comprehensive Encyclopaedia), trans. Phạm Trọng Điềm, ed. Đào Duy Anh. Hanoi: Social Science Publisher.

93. Tô, Ngọc Thanh & Hồng, Thao. 1986. *Tìm hiểu âm nhạc dân tộc cổ truyền* (An study on traditional music) (Vol.1). Hanoi: Culture.

94. Tô, Nguyễn & Trịnh, Nguyễn. 1981. *Kinh Bắc - Hà Bắc*, Culture Publisher, pp: 92-120.

95. Toan Ánh. 1943."Hát Quan họ, một lối chơi xuân thú vị ở vùng Bắc Ninh (Quan họ's performance: Bắc Ninh's New Year's entertainment)" In *Phong lưu đồng ruộng* (*Joys on the fields*), pp. 7-14. Hanoi .Culture Publisher.

96. Toan Ánh. 1969. *Cầm ca Việt Nam* (Vietnamese Music and Songs). Saigon.

97. Toan Ánh. 1974. *Nếp cũ: hội hè đình đám* (Old customs: festivals). Saigon, vol 1. Nam Chi tùng thư publishing, vol 2 published author

98. Toan Ánh. 1974. "Hội Lim với tục hát Quan họ (Lim Festival and Quan họ folk song performances)." *Oriental Monthly Review* 31 & 32.

99. Toan Ánh. 1992. *Phong lưu đồng ruộng* (Joys on the fields). Second edition. Hanoi: Culture Publisher.

100. Tử Phác. 1956. "Góp ý kiến về Quan họ (A Contributing Idea to Quan họ)". Music Journal Vol. 10.

101. Tô, Ngọc Thanh. 1986. *Tìm hiểu âm nhạc dân tộc cổ truyền* (An investigation into traditional music) (Vol.1). Hà Nội: Culture Publisher, pp. 74-181.

102. Trần, Chính. 2000. *Nghệ nhân Quan họ làng Viêm Xá (*Quan họ artisans of of Viêm Xá village). Hanoi: Science Society Publisher.

103. Trần, Linh Quý & Hồng Thao. 1997. *Tìm hiểu dân ca Quan họ* (A study on Quan họ). Hanoi.Ethnic Culture Publisher.

104. Trần, Linh Quý. 2005. "Dân ca Quan họ (Quan họ folk songs)." *Bắc Giang Folklore,* Bắc Giang. Bắc Giang Folklore Association.

105. Trần, Linh Quý. 2006. "Không gian văn hóa Quan họ và các làng Quan họ phía Bắc sông Cầu (Quan họ cultural space and Quan họ villages in the north of the Cầu River)." *Bắc Giang Folklore*, pp. 230-52. Bắc Giang: Bắc Giang Folklore Association.

106. Trần, Linh Quý. 2012. *Trên đường tìm về Quan họ* (On the way back to Quan họ). Hanoi.Culture and Information Publisher.

107. Trần, Minh Chính. 2016. *Sinh hoạt Văn hóa Quan họ làng (qua trường hợp làng Quan họ Viêm Xá)* (Cultural activities in Quan họ villages (Taking Viêm Xá Village as an example). Ph.D. Dissertation. Hanoi. Hồ Chí Minh Institute of National Politics. Printed in 2017. Hanoi: Writers Association.

108. Lê, Văn Kỳ. 1988. "Thử tìm hiểu một vài đặc điểm về hội lễ ở Hà Bắc (Let's try to explore some characteristics of the Hà Bắc festival)". *Hội xứ Bắc* (the Kinh Bắc region's festival), Bắc Ninh: Hà Bắc Culture and Information Department.

109. Trần, Văn Khê. 1958. "Quan họ Folk Song Performance." *Bách Khoa* Journal No.43.

110. Trần, Văn Khê. 1976. "*Sau khi thăm quê hương Quan họ - Vài nhận xét về quá trình nghiên cứu Dân ca Quan họ* (After visiting Quan họ homeland: some comments about the research process of Quan họ folk songs)." *Social Sciences* Journal 1.

111. Tú, Ngọc. 1956. *Các giọng trong Quan họ* (Voice types in Quan họ). Hanoi.

112. Tú, Ngọc. 1994. *Dân ca người Việt* (Vietnamese folk songs). Hanoi: Music Publisher.

113. Vietnam Institute of Cultural and Information & the Bắc Ninh Department of Cultural and Information. 2006. *Không gian Văn hóa Quan họ bảo tồn và phát huy* (The Quan họ Cultural Space: preservation and improvement). Hanoi.

114. Vũ, Bằng 1931. "Hội Lim (Lim Festival)", *An Nam tạp chí* (An Nam Journal).

115. Vũ, Ngọc Phan. 1971. *Tục ngữ ca dao dân ca Việt Nam* (Proverbs and folk songs of Vietnam) Seventh edition. Hanoi. Social Science Publisher.

RESEARCH GONG CULTURE OF CENTRAL HIGHLANDS: ACHIEVEMENTS AND PROBLEMS

1. Introduction

In November 2005, UNESCO included the Central Highlands Gong Culture Cultural Space of Vietnam in the list of Masterpieces of oral transmission and intangible heritage of humanity. In 2008, the UNESCO Convention on the Protection of the Intangible Cultural Heritage of 2003, together with the 89 Masterpieces of oral transmission and intangible heritage of mankind, which were recognized by UNESCO from 2001, 2003, 2005, The Central Highlands Gong Cultural Space was transferred to UNESCO's List of Representative Intangible Cultural Heritage of Humanity. In order to get UNESCO's recognition in 2005, the great merits of the ethnic minorities in the Central Highlands are very important, because they are the defenders of this intangible cultural heritage from their lifetime. At the same time, the effort of the gong culture researchers of the generations is also very valuable. Initially, we recognized the achievements of the authors through the works on the Central Highlands gong culture and raised the issues raised in this study.

2. Review some key works and national/international workshops in Vietnam

Gongs and cultural activities of gongs have been around for a long time, but researchers and collectors have not paid much attention. Before 1975, a number of overseas scientists were interested in gong culture in the Central Highlands of Vietnam such as Douriboure P. in the work *Les sauvages Ba-Hnars* (The wild Bahnars) (Paris, 1853), Guerlach R. in the article "Living with the barbarians in the Eastern Cochinchina: the Bahnar, the R'ngao, and the S'đăng" (1894), Guillemine P. in *The custom of stabbing buffaloes of the Bahnar* (BAVH, 1942), and *The Bahnar tribe in Kontum* (BEFEO, 1952), Jouln B.Y (*Cái chết và nấm mồ - Tục bỏ mả*, Paris,1949); Dournes J. in *La musique chex les Jorai* (Music of the Jo'rai, 1965) and *La culture Jorai* (The culture of the

Jo'rai, Paris,1972), Condominas G. in *Nous avons mangé la forêt* (We are eating the forest, Paris, 1982), etc. Initially, we would like not to mention these works but to the works in Vietnam of Vietnamese scholars.

The earliest of the works of Vietnamese scholars on the Central Highlands gong culture is the work of *Mọi Kontum* (The Bana ethnic group in Kontum) by Nguyễn Kinh Chi and Nguyễn Đổng Chi (1937). Nguyễn Kinh Chi and Nguyễn Đổng Chi wrote about Xoan dance: "Men and women both dance and each side has its own dance. A man's dance consists of several movements: taking a step forward, leaning forward, swinging twice, then leaning backwards and swinging away twice more. Just like that they stepped forward and continued to dance. A woman's dance is similar, but the difference is that when she takes one step, she turns her head to the left while swinging and hitting twice, then taking another step, she turns her head to the right shrugging and hitting away" (see Nguyễn Kinh Chi & Nguyễn Đổng Chi 1937, p. 126-7). They continue writing that:

"*Gong* - a set of three gongs, one large, one medium, and one small.

Đồng la (copper-made flat gong) - is like a gong but without a knob at the center. A set of *đồng la* includes seven or eight pieces. The first one is the biggest and then the smaller ones. Gong and đồng la must be purchased from Annam (Vietnam). After buying, they have to adjust the sound before playing.

The drum, the three gongs, the eight flat gongs all come together into a set of music. When playing gongs, there will be twelve people each holding one instrument each; first eight people hold the flat gongs, followed by three people holding the gongs and finally one person holding the drum. When playing, everyone has to beat the same rhythm. This set of music is usually only played during new rice cereal eating ceremony and peace ceremony funeral and graveyard-repudiation ritual" (see Nguyễn Kinh Chi & Nguyễn Đổng Chi 1937, p. 127).

After 1975, the study of gongs was well organized and managed by research and development agencies. In 1981, the Department of Culture and Information of Gia Lai-Kon Tum Province organized a scientific seminar on traditional culture, including gongs and published the book *Preserving and promoting the traditional cultural capital of the ethnic minorities* (Department of Culture and Information of Gia Lai-Kontum Province, 1981). In addition to the speeches of the provincial leaders, the remarkable speeches of the conference were the writings of the authors Rơmah Deh, Rơchơm Yơn about four days of a festival in the Central Highlands and about gongs of the ethnic of Jo'rai (J'rai, or Gia-rai). These are the presentations of ethnic minority intellectuals on their cultural heritage.

In 1985, the Institute of Music Research[77] and the Department of Culture and Information of Gia Lai-Kon Tum Province[78] organized the first scientific conference on Central Highlands gongs with 25 writers Among them, there are many scholars working on gongs of the Central Highlands ethnic groups such as Rơmah Deh, A Thiêng Xương, Rơchom Yơn, etc., then published the book *Art of gongs* by the Department of Culture and Information of Gia Lai-Kon Tum Province in 1985. Since then, the collection of research on gongs has been conducted by a number of specialized researchers.

In 1988, the Gia Lai-Kontum Department of Culture and Information published *The Bâhnar's Folklore* work by Tô Ngọc Thanh (editors), Đặng Nghiêm Vạn, Phạm Hùng Thoan, and Vũ Thị Hoa[79]. This work has mentioned aspects of festivals, dance, music and Hơ Amon art of the Bahna people in Gia Lai-Kon Tum province (now two

---

[77] This organization is now named the Vietnam National Institute of Culture and Arts.

[78] The province is now divided into two provinces of Gia Lai and Kon Tum.

[79] According to Prof. Tô Ngọc Thanh "[…] also in 1981, the work *The Bâhnar Folklore* was completed but it was not published until 1988 - Report at the Conference of the Central Highlands Gongs Cultural Space: the situation and the solutions measures to preserve and promote its values' (Tô Ngọc Thanh 2007, p. 9).

provinces: Gia Lai, and Kon Tum); however, it is mainly confined to An Khê district, Gia Lai province. It can be said that the project is the first treatise on the culture of the Central Highlands gongs through the case study of the Bahna ethnic group. In 1993, according to author Vũ Hồng Thịnh, *The 3rd Gong Scientific Conference and Gong Public Festival* was held in Buôn Ma Thuột, Dak Lak Province[80].

In 1993, Đào Huy Quyền published Chapter III entitled "Metal-based musical instruments" in the book: *The Ethnic Musical Instruments in Gia Lai* (see Đào Huy Quyền 1993, pp. 103-41) of mentioned 9 kinds of gongs of ethnic minorities living in Gia Lai province. This is the first contribution of the author Đào Huy Quyền to the study of the Central Highlands gongs, approaching from ethnographic music.

In 1995, Prof. Tô Ngọc Thanh published the book *Introduction on Musical Instruments of some Vietnam's Ethnic Minorities* (Tô Ngọc Thanh 1995), in which he introduced gongs as an instrument from page 116 to page 129.

In 1995, two authors Vũ Hồng Thịnh (chief writer) and Bùi Lẫm announced the work *Gongs art of the ethnic S'tiêng in Sông Bé province*, which is a provincial scientific research project "Monograph of the gongs art of the S'tiêng ethnic group in Sông Bé province" were accepted in 1993. Approaching from ethnographic music, the project contributes to the study of gong music in particular and the Gong culture of the S'tiêng people in general (Vũ Hồng Thịnh & Bùi Lẫm 1995).

In 1998, Đào Huy Quyền announced the works *Music Instruments of the Ethnic Jo'rai and Bahnar*. This is a continuation of the book that Đào Huy Quyền published in 1993 by Education Publishing House, so the author's approach is still ethnographic music.

In 2004, the Institute of Culture and Information organized an international scientific conference entitled "The cultural value of copper

---

[80] I have not had access to the proceedings of this conference.

percussion instruments of Vietnam and Southeast Asia". For the first time, Vietnam organized an international scientific conference on copper percussion instruments of Vietnam and Southeast Asia. In addition to national scientists, this conference also attracts the participation of foreign scientists such as ethnographic music experts such as Prof. Tokumaru Yosihiko (Japan), Prof. Sam Ang Sam (Cambodia), Prof. Jose Buenconsejo (Philippines), etc. It must be affirmed that this conference has had many effects for Vietnam to make a national profile of the Central Highlands' Gongs Cultural Space submitted to UNESCO for consideration and honoring (Institute of Culture and Information 2006).

In 2005, Phùng Đăng Quang announced the work of *Musical Instruments of the ethnic S'tiêng*. In chapter III (Phùng Đăng Quang 2005, p. 193-231), the author presented the gongs of the S'tiêng, and in chapter IV (p. 239-75), the author referred to the scale, the tones of S'tiêng instruments.

In 2006, the Institute of Culture and Information (now the National Institute of Culture and Arts of Vietnam) published the book *Masterpieces of oral transmission and intangible heritage of humanity: the Central Highlands Gong Culture Space*. This is a national record compiled by Prof. Tô Ngọc Thanh and Prof. Nguyễn Chí Bền, after being commented and approved by the competent authorities submitted to UNESCO for this organization to honor the Central Highlands Gong Culture Space as the Masterpiece of oral transmission and intangible heritage of humanity in November 2005. In addition to the Vietnamese version, there are many English and French versions of Vietnamese translators (Institute of Culture and Information 2006, p. 91-219).

In 2007, the People's Committee of Dak Lak province organized a national scientific conference on "Central Highlands cultural space and its state of conservation and promotion", with 27 presentations and scientific reports. Scientists such as Prof. Trần Văn Khê, Prof. Dr. Ngô Đức Thịnh, Dr. Buôn Krông Tuyết Nhung, Dr. Y Ghi Niê and a number of authors presented many issues from the status quo to the conservation solutions of Cultural Space of Gongs in the Central Highlands.

In 2009, the Ministry of Culture, Sports and Tourism coordinated with the People's Committee of Gia Lai Province to organize an international scientific conference on "Changing socio-economic life and conservation of gong culture in Vietnam and Southeast Asia". With the participation of 55 domestic and 13 foreign scientists, the conference was divided into 4 sub-committees. It can be said that, in the history of cultural studies of gongs culture of the Central Highlands of Vietnam and Southeast Asia, this is the first time that there has been a large gathering of scientists from the fields of ethnography, history, and anthropology, interested in researching gongs culture.

In 2010, the National Institute of Culture and Arts of Vietnam published a scientific theme of the Gongs culture of the Central Highlands by Master Đào Huy Quyền. The author divides the book into two parts: the Gong culture of the ethnic groups in the North Central Highlands and the Gong culture of the ethnic groups in the South Central Highlands. The author's approach is still the same ethnographic music approach as previous works such as *Traditional instruments in Gia Lai*, *The musical instruments of the ethnic Jo'rai and Bahnar* although they have focused on approaching the gong culture of local ethnic groups.

In 2017, the National Institute of Culture and Arts of Vietnam has selected 29 scientific works by authors who specialize in studying the Central Highlands gong culture and printed in the collection entitled *Cultural Heritage of Central Highlands Gongs*". The book is 510 pages thick and 16x24cm in size with three parts (Part 1: Context of the Central Highlands Gong Culture Area; Part 2: Culture of the Central Highlands gongs: the representative intangible cultural heritage of humanity; and Part 3: Making Central Highlands gongs echo to tomorrow). Among them, there are 12 works on gongs culture of each ethnic group, there are also works presenting the overall cultural space of the Central Highlands gongs as well as some basic artistic features and artisans of the Central Highlands gongs. It can be said that this is an intellectual synthesis of many scientists about the cultural space of the Central Highlands gongs, a representative intangible cultural heritage of humanity.

In addition to the works directly studying the culture of the Central Highlands gongs above, there are also studies on the Central Highlands provinces that refer to the Central Highlands' gong culture such as *Geographical Record of Gia Lai province* by Vũ Ngọc Bình, Nguyễn Chí Bền, Đào Huy Quyền, and Nguyễn Minh San; *Geographical Record of Đắc Nông province* by many writers; *Kon Tum: the land and the people* by many writers; or books on ethnic folklore such as *Folklore of the M'Nông* by Ngô Đức Thịnh (2nd edition, 1995), *Folklore of the Ê-đê* by Ngô Đức Thịnh and others (1995), etc.

3. Achievements of the study of the Central Highlands gong culture

If we count from the work of *Mọi Kontum* (The Bana ethnic group in Kontum) by Nguyễn Kinh Chi and Nguyễn Đổng Chi launched readers in 1937 by Mộng Thương thư trai (Huế), the process of studying gong culture of the Central Highlands has gone through more than 80 years. So, what are the achievements of the Central Highlands gong cultural research in recent years?

First of all, it can be seen that the pre-1945 research works of generations of researchers such as Nguyễn Kinh Chi (1899-1986), Nguyễn Đổng Chi (1915-1984) as well as the works of scholars of recent periods such as Đặng Nghiêm Vạn (1930-2016), Phạm Đức Dương (1930-2013), Trần Văn Khê (1921-2015), Nguyễn Từ Chi (1925-1995), Tô Vũ (1923-2014), Tô Ngọc Thanh, Nguyễn Chí Bền, Lê Thị Hoài Phương, Nguyễn Thụy Loan, Từ Thị Loan, Nguyễn Thị Mỹ Liêm, Đào Huy Quyền, Bùi Trọng Hiền, drew a complete picture of the Central Highlands gong culture. Remarkably, inheriting previous works of overseas researchers, Prof. Tô Ngọc Thanh and Prof. Nguyễn Chí Bền has completed a national scientific dossier submitted to UNESCO for this organization to honor the Central Highlands Gong Cultural Space as the Masterpiece of Oral Transmission and Intangible

Heritage of Humanity[81] along with 89 relics of other countries after 3 times of review: 2001, 2003 and 2005.

There are many high-quality works on the gong culture of 11 indigenous ethnic groups of both Austroasiatic and Austronesian linguistics families, such as Lều Kim Thanh's writing about the gongs of the Bahnar, Linh Nga Niê Kdam's about the Ê-đê, the late Rơmah Del's about the Jo'rai, the late Phạm Cao Đạt's about the M'nam group of the S'đăng people, Đào Huy Quyền's about the ethnic groups of Ch'ru, K'ho, Brâu, etc.

On the other hand, the works are approached from the perspective of ethnic music major and under the careful fieldwork perspective also have significant contributions. Three works of the late master Đào Huy Quyền, respectively, National musical instruments in Gia Lai (1993), Jo'rai and Bahnar ethnic musical instruments (1998) and Gong culture of the Central Highlands ethnic groups (2010), have contributed to the research process of cultural gongs in the Central Highlands thanks to his close attachment to the research area. Also in this approach, Bùi Trọng Hiền's work of researching and presenting the basic art features of the Central Highlands gongs is also the result of a fieldwork process when he joined the fieldwork group working for the national profile on Cultural Space of Gongs in Central Highlands led by Phạm Hùng Thoan in 2004.

Finally, there are a number of studies on the current status of the representative intangible cultural heritage of humanity, making recommendations to protect and promote the value of the Central Highlands Gong Culture Space. It is the works of domestic and foreign scientists who participated in the international scientific conference "The change of economic, social life and conservation of gong culture in Vietnam and Southeast Asia" co-organized by the Ministry of Culture, Sports and Tourism and the People's Committee of Gia Lai

---

[81] After 2008, this title changed into the Representative Intangible Cultural Heritage of Humanity.

Province in November 2009 which have contributed greatly to this issue. The scientific conference attracted important papers from domestic scholars such as Nguyễn Thụy Loan, Từ Thị Loan, Nguyễn Thị Mỹ Liêm and international scholars such as Trần Quang Hải (France), José G. Buenconsejo (the Philippines), Oscar Salemink (the Netherlands), Tokumaru Yosihiko, Oshio Satomi, Yumiko Nanaumi (Japan), etc.

4. Issues raised in the study of the Central Highlands gong culture

4.1. Considering the issues raised in the study of the Central Highlands gong culture, it is reasonable to start with the assessment of UNESCO: "The Central Highlands gong cultural space spreads in the area of five Central Highlands provinces: Kontum, Gia Lai, Đắc Lắc, Đắc Nông, Lâm Đồng and some surrounding areas of Vietnam. The owners of the Central Highlands gong cultural space are the residents of the ethnic minorities of the Austroasiatic and Austronesian linguistic families. The people here live mainly on agriculture and have developed traditional occupations, decorative arts, and housing architecture in their own way. Their beliefs are mainly forms of animism. This belief is closely linked to the life cycle of people and the crop cycle of traditional agricultural production. It has formed a mystical world in which the intervention of gongs is a language of communication between man and god, man and the supernatural. Behind each gong is hidden a god (male or female). The older the gong is, the more power the god has. Each family has at least one gong set, which represents the status, power, wealth, and prestige of that family. While there are many copper instruments used in various rituals, the gong itself is also present in all the community rituals and is the most important means of performing.

The Central Highlands gong culture is thought to originate from the ancient Đông Sơn (Dongsonian) civilization, which is known as a famous bronze drum culture in Southeast Asia. The Central Highlands gong is distinguished in its playing style. Each artisan carries a gong or flat gong with a radius of 25 to 80 cm. Groups of men or women are formed from 3 to 12 gongs and gongs depending on each village and each ethnic group. The arrangement and different melodies are coordinated to suit the context of each ceremony, such as buffalo stabbing ceremony, funeral rites or new rice/crop seasons, etc. Gongs in the Central Highlands are not made locally; instead, they are purchased from neighboring provinces in the plains or some neighboring countries and are tuned for use.

The change in farming methods of traditional agricultural production has greatly influenced traditional activities of ethnic minority communities. As a matter of fact, the context of cultural activities of the original gong has also changed. The transfer of customs, knowledge and know-how related to gongs and gong culture to the next generation was interrupted by decades of war. Now, that challenge is exacerbated by the death of elderly artisans and the charm and influence of foreign cultural currents on young people. Having lost their sacred meaning, gongs have been sold for recycling or traded for other goods"[82].

With such value of the Central Highlands Gong Culture Space, from the achievements of the Central Highlands' gong cultural research over the past 80 years, I think and share with Professor Tô Ngọc Thanh's opinion in his keynote speech at the Conference :*The Central Highlands Gong Culture and The Status Of Conservation And Promotion Solutions* organized by the People's Committee of Dak Lak province in November 2007. It is necessary to continue to thoroughly study the culture and art of gongs of all ethnic groups. Because, gongs in each ethnic culture have different roles, functions, personalities, and characteristics. Previously, we knew about gongs in some typical ethnic groups such as Ê-đê, Jo'rai, Bahnar, M'nông, etc. As for the gongs of other ethnic groups, either we do not know fully or almost nothing. It is essential that monographs about gong art and culture of each ethnic

[82] Translation of the Organizing Committee for UNESCO's Certificate of the Year 2006 in Pleiku, Gia Lai Province.

group"[83]. That orientation or the expectation of a leading expert on the Central Highlands gongs has gradually been implemented in the study of the Central Highlands Gong Culture Space, a representative intangible cultural heritage of humanity.

4.2. From the reassessment of the research process, to see the achievements of the Central Highlands gong culture and compare with the human value of the representative intangible cultural heritage of humanity (the Central Highlands Gong Culture Space), we will find some problems.

Firstly, it is necessary to have works on the Central Highlands gong culture studied from the holistic approach. The achievements of the past research process lively present the flip side of the Western approach, which is researched from the perspective of ethnographic music, ethnic culture but lacking the overall approach based on according to the valuable criteria of the Representative Intangible Cultural Heritage of Humanity given by UNESCO. Moreover, an approach from a cultural perspective to a representative intangible cultural heritage of humanity is necessary because it is possible to decode the symbols of Xoan dances and musical tones, as well as the philosophy of the creative subject of the Central Highlands gong culture.

Secondly, it is the protection and promotion of the value of the Central Highlands Gong Culture Space as committed by the Vietnamese Government 14 years ago to submit to UNESCO to honor this heritage. The state, the provinces in the Central Highlands, the community of local ethnic minorities have done too much work. However, when observing local reality, there are still many issues of concern if not weaknesses that need to be overcome. In particular, the role of the community as a UNESCO ideology is reflected in the 2003 and 2005 conventions that Vietnam has signed is very significant. The relationship between managers, researchers, and communities in the Central Highlands is somewhat different from Vietnam's intangible

---

[83] Proceedings of the conference, p. 10.

cultural heritages, which has been included in UNESCO's List of Intangible Cultural Heritage by mankind under the 2003 Convention of UNESCO.

Thirdly, it is the fact that scientific research originates from the need to protect and promote the value of the representative intangible cultural heritage of mankind: The cultural space of the Central Highlands Gongs in industrial revolution 4.0. Many issues are raised that need to be studied. Since 1997, the Ministry of Culture and Information, now the Ministry of Culture, Sports and Tourism, has built a data bank on the cultural heritage of 54 ethnic groups in Vietnam at the National Institute of Culture and Arts. Projects on collecting and preserving and promoting intangible cultural heritages, including the Central Highlands gong culture, have been implemented. Before making the national record of the Central Highlands Gong Culture Space, until later, the data of the Central Highlands Gong Culture includes 4 types of products such as text, photos, audio tapes and video tapes that have been collected and stored at the data bank of the Ministry of Culture, Sports and Tourism at the current National Institute of Culture and Arts of Vietnam. So, we can think of e-books 3D cultural space of the Central Highlands gongs to promote heritage and serve tourism development?

5. Conclusion

The Central Highlands gong cultural space is a cultural entity, a subject of research by many domestic and foreign scientific researchers. In accessing the works of domestic researchers, national and international scientific conferences held in the country, we have gained many achievements but also outlined some issues mentioned in this article.

Reference

1. Dak Lak Rubber Company, Center for Education and Training Technology Development (Office III: Central Highlands). 2007. *Không gian văn hóa cồng chiêng Tây Nguyên: thực trạng và giải pháp bảo tồn, phát huy* (The Central Highlands Gong Culture Space: conservation and promotion solutions). Buôn Ma Thuột.

2. Đào, Huy Quyền. 1993. *Nhạc khí dân tộc ở Gia Lai* (Traditional instruments in Gia Lai). Hanoi. Education Publisher.

3. Đào, Huy Quyền. 1998. *Nhạc khí dân tộc Jo'rai và Bahnar* (The Musical Instruments of the ethnic Jo'rai and Bahnar). Ho Chi Minh City: Young Publisher)

4. Đào, Huy Quyền. 2010. *Văn hóa cồng chiêng các dân tộc Tây Nguyên* (Gong Culture of the Central Highlands ethnic groups). Hanoi: Information Culture Publisher.

5. Department of Culture and Information of Gia Lai – KonTum province. 1981. *Giữ gìn, phát huy vốn văn hóa truyền thống của các dân tộc* (Preserving and promoting the traditional cultural capital of the ethnic minorities), Pleiku.

6. Department of Culture and Information of Gia Lai – KonTum province. 1986. *Nghệ thuật cồng chiêng* (The art of gong), Pleiku.

7. Institute of Culture and Information. 2004. *Vùng văn hóa cồng chiêng Tây Nguyên* (The Central Highlands gong cultural zone). Hanoi: Institute of Culture and Information.

8. Many authors. 2006. *Các nhạc cụ gõ bằng đồng những giá trị văn hóa* (Copper percussion instruments: cultural values). Hanoi: Ethnic Culture Publisher.

9. Many authors. 2009. *Sự thay đổi đời sống kinh tế, xã hội và bảo tồn văn hóa cồng chiêng ở Việt Nam và khu vực Đông Nam Á* (The change of economic, social life and conservation of gong culture in Vietnam and Southeast Asia). Proceedings of International Conference, organized in November 2009 in Pleiku city. The

manuscript is kept at the Vietnam National Institute of Culture and Arts.

10. Phùng, Đăng Quang. 2005. *Nhạc khí dân tộc S'Tiêng* (The musical instruments of the ethnic S'Tiêng). Ho Chi Minh City: Trẻ.

11. Nguyễn, Kinh Chi, Nguyễn, Đồng Chi. 1937. *Mọi Kontum* (The Kontum Montagnards). Huế: Mộng Thương thư trai Publishing.

12. Tô, Ngọc Thanh (ed.). 1988. *Folklore of the Bahnar*. Pleiku: Department of Culture and Information of Gia Lai - Kontum.

13. Tô, Ngọc Thanh. 1995. *Giới thiệu một số nhạc cụ dân tộc thiểu số Việt Nam* (Introduction on musical instruments of some Vietnamese ethnic minorities). Ho Chi Minh City: Văn nghệ Publisher & National Cultural Center.

14. Tô, Ngọc Thanh & Nguyễn, Chí Bền. 2006. *Kiệt tác truyền khẩu và di sản phi vật thể của nhân loại* (Masterpieces of Oral Transmission and Intangible Heritage of Humanity). Hanoi: Thế Giới Publisher.

15. Tô, Ngọc Thanh. 2018. "Vùng văn hóa Tây Nguyên (The cultural region of Central Highlands)". In *Cơ sở văn hóa Việt Nam* (*The basic of Vietnamese culture*), ed. Trần Quốc Vượng, pp.267 - pp.282, Hanoi: Education Publisher. 20th edition.

16. Vietnam National Institute of Culture and Arts. 2017. *Di sản văn hóa cồng chiêng Tây Nguyên* (Cultural heritage of the Central Highlands gongs). Hanoi: Ethnic Culture Publisher.

17. Vũ, Hồng Thịnh, Bùi, Lẫm. 1995. *Nghệ thuật cồng chiêng của dân tộc Xtiêng tỉnh Sông Bé* (The art of gongs of the ethnic S'tiêng in Sông Bé province). Thủ Dầu Một: Department of Culture and Information of Sông Bé province.

THE MARINE CULTURE-CHANGING, AN APPROACH FROM REGIONAL CULTURE THEORY

1. Open words

Vietnam has a long coastline of more than 3,260 km, ranking 27th out of 156 coastal countries in the world. The coastal zone of Vietnam stretches over 13 latitudes in the territory of 28 provinces and cities. That includes 125 towns and districts, 12 islands, and 2,773 islands of Hoang Sa, Truong Sa archipelagos. Therefore, Vietnamese marine culture is a changing entity in space and time.

2. The Vietnamese concepts about Marine culture

According to Prof. Dr. Tran Ngoc Them, "Marine culture concept is an attractive interest. With the keyword "Marine culture" through Google system in June 2011, we got about 188 million results"[84].

2.1. The concept among international research field

In 1973, Asahitaro Nishimura-Japanese anthropologist used the term *marine culturology* that perhaps evolved from the term culturology that the American anthropologist Leslie A. White used[85].

According to Prof. Dr. Akifumi Iwabuchi: "Even English-speaking countries do not have a clear definition of marine anthropology. In Japan, the term maritime anthropology and marine anthropology are used in parallel in the marine sector. The term marine anthropology includes a wide range of fields in European countries. In the second half of the twentieth century, people have new terms that cover broader meanings.

---

[84] *Culturology, theories and applies*, Culture Literature publisher, Ho Chi Minh city, 2013, p 128.

[85] Phan Thi Yen Tuyet, *The Social - Economic life of fishermen and residents in Southern coastal area*, Ho Chi Minh National University publisher, 2014.

That includes two areas: marine anthropology and anthropology of fishing. The anthropology of fishing divides into two fields: fishing tools and residents living on fishing. The Germans also use the term ethnology; however, they use *anthropology* in the United States. Both *maritime anthropology* and *marine anthropology* terms are used in the fields. Another evidence is the Journal of Marine Anthropology that researches on marine culture-related human activities at sea if it is narrow if limits on studying human activities need to expand because the field is much broader"[86].

"Marine anthropology and marine culture are vast research fields. This discipline includes *marine anthropology, fisheries anthropology*, fishing communities, fishery villages on the coast, Islands, or research on boats and fishing tools. *Marine anthropology* also studies *the ocean, history of marine areas, marine ecology, ocean voyages.* Marine anthropology also studies fisherman's and residents' behavior, the interaction, the customs, and the relation between coastal residents and the sea (such as marriage, funeral, and death anniversary) - the human relations related to ecological, environmental issues, marine natural resources. Marine anthropology and marine culture learn about different economic modes of fishing communities. For example, there are places where people specialize in processing seafood products such as fish sauce or dried fishes.

Nevertheless, there are many places; people do not know how to storage sea products because they simply have no salt at the location. *Marine anthropology* according to North American concept, does not exclude *Marine archeology and underwater archeology.* In the North America, archeology is a subject in the anthropology field. Concern about the spiritual life of coastal residents; therefore, *the marine anthropology and marine culture* research the religion, the beliefs, the

---

[86] Phan Thi Yen Tuyet, *The Social - Economic life of fishermen and residents in Southern coastal area*, Ho Chi Minh National University publisher, 2014, p 3,4.

taboos, the folklore culture, and marine art of fishermen and coastal residents, including music, painting, and visual arts related to the sea"[87].

Meanwhile, in 2006, according to *Marine tourism*, Chinese scholars supposed that "What is marine culture? It is living with the sea, exploiting the sea include philosophy and thinking about the sea. Marine culture is a culture created by humans and accumulated in existence living marine resources. Marine culture is an essential part of human resources: materialistic and spiritual civilization. Marine culture is a cultural phenomenon formed under the interaction of the marine environment on human life. It impacts on social values, on spiritual and material productions"[88].

According to *Shanghai World Expo 2010*, "Marine culture is the culture in a specific field - the marine and related to all activities humans do with the sea. Marine culture is a culture related to the ocean. It comes from creative cultural activities that are accumulated by coastal residents through time. In other words, humanity interacts with the sea, formed and influenced by the marine customs or other tangible and intangible cultural values and symbols"[89].

Also, in 2010, E. Ju. Tereshchenko, a Russian scientist, supposed that marine culture in theoretical literature became popular when scientists started to study people living and interact with the sea. In general, it is possible to categorize the marine culture survey into levels:

- The world level (civilization) - the level associated with the general rules in the exploitation of marine space.

---

[87] Phan Thi Yen Tuyet, *The Social - Economic life of fishermen and residents in Southern coastal area*, Ho Chi Minh National University publisher, 2014, p 4.

[88] Cited from Ha Dinh Thanh et al., *Marine Culture - preserve, promote marine culture values in the coastal area in the South - Central in the industrialized, modernized period*, Social Science publisher, 2016, p 48.

[89] Cited from Ha Dinh Thanh et al., *Marine Culture - preserve, promote marine culture values in the coastal area in the South - Central in the industrialized, modernized period*, Social Science publisher, 2016, p 48.

- The regional level assumes that every marine region all has its specific cultural characteristics.

- The level of an ethnic community to study ethnicity and ethnic groups in the coastal area.

The group level is interested in marine culture's professional fields (handicraft, commercial, navy, research field).

- The individual level is determined by the characteristics of the daily routine of people living in coastal areas[90].

"Marine culture can play a key role in developing a country and be a part of the socio-cultural system located in coastal territories."

From maritime history and culture perspective - it is a specific time in which a group or a community interacts with a coastal territory. It happens in a real geographical environment.

"In marine culture, the first factor is the adaptability to the natural - geographical environment. From the civilized perspective, the coastal territories have strategic significance for a country. On the other hand, each coastal territory contains unique historical-cultural characteristics from a cultural perspective. The general marine culture characteristics, including the marine geographical determinism, impact the operation and develop effective adaptive methods to ensure living behavior harmonizes with the sea's natural conditions. From that place, specialized fields and shaped culture associated with the sea."

Also, in 2010, in Japan, Professor Akafumi Iwabuchi presents a relatively complete viewpoint from a new perspective about marine cultural terminology. He suggested:

---

[90] Vietnamese translation version by Doan Tam, Social Science Information magazine, Nr. 8, 2011, p 46.

Coastal life culture/	Sea culture
Fishermen's culture	*Ocean culture*
(Anthropology)	(History)

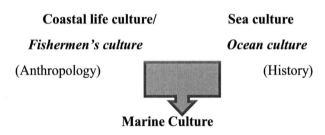

Marine Culture

(completed approach / interdisciplinary)

"From an interdisciplinary perspective, Prof. Akifumi Iwabuchi suggested that marine culturology refers to two parts: the marine culturology and ocean culture. The marine culturology use anthropological methods to study the culture of fishermen while ocean culture uses the historical approach of navigators' culture; Accordingly, marine cultural studies is to study the human adaptation to the sea, including four parts: marine anthropology, maritime history, underwater archeology, and marine art research"[91]. The concept defined by Prof. Akifumi Iwabuchi on marine culture is an advantage step on marine culture studies, an approach from a cultural perspective. He was applying the concept by Leslie Alvin White (1900 - 1975), an American scientist on the cultural studies.

2.2. The concepts used by Vietnamese scientists

The Vietnamese archaeologists used the term "Marine Culture" very early without definition. This term was mentioned in the researchers by Prof. Tran Quoc Vuong and Associate Professor Cao Xuan Pho published in 1996.

Assoc. Prof. Dr Nguyen Khac Su, the first researcher, credited to explain the connotation of marine culture term in Vietnam. In 1997, in his essay on *Prehistoric Marine Culture, a hypothetical model*, he admitted, "There no definition presented in Vietnamese documents

---

[91] Tran Thi An, *System of Marine Deities and the meaning of beliefs performance related to sea exploitation, clarify Vietnamese people's national sovereign in the North and North Central of Vietnam*, research, The Social Science Academy of Vietnam, 2016, digital version, p 25, 26.

regarding marine culture concept or prehistoric marine culture"[92]. He suggested: "Marine culture is the common denominator for collecting archaeological cultures or relic groups belonged to prehistoric inhabitants living in marine environments. In other words, this concept can be understood as the common denominator of the community's minds living in a marine environment represented externally by material and immaterial cultural traces"[93]. He identified three primary characteristics of marine culture: Dynamic - variability in space and in time; Exchange forever around; and Consistency in diversity. He presented four stages:

Approach => Formation => Outspread => Integrate

He also draws a development model of Vietnamese prehistoric marine culture.

The next researcher is Prof. Dr Ngo Duc Thinh, pioneering in marine culture research. In 2000, he was leading a research project *Folk culture in coastal villages*[94]. However, he never mentioned the marine culture term. In 2005, Prof. Dr Ngo Duc Thinh defined: "In his research project *"Vietnamese cultural forms"*, he suggested human cultural forms categorize into four groups, of which, *marine culture* belongs to the *Ecological Culture*", other forms such as delta culture, valley culture, highland culture, steppe culture.

In 2011, in the article *Traditional coastal culture of the Viet people*, presented in the national workshops *Exploiting the potentials of sea and islands, sustainable development in Quang Ngai province and the Central of Vietnam*. This time, Prof. Dr Ngo Duc Thinh officially defined the connotation of the *marine culture* concept: "A sea is an Ecology form associated with the origin of the organic world, and later, it associated with human society as cultural, thinking creatures. Marine

---

[92] Archeology magazine Nr. 3, 1997, p 16 – 28.

[93] Cited, p 18.

[94] Culture Ethnology Publisher, Hanoi, 2000.

ecology is a different ecology to compare with land ecology. Humanity has a rich and long-standing knowledge of the land, the forests, the rivers, and steppe. Moreover, the knowledge of the sea and ocean is not less than. The vast ocean contains enormous necessary resources for human life, but they are also hidden many dangers."[95]

In 2009, Dr Le Van Ky, in his *Marine culture in Central Vietnam* book, firstly a ministerial research project, later printed as a book. He did not annotate the term "Marine Culture" but cited the concept given by Prof. Dr Ngo Duc Thinh about *marine culture*, then affirmed, "We agree with this viewpoint."[96]

In 2011, Prof. Dr Tran Ngoc Them said: "Marine culture is a cultural element classified according to ecological conditions, formed under the-impact of the marine environment on human life and labor. It impacts the spiritual values and the material production capacity of society. Marine culture is a value system that human-created and accumulated in existence that makes the sea the primary source of life"[97]. In 2013, when published the work *Concerning the culture issues, theory, and application*, he also did not make any changes to the definition of marine culture:

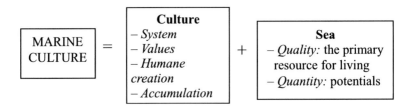

$$
\boxed{\begin{array}{c}\text{MARINE}\\\text{CULTURE}\end{array}} = \boxed{\begin{array}{l}\textbf{Culture}\\-\textit{System}\\-\textit{Values}\\-\textit{Humane}\\\textit{creation}\\-\textit{Accumulation}\end{array}} + \boxed{\begin{array}{l}\textbf{Sea}\\-\textit{Quality:}\text{ the primary}\\\text{resource for living}\\-\textit{Quantity:}\text{ potentials}\end{array}}
$$

[95] Different authors *Exploit the Marine potential for a Sustainable Development for Quang Ngai province and the Central*, National conference compiles Encyclopedia publisher, Hanoi, 2012.

[96] *Marine Culture in the Center of Vietnam*, Social Science publisher, Hanoi, 2015, p 76.

[97] *The opening essay of Marine Culture conference* Khanh Hoa, 15/6/2011, National conference compiles published by the Khanh Hoa People Committee, 2/2012, p 18.

In 2015, he quoted his explanation in 2011 in his presentation *Research on the island culture, education, and propaganda of the island sovereignty in Vietnam.* He participated in the national workshop *The Marine Culture, sustainable development resources*[98] organized by Hanoi University of Culture, Ho Chi Minh City University of Culture, and Quang Binh University held in Quang Binh province.

In 2011, Dang Vu Canh Linh, as the editor, published the book *Culture and people living on coastal land and islands of Vietnam.* The book bases on his state-level scientific research *"The characteristics of the coastal residents and coastal culture in the development process at present"* (code KX.03 / 06-10), led by Dr Tran Hiep[99]. In this book, the author used the marine culture concept a lot. He also explained the connotation of the term "Marine culture is the product of Vietnamese coastal residents living, working in associated with challenges, joys and sorrows in life attached with nature and society, setting up standards and values system through time generations"[100].

The author defined "The marine culture is a part of Vietnamese culture. It has the common features of Vietnamese culture. However, it has geographical nuances of specific residents living on the island and coastal areas"[101].

In 2016, in the research project *Marine culture and conservation, Promotion of marine cultural values in the South Central Coast in the industrialization and modernization period,* the author firstly cited the definition by Shanghai World Expo, by *Marine tourism* and by Prof.Dr Ngo Duc Thinh. Later, Assoc Prof. Dr Ha Dinh Thanh defined his connotation of marine culture "Marine culture is the material and spiritual value. The way it was created by a human being; And, how to

---

[98] Conference compiles, Labor publisher, Hanoi, 2015, p 108.

[99] Politic – Administration publisher, Hanoi, 2011.

[100] Politic – Administration publisher, Hanoi, 2011, p 10.

[101] Dang Vu Canh Linh chief editor, *Culture and people in Vietnam's coastal land*, Politic and Administration publisher, 2011, p 82.

perform these values during living, entertain, developing and adapting corresponding to marine and coastal environment"[102].

Going through referencing and analyzing the understanding of marine culture, in this paper, we choose to understand the marine culture as following:

Island culture is the sum of tangible and intangible creations of people living in the seas and islands in the living process, exploring and adapting the marine environment of Vietnam, exchanging and assimilating with other marine culture in the region. These cultural values are inherited through generations and identified characteristics of people living in those coastal environments.

3. Apply the regional culture theory

The study of regional cultures in the world has remarkably developed since the late 19th century. The studies by geographer Friedrich Ratzel (1844 - 1904) started with studies about "the cultural circle" theory. In the first half of the 20th century, F. Boas (1858 - 1942) published his work researched on the North American region's culture among American anthropologists. Then, his student Melville Jean Herskovits (1895 - 1963) presented the map of cultural regions in Africa. This theory was further developed and refined by Clark Wissler and Alfred Kroeber.

American anthropologists provided the theory "regional culture" to affirm that cultural forms resulted from random choices within relationships between cultural subjects and the natural environment. Nevertheless, the natural environment is not constant. Therefore, so the relationship between cultural forms and the surrounding natural environment is not constant.

In Vietnam, Prof. Ngo Duc Thinh is the most profound scholar who propagated the "regional culture" theory. Furthermore, he

---

[102] Social Science publisher, 2016, p. 48, 49.

persistently studied regional culture and cultural zoning in Vietnam[103]. Other scholars contributed to this subject are Prof. Dinh Gia Khanh, poet Cu Huy Can[104], and Prof. Tran Quoc Vuong.[105]

In order to study Vietnamese marine culture is changing from the North to the Center. The South of Vietnam, accompany theory and practical experiences provided by Prof. Ngo Duc Thinh, provided in his research *Regional Culture and culture zoning in Vietnam,* we apply other regional culture theories used by scholars in the former Soviet Union, Western scholars, chiefly North American scholars also.

3.1. The marine culture changing in Vietnam

Concerning the connotation of marine culture, we suggested that we have to take marine cultural subjects' activities and motivations into account. The marine culture subject in Vietnam has three activities:

- Exploiting the sea;

- Adaptation to the sea;

- Protect national sovereignty on the sea.

These primary activities lead to three types of marine culture. Each type has different components, and each type's appearance and development are also different.

Based on the specific characteristic of Vietnamese marine culture, we think Vietnamese marine culture consists of three types, and each type includes the following elements:

- *Exploiting the sea*

---

[103] See *Regional Culture and Cultural zoning in Vietnam,* Social Science publisher, Hanoi, 1993, Youth Publisher, 2004.

[104] Dinh Gia Khanh, Cu Huy Can, *Cultural Regions of Vietnam,* Literature publisher, Hanoi, 1995.

[105] See Tran Quoc Vuong et al, *The basis of Vietnamese culture,* Education publisher, Ha Noi, 1998, the 20th edition, 2018.

+ Manufacturing and repairing for fishermen go to the sea (shipbuilding and repair).

+ Fishing culture.

+ Aquaculture.

+ The processing and consuming seafood.

- *Adaptation culture to the sea*

+ Worship the natural forces; sanctifying natural forces; establishing a spiritual system on the coastal land.

+ To build cultural legislation, traditional beliefs, and cultural institutions.

+ Indigenous knowledge, artisans.

- *Protecting national sovereignty on the sea*

+ Protect national sovereignty at sea.

+ Rescue and aiding people in an accident at sea.

Based on the formation elements and concept of Marine Culture in Vietnam, this paper the author outlines the changes in the Vietnamese Marine culture of Vietnam.

In Vietnam, Vietnamese marine culture's changes from the cultural space perspective differ from the North to the South. In the North, from the farthest northern Mong Cai to Thanh Hoa province, this area faces the Gulf of Tonkin - the northwestern branch of the South China Sea as a part of the Pacific Ocean. The Gulf of Tonkin is relatively shallow, less than 60 meters in depth, therefore exploiting the sea or fishery is not an advantage characteristic as the coastal land in the Center and the South of Vietnam. In history, Nguyen Cong Tru (1778 - 1858) commanded to build dykes, expanded the rice land for agriculture in Nam Dinh, Thai Binh, and Ninh Binh provinces. In this area, the culture adapted to the sea also developed the historical figures worshiping. Remarkably, the number of King and Generals under the Tran dynasty (1225 - 1400) worshiped in the coastal strip of the

Northern. The whale-worshiping belief developed from Thanh Hoa province to the Southern. The cultural characteristic associated with national sovereignty on the sea emerged and developed in the Van Don area under the Ly dynasty (1009 - 1224) and the Tran (1225 - 1400). Nevertheless, the Red River's mouth flows into the Gulf of Tonkin has changed in history. Therefore, Van Don port no longer had a critical geo-economic, geopolitical position in the XII - XIV century.

On the other hand, in the Central and Southern coastal cultural regions, the marine cultures differ. The relations concentrated density that reflects on cultural behaviors and people's minds in the region.

"Whoever goes home and tell

Sending us Asparagus, we send back flying fish»

The verse shows that fishery and seafood became one major commodity in Central Vietnam while the mountainous residents have less, and they exchange. Whale / Ong Fish sanctified to become a worship figure for coastal residents from Thanh Hoa to Ca Mau province. The religious ceremony of going to the riverside greeting Ong Fish is indispensable for Coastal resident communities in the Central and the South of Vietnam.

In the South of Vietnam, in the number of worship Ong Fish temples, residents borrow a space to worship historical figures. The shrine worship historical Nguyen Trung Truc in Rach Gia city is an evident example (now Kien Giang province).

The culture of protecting national sovereignty on the sea developed strongly among residents living on the Ly Son islands (Quang Ngai province), Phu Quoc Island (Kien Giang province), Phu Quy island (Binh Thuan province), Hoang Sa, and archipelagos (Khanh Hoa province). The protection of national sovereignty on the sea imprints in the people's awareness on Ly Son island (Quang Ngai province) and make the *New Soldiers Ceremony* become a particularly sacred festival at the location. In history, under the regime of Nguyen Lords and King Nguyen, the citizens of Ly Son island had to join the army to protect the national sovereignty of Hoang Sa and Truong Sa islands. The soldiers left home for national sovereignty without knowing the return date. Generations of Ly Son people keep doing their duties until nowadays; therefore, the *New Soldier Ceremony* is essential. The family and the new soldiers are more proud of the duties rather than their lives.

From the above analysis, we can see Vietnam's marine culture corresponding to cultural space keep changing from the North, the Central to the South. However, Vietnamese marine culture's essence is the same if we approach from a cultural space perspective.

3.2. The changes in Vietnamese marine culture: subjective / objective

The subject of Vietnam's marine culture is the communities, different ethnic groups living on the mainland, islands, and archipelagos belonging to Vietnam's sovereignty several thousand years in history. In 2019, in volume 1 of a series of nine books about *Vietnamese Marine culture*[106], the author of this essay studied Vietnamese marine culture subjects and history and presented Vietnamese marine culture's subject according to ethnic groups, living space (coastal, on islands, or archipelago)[107].

Concerning the subject of Vietnamese marine culture, the living method of exploitation needed to consider. Around the 1940s, J.Y Claeys once said that "The fishing occupation and transportation developed in Annam. The abundance of canals, rivers, convex coastlines with safe lagoons always motivated people in Annam to become seamen, boat drivers, and fishermen. Before the French's

---

[106] Nguyen Chi Ben et al. National Politic and Administration publisher, Hanoi, Vol. 1, Nguyen Chi Ben edited, 2019; Vol.2: Tu Thi Loan edited, 2019; vol. 3: Vu Anh Tu edited, 2018; vol. 4: Do Thi Thanh Thuy edited, 2019; vol. 5 Bui Quang Thanh edited, 2018; vol. 6: Dinh Văn Hanh, 2019; vol. 7 Pham Lan Oanh edited, 2019; vol. 8: Bui Quang Thang edited, 2018; vol. 9: Bui Hoai Son edited, 2018.

[107] Vietnamese translation version by Phan Phuong Anh, archived in National culture and Arts Institute of Vietnam.

arrival, the vehicles have wheels almost unknown. On land, all goods carried on the shoulder with a pole, and people carried by palanquin. The coastal villages all have excellent seamen. They learned from father to son, from generation to generation, they inherited traditions and rituals related to fishing and boat building technique"[108] And: "The Annam people either farmer or fishermen. However, people of these two occupation groups do not mix. The dunes separate them. The fisherman usually has only a small garden on the dunes. If the fishing season is bad, there will be hunger. The farmer working with plow rarely see the sea. The dunes obscured their vision. Fishers bring fish to sell in the markets the canals in the delta. They buy rice and then return to the shadowless dunes, where the fishnets dried on the white sandbank. Sometimes farmers ask fishers to help them slap a pond or a lagoon to catch fish. The seaman returned home after a long binge in the disappointed mood of monsoons. The sea keeps the people dedicated to it, and treated these two groups is very different but somehow similar. That is the bond of the Gods, the domination of souls, and the observance of the divine will. The farmers held the procession to honor the coastal temple while the ship-builders go to the forest to offer ritual to the three kingdom Deities"[109].

The research area in J.Y Claeys's writing was Thanh Hoa province.

Thus, the fishermen's mode has changed according to cultural space. In the Northern cultural space, there is a difference between the rice farmers and the fishermen exploiting the sea - the rice field directed to the offshore. The fishermen's tools to exploit in the Northern are not able to go far offshore. It is called "offshore fishing" in the current language. Researches conducted in Hai Hau district (Nam Dinh province) showed that the people of this coastal area live on growing

---

[108] Vietnamese translation version by Phan Phuong Anh, archived in National culture and Arts Institute of Vietnam.

[109] See vol 1, p 153-168.

rice rather than fishing. The professional fishermen mode exploit sea transfer further to the Central and the South that remarkable differs from the fisherman model in the North of Vietnam.

Looking towards the sea, going offshore is the fishermen's posture, the subject Marine Culture in the Central and Southern Vietnam. That position makes the marine cultural Central and Southern coastal diversified and plentiful. The technic of crafting boats, the worshiping Whale/Ong Fish, are components of the cultural adaptation to the sea created by fishermen.

To study the migrations of Viet people moving towards the Southern "Carry the sword to expand the territory" (Huynh Van Nghe), fishermen's distinction becomes more and more obviously in change. Regarding the adaptation to the sea of the inhabitants of Phu Quoc island (Kien Giang province) is oyster farming for pearls and making fish sauce. Coastal residents in Bac Lieu province live on making salt in deep experience.

The distinction changes analyzed above related to the migrated journey towards the Southern explained that in the Central region, the Viet people absorbed the Cham people's marine culture. Then, when the Viet people arrived Mekong River Delta inherit the civilization of Oc Eo people. Therefore, the subject of Marine Culture changes with cultural environments. Looking at the cultural characteristic of Viet people in the North, it can see the changes. However, this cultural characteristic still originated from the Vietnamese. This opinion was remarked by J.Y Claeys nearly a hundred years ago. Nevertheless, it is still valid.

4. Conclusion

Vietnamese marine culture is an entity that developed through time and space. The geographical, economic, and social characteristics of each region from the North to the South differ much. The differences caused changes in Vietnam's marine culture. The changes enrich the value and the types that interest the cultural researchers. The paper is a small contribution that the author wants to add to the research field. However, this is an individual's initial opinion, we need to discuss further.

References

1.   *Culturology, theories and applies*, Culture Literature Publisher, Ho Chi Minh city, 2013, p 128.

2.   Phan ,Thi Yen Tuyet, *The Social - Economic life of fishermen and residents in Southern coastal area*, Ho Chi Minh National University Publisher, 2014.

3.   Phan ,Thi Yen Tuyet, *The Social - Economic life of fishermen and residents in Southern coastal area*, Ho Chi Minh National University Publisher, 2014, p 3,4.

4.   Phan, Thi Yen Tuyet, 2014, p 4.

5.   Cited from Ha Dinh Thanh et al., *Marine Culture - preserve, promote marine culture values in the coastal area in the South - Central in the industrialized, modernized period, Social Science Publisher*, 2016, p 48.

6.   Cited from Ha Dinh Thanh et al., *Marine Culture - preserve, promote marine culture values in the coastal area in the South - Central in the industrialized, modernized period,* Social Science Publisher, 2016, p 48.

7.   Vietnamese translation version by Doan Tam, Social Science Information magazine, Nr. 8, 2011, p 46.

8.   Tran ,Thi An, *System of Marine Deities and the meaning of beliefs performance related to sea exploitation, clarify Vietnamese people's national sovereign in the North and North Central of Vietnam*, research, The Social Science Academy of Vietnam, 2016, digital version, p 25, 26.

9.   Archeology magazine Nr. 3, 1997, p 16-28

10.   Cited, p 18.

11.   Ethnic Culture Publisher, Hanoi, 2000.

12. Different authors *Exploit the Marine potential for a Sustainable Development for Quang Ngai province and the Central.* National conference compiles Encyclopedia Publisher, Hanoi, 2012.

13. *Marine Culture in the Center of Vietnam*, Social Science Publisher, Hanoi, 2015, p 76.

14. *The opening essay of Marine Culture conference* Khanh Hoa, 15/6/2011, National conference compiles published by the Khanh Hoa People Committee, 2/2012, p18.

15. Conference compiles, Labor Publisher, Hanoi, 2015, p 108.

16. Politic – Administration Publisher, Hanoi, 2011.

17. Politic – Administration Publisher, Hanoi, 2011, tr 10.

18. Dang Vu Canh Linh chief editor, *culture and people in Vietnam's coastal land*, Politic and Administration Publisher, 2011, p 82.

19. Social Science Publisher, 2016, p 48-49.

20. See *Regional Culture and Cultural zoning in Vietnam*, Social Science Publisher, Hanoi, 1993, Youth Publisher, 2004.

21. See Tran, Quoc Vuong et al. *The basis of Vietnamese culture*, Education Publisher, 1998, 2018,

22. Đinh, Gia Khanh, Cu, Huy Can, *Cultural Regions of Vietnam*, Literature Publisher, Hanoi, 1995.

23. Nguyen ,Chi Ben et al.Truth National Politic Publisher, Hanoi, Vol. 1:Nguyen ,Chi Ben edited, 2019; Vol.2: Tu, Thi Loan edited, 2019; vol. 3: Vu, Anh Tu edited, 2018; vol. 4: Do, Thi Thanh Thuy edited, 2019; vol. 5 Bui, Quang Thanh edited, 2018; vol. 6: Đinh. Văn Hanh, 2019; vol. 7 Pham, Lan Oanh edited, 2019; vol. 8: Bui. Quang Thang edited, 2018; vol. 9: Bui, Hoai Son edited, 2018.

24. See vol 1, p 153-168.

25. Vietnamese translation version by Phan Phuong Anh, archived in National culture and Arts Institute of Vietnam.

26.   Vietnamese translation version by Phan Phuong Anh, archived in National culture and Arts Institute of Vietnam.

Bibliography

- Nguyen, Chi Ben, *Vietnamese Culture - studies and approaches*, Social Science Publisher, 2 vol., four books, 2018.

- Nguyen, Chi Ben et al., Vietnamese marine culture, *vol. 1 (General view on Vietnamese Marine culture)*, Truth National Politic publisher Ha Noi, 2019.

- *Đai Viet su ky toan thu* , Cao, Huy Giu translated, Dao, Duy Anh edited, Social Science Publisher, Ha Noi, second printed, vol. 1 (1972), vol. 2 (1971), vol. 3 (1972), vol. 4 (1973).

- Le, Qui Don, *Phu bien tap luc*, revised translation version by Tran Dai Vinh, Da Nang Publisher, 2015.

- Dinh. Gia Khanh, Cu ,Huy Can (Authors) *Vietnamese cultural regions*, Literature Publisher, Ha Noi, 1995.

- Le, Van Ky, *Marine Culture in the Central of Vietnam*, Social Science Publisher, Hanoi, 2015.

- Ha, Dinh Thanh et al., *Marine Culture and preservation, promotion marine culture values in South Central coastal region in the industrialization and modernization process*, Social Science Publisher, Hanoi, 2016.

- Phan, Thi Yen Tuyet, *Socio-economic life of fishermen and residents in the Southern coastal region*. Ho Chi Minh City National University, 2014.

- Phạm Lan Oanh et al., *Vietnamese Marine Culture, vol.7 (Southwestern Marine Culture)*, National Politic Publisher, Ha Noi 2019.

- Tran, Quoc Vuong et al, *The basis of Vietnamese culture*, Education Publisher, Ha Noi, 1998, the 20th edition, 2018.

- Tran, Quoc Vuong, *Vietnam – a geographic-culture view*, Culture Ethnic, Journal of Culture and Arts Publisher, Ha Noi, 1998,

VIETNAM SEA AND ISLAND CULTURE: VALUES AND APPROACH

1. Introduction

I was born and raised in a village in the middle of the Red River Delta, a country often referred to as ancient, with a temple of more than two thousand years of history, with a vague memory of an ancient citadel of Luy Lâu[110] dating from AD. In fact, in my whole childhood, I did not know the sea. I only knew rice fields and sweet potato fields. Then one day, in my visit to a friend, he led me to the beach, watching the open space to the horizon, with the waves of silver waves pouring into the shore and in the whispering of pine lines seaside. This scenery makes me go from surprise to surprise. On my way home, I was even more surprised looking at strange fish stalls with a strong smell at the local market. Staying overnight at his house, listening to the noisy waves from the sea and talking to his family members who have a loud voice that if in my hometown the old people presumed as if they 'swallow the waves and chase the wind'[111], I gradually enlightened that this place was not like my village of the Red River Delta, where the land is rich for only rice, potatoes, corn, peanuts and the rivers and ponds provide only freshwater fish and shrimps. From that moment, I began to understand that Vietnamese culture is not only plain culture in my village and wet rice-growing villages like mine but also the culture of coastal villages like my friend's one.

2. The subject of Vietnamese sea and island culture

Indeed it is! Vietnam is a country with a coastline of 3260 km, from Móng Cái,Quang Ninh Province (north) to Hà Tiên,Kien Giang Province (south), covering the east, south, and western part of the country; opens 12 nautical miles and the economic zone opens 200

---

[110] Today's Thuận Thành District, Bắc Ninh province.

[111] In Vietnamese: ăn sóng nói gió.

nautical miles, including a number of islands and archipelagos, especially the Paracel and Spratly Islands. According to the International Convention on the Law of the Sea (1982, 1994), Vietnam has sovereignty over an area of about 1,000,000 square kilometers (Lê Bá Thảo 1998, p. 54). Therefore, if looking from a career perspective, it can be seen that Vietnamese people have two ways of living: rice cultivation in the field, and coastal aquaculture and fishing in the open sea.

For Vietnamese residents living along the coast, the role of the sea for residents in each region is different. According to Professor Ngô Đức Thịnh (2000a, p. 22-4), Nghệ Tĩnh is the line to divide Vietnamese coastal residents into two parts: the Northern part from Nghệ Tĩnh to Móng Cái; the Southern parts from Nghệ Tĩnh to the South[112]. In the first part, residents are not fully aware of exploiting offshore resources, they fix one foot in the rice-field and only face the sea in half view. Prof. Ngô Đức Thịnh called them 'the bland-with-the-sea residents'. The second group of residents is more closely connected with the sea; for them, the sea plays a more important role in nurturing the fishermen's community, so the exploitation of aquatic products accounts for a higher proportion. However, if you look more specifically, coastal Vietnamese residents should be divided into three minor groups: the first group is residents from Móng Cái to Đèo Ngang where coastal residents look out to. the sea is somewhat faded; the second group includes the residents from Đèo Ngang[113] down to Ninh Thuận whose view towards the sea is somewhat clearer, though not completely deep; and the third group covers residents from Ninh Thuận to Cà Mau and Kiên Giang provinces in the South who prove to have the deepest view of the sea.

For the second and especially the third group of residents, the sea also plays an important role for them on the way to move and expand the country to the South. In the sixteenth, seventeenth and eighteenth

---

[112] Trần Ngọc Thêm (2012, pp. 15-46) divided into five zones.

[113] A pass between Hà Tĩnh and Quảng Bình provinces in Central Vietnam.

centuries, from the origins of the Red River Delta, the Vietnamese came to live in Central Vietnam and then "brought the sword to expand the country" (Huỳnh Văn Nghệ) to the South. In addition to gradual migration by road, there was a very important way the Vietnamese people migrated on their way to the south is to use wooden barges, boats or junks to cross the sea; in other words, the sea was their "way" to the south. The fundamental difference between this third group of residents and the residents of the Red River Delta in the North is clearly a sense of mind toward the sea. When still in the long strip of land in the Central, they absorbed the sea view of the Champa people, so that when they entered the South, their view of the sea became more profound and bold. Their lives are closer to the sea. The sea is like their "Thạch Sanh's rice-pot" [114], but the sea is also the source of their uncertainties and catastrophes.

In addition, more significant are the groups of residents living on offshore islands such as Cát Bà (Hải Phòng city), Cù Lao Chàm (Quảng Nam province), Lý Sơn (Quảng Ngãi province), Phú Quý (Bình Thuận province), Côn Đảo (Bà Rịa - Vũng Tàu province), Phú Quốc (Kiên Giang province), the Paracel islands (Đà Nẵng city), the Spartly islands (Khánh Hòa province) etc. Are they residents moving from the mainland to the island or are they local residents from ancient times to this day? From a contemporary perspective, the people living on these islands are residents who are intimately connected to the people on the mainland.

Regardless of the source, living on the coast or on offshore islands, they are the subjects of the cultural elements of Vietnam's sea and island culture, contributing to the overall Vietnamese culture.

---

[114] A metaphoric image appeared in the Vietnamese legend *Thạch Sanh – Lý Thông*. Accordingly, the foreign aggressors invade the country and present the challenge that if Vietnam can treat the meal to their troops they will withdraw to the country. Thanks to the miracles of the gods, Thạch Sanh brings the sacred rice pot to serve, the enemy try to eat all but can't run out of rice. Keeping their promise, they withdraw their troops back home.

3. Sea and island culture: elements

During his life of studying Vietnamese culture, Professor Ngô Đức Thịnh in his work *Vietnam Cultural Forms* (3) has divided the cultural forms of people into 4 groups, in which sea and island culture, like valley culture, highland culture, plateau culture, and steppe culture, belongs to the group of "ecological culture". Considering from the perspective of cultural creative subjects, the islanders have some relationships they have to handle as follows:

• Relationship with the natural environment

• Relationship with the social environment

• Their relationship with themselves

It is clear that sea and island culture is the result of a creative process by islanders and settlers.

Dealing with the natural environment of the sea and islands, these residents gradually mastered the techniques and know-how of shipbuilding, experience in sailing, and dealing with unforeseen situations at sea; techniques and know-how for farming and fishing seafood, etc.

In dealing with nature and themselves, the islanders gradually develop a unique set of folk beliefs, such as the worship of whales, worship of deified aquatic species, etc., and a series of festivals that demonstrate the sacred faith for the gods deified from fish in the open sea under three processes: historicalization, mythification, and localization (Ngô Đức Thịnh 2010, p. 313-30; 2012, pp. 170-85)

Dealing with the social environment, residents of islands have formed the unique organizational tradition of fishing groups and fishing communities that Nguyễn Duy Thiệu, Trần Hồng Liên, and others have presented deeply in their works (Nguyễn Duy Thiệu 2002; Trần Hồng Liên 2004; Nguyễn Chí Bền 2006). If applying the criteria of UNESCO, Vietnamese sea and island culture is divided into (1) tangible culture including the method of manufacturing and using boats and fishing tools; and (2) intangible culture including popular religions, festivals, know-how, indigenous knowledge, etc. However, if we base on the place of residence to classify, there must be two types: (1) the culture of coastal residents that Professor Ngô Đức Thịnh called "văn hóa cận duyên (near coastal culture)", and (2) the culture of offshore islanders and archipelagos. There are differences between these two groups of residents; therefore, their cultural creativity naturally also has different traits.

From a historical perspective, along with the sea and island culture that we can observe on the contemporary section, there is a cultural component located at the cultural base, which is the archaeological culture in the coastal areas such as the cultures of Hạ Long, Cái Bèo (Cát Bà), Hoa Lộc, Quỳnh Văn, Bàu Tró, Bàu Dũ, Sa Huỳnh, etc. In addition, in the coastal waters many shipwrecks of many countrics coming to trade with ancient inhabitants of cultures in Vietnam such as Đông Sơn, Sa Huỳnh, and Óc Eo recently discovered. Time-bound shipwrecks on these sunken ships only reveal value to the contemporary through the salvage of archaeologists and coastal residents. So far, no one has been able to predict how many such ships in the Vietnamese sea.

4. Value of Vietnam's sea and island culture

Thus, as part of the ecological culture, Vietnam's sea and island culture is an inseparable part of Vietnamese culture. It can be said that this is a cultural component rich in type, diverse in genres, and multi-valued.

4.1. First of all, we can scc thc sca and island culture truly reflects the soul and personality of Vietnamese people. Some scientists have divided Vietnam Sca and island culture into 5 areas to better see the difference in sea behavior of Vietnamese people from the North to the South. Even so, within the depths of their minds, the Vietnamese still have insight into the ocean. In that vision, the two extremes of fear of the sea and the spirit of daring to reach the sea coexist. It is this view that is the basis for creating the Vietnamese sea and island culture. We can see in the folklore treasures of Vietnamese compositions about or related to the sea. The Vietnamese proverb system also contains many sayings expressing Vietnamese folk knowledge and experiences about the sea[115]. In folk songs, legends, Vietnamese fairy tales, contain many stories related to the sea and islands, such as the legend of Lạc Long Quân – Âu Cơ, the legend of Mai An Tiêm, etc. The most notable is the traditional festivals associated with the worship of the whale of coastal fishermen from Thừa Thiên – Huế to the Cà Mau peninsula in the South. The figure that fishermen trust and worship is a large fish in the open sea that has been "legendized" to become the sacred figure: whales (Nguyễn Chí Bền 2006, pp. 585-624). Every year, people in the fishing villages respectfully celebrated the festival, expressing their gratitude to the figures they trusted in the immense water. At the same time, worship and festivals also contain the indigenous knowledge of fishermen: when they go to the sea, they expect to see the whales "rising" from the sea because they can catch a lot of anchovies where whales emerge.

4. 2. Historical value

In terms of historical value, it is significant to evaluate the culture at the seaports. The unique geographic position has created for Vietnam in the past and now many important seaports, such as Vân Đồn (12th – 15th centuries, in Quảng Ninh province), Hội An (16th – 18th centuries, in Quảng Nam province), Bến Nghé (present-day Hồ Chí Minh City), etc., and river port like Phố Hiến (present-day Hưng Yên province), which was once famous with the proverb "The first the capital city (Thăng Long, today's Hanoi), the second Phố Hiến". All of them have vestiges of both tangible and intangible sea and island culture. These cultural heritages represent a glorious time in the history of marine culture. In the eyes of Vietnamese people, Japanese Bridge Temple (chùa Cầu) and Japanese graves in Hội An, the statue of the

---

[115] According to the book Treasure of Vietnamese proverbs (Nguyễn Xuân Kính ed. 2002), 65 out of 16,097 proverbs have words "biển" or "bể" (sea).

Indian god, Kubera, later becoming a goddess of Vietnamese are not only mere cultural heritages but also historical witnesses to the economic exchange relations between Vietnam and Japan in the eighteenth century. In addition, the shipwrecks that we have unearthed recently are artifacts that show historical value. In this respect, it is impossible not to mention the festival of honoring the former soldiers going on missions on the Paracel islands[116] held annually by the people of Lý Sơn island (also known as Cù lao Ré), Quảng Ngãi province. Artifacts such as genealogy and ordinations of monarchial dynasties for people on Lý Sơn Island are historical evidence for Vietnam's national sovereignty with the Paracel and Spratly Islands.

5. A few thoughts on the approach

5. 1. As a part of Vietnamese culture, Vietnam's sea and island culture is characterized by multi-value, diverse types, genres, and richness in folklore reserves. Researcher Nguyễn Văn Kim, main writer and editor of the book *Người Việt với biển* (*Vietnamese people and the sea*) (8) made a reasonable suggestion that the study of Vietnamese sea and island culture must be based on a view of the sea with new methods and approaches. Obviously, this is an important issue to access Vietnamese island culture. The study of Vietnamese island and island culture must be viewed from many different dimensions and connected with many different issues. The assertion that Vietnamese people do not have a clear view of the sea by assessing the fact that Vietnam does not have large boats for offshore fishing or that the coastal residents built dikes to prevent the sea from taking rice land is incorrect.

5. 2. The coast as a border separating the land and the sea from Vietnam from Móng Cái to Cà Mau is not a constant factor. The position of the coast is probably not unchanged. The old Vietnamese verse "The blue sea has turned into a bride"[117] may be drawn from

---

[116] In Vietnamese: lễ hội khao thề thế lính Hoàng Sa.
[117] In Vietnamese: Thương hải biến vi tang điền.

the experiences of many previous generations. In the fifteenth century, Nguyễn Trãi (1380-1442) had poems of *Thần Phù hải khẩu* (The estuary of Thần Phù) and then *Hải khẩu dạ bạc hữu cảm* (Night boat parking at the estuary) and *Quan hải* (Closing the estuary) showing the image of a man hugging the pillow on the boat drifting along the waves all night to think about the life: "When the boat was overturned, the people knew the strength of the people like water"[100] Thần Phù estuary in the 15th century, where Nguyen Trai parked boats in the past, is now located inland. The translators of the book *Ức trai thi tập* (Collection of Nguyễn Trãi's poems) noted that: "The old estuary between Ninh Binh and Thanh Hoa has now been filled, it is now dozens of kilometers away from the current coast. This position in the past was a stormy sea gate, so people in the area have a saying: "Boats floating through the estuary of Thần Phù will be safe if the boatman is well-cultivated, and will sink if he is not in good manner" [118] (see Literature Institute 1969). The geologists have generalized the Pleistocene and Holocene periods with the times of sea rising and sea receding. ProfessorTrần Quốc Vượng and Associate Professor Cao Xuân Phổ have applied this theory to show the impact of the sea rising and sea receding on the lives of Vietnamese people in *Biển với người Việt cổ* (The Sea and the ancient Vietnamese) (Trần Quốc Vượng & Cao Xuân Phổ 1996). Researcher Cung Đình Thanh in Australia mentioned this issue in a chapter of his book, *Tìm về nguồn gốc văn minh Việt Nam dưới ánh sáng mới của khoa học* (Discovering the origin of Vietnamese civilization under the new light of science). Sea rising and receding have been an effective base for him to explain quite a lot of problems of Vietnamese sea and island culture from a contemporary perspective. According to Cung Đình Thanh, "there have been at least 20 times of glacier-forming and glacier-melting in the past 2 million years. Twenty times of glacier-melting caused 20 periods of sea rising and receding"

---

[118] In Vietnamese: "Lênh đênh qua cửa Thần Phù; Khéo tu thì nổi vụng tu thì chìm"

(Cung Đình Thanh 2003, p. 42). We must pay attention to two characteristics related to the rising and receding movements of the East Sea as well as the rise and subsidence of the Red River Delta. The interpretation of the values of Vietnamese island culture must take the sea rising and receding into account. Because there are areas that are now the "coastal areas"[119] but they used to be the sea; at the same time, there are areas that are now land, they used to be the sea. The present Việt Trì city is a piece of evidence. Among the interpretations of place names that have a special position with the ancient Văn Lang state, Hà Hữu Nga is very reasonable to claim that the city of Kattigara, a place used to be on the maritime map of the world before BC and now the confluence of the Việt Trì River, is the legendary Phong Châu capital of the ancient Vietnamese state (Hà, Hữu Nga 2012) Assessing the history of Vietnamese culture from sea rising and receding theory hopes to solve many problems of Vietnamese culture, including Vietnam's island and island culture, in order to avoid regretful confusion!

5.3. Vietnam has nearly 2,800 islands and archipelagos. It can be divided into two types: coastal islands and offshore islands (such as the Paracel and Spratly islands). Vietnamese people call the 'island' with many different names: đảo (island), hòn (islet), cồn (mid-river dune), and đá (rock), etc. The problem is that the inhabitants of these near-shore and offshore islands are now immigrants, they have moved away from the original land where their ancestors used to live and live for a long time. The inhabitants of Đầm Môn peninsula in Khánh Hòa province, whose records are the Đàng Hạ people (or Đẳng Hạ, Hạ, Hẹ). That's why the Việt people in the area call them 'the creolized Montagnards' (Lê Quang Nghiêm 1971; Trần Việt Kỉnh 1992; Nguyễn Duy Thiệu 2005)[120]. On Phú Quý island in Bình Thuận province, local residents are not indigenous. The ancestors of the

---

[119] In Vietnamese: "vùng cận duyên": the term used by Professor Ngô Đức Thịnh.

[120] Thanks to Assoc. Prof. Dr. Nguyễn Duy Thiệu for providing me with this manuscript.

current inhabitants came to these islands to establish their villages in the seventeenth century from the mainland. These communities generally have their own rules of cultural creation for the inhabitants of the islands from the North to the South: Cát Bà, Cồn Cỏ, cù lao Chàm, Lý Sơn, the Paracel, the Spratly, Côn Đảo, Phú Quốc : cultural belongings that these immigrants brought with them exist subconsciously; they have created a new culture to suit the natural and social conditions of the island. Are two essential parts of Vietnam's sea and island culture (the culture of the inhabitants on the shore and the culture of the inhabitants on the shore cultivated on the island) really just one?! This relationship between land and island culture in Vietnam can serve as concrete evidence to refute the ideas of F. Ratzel and Carl Schmitt (see Tereshchenko 2011) on territorial organization, and at the same time, it can be used as historical proof to prove that the Vietnamese people have owned these islands and archipelagos for a long time. The territorial space of the ancient and current Vietnamese inhabitants has encompassed both the mainland and the islands from ancient times to the present. Should the consideration of Vietnamese sea and island culture consider this feature as a theoretical starting point?

5.4. In some areas, such as Cửa Sót estuary (Hà Tĩnh province), there is a group of seaport residents; "The locals call them *Nôốc câu* people, *Bồ Lô* people or *Bố Chính* people. Before the August Revolution in 1945, "*Bồ Lô*" was used as a name to refer to the group of people whom Cửa Sót estuary residents called the "saltwater Mường people". In addition to Cửa Sót estuary, *Bồ Lô* people are also present at the nearby estuaries, for example, Nhượng estuary and Lò estuary" (Ngô Đức Thịnh 2000b, p. 389). In Đầm Môn peninsula of Khánh Hòa province, there is a group of Đàng Hạ people living among the Vietnamese (Kinh) surroundings. When studying Vietnamese people as the subject and object of Vietnamese sea and island culture, we need to see in the Red River Delta where Vietnamese people built a culture that always exists a layer of marine culture created by Malayo-Polynesian residents. In the ancient culture of Southeast Asia, marine culture is like sediment deep down to the unconscious floor of ancient Vietnamese inhabitants and exists to this day. For example, people often talk about sugarcane placed by Vietnamese people on the altar on Tết holiday; Some people also told about a jar of sardine sauce that residents of Chử Xá village (Văn Đức commune, Gia Lâm district, Hanoi city) offered to Saint Chử Đồng Tử during the village festival on January 17 of the lunar calendar each year as discovered by Đỗ Lan Phương in her MA thesis. People also mention the four sea goddesses (*Tứ vị đại càn thánh nương*) who are worshiped in many coastal places, the most typical of which is Cờn Temple (Càn Hải commune, Quỳnh Lưu district, Nghệ An province). These spirits were so "sacred and powerful" that the Nguyễn Dynasty (1802-1945) brought them to Vietnamese villages in the South in three groups of cults: *Tứ vị đại càn thánh nương* (the sea goddesses), *Thành hoàng bổn cảnh* (the Patron God of city/village), and Cao Sơn Đại Vương (the Mountain God). In the same way, it is possible to show more similar details or phenomena in the Vietnamese culture of North, Central, and South Vietnam related to marine culture. Many people like to lead the legend of Lạc Long Quân - Âu Cơ to remind that this myth has affirmed that marine culture is the origin of Vietnamese culture. A myth is still a myth; however, when placing the myth in relation to the phenomenon of the sea rising and receding in history, we have to reflect more on the role of marine culture in Vietnamese culture in the Red River Delta through the historical process. Perhaps, in the mind of the ancient Vietnamese, the attitude towards the sea was reasonable and bold as sediment, which can be presently determined through the artifacts of archaeological cultures such as Hạ Long, Cái Bèo, Hoa Lộc, Quỳnh Văn, Bàu Dũ, Sa Huỳnh (see Trần Quốc Vượng & Cao Xuân Phổ 1996).

The problem is that, in the past as well as in cross-sectional slices, Vietnamese people in the Red River Delta seem to express the feature of "non-profound behavior to the sea" as pointed by Ngô Đức Thịnh. That means there has been a fracture in the Vietnamese attitude towards the sea. There is an undeniable fact that when crossing the Hải Vân Pass to open the water to the South, the Vietnamese changed their attitude to the sea again. Is that change due to the natural conditions of the Central and Southern regions? I don't think so. The sea view is a mental imprint, even on the unconsciousness of the Vietnamese in the Red River Delta. That attitude of the sea arose again when Vietnamese people encountered suitable natural conditions. In this way, we can explain the change in the view of the sea when Vietnamese people migrated into the Central and the South. For a long time, many authors have argued that Vietnamese people living in Central Vietnam affected by the Cham will have a clear view of the sea. That statement is not wrong, but the problem is not entirely so. Indeed, explaining the cause of that phenomenon is not simple.

5.5. As a country with a long coastline, Vietnam has favorable seaports for foreign merchants to enter and trade. Ancient bibliography records a monumental period of Vân Đồn commercial port. From the time of King Lý Anh Tông (1136-1175), "traders from the three countries of Java, Lộ Lạc[121], and Siam entered Hải Đông area, asked to stay to do business, so they set up an entrepôt on the island, called Vân Đồn, to buy valuable goods and offer for the king of their local produce" (see Ngô Sĩ Liên 1972, p. 281) Another proof is Pho Hien, although this is a river port, not a seaport, foreign traders and goods still come from the sea. The Vietnamese used to say that "The first the capital, the second Phố Hiến"; the saying really reflects the prosperity of Phố Hiến in history. We can also mention Hội An (Faifo) prosperous when welcoming traders from countries such as Portugal, Netherlands, Japan, England, etc. These examples alone are not enough for us to make assessments about the acculturation of Vietnamese culture with the culture of countries coming from the sea. Therefore, when studying the value and the elements of Vietnamese sea and island culture, we cannot help but pay attention to those seaports because they act as a bridgehead and are the first to receive cultural flows from different horizons into Vietnam by sea.

---

[121] The name of an unidentified Southeast Asian state.

For conclusion

From a career perspective, Vietnamese villages can be classified into two categories: villages of wet rice farmers, and villages of people living on coastal marine raising and offshore fishing. Residents of these two types of villages have different cultural creations. However, from the core of the Vietnamese people, the two cultures are not opposed to each other but gather into the overall picture with two colors of wet rice culture and sea and island culture. Each of them has different components, different values, requiring us to have a unique approach. With island and island culture, this paper is at most an early outline.

Reference

1. Cung, Đình Thanh. 2003. *Tìm về nguồn gốc văn minh Việt Nam dưới ánh sáng mới của khoa học* (Discovering the origin of Vietnamese civilization under the new light of scienc). Sydney, Australia: Thought Publisher.

2. Hà, Hữu Nga. 2012. "Kattigara, kinh đô huyền thoại Việt" (Kattigara, the legendary capital of Vietnam), *Journal of Nghệ An Culture*, Vol. 1.

3. Lê, Bá Thảo. 1998. *Lãnh thổ và các vùng địa lý* (Territory and geographic regions), Hanoi: Thế Giới Publisher.

4. Lê, Quang Nghiêm. 1971. *Tục thờ cúng của ngư phủ ở Khánh Hòa* (the popular religions of the fishermen in Khánh Hòa) published author, Sàigon.

5. Literature Institute. 1969. *Nguyễn Trãi toàn tập* (Complete Collection of Nguyễn Trãi's works). Hanoi: Social Science Publisher.

6. Ngô, Đức Thịnh (ed.). 2000a. *Văn hóa dân gian làng ven biển* (Folklore of coastal villages). Hanoi: Ethnic Culture Publisher.

7. Ngô ,Đức Thịnh 2000b. "Vùng biển cửa Sót" (About Cửa Sót estuary). In *Văn hóa dân gian làng ven biển* (Folklore of coastal villages). Hanoi: Ethnic Culture Publisher, pp. 389.

8. Ngô, Đức Thịnh. 2010. *Văn hóa biển cận duyên của người Việt* (Near coastal culture of the Vietnamese people). In *Lễ hội đền Cờn, tục thờ Tứ vị thánh nương với văn hóa biển ở Việt Nam*. In Cờn temple festival: the worship of the four sea goddesses with sea culture in Vietnam). Vinh, Nghệ An: Conference proceeding, pp. 313-30. Officially printed in *Truyền thống văn hóa biển cận duyên của người Việt* (Coastal culture of the Vietnamese people), pp. 170-85. 2012. Hanoi: Encyclopedia Publisher.

9. Ngô, Sĩ Liên ,*Đại Việt sử ký toàn thư* (Complete Annals of Đại Việt), vol 1 Cao Huy Giu trans. & Đào Duy Anh ed. Hanoi: 1972, Social Science Publisher.

10. Nguyễn, Chí Bền. 2006. *Góp phần nghiên cứu văn hóa dân gian Việt Nam* (Contribution to the study of Vietnamese folklore). Hanoi: Social Science Publisher.

11. Nguyễn, Duy Thiệu. 2002. *Cộng đồng ngư dân ở Việt Nam* (Fishing communities in Vietnam). Hanoi: Social Science Publisher.

12. Nguyễn, Duy Thiệu. 2005. *Về nhóm người Hạ ở Khánh Hòa* (About Hạ people in Khánh Hòa), unprinted manuscript.

13. Nguyễn, Xuân Kính (ed.). 2002. *Kho tàng tục ngữ người Việt* (Treasure of Vietnamese proverbs). Hanoi: Social Science Publisher.

14. Tereshchenko, J. 2011. *Hiện tượng văn hóa biển và văn minh biển*, Vietnamese version translated by của Đoàn Tâm. *Social Sciences Information* vol. 8.

15. Trần, Hồng Liên (ed). 2004. *Cộng đồng ngư dân Việt ở Nam Bộ* (Vietnamese fishing communities in the South). Hanoi: Social Science Publisher.

16. Trần, Ngọc Thêm. 2012. "Văn hóa biển đảo và văn hóa biển đảo ở Khánh Hòa" (Study on sea and island culture and its presentation in Khánh Hòa). In *Văn hóa biển đảo ở Khánh Hòa* (Sea and island culture in Khánh Hòa), Nha Trang: Conference proceedings, pp. 15-46.

17. Trần, Quốc Vượng & Cao, Xuân Phổ eds. 1996. *Biển với người Việt cổ* (The Sea and the ancient Vietnamese). Hanoi: Information Culture Publisher.

18. Trần, Việt Kinh. 1992. *Người Đàng Hạ ở Khánh Hòa* (Đàng Hạ people in Khánh Hòa).

CONTROVERSIES VIEWS OF THE CẦU NHI TEMPLE IN HANOI CITY

1. Introduction

Holding the Decision 2646 dated November 21, 2007, of Ba Đình District People's Committee, approving the task of preparing the construction of a bridge on Trúc Bạch lake island (next to the famous West Lake in Hanoi), I dream that on the 1000th anniversary of Thăng Long-Hanoi's birth in 2010, there will be a bridge connecting Thanh Niên Highway to the island on the lake, and on the island like it used to be before 1986. That was Cầu Nhi Temple. According to a legend, Cầu Nhi Temple dedicated the dog and other spirits that the King Lý Công Uẩn (1009-1028), the founder of the Lý Dynasty (1009-1225), built on the island; however, it was then destroyed right at the time of the Reform in Vietnam in 1986. I imagine that from the rooms of the Sofitel Plaza hotel, visitors can see the bridge in the morning or sunset silhouetted against the surface of Trúc Bạch Lake. Visitors can also visit the lovely little island on the lake (from Thanh Niên street) without taking a boat, and the locals can also go to the island to burn incense for the gods they trust. I brought that dream to a my friend at a press agency, who replied firmly: I don't think like you. I don't think there's a bridge yet, so do not dream about the temple! Wait and see! Do you see, nearly a year has passed, everything is almost on a standstill? Nothing has changed yet! People waited exhaustedly, scientists argued fiercely, some agreed, some opposed. So, how can your dream come true?

Many questions appeared in my mind. Why are people's aspirations unfulfilled? Is it the truth that it is a relic attached to religion, therefore, it does not receive the support of the government (just like the case some overseas religious and political organizations, some Catholic churches and some foreign state institutions accuse the Vietnamese government of infringing religious freedom – see Philip

Taylor 2007, p. 7-15)? Or will the restoration of monuments violate Vietnam's Cultural Heritage Law?

My research aims to find answers to these questions. In fact, since the end of 2005, when the Organizing Committee of West Lake's Documents Valuation Conference invited me to read and comment on the work of two young researchers Nguyễn Ngọc Phúc, Phạm Đức Anh entitled "*Tây Hồ Chí* (Notes of West Lake) through the results of the survey of monuments around West Lake" (2005), I began to think about this temple. These two authors compared the records in *Tây Hồ Chí* to the results of field surveys to confirm the existence of 56 monuments around West Lake. 9 of the 56 monuments around the West Lake (with *Tây Hồ Chí*'s record) were lost due to historical ups and downs, so the authors had to note down "not found".

These cultural relics are not only related to the religion and belief of the Vietnamese people, but also to the history of the country, especially the Lý dynasty (1009-1225). They should have been preserved because the relics are the message of the ancestors left to today's generation. They should have been preserved because the carry the messages left by the ancestors to the contemporary. Therefore, it is sad to witness the historical-cultural relics of a bygone age lost or damaged at the hands of today's men. Therefore, I am more and more interested in the opposing views on Cầu Nhi Temple because I think these opposing views are the main reason for the postponement of the construction of this temple on the island.

2. The ups and downs of a temple

There is a small island in Trúc Bạch Lake, where there is a temple called Cầu Nhi Temple. At present, the north side of the temple is now the Sofitel Plaza Hotel, and the south side is the Quán Thánh Temple. In West Lake, near the opposite of Cầu Nhi temple is Trấn Quốc pagoda. Before 2005, this area of Trúc Bạch ward belonged to Ba Đình district; however, it currently belongs to Trúc Bạch ward (Tây Hồ district, Hanoi city). The temple is located in a cultural and religious space, surrounded by 56 cultural and historical sites.

Unlike the monuments around the West Lake, this temple has an unusual fate. In 1937, the owner of the Metropole hotel mobilized the city government to set up a bar with a stilt-house concert hall and a dance floor next to Cổ Ngư Street, close to the gate of Trấn Quốc Pagoda. The newspaper *L'Evelléconomique de l'Indochine* in 1937 once strongly protested that:

"Those who vulgarly plan to choose an ancient revered temple in the center of Hanoi as a place to dine, drink and dance in colorful lights and loud music are truly unconscious people. We, French people, often boast that we have brought civilization to indigenous peoples, so why are we not afraid of being despised by Vietnamese as a lack of culture?"

As a result, this project was quickly eliminated (see Trần Huy Ánh 2008). The temple remained on the island until 1985. In 1986, the Vietnamese government began to implement the national reform policy.

When economic thinking changes, people will compete to do business wherever they think they can use it. This wave of "doing business" has a strong impact on cultural heritage, enabling people to carry out economic development work in designated areas for the protection of heritage. They demolished many monuments for economic development, including the Cầu Nhi Temple on the island of Trúc Bạch Lake. Perhaps in order to increase the income of the area, the President of Ba Đình District destroyed the temple to establish a restaurant called Cổ Ngư Restaurant. At that time, many scholars shouted loudly and opposed the violation of this historical and cultural site in Hanoi. In the issue of Đinh Mão Lunar New Year in 1987 of the *Tổ Quốc* (Nation) newspaper, Professor Phan Huy Lê in the article "Hanoi in the protection and embellishment of historical-cultural relics" mentioned this incident as follows:

"... Cầu Nhi Temple on Trúc Bạch Lake which was associated with the relocation of the capital of King Lý Công Uẩn. It is a large landmark that has a long history in Hanoi and has now become the Cổ Ngư restaurant."

On April 12, 1987, in the *Nhân Dân* (People) newspaper, there was an article "Strictly obeying the law of protecting cultural heritage" by author Hoàn Nguyên with the remark that:

"Cẩu Nhi Temple on Trúc Bạch Lake is a relic associated with the relocation of the Lý dynasty, but local authorities have transformed it into a restaurant, Cổ Ngư. This is a serious violation."

The author also appreciated that the Ministry of Culture had promptly sent inspectors to review, verify and timely correct this incident. On October 13, 1987, the late Professor Trần Quốc Vượng published an open letter to the Chairman of the Hanoi People's Committee in the *Quân đội Nhân dân* (People's Army) newspaper to protest the destruction of the historical sites in Hanoi. He said, "a few months ago, some officials in Ba Đình district said that "Cẩu Mẫu Cẩu Nhi Temple" is not a historical monument but a "place of superstition". He had to prove directly to the officials of the Culture Department and to the public that this temple "was a historical memory of Thăng Long in the Ly Dynasty". Later, the district chairman who ordered the demolition of this temple to build a restaurant was disciplined and removed. Dr. Đặng Văn Bài, Director of the Department of Cultural Heritage, recalled that at that time, thanks to the National Assembly's Committee on Culture and Education, Cổ Ngư Restaurant was not built and the island was preserved. In 1988, the Hanoi Department of Culture built a stele on the site where the temple was demolished to record the legend of Cẩu Mẫu – Cẩu Nhi. The stele is still visible today, but no one has mentioned it for nearly two decades.

In recent years, starting from an unpredictable event, the event has been repeated more and more seriously. On December 9, 2002, residents of Ngũ Xá Village of Trúc Bạch (Ba Đình District, Hanoi city) wrote to the authorities at all levels requesting:

"Cầu Nhi Temple in the complex of relics and landscapes of Trúc Bạch Lake - West Lake is the place to worship King Lý Thai To. It is associated with the building of the country and relocating the capital of King Lý Công Uẩn 1000 years ago and is now a historical - cultural relic of the Capital. Now we earnestly expect that the Hanoi People's Committee, the Department of Culture, Sports and Tourism and the Ba Đình District Office of Culture will allow the reconstruction of Cầu Nhi Temple. We will submit blueprints and drawings of temples, bridges, gates and financial plans to the city authorities for approval. We will call for the contribution of funds for the construction and decoration of the temple through socialization. We will be responsible for mobilizing people inside and outside the ward to donate to the reconstruction work mentioned above".

Thus, the people of Trúc Bạch ward really want to rebuild Cầu Nhi Temple. Since people submitted petitions,3-4 scientific conferences have been held for debate, but the work of rebuilding the temple according to the wishes of the people has not been resolved. Four years later, in 2006, Mr. Nguyễn Văn Tiến, who are living at 12 Thanh Niên Street, Tây Hồ District, a resident who participated in writing an application for the government to reconstruct Cầu Nhi temple in 2002, wrote another letter to the Hanoi authorities. He said:

"We look forward to rebuilding the temple as it was in the 80s of the twentieth century (before it was demolished). We have to rebuild the temple to correct a mistake we have made to our ancestors. Other than that, we have no other requirements. Therefore, during the past 4 years, we have consistently waited and strictly followed the direction of the authorities and specialized agencies wait for permits. At the same time, we would like everything to be carried out under the close supervision and management of the city, district and ward leaders before, during and after the temple reconstruction process."

Thus, it can be said that the temple on the island of Trúc Bạch lake has a very ups and down fate. It was dismantled and replaced with a stele house. The local government and people had a plan to rebuild the temple, and there was another plan to build a bridge connecting the island and the mainland. However, they are now still on the paper. It seems that Vietnam have rare monuments of tragic fate like this temple.

3. Contending Views on Cầu Nhi Temple in Conferences and Newspapers.

Mr. Nguyễn Thanh Sơn, a former resident of Yên Phụ Ward, devoted himself to telling me about the demolition of a temple to open a restaurant on the island and a pontoon bridge connecting Thanh Niên street to the island before. Later, he witnessed the construction of a stele house and the placement of a stele on the island in 1988 (see photo). Recently, he was delighted to hear about the temple restoration and bridge construction projects, but then he was disappointed because he waited and saw no government action. He told me to ask at the Department of Culture, Sports and Tourism of Hanoi. Luckily, my friend at this Department lent me the entire minutes of the talks and seminars around the temple plan. Thanks to that, I was able to look through each of these thick folders.

A part of the Minute of the meeting of January 6, 2004 at the headquarters of the People's Committee of Ba Đình District recorded:

"+ Mr. Nguyễn Ngọc Thuận: This relic dates from the Lý dynasty but has now become a ruins.

+ Mr. Lưu Minh Trị: The restoration, conservation, and embellishment of monuments according to the wishes of the local people are very necessary. Cầu Nhi Temple has great spiritual and historical values associated with the historical relocation of Thăng Long capital of our country in the past. We should rebuild the temple and build another bridge so that the monument becomes proper..."

The Minute of the meeting on November 26, 2004 at the headquarters of the People's Committee of Ba Đình District recorded:

+Associate Professor Đỗ Văn Ninh: I think that there is no Cầu Nhi temple in fact. This temple only appears in *Tây Hồ Chí*. In my opinion, we should respect the historical truth, and should not associate the history of Thăng Long citadel with the story of King Lý Công Uẩn led by two dogs (to Thăng Long land). If you want to build a temple to serve your purely religious needs, I agree. As for architectural plans, I also agree. However, with the spirit of honoring the Thăng Long - Hanoi values, in my opinion, we should not build the temple with the purpose of worshiping dogs.

+ Associate Professor Trần Lâm Biền: We should respect the previous history. We should restore Cẩu Nhi Temple like it was."

The Minute of the meeting on August 20, 2005 at the headquarters of Hanoi Department of Culture and Information showed:

"+ Mr. Bùi Thiết: you need to tell us clearly the purpose of this meeting. If the City People's Committee, the Hanoi Department of Culture and Information, and the Ba Đình District People's Committee all assert that there was a Cẩu Nhi temple in the past, you need to show the documents. I myself think that there is no Cẩu Nhi temple in fact. We need to be fair. [...] If you have clear documents, we will go home.

+ Mr. Lê Cương: People's Committee of Hanoi decided to restore and embellish the temple of Cẩu Nhi which is in accordance with responsibility, law, and in accordance with people's wishes.

+ Associate Professor Đỗ Văn Ninh: In fact, there is no Cẩu Nhi temple because there is no scientific evidence.

+ Mr. Bùi Thiết: I assert that we should not believe in *Tây Hồ Chí* and documentary images by any reason. The state wants to do whatever it wants, but it cannot build a dog temple.

+ Associate Professor Phan Khanh: I support the People's Committee of Ba Đình District to restore this temple. People can add the worship of fish and/or others but cannot abandon dog worship.

+ Professor Phan Huy Lê: I affirm that there is a legend associated with King Lý Công Uẩn. This is a meaningful legend that has entered the history and text books through the ages and is popular everywhere. We cannot deny this legend. The view that Cầu Nhi Temple only appears in *Tây Hồ Chí* is arbitrary fabrication. We can conclude that the worship of Cầu Nhi(little dog) and Cầu Mẫu (mother dog) originated from the legend associated with King Lý Công Uẩn. [...]. The small temple there (the island on Trúc Bạch lake), in my opinion, was first to worship Cầu Nhi, later probably changed to Mẫu Thoải Goddess (Water Goddess), and finally to Fish God. So that relic has 3 layers of overlapping folklore".

I myself also look through each article that has been collected into a big folder. At that time, most famous newspapers were involved, including written ones such as Lao Động, Tiền Phong, Thanh Niên, Văn hóa, Thể thao và văn hóa, Pháp luật and electronic newspapers such as Vietnam Net,Viet Newspaper, etc. Along with the contradictions in the comment about Cầu Nhi Temple of researchers, the media also divided into two opposing groups. Some agreed while others opposed the construction of a temple on the island in the middle of Truc Bach Lake. Perhaps few temples have become the focus of the press and public opinion much like the situation of Cầu Nhi Temple for years.

4. Beliefs and legends about the founding king of a 1,000-year-old city

Lý Thái Tổ (974-1028) ruled Vietnam for only 19 years (1009-1028) and was a special king among Vietnamese monarchs. His name is related to the establishment of Thăng Long Citadel, which has a history of more than 1,000 years. In folk consciousness, historical figures can easily become cultural belief figures or sacred figures in the divine realm. In order to sanctify and transform historical figures into religious figures, people often use measures such as historicization (transforming non-historical figures into historical figures), localization, and legendization. Among them, legendary is the way people use to create magic for historical figures. Therefore, many historical figures are associated with one or more legends.

With King Lý Công Uẩn, the legendary divination on the stem of *cây gạo* (Kapok, 木綿) in the village of Cổ Pháp has already explained his future kingship. The legend also said that "In the past, the bitch gave birth to a small white dog with a black dot on the body expressing the words "Son of Heaven (Thiêntử, 天子)" at Cam Tuyền Hall of Ứng Thiên Tam Pagoda in Cổ Pháp Sub-District. Local scholars said it was an omen that someone born in the Year of the Dog would be king. King Lý Công Uẩn was born in the year of the Dog (GiápTuất) and later became the king. What a miracle!" (Ngô Sĩ Liên 1972, p. 190). Earlier, the book of *Việt Sử Lược* (越史略, Outlines of Vietnamese history) also noted: "Once upon a time there was a dog at Ứng Thiên Pagoda (Cổ Pháp sub-district). There was a pinch of black fur on the back of the dog that appeared the words "Son of Heaven (Thiêntử, 天子)" (see *Việt Sử Lược* 2005, p. 74). King Lý Công Uẩn was truthfully born in the year of the Dog (GiápTuất Year)." […] "It is unknown whether this motif from history goes into folk or vice versa. We only know that many writings about Lý Công Uẩn recorded this motif.

The legend of *Ngọc Phả cổ lục* (玉譜古錄, Ancient Records of Emerald Genealogy[122] of Tam Tảo commune (An Phú sub-district, Yên Phong district, Bắc Ninh province) said that Madam Phạm Thị Trinh dreamed of a Stone Dog God, becoming pregnant and giving birth to Lý Công Uẩn while working at Tiêu Sơn Pagoda. *Việt sử diễn âm* (越史演音, Phonetic annotation of Vietnamese History) written in Nôm scripts (unknown author)[123] also refers to the motif of the deified dog when talking about Lý Công Uẩn. It is said that when the mother and son came to the pagoda chaired by monk Lý Khánh Văn, the bronze dog of the temple suddenly barked out loud. The monk Lý Khánh Văn asked the reason and got to know:

---

[122] Recently stored at the Sino-Nôm Library, Serial no.VHv. 1236.

[123] Recently stored at the Sino-Nôm Library, Serial no. AB. 110.

In Vietnamese	English translation
Lão nhân ngày xưa đã truyền	Ancient men said that
Chó đồng hễ cắn thánh nhân đến nhà	If a bronze dog bites (or barks), the sage has come.

Thiên Nam ngữ lục (南天語錄, Quotations of the Southern Kingdom), an anonymous work, written in the second half of the seventeenth century[124] recalled the same thing:

In Vietnamese	English translation
Có thầy là Lý Khánh Văn	There is a monk named LýKhánhVăn
Gia truyền bảo bối một con muông đồng	His family passed down treasure as a bronze-made dog
Sấm truyền từ nẻo cha ông	His ancestors' divination said
"Hễ thiên tử đến muông mừng sủa lên"	"Whenever the king arrives, the dog will bark"

Therefore, when the mother and son Lý Công Uẩn went to the temple of the monk, "the bronze dog barked loudly, resonating throughout the area".

The relocation of capital by Lý Công Uẩn from Hoa Lư to Đại La (later renamed Thăng Long and Hanoi) is also associated with the dog. *Việt sử diễn âm* recorded:

In Vietnamese	English translation
Lại nghiệm cái chó lội sông	Let's imagine that a female dog swam
Bơi Ứng ThiênTự mà sang Long Thành	across the river From ỨngThiênTự to Long Thành.
Cắn lau làm tổ mới hoà	She bit the grass to make a new lodge
Sinh con thấy có hiện hình lạ song	Then gave birth to a puppy with a strange mark on his body
Nên chữ Thiên tử dòng dòng	It was the words "son of Heaven".

In addition to the above works, the legend of Ô Mễ commune (Tứ Kỳ district, Hải Dương province)[125] wrote:

"By the time Lý Thái Tổ (Lý Công Uẩn) became king of Lý Dynasty, this dog (mother dog) crossed the Nhị River in the north to Nùng mountain in Đại La Thành and stayed at the top of this mountain.

---

[124] Recently stored at the Sino-Nôm Library, Serial no.AB. 478.

[125] Recently stored at the Sino-Nôm Library, Serial no.AB. 478.AEa6/23.

Lý Thái Tổ confirmed this vestige [...], and moved the capital there." (see Đinh Khắc Thuân 2006).

Thus, the mother dog and puppet motif always appear in the process of sanctifying the character Lý Công Uẩn with details such as 1) Lý Công Uẩn's mother dreamed of seeing a stone dog, and thus gave birth to Lý Công Uẩn; (2) When he arrived at the temple, the bronze dog barked; (3) later, the mother dog and puppies crossed the river, the king followed the trail and chose the land to set up the new capital.

Tây Hồ Chí may have been derived from historical data and folklore. It wrote: "There is a temple in Châu Chử, to the northwest corner of the lake center. This place in the Trần dynasty was called Thần Cẩu Tân (Dog God Wharf). Arriving at the Lê Dynasty, this area belonged to Trúc Bạch village, so the new folk called Trúc Bạch lake.

When King Lý had not moved his capital to Thăng Long, there was a white dog at Thiện Tâm Pagoda on Ba Tiêu Mountain (in Bắc Giang Province) pregnant. She suddenly swam across the river up on Mount Khán and gave birth to a puppy. Everyone thought it was strange [...]. By the time the king moved the capital to Thăng Long, the two dogs were already dead. When the king heard this incident, he said it was two divine dogs and ordered to build a mother dog temple right on the mountain and a puppy temple in the middle of the lake. Now this temple is still available (the mother dog temple), in the territory of Trúc Yên village"[126].

It can be affirmed that the life of Lý Công Uẩn (Lý Thái Tổ) is legendized by a mother dog and puppies. Naturally, these are motifs of a myth that folk people use to sanctify historical figures. In folklore, this motif had previously appeared with the choice of the capital of King An Dương Vương (2nd century BC). According to Professor Trần Quốc Vượng and Vũ Tuấn Sán, King An Dương Vương was originally planning to build a capital in Uy Nỗ village (To village), but the king's precious dogs kept running to Cổ Loa mound to make its lodge and give

---

[126] *Tây Hồ Chí*, translated by Hoàng Tạo, computer manuscript, p. 18.

birth. Therefore, the king moved the capital to Co Loa. Besides, this motif also appeared with the character Vũ Thành, a famous general who fought against foreign invaders in Bồng Lai village, Phượng Sơn commune, Lục Ngạn district Bắc Giang province. The village legend also records that King Lý's Prince consort married King Lý Huệ Tông's second daughter but had no children. One day, he saw a dog who was about to give birth to a puppy swimming across the river to Bồng Lai village to find a good place. He followed the trail and build a house on that land. Shortly after, he gave birth to Vũ Thành, who later became a general in the court and had the merit of fighting foreign invaders. Admittedly, this is the mother and puppy dog's motif that folk used to sanctify a historical figure, turning that character into a figure in the sacred realm. I think of Philip Taylor (2007)'s idea that religion is a kind of 'nation's history' because the most widely accepted religious symbols encode popularly accepted community stories and its effectiveness. People of all generations have accepted the association of historical figure Lý Công Uẩn with the mother and puppy dog's motif and with the story of a mother dog crossing the river to find a place to give birth without thinking too much like some researchers today (see Bùi Xuân Đính 2008, pp. 34-40).

It can be seen that the mother and puppy dog's motif is just a motif that appears in the process of sanctifying a character, not at all a totem. The issue to consider is why people used this motif to associate with a king who founded Thăng Long capital. Is there anything absurd or offensive? I think it is necessary to distinguish the real dog that has been turned into a spirit with a pure totem symbol. Cẩu Nhi is simply a sacred object which emerged only in the process of sanctification. Vietnamese people burn incense before a dog statue, meaning that they burn incense for a sacred object, not an earthly animal considered by some to be inferior. Many villages today still maintain shrines dedicated to the dog. For example, villagers of Yên Lão Thị village (Mê Linh district, Hanoi) worship the dog in a local shrine. in 2005, Mr. Vũ Văn Nâu (86) said that on the first and first lunar month of each lunar month, villagers often lit incense to pray at this dog worship. They believe that by doing so, families can find their lost cattle. Another shrine dedicated to dog temple found at Địch Vĩ village of Phương Đình Commune (Đan Phượng District, Hanoi city). The Museum of Bắc Ninh Province, the home of Lý Công Uẩn, currently holds three remarkable stone dog statues. The first is a stone dog with the words "Cẩu tử linh thần (狗子灵神, Dog God)". The second statue is a stone dog with the words on its back "Cẩu Thần an thủ (狗神安守, Dog God, the Guardian)". The third statue is also a stone dog with the inscription on the stomach "Lang thần trấn thủ. Nhược mỗ nhân thảo thọ địa xứ, động thủ mỗ vật, tắc linh thần tru sát chi bất phân"(狼神镇守, Wolf (Dog) God, the Guardian. If anyone searches the grave site to steal something, the god kills immediately regardless of who it is)". In folk beliefs, many unreasonable, even immoral things in the eyes of contemporary people are still accepted by people (such as the case of the 18-king temple in Taiwan that Robert P. Weller analyzed in chapter 6 of the book *Asian Visions of Authority: Religion and the Modern States of East and Southeast Asia*). While the object that Robert P. Weller has studied is a phenomenon that has recently appeared, the worship of sacred dogs and the legendization of a historical figure with mother and puppy motifs in Vietnam are a long-standing tradition.

5.Heritages in the face of a 1,000-year-old city?

The cultural space around West Lake consists of rich and abundant amount of relics and which are remarkably noted are those relics dated back to the Ly dynasty. In 2010, Hanoi will reach the age 1000 years-old, and Temple Cau Nhi which is an important relic among these Ly dynasty's ones, it is widely known for its legendary stories and the respect with many believers who show and present the condolences towards these kings who founded and developed Thang Long citadel. From 9th Dec 2002, citizens of Ngu Xa village, Truc Bach ward, Ba Dinh district of Hanoi has submitted papers and proposals to the authorities to ask for constructing permission for rebuilding the Cau Nhi temple in the middle of the island of Truc Bach lake, until now it has been 6 years. There were 4 conferences and seminars which organized to discuss and come to conclusion of rebuilding the temple but the activities still being postponed and even stopped due to the strong reaction trike back of some individual scientists. 34 papers, documents from all stakeholders including authorities and citizens, scientists, researchers have been putting through, sending back and forth but the current issues are still in the same spot. At the moment, the south part of Cau Nhi temple is the Quan Thanh temple attract many visitors every day, and opposite to the right-hand side of Cau Nhi temple is the Tran Quoc pagoda with plenty visitors from Vietnam and other countries. Meanwhile, the island and the stele house on the island is still dreary, isolated and unfrequented visit and even lack of caring from people. It is such a critical issue that should be concerned, if we think about time toward 2010 the year that celebrate 1000 years-old of Thang Long Hanoi but Cau Nhi temple still being in the deserted area like this. The key point that should be considered here is the viewpoint toward the temple, the conceptual images of the mother dog and the baby in the legends and myths. Problem that the temple existed until 1986 therefore, rebuild the temple is inevitable. The attitude and standpoint of authority is clear: agree with the citizens to rebuild the temple.

6. Conclusion 1

Over the past twenty years, the small temple on an island in the middle of Truc Bach lake has had a struggled fate. It was demolished to build a restaurant, then built a stele house, but from 2002 until now, since the people of Truc Bach ward petitioned the authorities to rebuild the temple and build a bridge to the island. There are always conflicting views. Acknowledging the mistake of some officials when destroying the temple on the island just over a year later, the cultural department decided to build a stele house with a stele here recording the history of the temple and it is a real cultural act. Therefore, I think, rebuilding the temple on the island may be done. Because, making the capital spacious and modern, preserving historical and cultural relics, especially those associated with the Ly dynasty, is the consciousness of the government as well as the people of Thang Long - Hanoi. This awareness is even stronger when there are just over 700 days left until this city celebrates 1,000 years of age.

7. Conclusion 2

Finally, the wishes of the people of Ngu Xa ward in particular and Hanoi city in general have been recognized. In 2014, the temple restoration project was approved, in 2015, the project was implemented and on August 20, 2017, the newly restored temple was inaugurated. Now, from Thanh Nien Street, there is a concrete bridge connecting to the temple, instead of having to take a boat to cross the temple like before, or the rotten wooden bridge before. The bridge is 18m long and includes 5 spans, each span is 3.6m long and 2.25m wide. The temple architecture was restored in the style of the Ly Dynasty, the bridge is made of green stone embossed with dragons and phoenixes and reliefs with many connected motifs. The ancient Co Ngu street (now Thanh Nien Street) leading to the small temple is surrounded by many ancient trees on the mound. The ancient Cau Nhi Temple has now been given a new name, Thuy Trung Tien Temple. This is the result after the project's restoration process has been delayed for many years. Thuy Trung Tien Temple is located on a mound of land floating above the lake, which has caused a lot of scientific controversy among historians, cultural researchers and managers about whether a temple worshiping the God of God really exists or not. Previously, this place worshiped the God of Fish and Mother Thoai.

As the saying goes, better late than never. The fact that the temple is named Thuy Trung Tien does not fade people's memories of the previous name of the temple: Cau Nhi temple, with the legend of the first king of the Ly dynasty, with the dog worshiping religion that once existed. in folk consciousness. The debate about Cau Nhi temple is now only in archives, but the face of the relics in the Tay Ho area has shown a temple as expected by the people of the Tay Ho region in particular and Hanoi city in general. Notably, in August 2017, this relic was ranked and recognized by the Hanoi People's Committee as a city-level historical and cultural relic. It has been 13 years since Vietnam celebrated the thousandth anniversary of Thang Long, Dong Do, and Hanoi, debating the Cau Nhi temple, which at one time still had significance for cultural studies, research, and conservation. cultural heritage, and affirming the people's desire to always be a resource for developing the cultural heritage that previous generations leave for today and future generations./.

Hà Nội-New York, November 2008

Hà Nội, November 2023.

Reference

1. Bùi ,Thiết, Đinh ,Văn Nhật & Đỗ, Văn Ninh. 1999.*Đối thoại sử học* (*Historical Dialogue*). Hanoi: Youth Publisher.

2. Bùi, Xuân Đính. 2000. *"Người Việt có thờ chó không?" (Do the Vietnamese worship dogs?)* Journal of Ethnology 3: 34-40.

3. Cù ,Huy Hà Vũ. 2007. *"Đền cá hồ Trúc Bạch, ai nhớ ai quên* (*Fish Temple on Trúc Bạch Lake: Who still remember and who forget it?*). *Journal of Hồn Việt* 5: 32-5.

4. Dương ,Trung Quốc. 2005. *"Tổng hợp ý kiến các nhà khoa học về đền Cẩu Nhi (An Overview on the Ideas on the Cẩu Nhi Temple)"*. Việt Nam Net.

5. Đinh ,Gia Khánh & Trần,Tiến ed. 1991. *Địa chí văn hóa dân gian: Thăng Long-Đông Đô-Hà Nội* (*Geography of folklore in Thăng Long-Đông Đô-Hanoi*). Hanoi: Hanoi Department of Culture and Information.

6. Đinh, Khắc Thuân. 2006. *"Về thời điểm xuất hiện văn bản Tây Hồ chí và thần Cẩu Nhi trong Tây Hồ chí (About the time of writing of Notes of Tây Hồ and Cẩu Nhi Spirit in the Monograph)"*. Journal of Folklore 1: 42-6.

7. Kiều, Thu Hoạch. 2005. "Từ tục thờ chó của người Việt (From the Worship of the Viet)". Journal of Culture & Art 10: 37-45.

8. Kiều, Thu Hoạch. 2006. *"Tây Hồ Chí, đôi điều ghi nhận"* (*Notes of Tây Hồ*: some issues". Journal of Past and Present 255: 23-6.

9. Many authors. 2000. *Thực chất của đối thoại sử học* (The Essence of Historical Dialogues). Hanoi: Thế Giới Publisher.

10. Many authors. 2005. *"Đánh giá giá trị văn bản Tây Hồ chí"* (Evaluation of the Monograph *Notes of Tây Hồ*), Proceedings of the Conference held on December 31, 2005 by Hanoi Department of Culture and Information, the Directing Board of 1000 Year Celebration of Hanoi & the Association of Vietnamese History.

11. Many authors. 2005. *Một số vấn đề liên quan đến việc bảo tồn và phát huy tác dụng di tích đền Cẩu Nhi"* (Some Issues about the Conservation and Promotion of the Cẩu Nhi Temple), Proceedings of the Conference held on August 20, 2005 by Hanoi Department of Culture and Information & Association of Vietnamese History.

12. *Minute of the meeting of January 6, 2004* of the People's Committee of Ba Đình District.

13. *Minute of the meeting on November 26, 2004* of the People's Committee of Ba Đình District.

14. *Minute of the meeting on August 20, 2005* of Hanoi Department of Culture and Information.

15. Ngô, Sĩ Liên. *Đại Việt sử ký toàn thư* (大越史記全書, Complete Annals of Đại Việt). 1972. trans. Cao Huy Giu, ed. Đào Duy Anh. Hanoi: Social Science Publisher.

16. Nguyễn, Bá Lăng, 1972. *Kiến trúc Phật giáo Việt Nam* (Buddhist Architecture), Vol 1. Saigon: Vạn Hạnh University Institute.

17. Nguyễn. Xuân Diện. 2005. *"Sự thật về ngôi đền Cẩu Nhi trên hồ Trúc Bạch (The Truth about Cẩu Nhi Temple on Trúc Bạch Lake."* In Reports on Folklore Studies in 2005, pp. 34-43. Hanoi: Social Science Publisher.

18. Hoàng ,Đạo Thúy. 1978. *Đi thăm đất nước* (Exploring the Country). Hanoi: Culture Publisher.

19. Nguyễn Vinh Phúc & Trần Huy Bá. 1979. *Đường phố Hà Nội (Hanoi Streets).* Hanoi: Ha Noi Publisher.

20. Taylor, Philip. 2007. *Modernity and Re-enchantment Religion in Post – revolutionary Vietnam.* Singapore: ISEAS–Yusof Ishak Institute.

21. *Tây Hồ chí* (Notes of West Lake). Manuscript. Department of History, University of Social Sciences and Humanities, Vietnam National University - Hanoi.

22. Trần, Phương Hoa. 2005. "Miếu thần Cẩu Nhi ở hồTrúc Bạch (Cầu Nhi Temple in Trúc Bạch Lake)". Journal of Ethnic and contemporary.

23. Trần, Quốc Vượng & Vũ ,Tuấn Sán.1975. *Hà Nội nghìn xưa* (Hanoi for Thousand Years). Hanoi: Hanoi Department of Culture and Information.

24. Weller, P. Robert. 1994. "Capitalism, Community, and the Rise of Amoral Cults in Taiwan." In *Asian Visions of Authority: Religion and the Modern States of East and Southeast Asia*, ed. Charles F. Keyes, L aurel Kendall & Helen Hardace, Honolulu: University of Hawaii Press.

COMMUNITY AND ECOTOURISM DEVELOPMENT IN THE CENTRAL HIGHLANDS OF VIETNAM

1. Introduction

Ecotourism is one of the development directions of Vietnam's tourism industry. In the economic and cultural areas of Vietnam, the central highlands have many special features. It is home to 11 indigenous peoples belonging to two different language families, including Austro-Asiatic groups of Bahnar, Brau, K'hor (Cờ-ho), Giẻ Triêng, Mạ, M'nong, R'mam and S 'dang (Sơ-đăng); and Malayo Polynesian groups of Êđê, Jo'rai, and Ch'ru. The ethnic communities in the Central Highlands have many special features in terms of organizational structure and mode of operation. The area has a rich cultural heritage – both tangible and intangible, with very rich values, forms, and diverse creative themes. Therefore, the community plays an important role in the development of ecotourism and requires the participation of local residents. Starting from the regional characteristics, the requirements, and reality of ecotourism development, the author puts forward some issues that need to be discussed in order to enhance the role of the Highlanders in the development of ecotourism in the region.

2. The Central Highlands – Nature, Cultures and Ecotourism

The Central Highlands comprises five provinces: Kon Tum, Gia Lai, Dak Lak, Dak Nông, and Lâm Đồng. Its natural area is 54,638.4 square kilometers, accounting for 16.8% of the country's area, and its population is 5,842,681. It is one of the seven economic and ecological zones of Vietnam. The Central Highlands borders Quảng Nam province to the North, Quảng Ngãi, Bình Định, Phú Yên, Khánh Hòa, Ninh Thuận, and Bình Thuận provinces to the East, Đồng Nai, Bình Phước provinces to the South, and Atopeu province (Laos) and Ratanakiri and Mondulkiri provinces (Cambodia) to the West. The region has five cities, namely, Buôn Ma Thuột, Pleiku, Đà Lạt, Kon Tum, and Bảo Lộc;

four provincial towns of An Khê, Ayun Pa, Buôn Hồ, and Gia Nghĩa, and 52 districts.

There are many ways to classify cultural areas in Vietnam. I prefer the way Prof. Trần Quốc Vượng and his fellows did in the textbook *Cơ sở văn hóa Việt Nam* (Basis of Vietnamese Culture) (Trần Quốc Vượng ed. 1998, pp. 220–94). The Central Highlands is one of the six cultural regions in Vietnam but it is the most distinctive region. In terms of cultural heritage, the area has a gong cultural space, which was recognized by UNESCO as a Masterpiece of Oral and Intangible Culture on Nov. 25, 2005. When the 2003 Convention on Protection of Intangible Cultural Heritage of Humanity took effect in 2008, the Space of Gong Culture of the Central Highlands was inscribed by UNESCO in the Representative List of Intangible Cultural Heritage of Humanity in the first drive, without consideration by the Intergovernmental Committee under the UNESCO 2003 Convention. Because the gong represents the spiritual strength and creativity of the community, The Space of Gong Culture of the Central Highlands is considered a creative masterpiece of humanity. They were also purchased from the ethnic minorities of Laos and Cambodia or from the Kinh (Vietnamese) ethnic group on the coastal plains. After being creatively modified, it was transformed into a musical instrument by craftsmen and arranged to be an ensemble for each ethnic group. Craftsmen only play gongs in certain situations. Each ethnic group has its own gong system, which is closely related to the rituals of the human life cycle and crop life cycle, as well as other cultural and spiritual ceremonies. In gong performances, most ethnic groups perform Xoang dances (see Tô Ngọc Thanh 2006 for more information).

When talking about the gong cultural space of the Central Highlands and the intangible cultural heritage of the region, we should mention the cultural works that cultural entertainers and folklore researchers call *epic*, or *Hơ-amon* by the Bahnar, *Hơ-ri* by the Jo'rai, and *Khan* by the Êđê, etc. In the first half of the 20th century, *Khan Đam San* of the Êđê was translated into French and published in France.

There are a large number of works and their values in the treasure trove of customary laws of ethnic minorities in the Central Highlands.

The musical instruments of these ethnic groups are diverse in genres, use, and value. It is worth mentioning that the latest research by Vietnamese and international archaeologists found that An Khê Town of Gia Rai province is the birthplace of human history in Vietnam. Its history can be traced back to 800,000 years ago and it is one of the oldest cradles in the history of human development in the world. To date, the Ministry of Culture, Sports and Tourism have classified 60 cultural relics in the five provinces of Kontum, Gia Lai, Dak Lak, Dak Nông and Lâm Đồng as national historical, cultural and revolutionary relics.

Together with cultural heritage and natural beauty, the Central Highlands has many other characteristics. There are many beautiful and romantic lakes, including Dak Ke at Toong Dam in Mang Đen District, Kon Tum Province; T'Nung Lake in Gia Lai Province, Lak and EoKao Lakes in Dak Lak Province, West Dak Mil and Dak Rông Lake in Dak Nông province, and Xuân Hương and Tuyền Lâm Lakes in Lâm Đồng Province, etc. There are also many magnificent river waterfalls in the Central Highlands, which are very attractive to tourists. Visitors can visit the Dak Che waterfall in Kon Tum province, the Ya Ly waterfall in Kon Tum and Gia Lai province, the Xung Khoeng and Phú Cường waterfalls in Gia Lai province, the Thủy Tiên waterfall in Dak Lak province, Dray Nu and Dray Sap Waterfalls in Dak Nông province, and Prenn and Cam Ly Waterfall in Lâm Đồng province.

In addition, there are six national parks in the Central Highlands, including:

(1) Chư Mon Ray, located in the two districts of Sa Thầy and Ngọc Hồi, Kon Tum province, is considered to be the largest national park in Vietnam and has rich natural resources for biodiversity. There are 12 kinds of forest vegetation and 1,895 kinds of plants in this

national park, of which 48 are listed in the Vietnam Red Book and 63 are listed in the World Red Book.

(2) The Kon Ka King National Park in Dak Đoa, K'Bang, and Mang Yang districts has been recognized by the Association of Southeast Asian Nations (ASEAN) as an ASEAN heritage. Its flora is rich and diverse, and most of its forests are virgin forests. There are 34 precious species, which are of great value for genetic protection and scientific research. Its fauna also has 38 precious animal species, listed in the Red Book of Vietnam and the world, which is of great significance for genetic protection and scientific research.

(3) Yok Don National Park is rated as Grade A among the forests of international importance in terms of biodiversity as it is inhabited by some extremely endangered animal species globally with dipterocarp forests in the lowland. In terms of biodiversity, Yok Don National Park is rated A in forests of international importance because it is inhabited by some extremely endangered animals worldwide.

(4) Chu Yang Sin National Park has different vegetation, typical tropical and subtropical climates, and virgin forests, as well as the oldest existing vegetation in Vietnam. It is a standard sample of the central highland biodiversity ecosystem.

(5) Bidoup-Núi Bà National Park is located in the Lạc Dương district and is part of the Đam Rông district in Lâm Đồng province. In 2015, this national park became part of the Langbiang Biosphere Reserve recognized by UNESCO. Its flora has endemic and precious species, and the fauna also has precious animal species.

(6) Cát Tiên National Park was recognized by UNESCO as one of the world's biosphere reserves in Vietnam in 2005. It is inhabited by 40 animal species listed in the World Red Book, particularly the one-horned rhino.

Overall, on the plants in the Central Highlands, scientists such as Lê Văn Khoa and Phạm Quang Tú published statistical results of 3,480 species of plants, including 3,000 species of orchids and 400 species of flowers. According to Hoàng Ngọc Phong and Nguyễn Văn Phú, in terms of animals, "there are 525 terrestrial vertebrates in the Central Highlands, including 102 animals and 323 birds. In particular, the area is listed in the Red Book There are 32 precious wild animals" (Lê Văn Khoa, Phạm Quang Tú 2014, pp. 95, 98)

Therefore the Central Highlands is a natural and cultural area with many unique features. The climate is cool throughout the year and is typically in the temperate zone of the tropics. There are four seasons within a day: spring, summer, autumn, and winter. This is why it is very attractive to tourists who want to avoid the hot summer in the area. With rich natural resources, magnificent and spectacular landscapes, romantic mountain lakes, white waterfalls, national parks, and biosphere reserves, and precious animal and plant species, the Central Highlands has become a unique and outstanding tourism resource area, which is very conducive to ecotourism development of.

3. Ethnic minority groups and ecotourism

The understanding of ecological and cultural tourism differs between tourism and cultural managers and researchers. According to the United Nations Environment Programme (UNEP, 2002), ecotourism is a form of nature-based tourism with the following standards: (1) It is a form of tourism based on nature and native culture, usually organized in wild natural areas; (2) Ability to carry out environmental education activities and environmental interpretation; (3) It is important to carry out activities to mitigate the impact of natural resources and culture; (4) It is necessary to support nature conservation activities; and (5), It benefits local communities.

Recently, two forms of tourism have been identified, namely, mass tourism and alternative tourism. In recent years, alternative tourism has been further classified as natural tourism, rural community-based tourism, and cultural event tourism. Therefore, the concept of "ecotourism" comes from nature tourism. Today, Hall believes that eco-tourism is a convenient way to penetrate the niche market of the tourism industry because of its continuous supply of natural products and its development towards a sustainable environment and environmental awareness. However, Hall asserts that the specific meaning and meaning of the term is unclear. Fennell & Dowling have a more specific understanding of ecotourism, so at least three components of ecotourism are identified: (1) Experiencing in close contact with people of nature and different cultural backgrounds; (2) Choosing the form of tourism so that the poor, rather than large travel companies, can get the most income; (3) Comprehensively reducing the impact of tourism on the environment" (see Nguyễn Minh Đạo & Trần Quang Bảo 2018). Although the interpretation of the term ecotourism is inconsistent, the standards of ecotourism are clear. Close contact with wild nature helps people feel the beauty of nature. This is one of the goals of ecotourism, and the central plateau is an area that meets this requirement.

Furthermore, in the Central Highlands, there are now three ethnic groups: the native, the Kinh (Viet), and newly arrived ethnic minority groups. Native ethnic minority groups in the Central Highlands belong to the linguistic family of Malayo Polynesia including Jo'rai, Êđê and Ch'ru, and the Mon Khmer linguistic family including Bahnar, S'đang (Sơ-đăng), M'nông, Ma, Giẻ-Triêng, R'măm, and Brau. Both communities live in villages that differ according to each race. The Jo'rai and Ch'ru call their village *plei*, the Bahna plơi, the K'hor (Cờ-ho) *bon*, and the Êđê *buôn*, etc. In the languages of the native ethnic groups, there is no term to indicate a social unit higher than a village, although in the language of the Bahnar and Jo'rai the term *t'ring* refers to a village alliance and legends of *P'tao Ia* (King of Water), and *Potao Puih* (King of Fire) recalling a social unit higher than the village in the ancient times of these ethnic groups. However, according to ethnographers such as P. Guilemine, *t'ring* has no name and no head. Potao Puih and Ia are wizards, not heads of authorities. Therefore, from North Vietnam to South Vietnam, the local minority village community is different from most Kinh (Viet) communities. If the Kinh rural community on the plains (especially in the Red River Delta) lived on wet rice cultivation and lived in a self-sufficient village. Units higher than villages are communes. Some communes are developed from a single village. The indigenous minorities in the central highlands do not have such a system.

First of all, it is important to note that for the indigenous minority groups in the Central Highlands, "no matter what the group is, they live in an autonomous village or an independent village, mainly living on dry crop cultivation. In order to cultivate, people must settle in a complete village with the least population. Each village is located in a clearly defined area, and other villages cannot penetrate. If there is a violation, the outbreak is inevitable" (Nguyễn Từ Chi 1996, p. 521). When talking about the indigenous minority groups in the central highlands, one should mention their strong attachment to the forest. In their consciousness and daily actions, Yang (God) gave each village a specific area, a clear boundary, and inviolable, sacred, and constant space. In the words of scientists, the village is a community collective, "land and forest are the collective ownership of the village community." The forests of each indigenous minority village belong to at least four categories: (1) the forest has become a residential area; (2) forests for crop rotations; (3) forest used by villagers to collect daily necessities, such as honey, rattan, wood logs, etc., and (4) The sacred forest, considered to be the residence of the gods (and therefore untouched), is usually the watershed and is carefully preserved under a guise of religion or belief.

Only units with all these four types of forests can be called "villages" (Văn Khoa & Phạm Quang Tú 2014, p. 172). This is the real "social space" mentioned by G. Condominas (1921-2011) in his classic anthropology book Social space in Southeast Asia (1997). Therefore, ecotourism in the Central Highlands is closely linked to two platforms: forests and rural communities. The national parks in the Central Highlands, the premises, and ecotourism destinations are all forests, and of course, there are villages and rural communities.

4. The reality of the role of communities in the development of ecotourism in the Central Highlands

With the changes in the material and spiritual life of the minority villages in the Central Highlands, the economic panorama of the region has also changed. In the past few years, the Vietnamese government has allocated resources from the Programs of 168 and 135 and other national target plans for the development of the Central Highlands. It is based on a piece-rate work system for 116,470 hectares of forests consisting of 7,320 households lacking cultivated land. However, the relationship between people and forests is limited.

If in the past forests were an indispensable resource for people's livelihood, today's villagers will not be able to obtain forest resources, thereby worsening their livelihoods. If forests were once the spiritual space of indigenous minority communities, today they rarely show forest-based cultural and religious activities, and the role of forests in spiritual spaces gradually disappears. Forest resources have been narrowed down. The following table shows the results of the 2014 "Sustainable Development in Central Plateau" scientific research project in the region (Lê Văn Khoa & Phạm Quang Tú 2014, p. 188):

No	Activities of exploiting forest resources	Percent (%)
1	Upland farming	68.82
2	Hunting	1.61
3	Gathering	28.34
4	Collecting fire woods	64.44
5	Collecting logs	5.91
6	Organization of festivals	8.29

It is worth noting that land agriculture accounts for the largest proportion: 68.82%. When evaluating the real situation of the role of the community in the development of ecotourism, this caused us to think. In 2018, the total number of tourists visiting the Central Coast and the Central Highlands was 56 million, of which 9.5 million were foreign tourists (15.5 million nationwide). It is not easy to divide The Central Highlands and The Central Coast Regions in terms of the number of tourists by ecotourism; however, it is believed that the tourism industry in the Central Highlands has clearly developed in recent years, and the region is very conducive to the development of tourism. There are many types of landscapes in this area, e.g., highlands, plateaus, valleys, and deltas, all of which belong to sub climatic regions (subtropical, temperate, and cold), so they are very suitable for the development of ecotourism.

The problem raised here is the role of the community in the development of ecotourism in the region. In the "Vietnam Tourism Law 2005", *Clause 19 of Article 4* stipulates that ecotourism is a nature-based tourism industry with local cultural characteristics, and communities participate in sustainable development. At the same time, *Clause 16, Article 3* of the Law on Tourism 2017 stipulates that eco-tourism is nature-based tourism that combines local cultural identity with community participation and combines environmental protection education. The researchers emphasize that ecotourism is characterized by visiting natural destinations, reducing the impact on the environment, raising awareness of the natural environment, providing economic benefits for protected areas and local residents, and respecting local culture and people (Nguyễn Minh Đạo &Trần Quang Bảo 2018).

Therefore, the development of ecotourism in the Central Highlands must always pay attention to two aspects: the role of nature and the community. The natural environment of the Central Highlands is very suitable for ecotourism. Visitors to the natural destinations of the Central Highlands mean that they will come here to enjoy many beautiful and particularly interesting landscapes and national parks, such as Yok Đôn, Kon Ka King, and Chư Yang Sin, which are attractive destinations. It is worth noting the role of the community. Unlike the organizational village structure of other ethnic communities, villages of indigenous ethnic minorities operating in an autonomous manner with an old village regime, which is the remainder of the original communal time, as F. Angel put it: "In each commune, there is a certain common interest, that is, the right to protection should be allocated to individuals, although this protection is controlled by the collective. For example, judging/handling conflicts, punishing those who abuse power and religious functions due to primitive and brutal characteristics" (Angel 1971, p. 304).

The most obvious limitation of the development of ecotourism in the Central Highlands in the past few years is that it does not pay attention to the particularity of local communities. As an autonomous organization, villages of indigenous minorities include village heads and religious activists, also known as village patriarchs. In some villages of some ethnic minorities, it is not individuals but a group of people who are responsible for the village leadership (the council of patriarchs).

All collective activities in the village are gathered around the central figure, the village chief. The prestige and position of the village chief depend on their age, knowledge, and property. They are admired and respected by the villagers and become leaders of the entire village community. The Stieng called them *bù kuông* (elders, seniors with higher social status), the Ch'ru *tha ploi* (elderly people, understand the life and traditions of the village), and M'nong Gar *kro ver tom bri bon* (sacred people in forests and villages), etc.

After historical ups and downs and social changes, the system of autonomy and the system of village patriarchs have gradually disappeared, but they still occupy an absolute position in the lives of indigenous minorities. Therefore, in order to maintain the development of ecotourism, it is necessary to use the autonomous system and the village chief. Not to mention the religious activities of the village patriarchs, many of which are often organized in the forest, and the ethnic minorities call them "sacred forests." The process of non-religious activities has been carried out in national parks and nature reserves. For example, in the Bidoup-Núi Bà National Park, up to 300 ha of forests have been rented out to agencies to conduct ecotourism business activities. The position of sacred forests in the K'hor Cil villages has gradually declined. Thus, it is hard for village patriarchs to play their role in the community and for the community to have a position in ecotourism development. The community sense cannot rule over the thought and psychology of native ethnic minorities in the Central Highlands. The community's participation in ecotourism in the Central Highlands region is not as strong as in the plains, and when the community does not participate much, it is difficult to increase their income to meet the cultural traditions retained by the local people.

5. Development of special tourism products, ecotourism, cultural tourism, and community-based tourism in the Central Highlands

In terms of national management institutions, the Vietnamese government stated in its "Tourism Development Strategy to 2020 and Vision 2030"[127] that: "The central highlands include Kon Tum, Gia Lai, Dak Lak, Dak Nông and Lâm Đồng. Specific tourism products include eco-tourism and cultural tourism, which take advantage of the unique cultural values of the ethnic minorities in the central highlands." The Vietnamese government, when approving the Master plan for tourism development in the Central Highlands until 2020 and Vision 2030, determined: "The state regards the development of cultural tourism, ecotourism, and summer resort tourism as the core of the cultural value of its ethnic minorities in the central plateau as the basis for the development of various forms of tourism. The development of tourism must go hand in hand with the protection and development of the cultural values of ethnic minorities in the region". At the same time, tourism development must be associated with the prioritization of the following key products: (a) Tourism product group for researching and understanding the cultural heritage of ethnic minorities; (b) Ecotourism product group; and (c) Mountain- and lake-based resort tourism product group"[128].

At the same time, the Ministry of Culture, Sports and Tourism has also formulated a "Tourism Product Development Strategy by 2025

---

[127] See Decision No. 2473-QD-TTg dated 30 December 2011.

[128] See Decision No. 2162 QD-TTg dated November 21, 2013.

and a Development Orientation by 2030" emphasizes "developing cultural tourism products closely related to heritage, festivals, excursions, and cultural research as well as lifestyles of the local people; developing rural handicrafts and community tourism and family tourism by strengthening the development of ecotourism products, focusing on the development of biodiversity, caves, mountain tourism, agriculture, and rural ecotourism"[129]. More specifically, in the Central Highlands, three key tourist areas will form special tourism products, and four national tourist areas are expected to receive 1.2 million international tourists and 5.1 million domestic tourists by 2025.

However, the Central Highlands provinces are facing many challenges. The first challenge is the environment. The destruction of the forest has not yet been controlled, which has seriously affected the ecosystem; the area of the dipterocarp forests and the green forest is rapidly shrinking. Wild animal hunting and hunting of rare beasts, such as elephants and bison... reduced biodiversity. Due to the construction of hydroelectric power plants, water pollution, and reduced water flow in the Serepok, Sê San, and Đa Nhim rivers have greatly affected grandiose and imposing waterfalls in the region. Many natural lakes in the Central Highlands have important tourist values, for example, Great Lake/Biển Hồ (Gia Lai Province), Lak Lake (Dak Lak Province) and Tuyền Lâm Lake (Lâm Đồng Province); however, they are now facing the issue of water shortage. The second is to develop special tourism products closely related to nature in the region (forests, lakes, waterfalls, etc.), such as ecotourism and cultural tourism. The third is to adhere to the principles of ecotourism activities, including encouraging the role of communities and bringing benefits to communities.

The development of community cultural traditions of indigenous peoples has not yet been fully grasped and implemented in reality. For example, the Mang Đen district in Kon Plong district of Kon Tum province is an ideal place for ecotourism, with an altitude above 1200

---

[129] See Decision No. 2714 / QD-BVHTTDL dated August 3, 2016.

m, a mild climate throughout the year, ranging from 16 to 22°C, and considered to be the second Đà Lạt in the Central Highlands. However, it is still wild with three lakes, seven waterfalls and virgin forests covering more than 80% of the natural area. Here, Mang Đen National Eco-Tourism Zone was developed together with the Dak Ke – Mang Đen Eco Resort, Pa Sy Waterfall Eco-Tourism Zone, and Kampling Community Tourist Village. The ethnic minorities living in the region include R'mam, M'nam, S'dang, H're and K'dong (a branch of the S'dang).

In terms of indigenous festivals, the S'dang held Waterdrop Festival, the K'dong held Abundant Rice Festival. The K'dong and the M'nam (also called the H'rê) annually organize the new Communal House rites and Cross-Bow Shooting Festival. The S'dang held annual Buffalo Stable Construction Festival, Buffalo Killing Festival, and New Rice Eating Festival, and so on.

In addition, Mang Đen was classified as a historical, cultural and landscape relic by the Ministry of Culture and Information (now the Ministry of Culture, Sports and Tourism) in 2000. Therefore, the development of ecotourism in the Mang Đen district of Kontum province must be combined with cultural tourism, taking full advantage of the elusive nature of the local natural world as well as the culture of the local ethnic minorities and the history of this land. In general, taking Mang Đen as an example, I think the development of ecotourism in the Central Highlands of Vietnam should focus on solving the following problems:

Firstly, raising the community's awareness of the development of eco-tourism in the central plateau so that the community can clearly understand the requirements of eco-tourism development, especially the role of the community in maintaining the natural and cultural values of ethnic minority groups in the region. According to the requirements of ecotourism (as proposed by the Environment Agency (2002), creating high-income opportunities for the community is an important requirement, too. This is really a considerable challenge for the ethnic minorities in the Central Highlands.

Secondly, when developing tourism products, attention should be paid to the unique products unique to the region, which should include the natural, historical and cultural values of the ethnic minorities in the region. The value and price of tourism products should be placed in a socialist-oriented market economy in the context of Vietnam's economy.

Thirdly, training tour guides and giving priority opportunities to local ethnic minorities. In addition to tourism knowledge, traditional cultural knowledge should also be excavated in the minds and consciousness of indigenous peoples in order to illuminate and introduce this knowledge to tourists. We should return the forest culture to the community, and promote the community to introduce the forest culture of the local ethnic minorities to the tourists. We must brainstorm to attract and develop eco-tourists in the Central Highlands in a sustainable manner, overcoming the phenomenon of one-time tourist arrivals in tourist destinations.

Fourthly, formulating policies to solve current difficulties and constraints, limiting problems encountered in the process of developing eco-tourism in the Central Highlands. Attention is drawn to the development and implementation of policies related to the protection and development of the values of the natural and cultural landscape of ethnic minorities in the region. For example, under current circumstances, sacred forests of local ethnic minorities should be valued in national parks and nature reserves, and village patriarchs and the Council of Village Patriarchs should continue to play a role in forest-related activities, especially sacred forests. Opportunities for patriarchs to impart and spread local knowledge about forests and sacred forests to the younger generation should be created and respected.

From the development of databases and big data to the publication of 3D books on the forms and types of the tangible and intangible cultural heritage of indigenous minorities in the Central Highlands, the technological advancement of the Industrial Revolution 4.0 was applied to the development of ecotourism in the Central Highlands, from the use of traditional mass media To the new media to fully promote the tourism in the Central Highlands and the region, especially eco-tourism.

Last but not least, the application of technological advances of the industrial revolution 4.0 in ecotourism development in the Central Highlands should be promoted. This task could start from developing data banks and big data to publishing 3D books on the forms and types of the tangible and intangible cultural heritage of native ethnic minority groups in the Central Highlands. The use of both traditional mass media and new media in promoting the Central Highlands' tourism, including ecotourism, in particular, is highly appreciated.

Conclusion

The Central Highlands of Vietnam is an area with many features favorable for ecotourism development. The indigenous minority communities in the region bear many special characteristics, which bring opportunities and challenges to the development of the local ecotourism. In the past few years, the Vietnamese government has made every effort to the social and economic development of the Central Highlands. Overall, tourism, especially eco-tourism, is booming, but there are still difficulties and challenges. Many problems have emerged, which require the attention of scientists and administrators of culture, tourism, and community.

Reference

1. Angel, F. 1971. *Chống Đuy-rinh* (Anti Duyring), Hanoi, Truth Publisher.

2. Condominas, G. 1982. L'Espace social. A propos de l'Asie du Sud-Est) Paris, Flammarion,*(Social space in Southeast Asia)*, *(Không gian xã hội vùng Đông Nam Á)* Trans: Ngọc Hà, Thanh Hằng, Hồ Hải Thụy, Hanoi: Culture Publisher, 1997.

3. Lê, Văn Khoa & Phạm ,Quang Tú. 2014. *Hướng tới phát triển bền vững Tây Nguyên* (Toward sustainable development of the Central Highlands). Hanoi: Knowledge Publisher.

4. Ministry of Culture, Sport, and Tourism. 2016. Decision No. 2714 / QD-BVHTTDL dated August 3, 2016.

5. Nguyễn, Minh Đạo & Trần, Quang Bảo. 2018. "Du lịch sinh thái trong các vườn quốc gia, khu bảo tồn thiên nhiên khu vực miền Trung và Tây Nguyên, lý thuyết và thực tiễn (Ecotourism in national parks, nature reserves in Central Region and Central Highlands, Theory and practice)." In the Proceedings of *Bảo tồn đa dạng sinh học và phát triển bền vững miền Trung và Tây Nguyên lần thứ I* (The 1st International Workshop on Conservation of biodiversity and sustainable development in the Central Region and Central Highlands), Danang: manuscript.

6. Nguyễn, Từ Chi. 1996. *Góp phần nghiên cứu văn hóa và tộc người* (Contributing to research on culture and ethnicity). Hanoi: Culture and Information Publisher & Journal of Culture and Arts.

7. Prime Minister Office. 2011. Decision No. 2473-QD-TTg dated 30 December 2011.

8. Prime Minister Office. 2013. Decision No. 2162 QD-TTg dated November 21, 2013.

9. Tô ,Ngọc Thanh & Nguyễn, Chí Bền. 2006. *Kiệt tác truyền khẩu và di sản phi vật thể của nhân loại: Không gian văn hóa cồng chiêng Tây Nguyên* (Oral Masterpiece and intangible heritage of

humanity: the Gong cultural space in the Central Highlands). Hanoi: Thế Giới Publisher.

10. Trần, Quốc Vượng ed,1998. *Cơ sở văn hóa Việt Nam* (Basis of Vietnamese Culture). 20th edition,2018,Hanoi: Education Publisher.

THE ROLE OF COMMUNITY IN BEHAVIORS TOWARDS WATER IN THE RED RIVER DELTA AND THE CENTRAL HIGHLANDS OF VIETNAM

Introduction

Vietnam, as described by the late professor Trần Quốc Vượng (1934-2005) and his colleagues in a university textbook entitled *The Basis of Vietnamese Culture (Cơ sở văn hóa Việt Nam)* (1), is constituted of six cultural regions. The Red River Delta and the Central Highlands are two among these distinct cultural regions. Differences in geo-cultural and geo-economic positions of the two regions have led to dissimilarity in their inhabitants' attitude towards water, the natural agent familial to all human beings.

The community of the Việt in the Red River Delta and their water gods

The Red River Delta is also known as the Northern Delta, a delta spanning from 21°34' North latitude (Lập Thạch district, Vĩnh Phúc province) to the alluvial plain at 19°5' North latitude and from 105°17' East latitude (Ba Vì district, Hanoi capital city) to 107°7' East latitude (Cát Bà island, Hải Phòng city). The region measuring about 14860 square km occupies 4.5% of the whole area of Vietnam. Within the region there are two municipals, Hà Nội city and Hải Phòng city, and other provinces including Bắc Ninh, Hà Nam, Hải Dương, Hưng Yên, Nam Định, Thái Bình, Vĩnh Phúc and Ninh Bình. By 2016, the Red River Delta has a population of almost 21 million, accounting for 22% of the total population of Vietnam. Averagely, there were 1413 people living within a square km. The majority of population of the Red River Delta are the Kinh (Việt); whereas, several small groups of Mường people live in Ba Vì district (Hà Nội city) and Nho Quan district (Ninh Bình province). Therefore, it can be said that the Red River Delta is the land of the Việt (Kinh). As Pierre Gourou (1900-1999) described three decades ago, "a village does not appear in the landscape as a collection of houses, but a block of trees. It is surrounded by a bamboo fence with dense treetops forming a solid rampart, and the shaky bamboo branches bring a green and solemn scene to the village.

As a key element of the landscape, the village also plays a leading role in the spiritual and social life of the peasants. Peasants are not separated individuals nor citizens of a commune, who only participate remotely in the life of the commune, just like residents of the French countryside; on the contrary, the religious, political and social life of the Vietnamese village is very lively and daily, and every peasant participates sincerely and enthusiastically in it with an ambition to take on the role that gets more important day by day."(2). Each village, as such, included a number of families doing wetland rice cultivation and living together in a definite space. The entire farming land, rivers, lakes and ponds were possessed by the village. The village allocated its fields to families to use in compliance with the rule practiced and inherited through generations. The most common plant chosen by peasants of the Red River Delta was rice which was seen almost everywhere in the region. In 1936, Pierre Gourou published significant data stating that "total area of Bắc Ninh province is 110,367 hectares, of which land not used for cultivation (housing, rivers, mounds, etc.) occupies an area of 82,543 hectares, i.e. nearly 20% of the area of land not used for cultivation of the entire delta, rice fields occupy 82,543 hectares, and the land dedicated to other crops rather than rice accounts for 4,965 hectares, i.e. about 4.5% of the province's total area."(3). Also, Gourou himself further outlined in the footnote that "if the percentage of non-rice land in Bắc Ninh is applied to the whole delta, we have the following results: 68,000 hectares of non-rice land and 1,132,000 hectares of rice fields." (4).

Hence, rice was the plant closely attaching to the Red River Delta. Back then, the element that was most concerned by the peasants must be water. Pierre Gourou himself, when writing work *"The Peasants of the Tonkin Delta"* in 1935-1936, also dedicated the third chapter to the examination of this element: Water as part of material environment. To

Pierre Gourou, rice cultivation required a great amount of water. And water was an element that dominated every aspect of the life of peasants in the Tonkin Delta; it could make them rich or poor, gave them enough food for made them suffer from starvation, and it could bring them with wealthy lives or force them to leave their homeland. In dealing with water and rivers, the Việt in the Red River Delta have built up a dyke system. It is not the only way to deal with water; however, it is the decision made by the Việt in the Red River Delta. This behavior reflects the "adaptability" of the Việt, an attribute I mentioned in my 2008 book, where I borrowed an idea from Professor Cao Xuân Huy to describe the Vietnamese people as "smooth, flexible and fluid like water... the adaptability is preeminence and a survival secret of our people (5). Moreover, once placing the Red River in scale of space and time, we cannot see it as it is today. Rather, the river has brought many changes to the northern delta, especially since the Việt have decided to cope with its ferocity by building a dyke system. A consequence of such treatment for the aggressive Red River however was frequent dyke breaches happening before the 1970s, leading to the emergence of sunken areas along the Red River such as Hưng Yên and Hà Nam provinces. For wetland rice peasants, water is an object to worship. They have always asked Buddha and Gods for water and rain for their cultivation after a long time drought as some following folk songs:

I pray to God for a rain

to take water to drink

to have paddy fields to plough.

There are several ways to pray for water:

1/ having procession of worshipped statues from forbidden chamber to outside space such as in the festival of Tứ Pháp (four powers) in Thuận Thành district, Bắc Ninh province. Local residents have a procession of Pháp Vân (Cloud Goddess), Pháp Vũ (Rain Goddess), Pháp Lôi (Thunder Goddess), and Pháp Điện (Lightning Goddess) from the forbidden chamber to outside with a pray: *three goddesses visit the festival of Un pagoda, strong wind and rain to make easily earning.*

2/ taking worshipped statues out of the forbidden chamber to dry in the sun such as in the festival of Bối Khê pagoda (Thanh Oai district, Hà Nội city). However, water is also a subject to be conquered. Many traditional festivals have been held as a way to express the gratitude towards ancient heroes who protected communities from flood. Festivals, which worship Sơn Tinh (Mountain God) and Thủy Tinh (Water God) in Ba Vì, Hà Tây, have been manifestations of attempts made by wetland rice peasants to conquer water and control flood. Behind the legendary imagery of Lê Lợi, who returned the sacred sword at Hoàn Kiếm Lake, there is not only a desire for a peaceful country but also an image of a cultural hero who is capable of controlling water. On the other hand, for the Việt (Kinh) in the Red River Delta, water is a natural entity that is both gentle and aggressive, thereby it has been sacred into a deity: water god. Moreover, people in the Red River Delta express many different behaviors towards water.

Firstly, water is an environment where traditional festivals take place. The space of the Viet's traditional festivals is sacred and secular. Many of these festivals have sacred space which is a river or a sea body. For instance, the whale worship festivals of coastal residents from Ha Tinh province to Ca Mau province take place whether at river mouths, coastal areas or on the sea. To these festivals, all ceremonial activities, especially performances, are held on the river or on the sea. The most typical are boat racing and swimming contests. For example, in the festival of Bạch Hạc temple (the town of Việt Trì city, Phú Thọ province), festival of Chèm temple (Tây Hồ district, Hà Nội city), traditional festival in Khê Hồi village (Thường Tín district, Hà Nội city), Đồng Xâm festival (Kiến Xương district, Thái Bình province). Also, water is an environment where sacrifice offerings are absorbed. Villagers, after their ceremonies, usually float the offerings down the river or the sea as a way to express their respect to worshiped deities. For instance, during the festival of Bình Đà village (Thanh Oai district,

Hà Nội city), local residents bring Vía cakes to the river, crush them into pieces and throw them into the river. Moreover, water is an agent representing aspirations for innovation. It is the starting point of change. Việt people use water for washing ceremony (lễ mộc dục) – a required ritual essential to the process of festival. People believe that water in the middle of river is pure, and that it is the best to clean worshipped statues with this water. This ritual can be seen in many traditional festivals such as the festival of Bà Tấm temple (Gia Lâm district, Hà Nội city), the festival of Hóa Dạ Trạch temple (Khoái Châu district, Hưng Yên province), and the festival of Cuông temple (Nghệ An province), etc. On the other hand, water is subject to sacralization. It is transformed into holy figures representing community's beliefs and aspirations. Animals like snakes, dragons and whales are sacralized and worshipped in a number of traditional festivals. Many festivals of the Việt are central around the snake, including ones dedicated to the worship of Mother Goddesses, in which the snake appears under the name of Ông Lốt. Beside the snake, other animals worshipped by the Viet are all related to water environment. Water is the point of departure as well as the point of return to many worshipped animals in the Việt's traditional festivals. Meanwhile, coastal villages from Hà Tĩnh province to the southward of Vietnam adopt a certain cult dedicated to whales. Central characters in traditional festivals of these fishing villages are whales, creatures living in the open sea. To fishermen, the sea is a crucial resource of income essential to their lives, but it also contains a great amount of danger. For this reason, fishermen believe that whales are their guardian gods and they will rescue them whenever they have to face dangerous situations posed by the sea. Moreover, people from one generation to the next have sacralized many supernatural entities into historical – cultural figures being important to the Viet's spiritual life. Noticeably, before being mystified and historicized, many among these historical and cultural figures were entities associated with water. Result from an investigation into over 94 hagiographies of 94 villages in the Red River Delta showed that 25 villages' tutelary gods were mysteriously born as a result of the combination between a woman and a snake or a dragon. For instance, the figure of Linh Lang worshipped in festivals nearby Thăng Long imperial city and Lệ Mật village (Gia Lâm district, Hà Nội city) has his origin in the river. Other examples can be seen in the cases of Gods named Trương Hống and Trương Hát who are worshipped by residents living along the Cầu River (border line between Bắc Ninh and Bắc Giang provinces). Both of them are derived from snakes. As peasants living by wet rice cultivating or fishing, water is a vital element for Việt people. Thus, when people worship water spirits or historical figures – central elements of traditional festivals, they are actually worshipping water.

Because they live in a delta and have to deal with the Red River, an aggressive river, the role of their community in shaping the relation between human beings and water deities is of significance to Việt people. When speaking about the village community of the Việt (Kinh) in the Red River Delta, it is necessary to highlight the role of village convention. "Every village has its own convention and a given village convention often includes specific content which cannot be found in other conventions of other villages. Moreover, each convention has an aggregation of its own, that is, it is possible to mention a number of issues or aspects that will not be mentioned in other village conventions." (6) Researchers have agreed that the convention has many different names such as village custom, regulation, rules, or village agreement, etc.

In Vietnamese history, village conventions appeared as early as the 15th century. Until the 16th and 17th centuries, they were improved. In the 18th century, village conventions became very popular and were conceptualized as Confucian-inspired regulations applied to given villages. When characterizing Villages conventions and customs in particular and Villages autonomous mechanism in general, scholars usually use an folk idiom "*the rules of the King are secondary to the customs of the village.*" However, as showed by the aforementioned research outcomes, Villages could only enjoy their autonomy to a certain extent; whereas, the central state still sought to strengthen their controlling power. Regarding the relationship between village members with water and with water gods, the convention paid significant attention to the behavior of village members towards water. Interesting examples can be seen in conventions of some villages in Thái Bình province. In 1924 convention of Đại Hữu commune, Tân Định canton, Tiền Hải district, Thái Bình province, Article 3 mandated that: "Those who cause damage to the field edge must pay a fine ... and have to rebuild it". Article 4 in the same convention stated that "Anyone who waters the field without permission and do fishing that leads to the leak of farming water must be punished ... and forced to bail out water for the effected landlord "(7). Article 20 in the convention of Noi Trang commune, Hà Lý canton, Duyên Hà district, Thái Bình province, mandated that "The duty of the head of village guards and members of village associations are to patrol inside the village and outside in the field to urge tax collection, to look after planted crops, to repair roads and bridges, to ask younger guards to close and open water inlet sluice in order to appropriate provide water to farming fields, and to oversee village farming fields to make sure that no one lets their ducks go inside this area (8) Article 7 in the convention of Hoàng Nông village, Duyên Hà district, Thái Bình province, mandated that: "the head of village guards is responsible for pouring and draining water whenever it is necessary to do so. He must ask permission from the village administrative board before conducting his duties. Younger guards will immediately arrest those who open the water sluice and make the field dry up. Village administrative board will punish these people (9). Every year, in addition to the festival to worship the tutelary gods, villagers also hold several public rituals, such as the new rice ceremony in October and a ceremony to pray for rain (10) Thus, in the Red River Delta, the community attaches special importance to preserving water resources, organizing activities to express their beliefs in water gods and developing written agreements to protect water resources.

Ethnic minority groups in the Central Highlands and the Water Genie

Meanwhile, the indigenous ethnic minorities in Vietnam Central Highland have different behavior towards water and water Gods. It is to clarify that the Central Highlands comprises many highlands which are next to each other from North to South including Kontum, KonPlong, Kon Ha Nung, Pleiku, M'Drak, Buon Ma Thuot, M'Nong, Lam Vien, and Di Linh, with different height. While Lam Vien is the highest highland which is about 1500m, Di Linh about 900-1000m, and Plei ku about 800m, Kontum and Buonma Thuot Highlands are only 500m high. The Central Highlands with bazan soil includes five provinces: Kom tum, Gia Lai, Dak Lak, Dak Nong and Lam Dong. It borders Quang Nam to the north, Quang Ngai, Binh Dinh, Phu Yen, Khanh Hoa, Ninh Thuan and Binh Thuan to the east, Dong Nai and Binh Phuoc to the south, Attapeu (of the Lao People's Democratic Republic) and Ratanakiri and Mondukiri (of the Kingdom of Cambodia) to the west, covering an area of 54,000 km². As the Central Highlands has no borders with the sea and is rather close to the equator, it has two distinct weather seasons a year: the rainy season from April to October, and the dry season from November to April of the following year.

The indigenous ethnic minority groups in the Central Highlands of Vietnam comprise the Jorai, Ede, and Churu of the Malayo Polynesian linguistic family and the Bahna, Cohor, So dang, M'nong, Ma, Gie -Trieng, R'mam, and Brau of the Mon Khmer linguistic family. Both of these ethnic communities are inhabited in villages, with different names depending on the community and ethnic minority group. If the Jorai and Churu call their village *plei*, the Bahna calls it *ploi*, the Co ho *bon*, and the Ede *buon* etc. …The ethnic minorities in the Central Highlands "whatever group they belong to have settled in an autonomous or independent village and live on upland rice farming… For cultivation, they have to settle in villages which are complete populated and smallest units and each occupies an area with distinct borders that cannot be invaded upon by other villages, if not, conflicts would occur" (11) The economic activities of these indigenous ethnic minority groups are different in their behaviors to the water sources. If the Bahna, Brau, R'mam and Gie-Trieng live on upland rice farming (dry rice fields), the Churu and Co Hor live on wet rice cultivation. Also in the tribe that lives on upland rice farming, some groups of people live on wet rice cultivation. The Ede, for example, lives on upland rice farming, but the group of Ede Bih lives on wet rice cultivation; the So Dang people live mainly on upland rice farming, but the M'nam group lives on wet rice cultivation etc. Regardless of their rice cultivation modes - upland rice farming or wet rice farming, all these indigenous ethnic minority groups have strong attachment to the bazan soil highlands, thus water is very important for them. In their belief, these indigenous groups consider this natural phenomenon sacred and call it the Water Genie. The worship of river watering place is a sacred ritual for them. For example, for the Jorai the Water Genie (or *Yang Ia*) is very sacred but close to them which provides them with pure, fresh water sources. The ceremony of worshiping the river watering place is very important for them and is held anually after the harvest. The village oldest folk, who is the master of the ceremony prays for the Water Genie to come to the villages, to provide them with pure streams, brimful with water. And he is the first person to get water into a dried gourd and pour it into a wine jar and then he takes the first sip of wine from the jar through a bamboo pipe. At the end of the ceremony, women in the village (also called plei) fetch water home in their dried gourds. Talking about the Jorai people's behaviors to water, mention should be made to Potao Puih and Potao Ia – the religious leaders of Fire and Water. The historical books such as *Phủ biên tạp lục* by Lê Quí Đôn (1726-1784), *Lịch triều hiến chương loại chí* (Calendar of Constitutional Type) by Phan Huy Chú (1782-1840), and *Đại Nam thực lục tiền biên* và *chính biên* (Dai Nam Records of the frontier and the main border) by the National Historiographer's Office of the Nguyễn Dynasty (1802-1945) once mentioned them considering them as kingdoms: The Kingdom of Water region and the Kingdom of Fire region (12)

For Potao Puih, the ceremony pray for rain is the most important ritual. The Jorai people in the area influenced by Potao Puih believe that the sacred sword called by the villagers as oi Tha acts as a medium object and Po tao Puih is the only person who can contact Gods to ask them for rain to water their upland fields. The ceremony to pray for rain is held in April at the side where the sun rises of the house of Potao Puih. At the end of the ceremony, people splash water around.

The Ede organizes the river watering place ceremony annually after the harvest to express their gratitude to the Water Genie. The ritual is often held by the founder of the river watering place and presided by the village old folks. All villagers enthusiastically and voluntarily take part in the ceremony, expressing gratitude to the Water Genie for giving them pure and abundant water sources. For the Churu people who live on wet rice cultivation, cach plei designates a person in charge of irrigation and two assistants. The head of the irrigation work is elected by the villagers. He must be good at irrigation and impartial. His task is to distribute equally the water volume from public canals to each field of the village households. When necessary, he can ask the village head to mobilize villagers to renovate the irrigation works before the cultivation season.

So, the indigenous ethnic minority groups in the Central Highlands are always grateful to and respect the Water Genie. The role of the community to worship the Water Genie is very important. They all consider it sacred, respectful and grateful. Worthy of note is the role of the shaman and the village old folks in the ceremony to worship the Water Genie. In the history of the Central Highlands, only in the Jorai and the Ede ethnic minority groups, the shamans play the role of religious leaders of the Fire and Water Genie which were long time ago the Kingdom of Water and the Kingdom of Fire as recorded by Vietnamese historians. F. Angels remarks: "From the commencement of each of those communes, there were certain common interests whose conservation was assigned to every individuals, but controlled by the collective such as judging disputes; punishing those who abuse power;

and taking care of water sources..."(13). This suggests us to continue thinking of the role of shamans in the belief of water worship of the indigenous ethnic minority groups in Vietnam Central Highlands.

The Water Culture of Vietnam through two ethnic groups in two cultural regions

The Kinh (the majority Vietnamese) in the Northern Delta and the indigenous ethnic minority group in the central Highlands are two different ethnic communities living in two different spatial regions. Their behaviors to water are different. In their mind, the King in the Northern Delta fear water, but desire to conquer water. Yet, for the indigenous ethnic minority groups in the Central Highlands, they are respectful and grateful to water, considering it sacred. The water culture of Vietnam should be examined through historical evolutions and cultural space with changes. In Vietnam, the ethnic group playing the role of the subject is the Kinh (Viet), "Through ups and downs since the commencement of history, the ethnic group that will be the subject always settles in the delta while other ethnic groups settle in valleys or on mountain sides and the highlands. In the delta, people quicky turned to water rice cultivation with higher yield than subsidiary and upland rice crops in the uplands (14). The wet rice cultivation makes the Kinh have in their mind the two extremes: fearing water and conquering water. The legend of Son Tinh and Thuy Tinh (Mountain Genie and Water Genie) expresses the attitude of conquering water of the Kinh. The more the water rises, the higher the dykes will be embanked by them to prevent it. In 2008, at an international workshop on eco-culture of the residents living along the Red River from upstream to lower reaches, I presented a paper on the role and geographical and cultural position of the Red River Dykes from the three-crossroads of the River to the lower reaches (15). The Kinh always consider water an environment of rituals in their village festivals. In their ceremony, people take water from the middle flow of a large river to clean joss statues. The votive statues in the relics must be cleaned with the water fetched to the harem from the river after a ceremony worshiping the

River Genie and the Water Genie. People in each village have set their village regulations to protect water for their existence and for rice fields and designate people to manage the water sources. Of the 11 indigenous ethnic minority groups in the Central Highlands, only the Churu have behaviors to water similar to the King in the Northern Delta. They build canals, dykes and dams for wet rice cultivation irrigation. The water culture of the Churu in the Central Highlands is similar to that of the Kinh in the Northern Delta although these two ethnic groups live in two different geographical and cultural spaces. The remaining indigenous ethnic minority groups in the Central Highlands behave with water different to the Kinh in the Northern Delta. "Here the village is not attached to water as that in the Vietnamese society where the village is called "làng nước", meaning village and water... In many regions, there are chieftains ... at least there is a regime of religious leaders with the Kingdom of Water region and the Kingdom of Fire region " (16). The annual ceremony to worship the Deities of River Watering Place and the Water Genie after the harvest is a regular religious and cultural activity of the people of indigenous ethnic minority groups in the Central Highlands, whether they are Jorai, Ede or M'nong. The attitude of conquering water has not yet been seen in these ethnic groups.

Conclusion

The Kinh (Viet) in the Northern Delta and people of the 11 indigenous ethnic minority groups in the Central Highlands are two cultural subjects in two different cultural spaces in Vietnam. In the mind of the Vietnamese in the Northern Delta and the indigenous ethnic minorities in the Central Highlands there remain an attitude of respect and gratitude to water, fear of water but striving to conquer it. The behaviours with water of the ethnic groups in these two different cultural spaces in Vietnam have made the water culture of Vietnam unified but diversity, with different evolutions and changes in the space and time which need to be further studied by Vietnamese and foreign anthropologists and cultural researchers.

Note

(1) Tran, Quoc Vuong Ed,*The Basis of Culture Vietnam*, Education Publishes, 20th edition, 2018.

(2) Pierre Gourou,1936, *The peasants of the Tonkin Delta,* Nguyễn Khắc Đạm, Đào Hùng, Nguyễn Hoàng Oanh (trans.), Đào Thế Tuấn (ed.), Vietnam Association of History Science, École française d'Extrême-Orient, Young Publisher, 2003, p. 216.

(3) Pierre Gourou, 1936,*The Peasants of the Tonkin Delta,* Nguyễn, Khắc Đạm, Đào, Hùng, Nguyễn, Hoàng Oanh (trans.), Đào Thế Tuấn (ed.), Vietnam Association of History Science, École française d'Extrême-Orient, Young Publisher, 2003, p. 363.

(4) Pierre Gourou, *ibid., p.363*

(5) Nguyễn,Chí Bền, *(Vietnamese Culture: Studies and Approaches),* Social Sciences Publishes. Hà Nội, 2018, Vol.1, Issue 1, p. 920.

(6) Trần, Từ, *Organizational Structure of Traditional Vietnamese Villages in Northern Vietnam*, Social Science Publisher, H, 1984. p. 99.

(7) Nguyễn Thanh (ed.), *Village conventions in Thái Bình province*, National Culture Publishes, Hanoi, 2000, p. 140.

(8) Nguyễn ,Thanh, ibid, p. 146.

(9) Nguyễn, Thanh, ibid. p. 153.

(10) Nguyễn ,Thanh, ibid. p. 255.

(11) Nguyễn, Từ Chi, *Contributing to cultural and ethnicity Studies,* Culture and Information Publishes, Culture and Art Magazine, Hanoi,1996, p. 521).

(12) See also: + *Pơ tao Apuih, Documentation and Remarks*, many authors, published by Gia Lai Provincial Department of Culture and Information, Plei ku, 2004.

+ Jacques Dournes,1977, *Potao, a theory of the power of the Jorai in Indochina*,Paris,Flammarion, translated by Nguyên Ngọc, Knowledge Publishes, Hanoi, 2013.

(13)*Anti-Duhring*, Truth Publisher, Hanoi, 1971, p. 304)

(14)Nguyễn, Từ Chi, *Contributing to cultural and ethnicity Studies*, Culture and Information Publisher, Culture and Art Magazine, Hanoi, 1996, p. 518.

(15)See Nguyễn, Chí Bền, *Vietnamese culture-study and approaches*, Social Science Publisher, Hanoi, Vol. 1, Book 1, pp. 912-934.

(16)Nguyễn, Từ Chi, *Contributing to cultural and ethnicity Studies,* Culture and Information Publisher, Culture and Art Magazine, Hanoi, 1996, p. 527.

References

1. F. Angels, *Anti-Duhring*, Truth Publisher, Hanoi, 1971.

2. Nguyễn, Chí Bền, *Vietnamese Culture – Study and Approaches*, Social Science Publisher, Hanoi, 2018, Vol. 1, Book 1.

3. Nguyễn,Từ Chi, *Contributing to cultural and ethnicity Studies*, Culture and Information Publisher, Culture and Art Magazine, Hanoi, 1996.

4. Georges Condominas, *Chúng tôi ăn rừng*, the Vietnamese version by Trần, Thị Lan Anh, Phan, Ngọc Hà, Trịnh, Thu Hồng, Nguyễn, Thu Phương, edited by Nguyên Ngọc, The Gioi Publisher, Vietnam Museum of Ethnology, Hanoi, 2003.

5. Piere Gourou, *North Vietnam Delta peasants*, translated by Nguyễn, Khắc Đạm, Đào ,Hùng, Nguyễn, Hoàng Oanh, edited by Đào Thế Tuấn, Vietnam Historical Sciences Association, French Far East Institute, Young Publishing House, 2003.

6. Lưu ,Hùng, *Traditional Village in the Thuong upper land*, National Culture Publisher, Hanoi, 1994.

7. Many authors *Pơ tao Apuih, Document and Remarks*, published by Gia Lai Department of Culture and Information, Plei ku, 2004.

8. Jacques Dournes, *Potao, a theory on the power of the Jorai in Indochina*, 1977,Paris, Flammarion,translated by Nguyên Ngọc, Knowledge Publishing House, Hanoi, 2013.

9. Nguyễn, Thanh edited, *Thai Binh Village Regulations*, National Culture Publishing House, Hanoi, 2000.

10. Trần, Từ, *Orgaqnizational structure of a Vietnamese traditional village in North Vietnam*, Social Science Publishcr, Hanoi, 1984.

11. Trần, Quốc Vượng ed, *The Basis of Vietnamese Culture,* Education Publisher, Hanoi, 20th edition, 2018.

FROM THE RED RIVER DELTA TO THE CENTRAL HIGHLAND: WATER WORSHIP AND SUSTAINABLE DEVELOPMENT IN VIETNAM

In Vietnam, the Red River Delta region and the red soil plateaus in the Central Highlands experience dry seasons. Water is an extremely precious resource on which human beings depend for survival and development. Therefore, both Vietnamese and ethnic minorities from the delta to the plateau have a passionate and fearful attitude towards water. They all worship the god of water - the supreme god.

This article presents the water worship of the Vietnamese people in the Red River Delta and ethnic minority communities in the Central Highlands on the grounds of ritual developments, offerings, and sacrifice ceremonies. Based on that, the article analyzes the adaptability of the inhabitants to the ecology of two specific regions of Vietnam: the delta and the red-soil plateaus. At the same time, the paper also analyzes what water worship can help people in two places to be sustainable.

1. Introduction

Water is a natural ingredient closely related to human beings. In Vietnam, the relationship between people and water is different from the Red River Delta to the Central Highlands, although the Việt living in the Red River Delta and the ethnic minorities living in the Central Highlands share the same ancient Southeast Asian cultural foundation. Currently, both two communities are facing severe drought. So what is the role of water worship and how is it transformed?

2. The Red River Delta and the Central Highlands

From a cultural perspective, Vietnam is divided into six cultural regions (Trần Quốc Vượng ed. 1998/2018, pp. 220-94), which includes the Northwest, the Northeast (also called the Việt Bắc Region), the Red River Delta, the Coastal Central, the Central Highlands, and the South.

The cultural area of the Red River Delta, sometimes called the northern delta is an area formed by the sediments of the Red River and the Thái Bình River. The area covers areas such as provinces: Vĩnh Phúc, Bắc Ninh, Hà Nam, Hưng Yên, Hải Dương, Thái Bình, Nam Định, Ninh Bình, Hà Nội City and Hải Phòng City, a part of Bắc Giang province, a part of Phú Thọ province, and a part of Quảng Ninh province. Professor Trần Quốc Vượng regards the delta as an isosceles triangle, with Việt Trì city (Phú Thọ province) at the top, Móng Cái city (Quảng Ninh province), and Ninh Bình province at the other end. Geographically, this delta covers the area from attitude 21o34' North (Lập Thạch district, Vĩnh Phúc province) to attitude 19o5' North (Kim Sơn district, Ninh Bình province), from attitude 105o17' East (Ba Vì district, Hà Nội city) to attitude 107o7' East (Cát Bà island). The area of the delta is 15.000 square kilometers, accounting for 4.6% of the total area of Vietnam. The delta gradually decreases from northeast to southeast, changing from ancient sediment with the foundation of 10-15 meters high to alluvium ground of 2-4 meters high in the central part, and the coast is covered by rising tides every day.

The residents of the area are descendants of the ancient Vietnamese, which is consistent with Prof. Ngô Đức Thịnh's explanation: In the long history, the cultural development process from "Phùng Nguyên, Đồng Đậu, Gò Mun to Đông Sơn is also the process an ancient Mon-Khmer speaking group got connected to the ancient Tay-Tai community in the north and the Austronesian-speaking community from the southern coastal area. From this process, a new community emerged: ancient Vietnamese" (Vũ Tự Lập ed. 1991, p. 123). In the Red River Delta, until now, people have mostly made a living by growing rice. The agricultural area is about 760,000 hectares, accounting for 51.2% of the total area of the delta. Rice is the main plant, accounting for 82% of the total area of food crops. Before 1945, P. Gourou wrote in a survey of farmers in the Red River Delta: "Rice is grown in almost every field. Farmers have put a lot of effort into this, and other types of crops are only grown where rice cannot be grown in the field" (Gourou, trans 2003, p. 359). Rice is a crop that is vital to water, as can be seen from the saying "first water, second fertilizer, third diligence, and fourth seed variety" (nhất nước, nhì phân, tam cần, tứ giống). In other words, for the Việt in the Red River Delta, water is an integral part of their daily lives.

In terms of geographical and natural conditions characteristics, the Central Highlands is completely different from the Red River Delta. The total area of the central highlands is 53,471 square kilometers, 450 kilometers from north to south, and 150 kilometers from east to west (see map 2). This is not a separate highland but is composed of many adjacent highlands, such as Kontum Highlands, Kon Plông Highlands, Kon Hà Nừng Highlands, Plei Ku Highlands, M'Drăk Highlands, Buôn Ma Thuột Highlands, Mơ Nông Highlands, Lâm Viên Highlands, and Di Linh Highlands. These highlands cover the five provinces of Kon Tum, Gia Lai, Đắc Lắc, Đắc Nông, and Lâm Đồng from north to south. The highland is located at an altitude of about 500-600 meters above sea level. The main soil type is red basalt soil, so it is suitable for plants such as rubber, coffee, black pepper, and cocoa.

As for the climate, there are two distinct seasons in the Central Highlands: the rainy season lasts from May to the end of October, and the dry season lasts from November to April, with March and April being the driest and hottest months.

People living in the Central Highlands are divided into two categories: local people and people from the north after 1975. The local people consist of ethnic minorities belonging to the Mon-Khmer language group (Austro-Asiatic linguistic family), namely the Bahnar, Giẻ-Triêng, Sedang, Romam, M'nong, K'hor, Ma, Brau and ethnic minorities belonging to the Malayo–Polynesian language group (Austronesian linguistic family), namely the Êđê, Jo'rai (Gia-rai), and Churu. During the excavation in Gia Lai Province, archaeologists discovered that there was a culture called Biển Hồ culture, and confirmed that "the culture owner of Biển Hồ may be Malay-Polynesian speakers...", and these people came to the highlands about 4,000 years ago (Nguyễn Khắc Sử ed. 1995, p. 161).

Therefore, although the Việt in the Red River Delta and the ethnic minorities in the central highlands live in two regions with different natural conditions, climates, and farming methods, they still have the same water needs. Similar to the Việt in the Red River Delta, the ethnic minorities in the central highlands consider water as an important part of their daily lives.

3. An attitude of love and fear of water at the same time: the water worship

The Việt in the Red River Delta and the ethnic minorities living in the Central Highlands have some similarities in treating water: they both cherish water and fear water. However, the way they develop water worship is different.

The Việt in the Red River Delta experienced a long period of primitive communes, then approached 1,000 years under Chinese rule (111 AD- 938 BP), and another 1,000 years under the independent Viet dynasties (938-1945). Local water worship developed through three ways of sanctification: mythization, historicalization, and localization. People living in the Red River Delta have been always paying attention to rainwater awareness:

In Vietnamese	*English translation*
Lạy trời mưa xuống	I beg gods to offer rain
Lấy nước tôi uống	Give me water to drink
Lấy ruộng tôi cày.	And water the fields.

This worship began as part of daily life. Different dynasties of Đại Việt respected people's wishes, holding raining ceremonies at the national level. History books, for example, *Đại Việt sử ký toàn thư* (大越史記全書, Complete Annals of Đại Việt), *Đại Nam thực lục* (大南寔錄, Veritable Records of the Great South), written by Confucian scholars during the Lê Dynasty (1428-1789) and Nguyễn dynasty (1802-1945) recorded the details of many kings praying for rain. During the Lý (1010-1225) or Trần dynasty (1225-1400), people believed that gods could control rainfall, such as Đằng Châu Earth God or Hai Bà Trưng Goddesses (Two Trưng Kings), etc. In the praying season, the kings not only went to Dâu Temple whose central figure in the pantheon was not Shakyamuni Buddha but the goddess Pháp Vân (the goddess of Clouds, one of the four Dharmas[130] of the Việt people in the Red River Delta) but also ordered to set up an altar in Thăng Long capital to pray for favorable weather for the people.

This awareness has caused people in the villages to create rituals in their traditional festivals. Most festivals have a significant activity: the bathing ritual[131] (mộc dục, 沐浴). This sacred ritual must be conducted at mid-night moment. At Hát Môn temple festival dedicated to Hai Bà Trưng, an old man has to take a boat to the middle of the Red River to get water for the bathing rituals of God Chử Đồng Tử and his two wives in Chử Đồng Tử Temple. Prof. Đinh Gia Khánh discussed the water procession in Gióng Festival, which may represent many other festivals in the Red River Delta:

"We have seen Gióng Festival with ceremonial water parades in many different villages, which reflects the understanding of the importance of water in the very ancient period since the establishment of agriculture (especially the wet-rice agriculture) (Đinh Gia Khánh 1989, p. 86).

Accordingly, "Ceremonial water parades in many traditional villages have been explained by people in each place in a separate sense. However, not many people in the public understand that this ritual has

---

[130] Four Dharmas/Buddhas: Pháp Vân (Cloud Dharma), Pháp Vũ (Rain Dharma), Pháp Lôi (Thunder Dharma), Pháp Điện (Lightning Dharma) originated from the Banyan trees that the Indian master Kaudinya put his daughter named Man Nương in a local legendary story. After the tree fell into a river, the local people pulled the tree and made four statues from the tree log and installed the statures in four separate temples: Dâu, Đậu, Giàn, and Tướng Temples. In fact, the Four Dharma figures represent the four natural phenomena including Cloud (Vân), Rain (Vũ), Thunder (Lôi), Lightning (Điện) that were deified into Goddesses to be worshipped at the local temples. The Việt people in the Red River Delta tended to associate these temples with Buddhist pagodas.

[131] See pictures of the ritual ceremony at Đa Hòa Temple and Hai Bà Trưng Temple.

long popularized the festivals of Southeast Asia, and is related to wet rice civilization right at the dawn of history (Đinh Gia Khánh 1989, p. 182).

For the Việt people, water is both the object and the means of worship. On the Vietnamese altar, there may or may not be wine, but it is necessarily not lacking a glass of water. Water must be included on the altar because it is always available in nature and because it is the most precious thing for wet rice farmers (Diệp Đình Hoa 2000, p. 438).

It is worth noting that ancient aboriginal gods like water gods existed in abundance in the sacred space of the village. Tạ Chí Đại Trường (2000, p. 50- 64) emphasized the role of natural gods and spirits in the section of "Nhiên thần: các vị thần sông nước (Nature: the gods of water)"[132] in his well-known book *Thần, người và đất Việt* (The Gods, People, and Land of Vietnam). He provided many valuable bibliographical and field evidence and analyzed objectively that the water has been deified into gods that are both sacred and close to the people of the villages.

Meanwhile, the Central Highlanders until the seventies of the twentieth century were still at the end of the primitive communal period. Although some clues of the emergence of the social classes had been found, they did not shape the class distinction Therefore, the behavior of local people in this period belongs to the human behavior pattern in the late period of the original commune. Accordingly, all human daily activities must be witnessed and certified by the spirits. When building a new village, they had to build a water wharf and had to worship it regularly. For Êđê people, water is more important than food and clothing. They believe that they can still live without a meal for a month, and they will only catch a cold without clothes. But without water, they will not survive. Therefore, until today, when people in the central highlands are looking for land to build villages, they always pay

---

[132] In Chapter 2: Các hệ thống thần linh bản địa Việt cổ (The System of Local Gods of Ancient Việt People).

attention to finding water that can meet their needs for life and production (fieldwork note).

To perform this ritual, they selected talented men of the village to build a bamboo-made cây nêu (sacred pole). To avoid animals passing, the pole would be erected in a high position in front of nhà Rông (the communal house). Others would have to go to the head of the water to check and make sure that the fresh water will flow to the village. Before the ceremony begins, the village head would beat gongs from the early morning to inform the villagers that the village was about to hold a ceremony to worship the water wharf. That day, the waterfront was carefully decorated with a greeting gate with leaves, long grass, and hanging decorations. The collective worshiping ceremony consisted of three main parts. The first part was to organize a sacrifice at the wharf, praying that the water spirit would bring the villager's health. The second part was to set up the sacrificial activity at the fence before bringing water into the house. Finally, one more sacrifice was held at the home of the owner of the wharf. After the worshiping process was completed at the wharf, people would take water into water containers (usually dried gourds) and bring them home as blessing objects. Meanwhile, a group of people would follow the ceremonial master to the stairs of each house, singing to pray for peace and pour sacrificial blood drops at the foot of the stairs to pray for the owner. At the beginning of the ritual, the village head would stand at the head of the water, dropped a few blood drops of the sacrificial animal (usually buffaloes or cows) to flow down to the end of the water source, to the village. At that time, each villager, in turn, performed the ritual of worshiping the wharf. At the end of the ceremony, the entire village gathered in a longhouse (nhà Rông, public communal house) to participate in a group party, drink, and dance with lively gongs performance in the festive atmosphere. The sounds of gongs and jubilant dances brought people closer together. Ceremonial sacrifice to the water wharf and/or the water god was held every year after the harvest season to pray for favorable weather, good harvest, and happy life. This is one of the forms of community cultural activities that have many positive meanings in the spiritual life of the Êđê people.

During the ceremony at the water wharf, gongs are continuously performed at the longhouse. Gongs' sound functions as not only messages that people want to tell the gods about their concerns about life and death, but also the thoughts or the pursuit of the minds of different people in the entire village. Perhaps this is why the Êđê ethnic gong music in Dak Lak province fully embodies and reflects community activities; it is the material and means of sympathy (Victor Turner's 'communitas') and communication between man and god.

In the old time, ceremony to worship the water wharf was annually organized. The person in charge of the ceremony (also called the etiquette, hereafter: the ceremonial master) was usually the village head and also the owner of the water wharf. After preparing all the offerings, the ceremonial master and two ritual assistants dressing in ancient Êđê costumes proceeded to the water wharf to start the ceremony. People believed that the clothes they wear were very similar to those worn by their ancestors during the warfare. Each water wharf might require a different number of ritual assistants, however, this number must be consistent every year. The ceremonial master and two ritual assistants maintained their tools during the ceremony. During the ceremony, a person must hold a sword, knife, and wooden shield. These were the items delivered by the family of the wharf owner's wife and were only brought to the ceremony on this grand occasion. They believed that these were ancient objects and have sacred significance extremely important for family members, so they had to protect them well. After each offering, the ceremonial master watered the flesh placed in the leaves of Ê-nang tree. This action replaced the divine invitation to gods and spirits in the neighborhood to enjoy the offerings that day. Ending the ceremony at the water wharf, they returned to the village to do the ceremony under the old trees. They regarded that those trees functioned as an ancient fence protecting the residence of gods and earth spirits of the village. Afterwards, the ceremonial master instructed the owner of the water wharf, his wife, and all female family members to perform the ceremony in order. The offerings in the east are for the wharf owners. Part of the pig's body was used to thank the master of ceremony. All other items on the tray were evenly distributed by everyone present. In the end, people made sacrifices for the female owner of the water wharf with an offering as a rooster and a jug of wine. Both her husband and sons received a big jug of wine. Participants became more and more crowded, everyone was drunk in the sounds of gongs and drums and were given part of the offerings. Women were always given priority first, then men.

As we can see, the ritual dedicated to the water wharf is a form of community cultural activities with many positive meanings in the spiritual life of the Êđê people that need to be preserved and promoted. It is not just a belief, this custom helps people to raise awareness about the importance of water in their daily life to conserve and protect water sources.

The neighboring Jo'rai (Gia-rai) call the rain praying masters (shamans) to be pơtao apuih. According to Nguyễn Kim Vân (2007), pơtao apuih in the old time conducted rain prayers at the beginning of the planting season around April every year. In addition, pơtao apuih also prayed for rain whenever a certain area was in a drought, and people in that area brought gifts to ask for help from pơtao apuih. Also according to Nguyễn Kim Vân, the last rain praying ceremony was carried out by Siu Luynh, the last pơtao apuih, on the floor of his house according to the following procedure:

(1) *Tlăo đing* (the person who put the stem into the wine jug, also the most important assistant of the *pơtao apuih*) must have prepared an offering, including one jug of wine, some beeswax candles rolled into sticks, one vase of rice and one cooked roaster cut into pieces. All were placed on a mat, spread on the north side door of Mr. Siu Luynh's house;

(2) At the beginning of the ceremony, Tlăo đing sat correctly

facing the offering (side door) and put the wine stem (straw) into the wine jug (for the potao apuih) with the top of the stem facing his side. After all the preparations were ready, *Tlăo đing* turned the stem towards the other side, bowed 3 times, and then lighted the candle.

Potao apuih came over and sits down at *Tlăo đing*'s original position, bowed three times to the altar of gods, then took some water from the copper pot with a copper cup and poured it into a wine bottle with his right hand. Meanwhile, His left hand held the wrist of his right hand to show respect to the gods. At the same time, while praying, he and took the rice from the jar and threw into the mat to invite the mountain gods, wood gods, stone gods, to participate in the ritual. Still holding the right hand with his left hand, potao Apuih picked up the meat with his right hand and threw it forward three times. Every time he threw the piece of meat forward, he read the praying spell.

(3) Next, Fire Lord (Potao Apuih) drank wine from the jug and poured it into his hands, where there were a piece of chicken, a piece of chicken liver, a piece of beeswax, and some rice. A rice bowl was always available under the Fire Lord's (Potao Apuih's) hand. Fire Lord (Potao Apuih) carefully placed the rice used in the ceremony in a closed place, and then used it as a spiritual weapon. Fire Lord (Pottao Apuih) and his representatives believed that they had fled the profane world during the ceremony. So people thought that these people's actions were now representative of the divine world. It was believed that the divine world was the opposite of the living world in which the gods could eat raw meat (which was believed to be cooked meat in the divine world). . Fire Lord (Potao apuih) then poured the wine and meat into a copper bowl and poured it into the tomb of dead Lords (Potaos). According to the Fire Lord (Potao Apuih), this ritual was to pray for the dead Lord (Potao) who would answer the prayers: it would bring rain (see Nguyễn Kim Vân 2007, p. 135).

Therefore, it can be seen that for the ethnic minorities in the Central Highlands, the water god is their sacred god.

4. In an increasingly dry nature, is the worship of water still a spiritual prop?

In recent years, like other regions, the Red River Delta and the highlands in the Central Highlands of Vietnam have endured tremendous changes in nature. At this time, government agencies play a big role in providing water for people to cultivate wet rice. In the Red River Delta, Vietnamese people do not have to face severe drought and water shortage, but the Central Highlands situation is quite tragic. In the first few months of 2016, the whole Central Highlands is in drought. To quickly help localities overcome the consequences of drought (and saltwater intrusion in the coastal regions), Prime Minister Nguyễn Xuân Phúc recently issued Decision No. 604/QD-TTg supporting 21 provinces, in which Đắk Lắk province received 57 billion VND (approximately, 25,5 million USD); Gia Lai province received VND 17.9 billion (7.6 million USD).

However, the whole Gia Lai province with 17/17 districts and towns suffered losses due to drought. Up to now, nearly 22,000 hectares of crops have been damaged, amounting to about VND 375 billion (15 million USD). Currently, the water level in rivers, streams, and ponds in this province has reached a record low. Most small-scale irrigation reservoirs have run out of water. Drought is getting more and more serious.

In Đắk Lắk province, data from the Provincial Steering Committee for Disaster Prevention and Search and Rescue shows that up to now, the whole province has 36,961 hectares of drought crops including 3,932 hectares of wet rice (of which 864 hectares are completely lost); 29,348 ha of coffee (of which 3,958 ha are completely lost); 1,494 ha of pepper and some other crop areas. Total damage estimated at VND 1,110 billion (47.5 million USD).

In Kon Tum province, there were more than 2,100 hectares of crops that were drought and lack of water, of which 900 ha were completely lost, estimated damage caused by drought to agricultural production was about VND 93 billion (4 million USD). Drought makes 10,000 households lack of water for living.

Thus, nature is in a period of a formidable, terrible transformation. So what function does the water worship have for the locals? Quietly, people still worship water wharf as an unconscious habit. In fact, it is conscious behavior (see Illustration). Deep inside, people of the Êđê, Jo'rai, Bahnar, and other ethnic groups are still organizing sacrificial ceremonies dedicated to water gods and praying for their help. In a world where everything can be transformed, a spiritual prop in the depths of the mind is extremely important.

5. Conclusion

From the Red River Delta to the red soil plateaus in the central highlands, it is a long journey from the lowlands to the highlands. In these two places, we can hardly predict where the water worship took place earlier or are playing a more important role in the spiritual life of the community. Changes in nature will naturally lead to cultural changes, including popular religions. Water worship in Vietnam is currently strongly influenced by natural changes, but it still functions as a spiritual pillar in local people's mindset.

Reference

1. Diệp, Đình Hoa. 2000. *Người Việt ở đồng bằng Bắc bộ* (The Viet People in the Red River Delta). Hanoi. Social Science Publisher.

2. Đinh, Gia Khánh. 1989. *Trên đường tìm hiểu văn hóa dân gian* (Understanding Folklore). Hanoi. Social Science Publisher.

3. Vũ, Tự Lập et al. 1991. *Văn hóa và cư dân vùng đồng bằng sông Hồng* (Culture and People of the Red River Delta). Hanoi: Social Science Publisher.

4. Gourou, Pierre. 1936. *Người nông dân châu thổ Bắc Kỳ* (Peasants of the Red River Delta). Maison d'édition d'art et d'histoire,Paris. Vietnamese translation by Nguyễn Khắc Đạm, Đào Hùng & Nguyễn Hoàng Oanh. Hanoi.2003. Youth Publisher.

5. National History Bureau of the Nguyễn Dynasty. 2004. *Đại Nam thực lục* (大南寔錄, Veritable Records of the Great South), vol. 2, 3 & 4. Hanoi: Education Publisher.

6. Ngô, Sĩ Liên. 1479,*Đại Việt sử ký toàn thư* (大越史記全書, Complete Annals of Đại Việt), trans Cao Huy Giu,ed Đào Duy Anh ,1971, Hanoi. Social Science Publisher.

7. Nguyễn, Khắc Sử (ed.), Vũ Ngọc Bình, Đào Huy Quyền. 1995. *Tiền sử Gia Lai* (Pre-history of Gia Lai). Pleiku: Gia Lai Department of Culture, Information and Sports.

8. Prime Minister of the Socialist Republic of Vietnam. 2016. *Decision No. 604/QĐ-TTg supporting 21 provinces during the drought season of 2016.*

9. Trần, Ngọc Thêm. 2006. "Văn hóa nước của người Việt (The Water Culture of the Viet People)." In *Văn hóa sông nước miền Trung* (The River and Waters culture of the Central Region), Hanoi. Social Science Publisher.

10. Tạ, Chí Đại Trường. 2000. *Thần, người và đất Việt* (Gods, People and the Land of Viet), new edition. California. USA. Literature Publisher.

11. Nguyễn, Kim Vân. 2007. *Đến với lịch sử-văn hoá Bắc Tây Nguyên* (Understanding the History-Culture of the North of the Central Highlands). Đà Nẵng: Đà Nẵng Publishing House.

12. Trần, Quốc Vượng ed. 1998/2018. *Cơ sở văn hóa Việt Nam* (The Basis of Vietnamese Culture). 20th edition. Hanoi: Education Publisher.

CHINESE COMMUNITY IN THE SOUTH OF VIETNAM CULINARY CULTURE, FROM THE THEORY OF CULTURAL EXCHANGE

1. Forewords

Southern Vietnam refers to the southernmost region of Vietnam. The Chinese began immigrating to the region at different points in history; however, records indicate that their settlements truly took root from the end of the 17th-18th centuries onwards. Alongside the Viet (Kinh), the Khmer, and the Cham, the Chinese have contributed greatly to the cultural history of southern Vietnam, among which culinary cultures set a notable example. The culture of cuisine among the Chinese settling in Southern Vietnam is their cultural invention, co-produced through reciprocal exchanges with the Viet, the Khmer, the Cham, and other ethnic groups. This paper examines the socio-cultural functions of Chinese culinary cultures from the following groups: Mạc Cửu (in Hà Tiên, now part of Kiên Giang province), Dương Ngạn Địch and Hoàng Tiến in Mỹ Tho (now Tiền Giang province), Trần Thượng Xuyên, Trần An Bình in Bàn Lân, Biên Hòa (now Đồng Nai province), as well as the overall culinary culture of the Chinese in Southern Vietnam. Drawing on the theory of cultural exchanges, especially the exchange between Khmer, Khmer, and Cham in southern Vietnam, this article uses Southeast Asian culture as the background to locate the culinary culture in southern Vietnam.

2. The Chinese in southern Vietnam and Vietnamese re-settlers in the new land

Southern Vietnam (Nam Bộ) comprises two sub-regions: the Eastern Subregion (including the provinces of Bình Dương, Bình Phước, Đồng Nai, Tây Ninh, Bà Rịa – Vũng Tàu and Ho Chi Minh City) and the Western Sub-region (including the provinces of Long An, Tiền Giang, Bến Tre, Trà Vinh, Vĩnh Long, Đồng Tháp, Hậu Giang, Kiên Giang, An Giang, Sóc Trăng, Bạc Liêu, Cà Mau and Cần Thơ City).

Unlike the north, there are four main ethnic groups in southern Vietnam, namely Viet (Kinh), Khmer, Hoa (ethnic Hoa, or Vietnamese of Chinese origin), and Cham.

The geo-historical position of the region has made a fracture in its evolution. In early centuries AD, the region was inhabited by the Óc Eo-Phù Nam inhabitants, who created the Óc Eo-Phù Nam culture, but after the 7th century, those residents and their culture disappeared, leaving behind only the legacies underground. In the 8th century, Chinese Yuan Dynasty officials Zhou Daguan (Châu Đạt Quan, 周達觀, 1266-1346) passed by this region during his visit to the Kingdom of Angkor (the present Thai-Cambodian border area) and found that "the whole area is covered with low forests, hundreds of miles of large estuaries-long and wide rivers, ancient trees and lush shadows of rattan forming many dense shelters. The sounds of birds and animals are everywhere. Halfway down the estuary, wild fields were seen without any crops. Only grass can be seen, thousands of wild buffaloes in the area gather in the herd. Besides, some bamboo slopes are of hundreds of miles long" (Châu Đạt Quan 1973, p. 80). And "Looking at the river, we see long ancient rattan, golden sand, and white reeds." (Châu Đạt Quan 1973, p. 20).

The Khmer started immigrating to the wild area of southern Vietnam to make a living and avoid the war conflict between the Kingdom of Angkor and the Siamese (now Thailand) in the late 13th century. The Viet (Kinh) people gradually arrived in southern Vietnam to reclaim arable land from the late 16th century (mainly the 17th century). The Chinese also settled in the area in the late 17th century. In 1671, Mạc Cửu (鄭玖, 1655-1735), a businessman from Leizhou and Guangdong, China, specialized in long-distance maritime trade, led a group of Chinese immigrants to the Hà Tiên area to cultivate the land. In 1679, a group of Chinese from the Ming Dynasty (1368-1644) led by Dương Ngạn Địch (楊彦迪, Yang Yan Di) and Trần Thắng Tài (陳勝才, Chen Sheng Cai) left China for southern Vietnam to avoid the pursuit of the Qing Dynasty (1644-1912) in China and asked the

Nguyễn Lord to settle down in this region. Lord Nguyễn Phúc Tần (1620-1687), also known as Nguyễn Phước Hiền, allowed them to settle in southern Vietnam.

So far, there are five local groups in southern Vietnam: Cantonese, Chaozhou, Fujianese, Hakka and Hainanese. Statistics from the 2009 General Population and Housing Census show that the Vietnamese population of Chinese descent is 823,071, spreading across all 63 provinces and cities in the country. In southern Vietnam, they live in 21 provinces and cities (see Annex).

Therefore, the Chinese in southern Vietnam, whether they belonged to the group led by Mạc Cửu or Dương Ngạn Địch and Trần Thắng Tài, whether they were from Guangdong or Fujian, had left their hometowns and lived on a strange land, not their home country. Being new immigrants in the region like the Khmer, the Kinh (Victnamese), and the Cham, they must have delt with several issues to create their own culinary culture. The first is the subconscious cultural capital and natural and social resources on the new land, which is completely different from their motherland. The early Chinese came from different parts of China's southeastern coastal area. When they left their hometowns to settle in this new land, they could not take away their local culinary culture but took their sub-consciousness of the native culinary culture. In this new land, they created their own cooking culture suitable for natural and social conditions with their subconscious cultural capital. The second is the relationship with other races that coexist in the same area. Looking back on the history of the region, the Kinh (Viet), Chinese, Khmer, and Cham people have coexisted for hundreds of years with no ethnic wars occurred. On the contrary, cultural exchange and development have become very powerful.

3. Acculturation and cultural exchange in creating the culinary cultures of Southern Vietnam

The concepts of acculturation and cultural exchange are used widely in social sciences in Vietnam and the world. However, in Vietnam, the understanding and interpretation of the term "acculturation" are not the same as elsewhere in the world. The author of this paper would like to use this term to refer to both acculturation and cultural exchange. Professor Trần Quốc Vượng once said: "According to Professor. Hà Văn Tấn and American scientists such as R. Redfield, R. Linton, and M. Herskovits, this concept [acculturation] was defined in 1936 as follows: under the term acculturation, we understand it is a phenomenon occurred when a group of people has different cultures, its long-lasting contacts caused changes of the initial cultural patterns of the group or both groups" (Trần Quốc Vượng ed. 1998/2018, p. 51).

As mentioned above, Viet, Khmer, Chinese, and Cham are all immigrants, and they have coexisted in the region for the past few hundred years. In this area, there is a natural cultural exchange between these ethnic groups. This process has always raised questions for each ethnic group in order to properly handle the relationship with the culinary culture of other ethnic groups in the area. I think that the term "double acculturation" of Jean Cazeneuve that Phan Thị Yến Tuyết used to be correct in this case because "If the two ethnic groups have cultural contacts in both directions, and their cultural exchanges are interactive, rather than unilateral, then this cultural contact can be regarded as "double inclusion"... This phenomenon occurs when these two ethnic groups know how to choose the appropriate factors from each other's culture to make up for their cultural traditions. They know how to "modify" and "improve" their cultural model to "adapt" to the local natural environment and socio-economic conditions and the culture of the race they are exposed to" (Phan Thị Yến Tuyết 1993, p. 296). The term "double acculturation" proposed by Phan Thị Yến Tuyết in the process of studying the three races of Kinh, Chinese, and Khmer in southern Vietnam can be used in this case studies.

The culinary culture of the Viet (Kinh) →The culinary culture of the Chinese → The culinary culture of the Khmer

(see Phan Thị Yến Tuyết 1993, p. 298)

For example, three ethnic groups use fish sauce, different types of sauce, and dried fish and shrimp. On their original land, the Chinese are used to making soy sauce, but nowadays, they use fish sauce in their meals, such as Viet (Kinh). Sour soup is a Khmer dish, the Viet (Kinh), and then the Chinese, used as a popular dish in their restaurants and food courts. Chinese people in southern Vietnam prefer sour soups made with different kinds of fish because they think this dish is suitable for the hot weather in the area. During the New Year or ancestral anniversaries, all cook ordinary and glutinous rice as offerings. The Viet provides cooked ordinary rice, *bánh tét* and *bánh ít* cake (made with glutinous rice), Khmer provides *bánh tét* (ansan), *bánh ít* (nùm krom) and a handful of sticky rice and ordinary rice (bai bánh), Chinese cooked rice, sweet porridge, and cake (made with glutinous rice) are used as offerings. It is worth mentioning that these four ethnic groups all use betel nuts and areca. This is a very typical product and is an important ritual indispensable in the engagement and wedding ceremonies of the ethnic groups. Betel nut and betel nut are not used in the life cycle of the Chinese in China, but for Cantonese and Chaozhou people in southern Vietnam, they have got used to it. In other words, the integration of culture has transformed betel nut and areca into essential offerings for the engagement and wedding ceremonies and life cycle ceremonies of the local Chinese in southern Vietnam. Similarly, tea, daily drinking, very common in all families, has become an offering for the rituals of all the four ethnic groups in the region. The four ethnic groups like to use diluted lotus tea and jasmine tea instead of ordinary tea and drink hot teas like the Vietnamese in the northern delta.

However, after June 1862 and 1867, the entire area was occupied and ruled by French colonialists. All ethnic groups in the region must deal with the relationship between Western culinary culture (mainly the French) and their own culinary culture. There is a dialectical relationship between endogenous factors and exogenous factors, and they are always interchangeable. In southern Vietnam, cooking culture and immigration culture are not separated from each other. In general, local communities have applied two extremes in accepting external factors: voluntary and mandatory. Besides, the reception is also divided into two levels: whole reception and creative reception. Some cultural scientists believe that creative acceptance is divided into three levels. First, instead of accepting all systems, the recipient selectively accepts the values of another group's culinary culture that suits them. The second is the acceptance of the entire system, but then it will be rearranged according to the value of its country. The third method is to simulate and accumulate some cultural achievements of other groups (see Trần Quốc Vượng ed. 1998/2018, p. 53).

Since the French invaded and ruled the South from 1867 to 1954, the culinary culture of the Viet (Kinh), Chinese, Khmer, and Cham ethnic groups in the South, concerning the Western culinary culture (mainly French culinary culture), all three trends appear simultaneously. When the French invaded southern Vietnam, the Vietnamese showed their attitude of not accepting bread, thinking it was the product of the aggressor, and the patriotic Vietnamese did not use the product of the aggressor. Patriotic poet Nguyễn Đình Chiểu (1822-1888) ridiculed "sharing unflavored wine and chewing bread, how ashamed it is!" (*Văn tế nghĩa sĩ Cần Giuộc*, Funeral Oration for Cần Giuộc martyrs).

Since 1859, various foods have been imported into southern Vietnam but were mainly processed and manufactured by the French. In the 1940s, the Chinese learned to make bread with the French. Since then, bread has gradually become a common food for the four groups in the region. Since 1954, the bread processing method in northern Vietnam has been transferred to Saigon (now Ho Chi Minh City) and the entire southern region. The married couple Mr. Lê Minh Ngọc and Ms. Nguyễn Thị Tình's Hòa Mã Bakery was established in 1958 and has developed rapidly due to their special products and long-term reputation. Therefore, for more than 150 years, French bread has been transformed into Vietnamese-styled bread. Historically, the Vietnamese localized French-styled bread through two extremes: first rejected, then voluntarily accepted but improved its processing techniques to satisfy the tastes of local people, no matter what group they belong to. Vietnamese-style bread has long been an important part of southern Vietnamese cuisine, expressing the characteristics of local communities and their culinary culture. The culinary culture of southern Vietnam for more than 300 years is indeed a joint innovation product of the local immigrant groups and plays a very important role in the culture and cultural exchange of local ethnic groups.

4. The Chinese cuisine and Southern Vietnam culture

In southern Vietnam, the Chinese are immigrants like the Viet (Kinh), Khmer, and Cham. Therefore, Chinese cuisine is a cultural reality of an immigrant group. The nature of the new land (Southern Vietnam) is somewhat similar to the coastal areas of their homeland (Southeastern China), but the weather is different. When people talk about the southern part of Vietnam they mean talking about the canal and river system that crosses the region. Trịnh Hoài Đức in his book *Gia Định thành thông chí* (嘉定城通志, Gazetteer of Gia Định Citadel) described the region in the early 19th century: "There are many rivers, streams, and islands on the land of Gia Định. Nine out of every ten people are used to boating, swimming, and using fish sauce in their meals"; or "In Gia Định, boats can be seen everywhere. People use it as a shelter or a means of hanging out to visit relatives or transport rice and firewood. In fact, waterway transportation is very convenient" (Trịnh Hoài Đức 1972, pp. 12, 14-5).

In the past, the literature has often shown that the total length of digging channels in southern Vietnam is about 2500 kilometers, while the total length of rivers and natural canals is 2,400 kilometers. Ms. Lê Bá Thảo pointed out in Vietnam Nature that there are 4,900 kilometers of digging channels, including 1,575 kilometers of 18-60m wide canals. Mr. Trần Đình Gián said: "Over the centuries of land reclamation, people have added irrigation, drainage, transportation, and fish farming systems to the natural hydraulic system, and have grown 5,000 kilometers of canals in the southwest-northeast intersection (Trần Đình Gián 1982, pp. 53-4). During the two rainy and dry seasons, in such criss-cross river and canal areas, southern Vietnam has rich and diverse seafood resources, as described by Nguyễn Liên Phong (1908, p. 83) in *Nam Kỳ phong tục nhơn vật diễn ca* (The Ballard of the Customs and People of the South):

In Vietnamese	English translation
Cá đồng, cá biển, cá sông	Freshwater fish, sea fish and river fish
Ốc, đuông, ba khía, chim cùng tôm cua	Snail, weevil, birds, crayfish and crabs, all are abundant.

Of course, Southern Vietnam is different from the native land of the Chinese in this region, thus their creation of culinary culture from the culinary cultural capital of their ancestral generations hidden in their sub-consciousness becomes the culinary culture of the Chinese in this new land. For example, the tenderly cooked pork with brine dish is not only common among the Chinese but accepted by the Viet (Kinh) in Bến Tre, adding coconut milk to it to become Chinese tenderly cooked pork dish. Bến Tre is the land of coconut growing in Southern Vietnam. Among its uses, coconut is a source of food for the southerners to create many dishes. Bến Tre is famous for its coconut candies. People in this province of three isles Bảo, Minh, and An Hòa think that the creator of the Bến Tre coconut candy processing technique is Mrs. Nguyễn Thị Ngọc, but some people think that along with Mrs. Ngoc, there is a Chinese man who also has the creative merit: Mr. Hữu. Southern Vietnam has many other products than southern China, such as fruits, vegetables, fruits, animals, pepper, chili, onions, garlic, ginger, lemongrass, various kinds of sour leaves and fruits, etc., so the local Chinese are forced to use new spices in their dishes compared to the traditional.

The authors of the book *Văn hóa người Hoa Nam Bộ* (The culture of the Chinese in Southern Vietnam) noted that "The Chinese cuisine in southern Vietnam is very rich and special in the use of materials, spices and processing techniques. Their cuisine combines the Chinese culinary tradition with the culinary culture of other ethnic groups and various natural environments on the land of southern Vietnam" (Lưu Kim Hoa et al. 2016, p. 106). Without the local Chinese cooking culture, the entire cooking culture in southern Vietnam will be incomplete.

The structure of the Vietnamese meal in the north (Vietnam) is rice + vegetables + fish, while the pattern in the south becomes rice + pickles + liquid dishes (soup, fried or boiled). Sometimes, a plate of fried meat and vegetables is added. *Khô quẹt* (well-cooked fish or shrimp sauce) and uncooked fish sauce are indispensable in the meals of the Viet (Kinh) as well as the Chinese in Southern Vietnam. In addition to rice, the Chinese also use food processed from wheat flour into *hun-tun* noodles (*hoành thánh*, or *vằn thắn*, 餛飩) and other types of noodles. Different groups of Chinese create different types of noodle dishes such as the Cantonese noodle with lean meat and pork mince, the Fujianese noodle with fish balls, tofu, and the small round shrimp cakes; the Chaozhou long salty thread noodles (being boiled to release salt before eating), etc. Foods offered to gods and ancestors during the Lunar New Year festival by local Chinese include *bánh tổ hấp* (steamed sweet rice cake), which adds to the richness of culinary culture in southern Vietnam. Chinese people prefer meat to fish. They process meat into different forms of different dishes, such as cooking with brine, frying, grilling, and roasting, the most typical of which is roast pork and roast duck. Roast pork is served with *bánh hỏi* (a type of rice noodles) and salad. Roast duck and stewed duck are the first choices of Chinese people in important sacrifices and formal meals. Duck stew with salty lemon or orange, stuffed with minced pork. Roast chicken is also preferable to the Chinese. All of these dishes strongly improve the diversity of Chinese cooking culture in southern Vietnam.

The Chinese in southern Vietnam received fish, dried freshwater fish, and fish sauce from the Viet (Kinh). They also like fried anchovies and steamed bluefish. Regarding soup, the Chinese brought Chinese herbal soup from China, which later became a specialty herbal soup in the region. Anyone can buy herbs for cooking in any local pharmacy store. The herbs are cooked from pork bones (and some meat) to make medicine soup. The Chinese also have soups made from herbs stewed with black chicken, pig brain soup cooked with ginger eggs, and red bean soup cooked with catfish. Overall, the culinary culture of the Chinese in southern Vietnam has enriched and diversified the local food culture.

5. Preservation and development of the values of the culinary culture of the ethnic Chinese in Southern Vietnam

The food culture in southern Vietnam is a combination of four ethnic groups: Viet (Kinh), Khmer, Chinese, and Cham. The preservation and development of the food culture values of these four groups must not only take place today but also in the future. In particular, the Chinese people's food culture in southern Vietnam and the general food culture in southern Vietnam must do a lot of things, but the author of this article suggests the following things to be done shortly:

First, it is necessary to record the food culture of the Chinese in southern Vietnam. In the 1990s, the late Professor Trần Quốc Vượng (1934-2005) suggested:

• Conduct a general inventory survey of Vietnamese food and beverages;

• Compose a Vietnamese food dictionary.

• Organize the Vietnam cuisine festival on the occasion of the Hung King Ancestral Anniversary" (Trần Quốc Vượng 2000, p. 405). In the current social context of a flat world, the 4th industrial revolution poses to the generation today many opportunities, but also lots of challenges. General inventory of the culinary culture of the Chinese in particular and Southern Vietnam, in general, is essential. Information technology should be used in information storage of Chinese food in Southern Vietnam. There should also be CDs and DVDs available about their culinary culture. For this reason, we must do a general survey and study of the Chinese cuisine in southern Vietnam and the cuisine of Viet (Kinh), Khmer, and Cham. The work not only lists dishes and drinks but also records the creative techniques and creative artists of various creative cuisines in the South.

The second is the study of the food culture of the Chinese in southern Vietnam. So far, some scientific research has been conducted on the Chinese culinary culture in southern Vietnam and the culinary culture throughout southern Vietnam. Trần Thị Kim Oanh of the National Academy of Social Sciences of Vietnam said in a doctoral thesis defended by the Vietnamese Academy of Social Sciences in 2019 that there are some sporadic studies on the culinary culture of Chinese in southern Vietnam (Trần Thị Kim Oanh 2009). The most common are studies on the culinary culture of the Chinese in southern Vietnam, such as ceremonies hosted by Trần Hạnh Minh Phương, and ethnic cultural ceremonies, such as those for Phan An and Nghị Đoàn. It is worth mentioning that, there is not so much research on food culture in the Mekong Delta, except Phan Thị Yến Tuyết (1993)'s *Housing, clothing, and ethnic food in the Mekong Delta*. Therefore, until now, there are still many issues in the study of the culinary culture of Chinese people in southern Vietnam, especially in southern Vietnam.

The third is to preserve and teach the knowledge of the ethnic Chinese culinary culture in southern Vietnam and to enhance the role of the community in inheriting and teaching the culinary culture of the present and future generations.

The fourth is to promote the food culture of the Chinese nation in southern Vietnam, develop the food culture tourism industry in southern Vietnam, and turn it into a tourism resource. In general, we need to accelerate the adaptation and culinary cultural exchanges of the ethnic groups in the region, the country, and all Southeast Asian countries. The lesson of history will always be valuable in today's life if we consider thoroughly the role of ethnic groups in Southern culinary culture in particular, the whole country in general.

6. Conclusion

In the theory of culture and cultural exchange, the culinary culture of southern Vietnam is a combination of the culinary cultures of the four ethnic groups of Viet (Kinh), Chinese, Khmer, and Cham. Each ethnic group has its treasures of culinary culture; however, as immigrants, various ethnic groups in southern Vietnam created their own cooking by using the natural, social and historical conditions of the new land and experience in treating other fellow ethnic cultures coexisting in the region. The culinary treasures of southern Vietnam should be further studied by many other scholars because this article is limited to one sketch.

Annex

Statistics of the Chinese population in Southern Vietnam in 2009

Unit: person

Locality	Population	Locality	Population
Ho Chi Minh City	414.045	Vĩnh Long	4.879
Bình Phước	9.970	Đồng Tháp	1.855
Tây Ninh	2.495	An Giang	8.075
Bình Dương	18.783	Kiên Giang	29.850
Đồng Nai	95.162	Cần Thơ City	14.199
Bà Rịa - Vũng Tàu	8.730	Hậu Giang	6.363
Long An	2.950	Sóc Trăng	64.910
Tiền Giang	3.863	Bạc Liêu	20.082
Bến Tre	5.213	Cà Mau	8.911
Trà Vinh	7.960	**Total**	**728.295**

(Source: Lưu Kim Hoa et al. 2016, p.22)

Reference

1. Châu ,Đạt Quan (周達觀). 1973. *Chân Lạp phong thổ ký* (真臘風土記, The Customs of the Kingdom of Chenla), trans. Lê Hương. Saigon: New Era Publishing.

2. Lưu, Kim Hoa et al., 2016. *Văn hóa người Hoa Nam Bộ* (Chinese culture in Southern Vietnam), Ho Chi Minh Culture and Arts Publisher.

3. Many authors. 1982. *Một số vấn đề khoa học xã hội về đồng bằng sông Cửu Long* (Some social science issues in the Mekong River Delta). Hanoi: Social Science Publisher.

4. Many authors, *Bản sắc ẩm thực* (Cuisine Identity), Hanoi: News Agency Publisher. 2009

5. Ngô, Đức Thịnh. 2010. *Khám phá ẩm thực truyền thống Việt Nam* (Discovery of traditional cuisine of Vietnam). Hanoi: Young Publisher.

6. Nguyễn, Đình Chiểu,*Văn tế nghĩa sĩ Cần Giuộc* (Funeral Oration for Cần Giuộc martyrs).

7. Nguyễn, Liên Phong. 1908. *Nam Kỳ phong tục nhơn vật diễn ca* (The Ballards of the Customs and People of the South). Tom 1, Phát Toán Publishing, Saigon.

8. Phan ,Thị Yến Tuyết. 1993. *Nhà ở, trang phục và ẩm thực các dân tộc Đồng bằng sông Cửu Long* (Housing, costumes and eating of ethnic groups in the Mekong River Delta). Hanoi: Social Science Publisher.

9. Trần, Đình Gián. 1982. *Tìm hiểu đặc trưng môi trường tự nhiên và tài nguyên cùng với môi trường sinh thái,tiến tới định hướng phát triển kinh tế hợp lý kết hợp với bảo vệ tốt hơn hệ sinh thái đồng bằng sông Cửu Long*, "Study the characteristics of natural environment, natural resources and eco-environment, toward orientations for economic development relevant to ecological system in the Mekong River Delta." in trong tập *Một số vấn đề khoa học xã hội về đồng bằng sông Cửu Long* ,In *Some social science issues in the Mekong River Delta*), pp.53,54. Hanoi: Social Science Publisher.

10. Trần, Quốc Vượng. 2000. *Văn hóa Việt Nam: tìm tòi và suy ngẫm* (Vietnamese Culture: Study and Reflection). Hanoi: Ethnic Culture Publisher & Culture and Arts Journal.

11. Trần, Quốc Vượng. 2000. *"Văn hóa ẩm thực Việt Nam-Hà Nội đôi ba vấn đề lý luận*, (Vietnam-Hanoi culinary cultures, some theoretical issues)." In trong tập *Văn hóa Việt Nam tìm tòi và suy ngẫm* (Vietnamese culture, study and reflection), pp. 405, Hanoi. Ethnic Culture Publisher & Culture and Arts Journal.

12. Trần, Quốc Vượng ed. 1998/2018. *Cơ sở văn hóa Việt Nam* (Basis of Vietnamese Culture). 20th edition. Hanoi: Education Publisher.

13. Trần, Quốc Vượng & Nguyễn, Thị Bảy. 2010. *Văn hóa ẩm thực Việt Nam, nhìn từ lý luận và thực tiễn* (Vietnamese Culinary Culture, from theory to practice). Hanoi. Encyclopedia Dictionary & Culture Institute Publisher.

14. Trần, Thị Kim Oanh. 2019. *Văn hóa ẩm thực của người Hoa Quảng Đông ở thành phố Hồ Chí Minh hiện nay* (Culinary culture of the Chinese from Guangdong in Ho Chi Minh City at present). Ph.D. Diss. in Culture. Hanoi.Vietnam National Academy of Social Sciences.

15. Trịnh, Hoài Đức. 1972. *Gia Định thành thông chí* (嘉定城通志, Gazetteer of Gia Định Citadel), trans. Nguyễn Tạo. Saigon. Bureau of Cultural Affairs, Board of Culture Publishing.

16. Vietnam Department of Statistic. 2009. *The 2009 General Population and Housing Census*.

THE STATE AND THE PROTECTION AND USE OF INTANGIBLE CULTURAL HERITAGE AND THE USE OF ITS VALUE IN VIETNAM: LESSONS FROM HISTORY

1. Preface

In 2010, I was assigned to be the head of building a national file on *Hùng Kings Worship in Phú Thọ province* to submit to UNESCO for evaluation and recognition as a representative intangible cultural heritage of humanity. Despite some experience, I still could not help but worry. The great pressure on me and my colleagues is not only because the worship of Hong Wu is the sacred tradition of the Viet/ Vietnamese people or the common ancestor worship of the entire people/nation of Vietnam but from another perspective. According to the historical records of Confucian scholars, at least for more than six centuries, the worship of Hùng Kings has been the concern, management, and even intervention of the monarchy. Meanwhile, UNESCO appreciates the role of communities and emphasizes that policies to protect and promote the value of cultural heritage must be community-based.

Has the intangible cultural heritage of the Viet and other ethnic groups in Vietnam always been inseparable from the monarchy? Has the existence of Vietnam's intangible cultural heritage been always related to the role of the state?

2. State model before August 1945

Except for the primitive period, the traditional festival in Vietnamese history is a cultural phenomenon that has been moving and operating between two forces: the bottom-up influence of the people and the top-down influence of the state (including monarchial dynasties from the beginning of the 10th century to 1945 and the Democratic Republic of Vietnam/Socialist Republic of Vietnam from 1945 to the present). Therefore, along with the three basic subjects of farmers, fishermen, and urban residents, the traditional festival of the Vietnamese people has another subject, the past monarchial dynasties and the present government.

To understand the relationship between the state and the conservation of intangible cultural heritage, it is necessary to determine the nature of the model of the two types of government. In the context of this essay, I will focus only on the subjectivity of monarchial dynasties before 1945.

Vietnamese monarchical dynasties, namely, the Ngô(939-965), the Đinh(968-980), the pre-Lê (980-1009), the Lý (1009-1225), the Trần (1225-1400), the Hồ (1400-1407), the Lê (1428-1527) to the Lê-Mạc (1527-1592), the Lê-Trịnh (1533-1789) in Tonkin and the Nguyễn Lords (1558-1777; 1780-1802) in Cochinchina, the Tây Sơn (1778-1802) and finally the Nguyễn (1802 -1945), express certain common characteristics despite differences in the ideological choice between them. First of all, these monarchies have a model of secular power governance. The king was always independent of the gods, standing above the gods while being able to command and assign tasks to the gods. Despite the importance of Buddhism, the Lý Dynasty still identified the gods as their invisible servants. The dynasties from the Lê Dynasty to the Nguyễn Dynasty, which held high regard for Confucianism in the social-ideological life, clearly defined that gods are the servant of the court and the protectors of the people, and thus the people are responsible for sacrificing and serving the gods. Secondly, these are the dynasties of the paddy rice farmers. Thirdly, these dynasties always faced the need to affirm the independent existence of Đại Việt nation. Nguyễn Trãi (1380-1442) in *Bình Ngô đại cáo* once wrote:

In Vietnamese	*English translation*
Núi sông bờ cõi đã chia	Mountains and rivers and the territories have been divided in two
Phong tục Bắc Nam cũng khác	North (Chinese) and South (Vietnamese) customs are also different
Tự Triệu, Đinh, Lý, Trần đã bao đời gây nền độc lập,	Vietnam has built an independent state from the periods of the Triệu, the Đinh,
Cùng Hán, Đường, Tống, Nguyên, mỗi bên làm để một phương	the Lý and the Trần. Together with the Han, the Tang, the Song and the Yuan, each ruled one side.

At the same time, these dynasties must comply with the requirements of protecting national independence from the Chinese dynasties' desire to annexing the country of Đại Việt (Vietnam). Therefore, the Confucian scholars, especially from the Lê Dynasty onwards, while "compiling" the legends, they used the 'historicalization' method to associate the tutelary gods and other worshiped figures with the history of the building and defending the nation. One can imagine traditional Vietnamese society as a triangle as follows:

King

Dynasty

Village   Family

However, the link between the family and the king/the court is almost indirect through villages. All three subjects (the king, village, family) are three subjects/objects of Vietnamese intangible cultural heritage. The impact of these objects on intangible cultural heritage is naturally different. The relationship between the court/king and the village is the relationship between the ruler and the ruled.

When discussing this relationship in Vietnam, people often rely on the seemingly "permissive" attitude of the court concerning villages to assert that Vietnamese villages were autonomous. For example, one Westerner once said that every village in the Northern Delta (the Red River Delta) was a small "autonomous republic". However, that does not mean that monarchs did not care about preserving and promoting the value of intangible cultural heritage in the village. Although villages had the right to make certain decisions such as allocating land to village farmers, controlling farming activities, and managing social activities and rituals related to the life cycle, etc., the state agencies in the village handled all the important works. They worked under motto called "The king's law loses to the village rules." Therefore, the roles of both the state and the community in developing works related to the protection and promotion of cultural heritage values have always been "equivocal". Both are powerful but seemingly powerless, and their 'power' is virtually 'real'. Many scholars believe that the community is the opposite of the ruling class and that this kind of folklore creations belongs only to the people.

Importantly, the concept of "people" needs to be properly understood and defined. I find that the judgment of V. Guxep, a folklore researcher in the former Soviet Union, is correct in this case. He said: "People are a community of social groups and a class of people formed according to history. They constitute the basis of each society. The social structure of the people in different stages of human social history is not invariant; on the contrary, it changes from one age to another within the context of a social form. This determines the content and form of specific folklore in each era (cited in Guxep 1999, p. 32). In other words, "people" is not an "immutable" concept. Its content has changed through historical periods. During the times of the monarchial dynasties, besides farmers, fishermen, and urban residents, the rural Confucianists were also important. They were both the subjects and the objects of cultural heritage. Rural Confucianists should not be grouped in the farmers, fishermen, or urban residents and their role in traditional festivals in the village should not be ignored. The Confucianists played a special role in mediating the relationship between the state and the community, as well as between the central monarchy and the "autonomous" villages. On the one hand, they played the role of the court's unofficial "agents" in the village, directly interpreting the court's texts (such as royal edicts and ordains, God legends, civic laws, etc.) and acting as orthodox Confucian spokespersons (e.g., in education and state-sponsored ceremonies); on the other hand, they represented the community to express their desires and aspirations.

The political and social status of the Vietnamese Confucianists was significantly affected when the French rulers abolished the Han script-based imperial examination in the late nineteenth - early twentieth centuries. However, the villagers still needed the Confucianists to work as cultural figures who conveyed Confucian values to the community. It must be admitted that the Confucianists in traditional society were the special subjects of Vietnam's intangible cultural heritage.

3. The impacts of monarchial dynasties on intangible cultural heritage

As a government of secular power, Đại Việt's monarchial dynasties did a lot of work in the field of cultural heritage during the period from the 10th century to 1945. Generally, all dynasties carried out the following activities in villages that influenced the cultural tradition.

The first is to bestow ordinations to significant gods, tutelary gods, and deceased meritorious officials who had made great contributions to the court and the country. It functioned like the king's "officer appointment" when he assigned the gods to "rule" the sacred space of a village. This is the court's confirmation of the gods in the village. According to Trương Hán Siêu's study on stele records, the ordination for the gods in Vietnam probably dates back to the Lý dynasty. However, most of the remaining ordinances date from the seventeenth century onwards. In Hanoi, the earliest ordination dates from the Vĩnh Tộ reign (1619) while the latest from the 9th year of the

Khải Định reign (1924). In Vĩnh Phúc province, the earliest ordination was made in the 7th year of the Phúc Thái reign (King Lê Chân Tông, 1646) while the latest was in the 19th year of the Bảo Đại reign (November 19, 1944) (see Lê Kim Thuyên, Sđd, p. 12). In Hưng Yên province, we surveyed and collected 2. 345 ordinances, of which the earliest one was in the second year of the Vĩnh Tộ reign (1620) and the latest was in the 9th year of the Khải Định reign (1924) (see Nguyễn Chí Bền....). Most of the ordinations (for deities) still present in this province are those of the Nguyễn Dynasty (1802-1945). According to author Nguyễn Mạnh Hùng (2008, p. 568), in the fifth year of the Tự Đức reign alone (1852), the king granted 13.069 ordained titles for gods in the whole country.

Along with the bestowing of ordinances, the dynasties also deployed the re-edition / re-compilation of god legends in the villages. This is an important "push" for the development of the festivals - an element of intangible cultural heritage. There were a few facts that should be mentioned in the study of god legends' formation. The first was that Dr. Nguyễn Bính, a scholar of the National Hanlin Academy, compiled nationwide god legends in the first year of the Hồng Phúc reign (1572). The second was that the scholar Nguyễn Hiền copied and re-edited these legends in 1736.

Statistics from the lookup table of god legends sorted by village names by École française d'Extrême-Orient (French School of the Far East) in Hanoi in 1938 show that of the total of 2.121 god legends, 259 were compiled by Nguyễn Bính, 1.137 were compiled by Nguyễn Bính and copied/further re-edited by Nguyễn Hiền, and 78 others were re-edited by Nguyễn Hiền alone.

In addition to the god legends compiled by Nguyễn Bính and copied/re-edited by Nguyễn Hiền, a number of other Confucian scholars also participated in this work in the villages. For example, in 1466, Đào Cử compiled a legend of Lỗ Khê commune; in 1470 Nguyễn Cố composed Hùng Kings legend for Hy Cương commune, and Lê Tung compiled legends for Nội Xá, Đông Xá, Dị Nậu, and Phúc Lâm communes. Similarly, Nguyễn Bảo compiled legends for Yên Vĩnh hamlet of Mậu Công commune in 1472 and Lê Tùng wrote legends for An Trực and Thanh Khê communes in 1510. At that time, the Lê Dynasty requested people to report and register god legends of their village. Most of the god legends remaining to this day were compiled and edited by Nguyễn Bính in the first year of the Hồng Phúc reign (1572), while there were only 7 legends ordained during the Thiên Phúc reign period (King Lê Đại Hành's reign, 980-988) (see Nguyễn Duy Hinh 1996, p. 81-2).

The second is the royal orders of title ordination, setting up places of worship, and offering sacrifices for the gods. These activities took place from the Lý dynasty. Therefore, we must accept the fact that the sacrifices to the gods in the village were closely related to the ideology of monarchial dynasties such as the Lý Dynasty (1009-1225) and the Trần Dynasty (1225-1400).

Among the monarchs of Đại Việt, the Lý dynasty valued Buddhism the most. Not only the monks who had an important role in the court but also the Lý kings themselves appreciated Buddhism. For example, King Lý Thánh Tông (1023-1072) founded the Thảo Đường sect in Buddhism and King Lý Cao Tông (1173-1210) proclaimed himself a Buddha. In 1031, King Lý Thái Tông (1000-1054) "issued the edict to hire workers to build 150 pagodas (temples) in villages" (see Ngô Sĩ Liên 1973; 2010, p. 157). In 1115, during the reign of King Lý Nhân Tông (1066-1128), the Mother Queen Ỷ Lan (1044-1117) ordered to "erect over a hundred Buddhist temples" (see Ngô Sĩ Liên 1973; 2010, p. 177).

The choice of Buddhism by the Lý kings made the number of pagodas grow so much that some people called the culture of this period a "pagoda culture". There are three basic forms of the pagodas in the Lý Dynasty, respectively, massive state-sponsored monasteries, non-state monasteries, and popular village pagodas. Since then, Buddhist temples became increasingly popular in the villages.

Buddhism in North Vietnam changed due to the process of acculturation of Vietnamese people and profoundly intertwined with Vietnamese folk beliefs. In the temple that is believed to have the longest history of Buddhism in Vietnam is Dâu Temple (Thanh Khương commune, Thuận Thành district, Bắc Ninh province), the central figure is not Shakyamuni but the Cloud Dharma Goddess (Pháp Vân). In Vietnamese folk beliefs, natural phenomena such as clouds, rain, thunder, and lightning have been "transformed" into the Four Dharmas, namely, (goddesses) of Pháp Vân (Cloud Dharma), Pháp Vũ (Rain Dharma), Pháp Lôi (Thunder Dharma), and Pháp Điện (Lightning Dharma), which are closely associated with mass Buddhism. In this way, Cloud Dharma has become the central figure of festivals in the area of Dâu Temple. The fusion and integration between Buddhism and the indigenous beliefs of the Vietnamese people created Buddhism in Giao Châu (交州, Jiaozhou, today's North Vietnam) in the early historical period or Đại Việt in later periods a distinct feature.

All major religions, especially Buddhism and Confucianism, were promoted at the time. In the third year of the Kiến Trung reign (1227), the Trần Dynasty opened the royal exam of Three Teachings (to select the best scholars of Confucianism, Buddhism, and Taoism) (see Ngô Sĩ Liên 2010, p. 215). In the second year of the Kiến Trung reign (1231), "the Emperor issued a decree to regulate that all communal houses (state-sponsored public houses) in the country must build/erect Buddha statues and the villagers must perform regular rituals" (see Ngô Sĩ Liên 2010, p. 216). Besides, the Lý Dynasty founded the National Academy (Quốc học viện, 國學院) in the third year of the Nguyên Phong reign (1253) and ordered to build the statues of Confucius, Zhugong and Mencius, and painted 72 prominent Vietnamese scholars" (see Ngô Sĩ Liên 2010, p. 223). Thus, for the Trần dynasty, both Buddhism and Confucianism were highly valued and created favorable opportunities for development..

The Lê Dynasty (1428-1788), founded by Lê Lợi (1385-1433) after the victory of the Lam Sơn Uprising against the Ming aggression

(China), chose Confucianism as the most important ideology for the country. Starting from Lê Thái Tổ to his descendants, Confucianism gradually gained a high position in the court, pushing Buddhism out of the dominant posture that had existed in the earlier Lý and Trần dynasties. In the second year of the Thuận Thiên reign (King Lê Thái Tổ, 1429), the court intentionally organized a separate examination for Buddhist monks in the provincial administration offices and stipulated that those who passed the exam would be issued with a monk card, and those who failed would be required to secularize (return to laity). In 1431, the Lê Dynasty opened the Hoành Từ examination at the Bồ Đề (Bodhi) Monastery. Then, King Lê Thái Tông (1433-1442) opened a doctoral examination in 1442 to select officials.

The choice of Confucianism to support the state's official ideology caused the Lê kings a responsibility to prove the fact that the Dynasty was naturally assigned by the Heavenly Emperor to ascend the throne and perform the task of ruling the people (on behalf of the Heavenly Emperor). Nguyễn Trãi (1380-1442) in *Bình Ngô Đại Cáo* (平吳大誥, Great proclamation upon the defeat of the Wu) had a very special opening sentence that most of the modern Vietnamese translators ignore (intentionally or unintentionally): "Working on behalf of the Heavenly Emperor, the King announces that..." (承天行化，皇上若曰, thừa thiên hành hóa, hoàng thượng nhược viết). Therefore, the Lê kings determined that they had an "obligation" to govern both the people and the gods. This led to two inevitable consequences. The first is the court's need to build/set up separate 'offices' (temples) for the gods so that they could rule the sacred space of the villages on the behalf of the king. The Lê Dynasty "had an order to give the village the task of managing private communal houses in 1496" (Tạ Chí Đại Trường p. 155). This is a decision that greatly influenced the intangible cultural heritage of the Vietnamese people after the 15th century. Earth god (in the family called Mr. Thổ Công, in the village called Mr. Thổ Địa), as the tutelary god of the village, needed a place to "shelter"[133]. He could not "shelter" in a non-public place, but in the village's communal house because he was the official tutelary god of the village. That decision of King Lê Thánh Tông really "led to the development of a spiritual structure of the village, creating a sense of distinct consciousness of Vietnamese society, which is still preserved today" (see Tạ Chí Đại Trường p. 155).

The village communal house (đình làng) emerged early in Vietnamese history, before the Lê dynasty in the 15th century. Khương Tăng Hội[134] in the *Lục độ tập kinh* (written at the end of the 2nd century - early 3rd century) mentioned the communal house and his request for sleep in it. But it was until the court needed a god to govern a sacred space in the village on behalf of the court and the people in the village wished that their village god was recognized by the state, the communal house fully developed the function of a Confucianized communal house.

It is difficult to study the village communal houses that existed before the 16th century due to the shortcoming of historical data. The earliest establishment is Lỗ Hạnh communal house in Hiệp Hòa district, Bắc Giang province; the record on its structure shows the date of June 7, the 11th year of the Sùng Khang reign (1576). Professor. Hà Văn Tấn (1998, p. 44) asserted: "We can call the 17th century as the century of the communal house". Obviously, the dynasties' choice of Confucianism either accidentally or intentionally made the Confucian cultural heritage flourish. On the other hand, King Lê Thánh Tông intentionally ordered to establish Hùng Kings' official legend(s). During our investigation, we found a typical version of Hùng Kings legend in the Nghĩa Cương and Hy Cương communes in Phú Thọ province, that is, *The Holy Genealogy of 18 Hùng Kings*[135]. This legend was written (compiled) by Nguyễn Cố - a scholar of the National Hanlin Academy in March of the first

---

[133] Tạ Chí Đại Trường used the term "trú sở", meaning "shelter".

[134] A Sogdianan monk who came to North Vietnam to spread Central Asian Buddhism in the third century AD.

[135] In Vietnamese: *Hùng đồ thập bát diệp thánh vương ngọc phả cổ truyền*; in Chinese: 宏圖十八葉聖王玉譜古傳.

year of the Hồng Đức reign (the Year of Dragon), edited by Nguyễn Trọng on October of the first year of the Hoằng Định reign (the Year of the Rat, 1600), and later copied by Lê Đình Hoan. It can be said that the compilation of Hùng Kings legends of the Lê Dynasty strongly motivated the god-kings legends system to develop intelligently. Without this event, there would be no basis for Nguyễn Bính to compile the divine legends of the gods in Vietnamese villages later in the first year of the Hồng Phúc reign. By choosing Confucianism as official ideology, the Lê Dynasty became different from the Lý and Trần dynasties in acquiring theocracy throughout the country into the hands of the king.

The Lý, Trần, and Lê dynasties treated the gods on the basis of Confucianism. "While accepting an orthodox ideology as a basis for dynasty building and seeking to systematize the gods in a pattern evoked by a unified secular structure, the kings encountered obstacles from the same forms of beliefs that they had shared before they were crowned and could not abandon them once they were kings" (see Tạ Chí Đại Trường, p. 129). Therefore, the dynasties had to regularly perform sacrifices for the gods. The book *Đại Việt sử ký toàn thư* (大越史記全書, Complete Historical Annals of Đại Việt) recorded that "[The court] performed the Mountain God of Lý Phục Man sacrificial ceremony in the 7th year of the Thuận Thiên reign (1016)" and "conferred the title of "king" for the god of Đồng Cổ mountain and ordered the establishment of Đồng Cổ Temple, making it the place of the annual oath ceremony" in the 19th year of the Thuận Thiên reign (1028) (see Ngô Sĩ Liên 2010, p.150). Later, in the 5th year of the Đại Định reign (1144), heavy rains lasted throughout April, [the court] prayed for the sunshine. Later, "in July, [the King ordered] to erect the temple of Mount Tản Viên and the temples of Bố Cái, Ông Nghiêm, and Ông Mẫu" (see Ngô Sĩ Liên 2010, p. 195). Furthermore, "in the 5th year of the Thái Ninh reign (1076), [the court] establishes the temple of Trương Hống & Trương Hát at the estuary of the Như Nguyệt River (Nam Quận district)" (see Ngô Sĩ Liên 2010, p. 173). By the fourth year of the Thiên Tư Gia Thụy reign (1189), the King traveled 'across mountains and rivers' in March. In the villages where he visited, the gods were granted titles, and the villagers were allowed to build temples to worship the gods" (see Ngô Sĩ Liên 2010, p. 205).

This work was followed by the Trần dynasty. Although the Trần dynasty, which is different from the Lý dynasty, simultaneously promoted the development of Buddhism, Confucianism, and Taoism, the sacrifices to tutelary gods were still strictly performed in the Confucian way. For example, the king sacrificed all the gods of the mountains and rivers in 1299. In 1312, the king "superscribed the names of the earth gods and established a temple at the estuary of Cần Hải" (see Ngô Sĩ Liên 2010, p. 267).

In 1370, "[the king] brought buffalo and silk offerings to Tản Viên and the water gods of the Lô River in the spring (January)" (see Ngô Sĩ Liên 2010, p. 298). In 1428, "[the King] sent his mandarins to offer sacrifices to mountain and river gods, important tutelary gods in certain districts (villages) as well as tombs of previous dynasties" (see Ngô Sĩ Liên 2010, p. 381). The Lê Dynasty continued this work. The Lê king "established the temple of the capital's tutelary God, built a temple to worship the gods of wind, cloud, thunder, and rain, and set up a shrine to worship the demons that no one sacrificed" (see Ngô Sĩ Liên 2010, p. 426). In 1427 the king "ordered all regions to establish temples of meritorious officials and conduct regular sacrifices" (see Ngô Sĩ Liên 2010, p. 304).

Thus, the main impact of the above-mentioned policy was the promotion of forming a rather powerful force and worshipped figures in the villages. Every village became like a sacred space and had its own god(s). Gods functioned as "officials" of the government, "ruling" the villagers on behalf of the court. They could be tutelary gods, blessing gods, water gods, sea gods, mountain gods, etc., or officials who had made great contributions to the court and the community. However, the god ordained and arranged by the court for the village might not get the acceptance of the villagers. Prof. Nguyễn Văn Huyên in his research on tutelary gods in Bắc Ninh province before 1945 commented that "In this Bắc Ninh province, both the Lê dynasty ruling for nearly four centuries in history and the current Nguyễn dynasty were all able to impose new gods on the villagers. Heroes, whether heavenly or earthly, are worshiped for the cause they accomplished in their lifetime, and for the miracles they performed for the interests of the people" (Nguyễn Văn Huyên 1996, p. 462). Interests of the court and the attitude of the people may or may not meet in the figures worshiped in the village. In fact, there were some cases where two types of gods were worshiped in the same temple, including the god granted by the king and the god selected by the villagers.

However, as the leaders of the secular state, Vietnamese kings had the supreme power to rule all peoples, responsible for taking care of all affairs. Since the subjects of the king were farmers who lived on wet rice cultivation, there were two activities that all kings paid attention to, namely, the new-year plowing ceremony and rituals of rain praying.

The first king to perform a land plowing ceremony was King Lê Đại Hành. The book *Đại Việt sử ký toàn thư* wrote: "In the spring of the Year of the Pig (the 8th year of the Thiên Phúc reign, 987 AD), the king performed the first ploughing ceremony on the Đọi mountain[136] (Ngô Sĩ Liên 2010, p. 137). In the Lý dynasty, this ritual was continued. In 1038, "the king came to Bố Hải estuary to hold a farming ceremony. He ordered the clearing of grass and the building of an altar. He personally sacrificed Thần Nông (神农, the Farming God) and then personally plowed the land" (Ngô Sĩ Liên 2010, p. 160). During the Lê Dynasty, in the spring of 1473, "the king personally performed the plowing ceremony and urged the officials to perform one by one. The king celebrated the Giao ritual" (Ngô Sĩ Liên 2010, p. 477). This ceremony was maintained by the later kings of the Lê Dynasty in 1499, 1509, 1514, etc. During the Nguyễn Dynasty, the plowing ceremony remained until August 1945.

---

[136] now in Duy Tiên district, Hà Nam province.

If the plowing ceremony functioned as a visionary act at the new year to "awaken" the land and set an example for all peasantry, the kings also performed rituals to pray for rain and sunshine on demand. *Đại Việt sử ký toàn thư* recorded the event that the King personally performed prayer ceremonies to pray for rain and/or to stop rain in 1118, 1127, 1130, 1131, and so on. Prior to this, the Lý king "built an altar at the mouth of the Trường Quảng River in 1048 to pray for rain and for the wealth of the crops" (Ngô Sĩ Liên 2010, p. 165). Even the king ordered to take Cloud Dharma Buddha (Pháp Vân) from Dâu Temple to the capital to conduct a rain praying ceremony on the second year of the Thái Ninh reign (1073) (Ngô Sĩ Liên 2010, p. 171). Similarly, in the first year of the Thiệu Bình reign (1434), the King ordered his ministers to take Cloud Dharma Buddha to the capital to pray for rain" (Ngô Sĩ Liên 2010, p. 392). In other cases, the king personally went to the Buddhist temple to pray for rain, such as the case that the Lý king personally went to Pháp Vân Temple in Duềnh Bà to pray for rain on the third year of the Thiên Tư Gia Thụy reign (1188) (Ngô Sĩ Liên 2010, p. 205).

The third is to allocate land for villages to cultivate for the benefit of organizing spiritual offerings. This is the correct decision of the government, especially in the Red River Delta, where there were a large population in limited land area. The royal decrees to the villages around Hùng Kings Temple area (Việt Trì city, Phú Thọ province) can serve as an evidence. *The Hùng Kings Legend* written in the first year of the Hồng Đức reign (1470) and later re-edited and copied by Nguyễn Cố in the first year of the Hoằng Định reign (1600) noted that: "[The king] granted 500 acres of land to Hy Cương village and provided the village with land tax money collected from the surrounding areas. The population living upstream of the Red River from Tuyên Quang and Hưng Hóa down to the communes of Việt Trì must pay land taxes for sacrificial offerings to 18 Hùng Kings."

The successive dynasties, such as the Lê-Trịnh, Tây Sơn, and Nguyễn dynasties, continued ordaining the king gods and issuing decrees to prescribe that the people of the communes in the vicinity of Hùng Kings Temple had to worship the kings. The courts allowed local people to be exempt from taxes and public labor services, instead, they had to use the tax money to "modify/reconstruct the temple carefully and graciously serve the worship of the king gods so that the country could develop sustainably and the rivers and mountains could last forever". The stele No. 5 at Thượng Temple - the stele *Hùng miếu điển lệ bi* (雄廟典例碑, Model Stele of Hùng Kings Temple, erected in the 8th year of the Khải Định reign, 1923), recorded the statement that the people of Lâm Thao county had to offer sacrifices on the annual anniversary of the Kings' birthday as follows:

Hy Cương commune [pays the interests of] 10 mẫu 1 sào 10 thước; Tiên Cương commune 1 mẫu 9 sào 7 thước 5 tấc; Hy Sơn commune 7 mẫu 8 sào 3 thước[137]; Do Nghĩa commune 1 mẫu 9 sào 3 thước; Cao Mại commune 2 mẫu 5 sào 3 thước; and Lâm Nghĩa commune 1 mẫu. A total of 25 mẫu 8 sào 22 tấc 4 thước was assigned to Lâm Thao county for management. In 1917, Phú Thọ's Governor Lê Trung Ngọc sent a letter to the court asking the Ministry of Rites to "set the date of the 10th of the third month of the lunar year to be the National Ritual Day (the State Ritual Ceremony at Hùng Kings Temple)".

The fourth is the rules on pattern of rituals of worship. The monarchial dynasties strictly prescribed codes pf ritual ceremonies in god temples. In 1456, King Lê Thái Tông "personally led hundreds of officials to the worship of the gods in Sơn Lăng and issued an order to the guardian officials of the tomb in Lam Sơn to regulate that "everything in the temple must be done respectfully, such as cutting trees, splitting bamboos, collecting firewood, etc. When the ritual is organized, the temple have to sacrifice 4 buffaloes, beat the drums, and prescribe the soldiers to shout and cheer. In terms of ceremonial music, it is necessary to organize the literary dance of *Chư hầu lai triều* (諸侯

---

[137] In traditional Vietnamese measurement, 1 mẫu = 3,600 m²; 1 sào = 1/10 mẫu = 360 m²; 1 thước = 1/15 sào – 24 m²; 1 tấc = 1/10 thước = 2.4 m².

來朝, The vassals come to pay tribute) and the military dance "*Bình Ngô phá trận*" (平吳破陣, Defeating the Wu on the battlefield). When Mr. Lê Bí, Minister of Education, went to worship at Chiêu Hiếu Vương and Trung Dũng Vương Temples, he used 3 buffaloes. Mr. Lê Khang, Minister of Interiors, used 1 buffalo" (Ngô Sĩ Liên 2010, p. 432). King Lê Thánh Tông prescribed the sacrifices of the wandering souls in 1464 and the rites at the Confucius temples in all regions in 1465. He "began to fix the annual sacrifices to the gods in the spring and regulated not to offer vegetarian foods..." (Ngô Sĩ Liên 2010, p. 451). In 1468, the king prescribed the ceremonial mantra in the rituals to pray for rain and sunshine. In 1572, the king held a sacrifice to worship the heavens and the earth in Nam Giao Temple (Temple of Heaven). All these rituals were clearly stated. Phan Huy Chú (1961, p. 201-6) recorded these rituals quite adequately in *Lịch triều hiến chương loại chí* (歷朝憲章類誌, Charters of the Vietnamese dynasties). It is noteworthy that in 1669, the Lê – Trịnh dynasty issued a "regulation of doing good deeds and abolishing bad practices with a total of 18 articles. The king "assigned the Ministry of Rites to examine and perform the rituals that have previously existed in the temples of the kings and significant gods. Sacrificial activities in district-level temples and shrines were assigned to the governors of prefectures and districts as they were normally held in previous years" (Ngô Sĩ Liên 1973, vol. 4, p. 317).

Fifth, the monarchial dynasties were sometimes "cruel" to certain intangible cultural heritages which were judged to be "incompatible" with the state orthodoxy. Both the Lý and the Trần dynasties promoted the development of folk beliefs; on the other hand, they treated the beliefs very strictly and even restricted their development.

Việt điện u linh by Lý Tế Xuyên recorded the fact that the Trần Dynasty bestowed titles to tutelary gods in the first year of the Trùng Hưng reign (1285) as well as in the fourth year and the twenty-first year of the Hưng Long reign (1288 and 1313). The Lý and Trần Dynasties both expressed their "resolute" attitude towards traditional fertility beliefs (reproductive beliefs), which, according to them, were the heterodox worships. Lý Tế Xuyên wrote about general Lý Thường Kiệt in *Việt điện u linh* as follows:

"Those who took advantage of heterodox cults and medium spirits to deceive others were severely punished by the general [Lý Thường Kiệt]; more than half were fired and thus dirty habits were washed away. So at that time, the heterodox temples were turned into orthodox ones" (Lý Tế Xuyên 1972).

During the reign of King Trần Anh Tông, a senior master "visited the mountains, rivers, and villages". Whenever he discovered heterodox and/or non-standard spirits that "harmed the civilization of people", he strictly requested to remove them. "Some sacred but 'fierce' deities begged him to 'formalize' them, he ordered the villagers to reduce the sacrifices to these deities and forced them to fulfill the mission of protecting the people..." (see Hồ Nguyên Trừng 1978, p. 711). This policy of the Trần Dynasty made the ancient Southeast Asia-originated fertility beliefs severely destructured/decomposed". When people were not allowed to publicly worship their fertility deities, they had to hide them in a secret and/or informal way. The "hèm" phenomenon as an unofficial ritual of monarchial dynasties appearing in traditional festivals of Vietnamese people probably originated from that reason. In the Lê Dynasty, the *rí ren* dance of the people in Lam Kinh (Thanh Hóa) was considered to be heterodox, so it was abandoned and no longer performed when the King and his ministers visited their homeland[138] (Ngô Sĩ Liên 1972, p. 139).

4. The return of cultural heritage to the community and the role of the state

In comprehensive studies of the policies that monarichial dynasties implemented to Vietnam's intangible cultural heritage, we identify both positive and negative aspects. The lesson that we can learn

---

[138] The founding king of the Lê Dynasty, Lê Lợi (1385-1433), was born in Lam Sơn district of Thanh Hóa province.

from the attitudes and practices of the forerunners is still valid and effective for today's generation.

First, it should be noted that the Vietnamese monarchial dynasties used to have policies that "did not support" certain types of people's popular beliefs but, instead, required the people to worship state-sponsored orthodox deities. For example, a king of the Trần Dynasty, Trần Thừa, once requested the villagers to build Buddha statues and set up the worship of Buddha in the communal house, forbid them from worshiping 'heterodox' spirits, and ordered the abolishment of 'heterodox' cults. This kind of policy was not completely effective. When it was not allowed to worship the non-standard deities in the official system, villagers worshipped them in their "unofficial" way. Therefore, along with the "gods bestowed by the king", people had their own deities.

However, the central point of the dynasties' emphasis is that every sacred realm in the village must be ruled by a state-sponsored tutelary god. At the same time, the dynasties always created conditions to facilitate the worship 'orthodox' gods in every village. Among various state-sponsored gods, the village tutelary god converged the sharing point between the court's desires and the wishes of the villagers.

The process of sanctification made the deities become more sacred in the village, which was associated with community cultural activities. That has made the village festivals become a 'spiritual museum' that preserves many intangible cultural heritages. Therefore, it can be affirmed that the monarchial policies of pre-modern Vietnamese dynasties by the one hand created opportunities and empowered the villagers to protect their own cultural heritage, but in the other hand strictly tightened the on-site management.

Historically, the village community has played a large role in the transmission and conservation of cultural heritage. Today, in view of UNESCO's advocacy of upholding the role of the community in protecting intangible cultural heritage, we need to fully and actively assess the valuable lessons of our ancestors.

5. Conclusion

There is a sensitive relationship between the village community and the secularized monarchs in Vietnam throughout the history. It requires a dialectical perspective to study this relationship. The success of the preservation of heritage values completely depends on how this relationship is handled. We cannot take advantage of upholding the role of the community to ignore the responsibility of the state and vice versa. It is clear that we can draw useful historical lessons for the preservation and promotion of the intangible cultural heritage at present. History is not a silent past, it always offers new and valuable lessons for today's development.

Reference

1. Guxep, V. *Mỹ học folklore*. Trans Hoàng, Ngọc Hiến, Đà Nẵng Publisher, 1999.

2. Hà, Văn Tấn and Nguyễn, Văn Kự, 1998. *Đình Việt Nam* (Vietnamese communal house). Ho Chi Minh City Publisher.

3. Hồ, Nguyên Trừng. 1978. "Nam Ông mộng lục (南翁夢錄, Dream memoir of Southern Man)." In *Thơ văn Lý Trần* (Poetry of the Lý and Trần Dynasties), vol. 3, Hanoi: Social Science Publisher.

4. Lê, Kim Thuyên, *Sắc phong tỉnh Vĩnh Phúc (The royal ordinations in Vĩnh Phúc province)* Sở văn hóa,thể thao và du lịch tỉnh Vĩnh Phúc (Department of culture, sports and tourism of Vinh Phuc province), 2012.

5. Lý, Tế Xuyên. 1972. *Việt Điện U Linh Tập* (越甸幽靈集, Collection of Stories on the Shady and Spiritual World of the Viet Realm), trans. Trịnh Đình Rư, ed. Đinh Gia Khánh. Hanoi: Literature Publisher.

6. *Sắc phong trên địa bàn tỉnh Hưng Yên* (The royal ordinations in Hưng Yên province), Department of Culture, Sports and Tourism of Hưng Yên province (4 vols).

7. Nguyễn, Duy Hinh. 1996. *Tín ngưỡng thành hoàng Việt Nam* (The cults of tutelary gods cults in Vietnam). Hanoi: Social Science Publisher.

8. Nguyễn, Mạnh Hùng. 2008. "Khảo sát văn bản sắc phong thuộc triều đại nhà Nguyễn (Điều tra về các tài liệu phong chức của nhà Nguyễn)", Proceedings of scientific workshops *Chúa Nguyễn và vương triều Nguyễn trong lịch sử Việt Nam từ thế kỷ XVI đến thế kỷ XVIII* (Nguyễn lords and the Nguyễn Dynasty in Vietnamese history from the sixteenth century to the eighteenth century), Thanh Hóa.

9. Ngô, Sĩ Liên. 1973. *Đại Việt sử ký toàn thư* (大越史記全書, Complete Historical Annals of Đại Việt), trans. Cao Huy Giu, ed. Đào Duy Anh. Hanoi: Social Science Publisher.

10. Ngô, Sĩ Liên. 2010. *Đại Việt sử ký toàn thư* (大越史記全書, Complete Historical Annals of Đại Việt), trans. Ngô Đức Thọ & Hoàng Văn Lâu. Hanoi. Social Science Publisher.

11. Nguyễn, Trãi, *Bình Ngô Đại Cáo* (平吳大誥, Great proclamation upon the defeat of the Wu). Hanoi.

12. Nguyễn, Văn Huyên. 1996. "Về một bản đồ phân bố các thành hoàng ở tỉnh Bắc Ninh, Bắc Kỳ (About a map of the tutelary gods' distribution in Bắc Ninh province of Tonkin)." In *Góp phần nghiên cứu văn hóa Việt Nam* (A contribution to the study of Vietnamese culture), vol. 1, Hanoi: Social Science Publisher.

13. People's Committee of Quảng Nam province & Department of Culture, Sports and Tourism. 2015, Hanoi: Khoa học kỹ thuật.

14. Phan, Huy Chú. 1961. "Lễ nghi chí: các lễ tế cầu đảo và ăn thề (Records on rituals: rain prayers and oath ceremonies)." *Lịch triều hiến chương loại chí* (歷朝憲章類誌, Charters of the Vietnamese dynasties), trans. Vietnam Institute of History. Hanoi: History Publisher.

15. Tạ, Chí Đại Trường,*Thần,người và đất Việt(Gods, people and land of Vietnam)*, California, USA,Literature (Văn học) Publishing, 1989.

PROSPECTS OF PRESERVING INTANGIBLE CULTURAL HERITAGE IN ASIA (A CASE STUDY OF VIETNAM)

1. Introduction:

Asian countries, including Vietnam, possess various forms of treasures of intangible cultural heritage, with deep national and ethnic characteristics. In recent years, Asian countries have attached great importance to the protection of intangible cultural heritage and have made many valuable achievements, but at the same time, practical problems have also arisen. Through the case of Vietnam, one can see the view of protecting Asian intangible cultural heritage.

2. Views from the definition of intangible cultural heritage

The Convention on the preservation of intangible cultural heritage approved by UNESCO in the 32nd meeting (October 2003) stated: "Intangible cultural heritage is the practices, representations, expressions, knowledge, skills – as well as the instruments, objects, artifacts and cultural spaces associated therewith – that communities, groups and, in some cases, individuals recognize as part of their cultural heritage. This intangible cultural heritage, transmitted from generation to generation, is constantly recreated by communities and groups in response to their environment, their interaction with nature and their history, and provides them with a sense of identity and continuity, thus promoting respect for cultural diversity and human creativity".

In Vietnam, the Cultural Heritage Law defines "Intangible cultural heritage is a spiritual product with historical, cultural and scientific significance, which is preserved through people's memories, writing, or passed down orally such as traditional handicraft's know-how, performances and other forms of oral heritage. Preservation and circulation, including language, writing, artwork, science, oral literature, folk performing arts, lifestyle, festivals, traditional craftsmanship, food, traditional costumes, and other folk knowledge (the Cultural Heritage Law 2001).

3. Achievements and emerging issues in the protection of Vietnam's intangible cultural heritage

a. Achievements

The first achievement that should be recognized is the understanding of intangible cultural heritage. This awareness is reflected in cultural policies including intangible cultural heritage. When considering the policies of the Party and the Government on intangible cultural heritage, it is recommended to consider President Hồ Chí Minh's cultural ideology, including considering folklore as an important part of intangible cultural heritage. At the Cultural Workers Conference in 1958, President Hồ Chí Minh announced: Interesting proverbs and songs were created by the masses. These works are concise and meaningful, not as long as the novel. Cultural workers should help promote the creation of the masses. These works are indeed cultural treasures" (Hồ Chí Minh 1997).

The Communist Party of Vietnam has always reiterated in its parliamentary documents that "The state works with the public [...] to protect and modify cultural and historical heritage sites [...]; [the State and the people will] complete the collection of the capital of national culture and art" (Documents of the 6th National Congress 1986, p. 92). In order to institutionalize the party's views, the Vietnamese Prime Minister issued Decision No. 25/TTg on January 19, 1993, on the formulation and reform of certain cultural and artistic policies. Regarding the collection and preservation of cultural heritage, the Decision states that "100% of the funds will be used to collect, correct works, long-term preservation, and dissemination of spiritual and cultural products, such as folk literature, traditional dance, folk singing, and traditional handicrafts".

The resolution of the Eighth Meeting of the Central Committee of the Vietnamese Communist Party said: "Cultural heritage is a valuable property that links one ethnic community with another. They represent the core of our national identity and are the basis for recreating new valuable works and cultural exchanges. The preservation, inheritance, and development of tangible and intangible cultural values, traditional cultural values, academics, folk cultural values, and revolutionary cultural values are extremely important".

In order to institutionalize the guidelines and viewpoints of the Party and President Hồ Chí Minh on the protection and development of the value of intangible cultural heritage, the Cultural Heritage Law reserves the entire Chapter 3, namely Articles 17 to 27, to deal with this issue. These articles vividly demonstrate the responsibility of the state and state-owned institutions for the principles of preservation and promotion of cultural heritage. For example, Article 20 states: "National authorities must take necessary measures to protect intangible cultural heritage from improper use, disappearance and loss" (the Cultural Heritage Law 2001). Article 26 stipulates that "The State expresses its appreciation to artists who master, preserve and disseminate traditional art and professional knowledge" (the Cultural Heritage Law 2001).

In Vietnam, the protection of intangible cultural heritage has a long history. This process can be divided into two phases: the spontaneous phase and the active and voluntary phase. In the spontaneous phase, i.e., in the monarchial periods, Confucian scholars contacted and recorded elements of intangible cultural heritage, such as folk songs and legends. From 1858 to 1945, some Confucian scholars and Western scholars published many research results on intangible cultural studies, especially folk literature. From the beginning of 1954 to the present period, the protection of intangible cultural heritage has been taken care of on an active and voluntary basis, and many achievements have been made.

An advantage at this phase is that folk literary works have been written and printed in books. Various folklore works of different ethnic groups came into being, such as *Tục ngữ, ca dao, dân ca Việt Nam* (Vietnamese proverbs and folk songs) by Vũ Ngọc Phan (1956), *Kho tàng truyện cổ tích Việt Nam* (Treasure of Vietnamese Legends) by Nguyễn Đổng Chi (1957), *Kho tàng ca dao người Việt* (Treasure of Vietnamese folk songs) by Nguyễn Xuân Kính and Phan Đăng Nhật (1995); *Kho tàng truyện trạng Việt Nam* (A treasure of talent stories in Vietnam) by Thạch Phương, Nguyễn Chí Bền and Mai Hương (1996), etc. Recently, after the second re-publishing of the Vietnamese literary works collection, different literary works by different authors were collected, and the National Social Science and Humanities Center (now known as the Academy Vietnam Social Sciences) is compiling the book *Tổng tập văn học dân gian người Việt* "General Collection of Vietnamese Folk Literature Works" by the Vietnamese people Literature with 19 volumes. Until now 19 volumes of this General Collection printed in 20 books are published. *Tổng tập văn học dân gian các dân tộc thiểu số Việt Nam* (The General Collection of folklore of Vietnam's ethnic minorities) is about to be published. In addition, many other research results of folk literature studies of different ethnic groups have been introduced to readers in the past few years (see Lê Hồng Lý 1999).

Under the guidance of national institutions and professional research institutions, Vietnam voluntarily and vigorously developed Vietnam's intangible cultural heritage protection activities to adapt to UNESCO's definition of intangible cultural heritage and respond to its "Convention on the Protection of Intangible Cultural Heritage". The achievements in the research, collection, preservation, and promotion of Vietnam's intangible cultural heritage can be seen from the following aspects:

First of all, most of staff in this field have been trained on the working methods, experience, and perspectives of intangible cultural heritage. In collaboration with the National Center of Social Science and Humanities (now known as the Vietnam Academy of Social Sciences), UNESCO organized a workshop on the collection and protection of the intangible cultural heritage of different ethnic groups in Vietnam from November 23, 1995, to December 12, 1995. The National Goals Plan on Culture assigned by the Vietnamese government to the Ministry of Culture and Information (now called the Ministry of Culture, Sports and Tourism) has been in progress since 1997. Under this policy, the Vietnam Institute of Culture and Arts (VICAS) has paid special attention to the training of staff for the collection and preservation of intangible cultural heritage. VICAS organized six training courses nationwide in Yên Bái, Tiền Giang, Huế, Quảng Ninh, Ninh Bình, Gia Lai, Quảng Bình, and Đồng Nai provinces, and 325 employees from 64 provinces and cities received training in planning and implement intangible cultural heritage protection projects. Thankfully, 325 employees from 64 provinces and cities received expert training to plan and implement intangible cultural heritage protection projects. Besides, the Vietnam Folklore Association has also held many training courses in this field. The association organizes 7-10 training courses for its members on the collection and protection methods of intangible cultural heritage every year.

Secondly, the intangible cultural heritage of the ethnic minorities of Vietnam was collected and recorded through special equipment, which is one of the four major goals of the National Goals Plan on Culture. Its implementation is directly guided and informed by the Ministry of Culture and Information (now called the Ministry of Culture, Sports, and Tourism) since 1997. So far, the number of projects per year is as follows:

Year	Total number of projects	Number of local projects	Number of national projects
1997	18	13	5
1998	79	65	14
18999	75	61	14
2000	61	41	20
2001	72	40	32
2002	72	61	11
2003	78	61	17
2004	88	63	25
2005	90	64	26
2006	18		
2007	26		
2008	24		

2009	35		
2010	34		
2011	20		
2012	25		
2013	22		
2014	16		
2015	13		
2016	7		
2017	14		
2018	8		
2019	8		

There are a total of 640 projects (469 local projects and 171 national projects). Total year 1997- year 2019 has projects 833. After 2019, Vietnam no longer has a national target program on culture. It is worth noting that these projects have been widely promoted in 64 provinces and citics nationwide. Special attention has been paid to the protection of the intangible cultural heritage of ethnic minorities such as the Ơ-đu, Brâu, Chứt, and other ethnic groups. Each project produced four products: written scientific reports, a set of BETACAM videotapes, photo albums, and audiotapes.

From September 1997 to the end of 2005, the Ministry of Culture and Information invested 29 billion Vietnamese dongs (equivalent to 1.25 million USD) and 500 million Vietnamese dongs (21.5 thousand USD) in the non-administrative budget of the target cultural plan to collect, protect and promote the intangible cultural heritage of the ethnic minorities of Vietnam.

In addition to collecting and recording, attention should also be paid to the storage of intangible cultural heritage. The Ministry of Culture and Information has instructed VICAS to establish a database of Vietnamese ethnic intangible cultural heritage through modern means and technologies. VICAS staff recorded thousands of hours of documentaries. To date, VICAS has recorded nearly three hundred movies on CD-ROMs. These movies will be stored on DVDs. In addition to the storage carried out by the Ministry of Culture and

Information (now the Ministry of Culture, Sports and Tourism), the Vietnam Institute of Social Sciences also carried out projects to collect, translate and introduce the epics of the ethnic minorities living in the Central Highlands. At present, hundreds of epics have been collected, recorded, and many have been translated and introduced to readers in the national official language.

The spread and introduction of intangible cultural heritage have attracted the attention of the Vietnamese mass media. Vietnam TV and Hanoi TV set up a special program called "*Không gian văn hóa: Gìn giữ cho muôn đời sau* (Cultural space: preservation for future generations)" to introduce to the audience the intangible cultural heritage of various ethnic groups in the country.

b. Emerging issues

Despite tremendous efforts, the collection and preservation of Vietnam's intangible cultural heritage still face many difficulties.

First, it is the focus on craftsmen. On August 10, 1993, the UNESCO Executive Board recommended the establishment of a human living treasure system. It is recognized that Vietnam has not given due attention to this matter. So far, people have paid attention to the intangible cultural heritage itself, but have not paid attention to the people who created it. They are artisans - the creators, preservers, and inheritors of intangible cultural heritage. In recent years, the Vietnam Folklore Association has granted the title "folk artisan" to certain artisans, but this practice has been limited. This is a weakness in the collection and preservation of Vietnam's intangible cultural heritage.

Another more important issue is to enhance the role of artisans in the community. For example, policies should be developed to encourage artisans to pass on their consciously owned heritage to the community. Vietnam has not yet formulated an effective policy on this matter.

In addition, an overall inventory of intangible cultural heritage needs to be conducted across the country, across regions, and in different ethnic groups to provide plans for collection, research, preservation, and promotion. Local administrators must know exactly the amount of intangible cultural heritage in their place. UNESCO's warning to all countries is very valuable, especially Vietnam and similar countries. Currently, conducting surveys and inventory of intangible cultural heritage of localities and ethnic groups in Vietnam is significantly urgent because it will provide the basis for mapping intangible cultural heritage in Vietnam and design collection, conservation and promotion plans.

Second, it is the management of intangible cultural heritage. Vietnam has not yet implemented the classification of intangible cultural heritage in order to decentralize it. In addition to Vietnam's two oral and intangible heritage masterpieces designated by UNESCO, namely *Nhã nhạc cung đình Huế (Huế Royal Court Music)* (2003) and *Không gian văn hóa cồng chiêng Tây Nguyên (the Gong Cultural Space in the Central Highlands)* (2005), two other heritages are preparing national candidate files for submission to UNESCO as *Không gian văn hóa Quan Họ tỉnh Bắc Ninh (Cultural Space of Quan họ Folk songs in Bắc Ninh province)* and *Nghệ thuật ca trù của người Việt (Ca trù singing of the Việt)*. Many other intangible cultural heritages in the country have not yet been ranked and fully researched by cultural managers and scientists.

In promoting the intangible cultural heritage, the most important thing is to make heritage exist in daily life. It is essential to increase the community's awareness and pride of the intangible cultural heritage to ensure that the heritage exists in the community as its nature. It is also related to the spread and inheritance of intangible cultural heritage. Therefore, the folk works of the community must be brought back to the community who created and delivered them. Education and communication, especially for the younger generation, are essential to understanding and preserving intangible cultural heritage. This is an essential task because it can function as a bridge that can bring intangible cultural heritage back to the community. The collection, recording, and filming of intangible cultural heritage are necessary, but it is more important to return the cultural heritage to the owners. Both Vietnamese researchers and managers are concerned about this work, but to be fair, it is not effective.

Another concern for the protection of intangible cultural heritage is to make it an internal factor for sustainable development and this kind of development does not perform well in Vietnam and remains a weakness. Much intangible cultural heritage can contribute to the development with high economic value, for example, through tourism. However, it did not perform well in Vietnam. Various products of the system, such as books and pictures, CD-ROMs, VCDs, DVDs, and leaflets introducing the intangible cultural heritage of Vietnamese ethnic groups, have received little attention.

4. Globalization and the Protection of Asian Intangible Cultural Heritage

Asian countries, including Vietnam, cannot stop the ongoing globalization. Globalization may have different effects on the protection of intangible cultural heritage in each country, and no one can deny it. Intangible cultural heritage is mainly preserved in oral and intangible form, so there is a risk of being changed or extinct. Besides, most Asian countries are developing. Industrialization and modernization have changed the existing space of traditional culture, including intangible cultural heritage. The human oral and intangible masterpiece of the Gong Cultural Space in the Central Highlands of Vietnam is a piece of obvious evidence. Natural and social changes and traditional farming methods put this masterpiece's existing space at risk. The indigenous communities in Central highland of Vietnam do not value gong-related ceremonies as important as before.

In addition, Asia is a continent with a rich and intangible cultural heritage. Over the years, Asia and Africa have more UNESCO cultural heritage than other continents, such as 6 of 19 heritages in 2001, 12 of 28 in 2003, and 43 of 43 in 2005, etc. Therefore, UNESCO designated

Asia and Africa as human oral and intangible masterpieces, and that Asian intangible cultural heritage has great potential.

Therefore, some Asian countries have long attached great importance to the protection of intangible cultural heritage. For example, since the Law on the Protection of Cultural Property was promulgated in 1950, Japan has aroused great interest in this matter. It is worth noting to learn theory and practical experience from Japan.

South Korea established its "Living Human Treasures' Systems" before the "Proposal" was issued by the UNESCO Executive Committee in 1993. China has also implemented a master project for the protection of intangible cultural heritage. The project has been implemented since 2003 and has completed about 800 masterpieces of the List of National Intangible Cultural Heritage (Zhang Min 2005). Through the "Museums: Intangible Heritage and Globalization" seminar held in Shanghai in 2002, you can see that museums and nature conservation organizations in Asian countries are very interested in this field. Through these pieces of evidence, we can see the perspective of protecting Asian intangible cultural heritage.

5. Conclusion

The intangible cultural heritage has always been the source flowing from the past to the present, and it is the foundation for establishing the national culture of every Asian country today. In the past few years, Vietnam has made many achievements in the collection, preservation, and promotion of intangible cultural heritage, but it has also shown limitations. Every Asian country faces certain challenges in the preservation of intangible cultural heritage since each has its own achievements and limitations. Taking Vietnam as an example, I make the following suggestions:

(1) UNESCO or ACCU should organize forums and seminars to exchange the theoretical and practical experience of protecting intangible cultural heritage between different countries;

(2) A network of Asian intangible cultural heritage protectors should be established and a special journal/magazine on the protection of Asian intangible cultural heritage should be established and regularly issued.

(3) Cooperation among Asian countries in the protection of intangible cultural heritage should be effectively strengthened through practical programs and projects.

Reference

1. Communist Party of Vietnam. 1998. *Documents of the 5th Central Committee Meeting* (Session VIII). Hanoi: National Politics.

2. Hồ, Chí Minh. 1997. Culturally. Hanoi: Hồ Chi Minh Museum Publishing.

3. National Assembly of Socialist Republic of Vietnam. 2001. *The Cultural Heritage Law*. Hanoi: National Politic Publisher.

4. Lê, Hồng Lý (ed.). 1999. *Thư mục văn hóa dân gian* (Folklore Culture Directory). Hanoi: Social Science Publisher.

5. National Center for Social Sciences and Humanities (Institute of Literature). 2007. *Tuyển tập Văn học dân gian Việt Nam* (Vietnamese Folk Literature Collection). Hanoi: Education Publisher.

6. Nguyễn, Đổng Chi. 1957. *Kho tàng truyện cổ tích Việt Nam* (Treasure of Vietnamese Legends). Hanoi: Education Publisher.

7. Nguyễn, Xuân Kính & Phan, Đăng Nhật. 1995. *Kho tàng ca dao người Việt* (Treasure of Vietnamese folk songs), 2 vols. Hanoi: Culture & Information Publisher.

8. Thạch, Phương; Nguyễn, Chí Bền & Mai, Hương.1996, *Kho tàng truyện trạng Việt Nam* (A treasure of talent stories in Vietnam), 6 vols, Hanoi, Social Science Publisher.

9. Vũ, Ngọc Phan. 1956. *Tục ngữ, ca dao, dân ca Việt Nam* (Vietnamese proverbs and folk songs). Hanoi: Literature Publisher

10. Zhang, Min. 2005., Paper at the Seminar *Methods of Developing Inventory List and Heritage Preservation*, December 2005, Kingdom of Thailand.

ILLUSTRATION

The space of Gong culture in the cultural highland

Picture 1: Đrây Sap Water Fall (Dak Nong province) - one of the most
famous landscapes in the central highland;
Source: Vicas documents

Picture 2: Communal longhouse;
Source: Vicas documents

Picture 3: Longhouse of Ede ethnicity;
Source: Vicas documents

Picture 4: Gongs performance by artisans;
Source: Vicas documents

Illustration   343

Picture 5: Collection of Gongs;
Source: Vicas documents

Quan ho Bac Ninh folksong

Picture 1: Cau River - river of Quan ho Bac Ninh folksong;
taken by Truc Tan

Picture 2: Performance by Quan ho sisters;
Source: Vicas documents

Picture 3: Quan ho singing on boat;
taken by Vu Giang Binh

Illustration   345

Picture 4: Traditional meal set of Quan ho Bac Ninh;
taken by Duong Thanh Giang

Picture 5: Vietnam's leaders, diplomats with Quan ho artisans;
Source: Vicas documents

Giong festival at Phu Dong temple and Soc temple

Picture 1: Offerings presented to Saint Giong at Soc temple;
Source: Vicas documents

Picture 2: Little girl who act as invader's head;
Source: Vicas documents

Illustration   347

Picture 3: The festival celebrant wave flag to wipe out Northern enemies;
Source: Vicas documents

Belief in worshiping Hung Vuong

Picture 1: Ha temple at Nghia Linh mountain;
Source: Vicas documents

Picture 2: Trung temple at Nghia Linh mountain;
Source: Vicas documents

Picture 3: Thuong temple at Nghia Linh mountain;
Source: Vicas documents

Illustration   349

Picture 4: Hung Vuong tomb at Nghia Linh mountain;
taken by Hoang Son

Picture 5: People making Chung cake offering Hung Kings;
taken by Hoang Son

Picture 6: Vietnamese people come to worship Holy ancestor Hung Kings;
Source: Vicas documents

Vi Giam Nghe Tinh folksong

Picture 1: Vi Giam singing in Lam River;
Source: Vicas documents

Illustration   351

Picture 2: Vi Giam singing at corn field;
Source: Vicas documents

Picture 3: Learning Vi Giam from the senior;
Source: Vicas documents

The Viet belief in the Mother Goddesses in Three Realms

Picture 1: Word formation at Phu Giay festival;
Source: Vicas documents

Picture 2: a form of mediumship ritual;
Source: Vicas documents

Illustration   353

Picture 3: a form of mediumship ritual is performed by a young artisan
Source: Vicas documents;

Marine culture

Picture 1: A corner of the sea;
Source: Internet

Picture 2: A landscape on Ly Son Island;
taken by Truc Tan

Picture 3: Festival of appraising Hoang Sa warriors at Ly Son Island;
taken by Dang Vu

Illustration   355

Preservation and Promotion of heritages

Picture 1: Reception ceremony of UNESCO "The space of Gong culture
in the cultural highland of Vietnam";
Source: Vicas documents;

Picture 2: Reception ceremony of UNESCO for Quan ho Bac Ninh folksong;
Source: Internet